KABBALAH

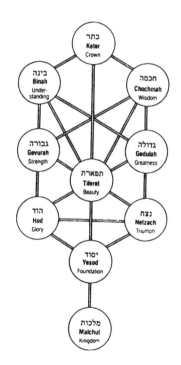

KABBALAH

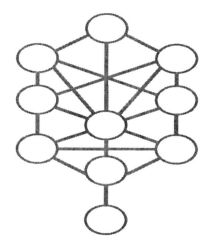

Selections from Classic Kabbalistic Works
from *Raziel HaMalach* to the Present Day

RABBI AVRAHAM YAAKOV FINKEL

TARGUM/FELDHEIM

First published 2002
Copyright © 2002 by Avraham Yaakov Finkel
ISBN 1-56871-218-9

All rights reserved

No part of this publication may be translated, reproduced, stored in a retrieval system, or transmitted in any form or by any means, electronic, mechanical, photocopying, recording, or otherwise, without prior permission in writing from both the copyright holder and the publisher.

Published by:
TARGUM PRESS, INC.
22700 W. Eleven Mile Rd.
Southfield, MI 48034
E-mail: targum@netvision.net.il
Fax: 888-298-9992
www.targum.com

Distributed by:
FELDHEIM PUBLISHERS
202 Airport Executive Park
Nanuet, NY 10954

Printed in Israel

אגודת הרבנים דארצות הברית וקנדה
THE UNION OF ORTHODOX RABBIS
OF THE UNITED STATES OF AMERICA
235 EAST BROADWAY
NEW YORK, N.Y. 10002

964-6337 964-6338

20 Menachem Av, 5762/2002

New York

My friend Rabbi Avraham Yaakov Finkel showed me the *sefer* he wrote about the lives and teachings of the great Kabbalists, together with selections from their writings, ranging from the earliest masters of Kabbalah to the more recent great *Mekubbalim*. The work is written in a conversational, easy-to-understand style of English, making it accessible to the widest circle of readers.

The author has earned his reputation with his many previous books on Torah themes, which were widely aclaimed by Torah scholars and laymen alike.

The present *sefer* is an important work, written with *tuv taam vadaas*, "good reasoning and knowledge." The book is the fruit of a great deal of labor and is written with judicious discernment and insight.

My *berachah* is that the author's "springs may spread outward," and that, with the help of Hashem, this important work will be welcomed in the halls of the yeshivah and the *beis midrash*.

With Torah greetings,

אגודת הרבנים דארצות הברית וקנדה

Rabbi Tzvi Meir Ginsberg
Chairman and Director
The Union of Orthodox Rabbis
of the United States and Canada

Machon L'Torah
The Jewish Learning Network
15221 West Ten Mile Road
Oak Park, MI 48237
(248) 967-0888 Fax 967-0412

Jewish Resource Center of Ann Arbor
at the University of Michigan
1335 Hill Street
Ann Arbor, MI 48104
(734) 996-2000

With his remarkably clear and uniquely articulate style, Rabbi Avraham Yaakov Finkel enables us to comprehend difficult and complex Kabbalistic concepts. While traditionally the study of Kabbalah is reserved for qualified Torah scholars knowledgeable in all aspects of Torah, recently premature study of Kabbalistic writings coupled with published misinformation and distortion about the Kabbalah have become commonplace. As a response to this trend, this monumental work is a great contribution to the world of Jewish literature.

Rabbi Avraham Jakobovitz
Director, Machon L'Torah
The Jewish Learning Network

BETH AVRAHAM YOSEPH OF TORONTO CONGREGATION
THE JOSEPH AND FAYE TANENBAUM SYNAGOGUE CENTRE
A FAMILY SYNAGOGUE EMPHASIZING THE WARMTH OF TORAH TRADITION
513 Clark Avenue, West, Thornhill, Ontario L4J 5V3
Telephone: (905) 886-3810
Fax: (905) 886-5103

י"ג תשרי, תשס"ג
September 19, 2002

We are witnessing a phenomenon today whereby people are experimenting with "New Age" religious expression. Mysticism is "in." Sophisticated bookstores which present a small number of volumes in the "Judaism" category offer an endless selection of New Age spirituality, witchcraft, and, yes, Kabbalah. From the Hollywood salon to the corporate offices of New York, Kabbalah has been discovered.

As happens with all popular intellectual fads, this climate of "popular Kabbalah" has resulted in a genre of literature on the subject that is transparent, superficial, and lacking in the area of genuine scholarship.

There has been a need for some time for an authentic introduction to the major institutions, themes, and personalities of Jewish mysticism. This volume serves that purpose with grace. It is not designed to teach Kabbalah, but to provide a concise overview of this most precious area of Jewish theology.

The reader will be inspired by the biographical presentations of the Masters of Kabbalah and Chassidut. The selections of their teachings will surely touch the reader's heart and soul, inspiring further exploration into the sources of Jewish traditions and a meaningful search for the truth in Torah.

The noted author Rabbi Avraham Yaakov Finkel has offered up yet another indispensable literary offering on the table of the Jewish world.

Rabbi Baruch Taub
Rabbi of Beth Avraham Yoseph of Toronto (BAYT)

BROOKLYN LAW SCHOOL

AARON D. TWERSKI
Francis Newell DeValpine
Professor of Law

Rabbi Avraham Yaakov Finkel has authored a book introducing the reader to the masters of Kabbalah. Few in our generation have any appreciation of what the study of Kabbalah entails. To be sure this book will not turn the reader into a student of this all important aspect of Torah. What it will do is provide a window into Kabbalah and to the masters throughout the ages who wrote the leading words on the subject. The biographical material on each of the Kabbalists is fascinating and the excerpts from their works is engaging. This book will deeply move you. You cannot escape the confrontations with the overwhelming spiritual nature of the soul and the cosmic significance of every human act.

Professor Aaron D. Twerski

To my dear wife, Suri

CONTENTS

Acknowledgments xvii
Kabbalah: An Overview xix

Part I: CONCEPTS OF KABBALAH

Chapter 1: Creation and *Tzimtzum* 3
Chapter 2: The *Sefiros* 7
Chapter 3: *Sheviras HaKeilim* 15

Part II: THE EARLIEST KABBALISTIC WORKS

Introduction 21
Chapter 4: *Raziel HaMalach* 23
Chapter 5: *Sefer Yetzirah* 31
Chapter 6: *Sefer HaBahir* 40
Chapter 7: *Sefer HaZohar* 47

Part III: THE KABBALISTS OF SPAIN, ITALY, AND PROVENCE

Introduction 63
Chapter 8: Rabbi Shabsai Donnolo 65

Chapter 9: Rabbi Avraham ben David of Posquieres (Ravad III) 70
Chapter 10: Rabbi Yitzchak Sagi Nahor. 72
Chapter 11: Rabbi Azriel of Gerona 74
Chapter 12: Rabbi Moshe ben Nachman (Ramban). 79
Chapter 13: Rabbi Avraham Abulafia. 87
Chapter 14: Rabbi Yosef Gikatilla. 91
Chapter 15: Rabbi Moshe de Leon 99
Chapter 16: Rabbi Bachya ben Asher (Rabbeinu Bachya). 102
Chapter 17: Rabbi Menachem Recanati. 110
Chapter 18: Rabbi Meir ibn Gabbai. 112
Chapter 19: Rabbi Shlomo Molcho 119

Part IV: THE MEDIEVAL EUROPEAN KABBALISTS

Introduction. 125
Chapter 20: Rabbi Yehudah HeChassid 127
Chapter 21: Rabbi Elazar Rokeach of Worms 141
Chapter 22: Rabbi Yehudah Loeve (Maharal of Prague). 145
Chapter 23: Rabbi Menachem Azaryah of Fano (Rama of Fano) 154
Chapter 24: Rabbi Shabsai Sheftl Horowitz (Shefa Tal) 157
Chapter 25: Rabbi Yeshayah Horowitz (Shelah HaKadosh). 161
Chapter 26: Rabbi Nassan Nata Shapira (Megaleh Amukos) 169

Part V: THE KABBALISTS OF ERETZ YISRAEL

Introduction. 179
Chapter 27: Rabbi Shlomo Alkabetz 181
Chapter 28: Rabbi Moshe Alshich. 184
Chapter 29: Rabbi Moshe Cordovero (Remak). 190
Chapter 30: Rabbi Yitzchak Luria Ashkenazi (Ari HaKadosh) 198
Chapter 31: Rabbi Chaim Vital 208
Chapter 32: Rabbi Avraham ben Mordechai Azulai 213

Chapter 33: Rabbi Chaim ibn Attar (Or HaChaim) 218
Chapter 34: Rabbi Shalom Mizrachi Sharabi (Rashash). 225
Chapter 35: Rabbi Chaim Yosef David Azulai (Chida) 227

Part VI: EUROPEAN KABBALISTS OF THE SEVENTEENTH AND EIGHTEENTH CENTURIES

Introduction. 239
Chapter 36: Rabbi Menashe ben Israel (Nishmas Chaim). 241
Chapter 37: Rabbi Yonasan Eibeschutz. 248
Chapter 38: Rabbi Moshe Chaim Luzzatto (Ramchal). 254
Chapter 39: Rabbi Eliyahu of Vilna (The Vilna Gaon). 262
Chapter 40: Rabbi Chaim Berlin of Volozhin (Reb Chaim Volozhiner). . 271

Part VII: KABBALISTS OF THE CHASSIDIC WORLD

Introduction. 283
Chapter 41: Rabbi Yisrael ben Eliezer (Baal Shem Tov). 285
Chapter 42: Rabbi Dov Ber (The Maggid of Mezritch). 294
Chapter 43: Rabbi Yaakov Yosef of Polnoye (Toldos Yaakov Yosef) . . 302
Chapter 44: Rabbi Elimelech of Lizhensk (No'am Elimelech) 309
Chapter 45: Rabbi Baruch of Kossov 316
Chapter 46: Rabbi Shneur Zalman of Liadi (Baal HaTanya) 324
Chapter 47: Rabbi Chaim Tirer of Chernovitz (Be'er Mayim Chaim) . 331
Chapter 48: Rabbi Nachman of Breslov 339
Chapter 49: Rabbi Shlomo Rabinowitz of Radomsk (Tiferes Shlomo). . 348
Chapter 50: Rabbi Yitzchak Eizik Safrin of Komarno 355
Chapter 51: Rabbi Tzadok HaKohen of Lublin. 361

Part VIII: KABBALISTS OF THE TWENTIETH CENTURY

Introduction. 371
Chapter 52: Rabbi Yosef Chaim of Baghdad (Ben Ish Chai) 373

Chapter 53: Rabbi Shem Klingberg of Zaloshitz (The Zaloshitzer Rebbe) . . 376
Chapter 54: Rabbi Yehudah Leib Ashlag 383
Chapter 55: Rabbi Yisrael Abuchatzeirah (Baba Sali) 392

    Glossary 401
    Name Index 411
    Other Books by the Author 415
    Translations by the Author 416

ILLUSTRATIONS

1. Title page of *Shaarei Orah* by Rabbi Yosef Gikatilla, with a representation of the ten *Sefiros* 1
2. Title page of *Raziel HaMalach*, which reads, "This is the book that Raziel HaMalach gave to Adam, the first man". . . . 19
3. Title page of *Maros Elokim* by Rabbi Meir ibn Gabbai, printed in Venice, 1546 61
4. Title page of *Amaros Tehoros* by Rabbi Menachem Azaryah of Fano, printed in Frankfurt am Main, 1698 123
5. Title page of *Toras Moshe*, Rabbi Moshe Alshich's commentary on the Torah 177
6. Portrait of the Vilna Gaon, Rabbi Eliyahu of Vilna. 238
7. Title page of the first edition of *Likutei Moharan*, a compilation of commentaries by Rabbi Nachman of Breslov, printed in Ostroh, 1808 281
8. Portrait of the Ben Ish Chai, Rabbi Yosef Chaim of Baghdad . . . 369

ACKNOWLEDGMENTS

How can I repay Hashem for all His bounties to me?
(Tehillim 116:12)

First and foremost I want to give thanks to Hashem for enabling me to complete this *sefer* and thereby afford you, the discerning reader, the opportunity to savor the wisdom of the great Kabbalists straight from the source. While the text does not even scratch the surface of the rich spiritual treasures contained in the *sifrei Kabbalah*, I hope, nevertheless, that the teachings and biographical sketches of these Torah giants will uplift you and stimulate in you a great thirst for Torah knowledge and a deeper commitment to mitzvos and *maasim tovim*. For the primordial Light of the first day of Creation is hidden in the Torah, to be discovered and delighted in by the students of Torah.

I want to thank Rabbi Moshe Dombey, the astute and discerning director of Targum Press, for taking on the publication of this book.

I am grateful to Mrs. Miriam Zakon, editor-in-chief of Targum Press, for her insightful suggestions and for piloting the project from manuscript to finished product.

My special thanks to Mrs. Chaya Baila Gavant for her expertise and meticulous editing of the text and the care and concern she has devoted to this project.

Many thanks to Mrs. Liff for her graphics design and for creating the impressive cover.

A special word of gratitude to my son Rabbi Chaim Finkel, founding *menahel* of Bnos Bais Yaakov High School of Toronto, for his perceptive and valuable advice regarding the selections of the *sifrei Kabbalah*.

My appreciation goes to my friend Arthur Kurzweil, the well-known personality in the literary world, for proposing and encouraging me to write this book.

I want to thank my children, grandchildren, and great-grandchildren for being such a great source of genuine *nachas*, and for showing such a lively interest in the progress of the work. They are living proof of the verse, "*Ateres zekeinim benei banim* — Grandchildren are the crown of their elders" (*Mishlei* 17:6).

Most importantly, I want to express my gratitude to my dear wife, Suri, who exemplifies the virtue and kindness of a Jewish wife and mother. Her devotion, patience, and encouragement have helped me greatly in bringing this work to fruition. May we merit to see children and grandchildren engage in Torah and mitzvos, bringing peace upon Yisrael.

Introduction

Kabbalah: An Overview

As a child of the age of science and technology, your life is swept up in a relentless quest for material success. You live in a society where every product or service is geared to providing fun, where making money is the highest value. You tend to be pragmatic, and your mind is attuned to solving nuts-and-bolts problems. Even your leisure hours are filled with down-to-earth pastimes accompanied by the din of discordant music. The net effect is that your activities and diversions drown out your inner voice that asks: *Is this what life is all about?* Something seems deeply amiss.

The brief intervals of prayer are your only reminders that there is more to life than the pursuit of physical pleasure. Then there are the fleeting moments of quiet reflection. It may be the serenity of Shabbos, the immensity of the star-studded sky, a majestic mountain, a placid lake, or a delicate butterfly, that set you to thinking. Awestruck by the grandeur of God's creation, you feel your soul is stirred. A sudden jolt whisks you out of your daily grind. Your thoughts begin to soar, questions pile up. How did God bring all this splendid bounty into existence? And for what reason?

You remember the story of Creation, when God said, "Let there be light, and there was light. Let the earth bring forth living creatures. And so it was." And you ponder how God who is One, an intangible, infinite Being, created the universe that is physical, multifaceted, and finite. How did the Divine Spirit evolve into tangible matter? How is it that kindness and strictness, mercy and justice, all come forth from one indivisible, beneficent, compassionate Creator? A storm of thoughts is blowing through your head.

You have touched the core of existence. It is questions such as these — the mysteries of God, man, and the world — that form the subject matter of Kabbalah. (Kabbalah, from the root *kibbeil*, "to receive," means "Tradition." It is the secret knowledge of the unwritten Torah that was communicated by God to Moshe and Adam and was transmitted to the wisest and saintliest sages of each generation.)

Of course, knowledge of God and His ways is beyond man's reach. Not even Moshe, the greatest human being who ever lived, was capable of comprehending the Divine Essence. He wanted to know the true nature of God and asked, "Show me Your glory" (*Shemos* 33:18). God replied that this was impossible, telling Moshe, "You cannot see My face, for no man can see Me and live" (*Shemos* 33:20).

To a certain extent, however, Kabbalah lifts the veil that shrouds these mysteries and reveals some of the secrets of the higher world. This esoteric body of knowledge is accesible to *yod'ei chein*, "those that understand *chein* [an acronym of '*chochmas nistar*'], the hidden wisdom of mysticism." The *yod'ei chein* are the great and saintly Kabbalists who live a life devoted to Torah study, benevolence, piety, prayer, and contemplation. They yearn to achieve a state of *deveikus*, closeness to God. For all others — including the author of this book — this wisdom remains an unfathomable secret, an inscrutable enigma that can be touched upon in only the most cursory and oversimplified terms.

In this book I humbly offer a sampling of the teachings of the masters of Kabbalah. The selections, prefaced by short biographical notes, are listed in chronological order, ranging from the venerable ancient texts to the writings of the medieval Kabbalists, followed by the more recent Kabbalistic insights of the great chassidic masters. The list of sages is by no means complete, but the constraints of space and time forced me to make choices. Rather than learn about Kabbalah from second-hand sources, you hear the authentic wisdom of the Kabbalists themselves — in their own words — as they speak to you across the millennia. I hope that their message will give you a deeper appreciation of the wisdom of the Torah, awaken in you a love of God, and inspire you to a more intense fulfillment of the mitzvos. As Shlomo said, "The sum of the matter, when all is said and done: Fear God and keep His commandments, for that is man's whole duty" (*Koheles* 12:13).

Part I
CONCEPTS OF KABBALAH

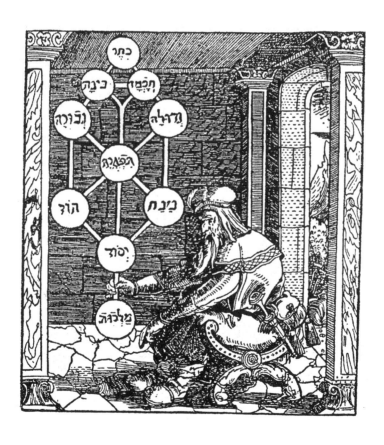

Chapter 1
CREATION AND *TZIMTZUM*

To what purpose did God create the world? How did the universe come into being?

Kabbalah finds an indication in the verse, "*Olam chesed yibaneh* — The world is built on kindness" (*Tehillim* 89:3). God, in His infinite love, desired to bestow *chesed*, kindness, on a being that would deserve His bounty by freely choosing to serve Him. To that end He created the universe for the sake of man,[1] whom He endowed with *bechirah*, the freedom to choose between good and evil. Unlike angels who have no free will, man is given both the *yetzer hatov* (the good impulse) and the *yetzer hara* (the evil impulse). By freely choosing to do good and resisting evil in spite of its powerful allure, man earns the boundless flow of kindness God wants to bestow on him.

How does the flow of Divine kindness make the transition from the spiritual realm down to the coarse physical earth? How does intangible spirit become tangible matter?

Kabbalah teaches that before Creation, God's Infinite Light filled all existence; as it says, "There is no place empty of Him" (*Midrash Rabbah* 12:4).[2] Within the all-encompassing Divine Light nothing else could exist. Therefore, in order to create the universe God made "room" for it by yielding

---

1 Rabbi Chaim Volozhiner, *Nefesh HaChaim* 1:17, end of chapter (see ch. 40).

space, in a process called *tzimtzum*, which means stricture, or contraction of His Infinite Light. To put it another way, God withdrew into Himself, leaving a vast primordial void in the center of His Infinity. Into this newly created space flowed a thin ray of the *Or Ein Sof*, the Divine Infinite Light, descending through a series of ten *Sefiros*. For lack of a better term, the *Sefiros* commonly are called "attributes," "vessels," or "emanations." It was through this thin ray of Divine Light that all Creation took place.

It should be understood that *Sefiros* are purely metaphysical in nature and not in any sense material; their essence completely transcends human comprehension.

The Divine Light flows from the higher worlds to our physical universe by way of the *Sefiros*. The *Sefiros* are the channels through which the divine flow of plenty surges from the lofty heights of the spiritual domain to our crude material world. It is a stream of divine bounty through which God continually sustains His world and keeps it going, as we say in *Tefillas Shacharis*, "In His goodness He renews daily, perpetually, the work of Creation." If this divine stream of kindness would cease to flow even for a split second, the world would instantly revert to nothingness.

Simply put, the *Sefiros* are the divine attributes through which God reveals Himself to a limited degree. As the Infinite Light flows from the higher to the lower *Sefiros*, its intensity progressively diminishes; its splendor is concealed more and more.

The Mystery of the Ten *Sefiros*

One of the fundamental principles of the Jewish faith is that it is impossible to comprehend God. As the Rambam[1] puts it:

We believe that God is totally nonphysical. He is not a body or a physical

---

2   *Sefer HaBahir,* by Rabbi Nechunya ben HaKanah, a Talmudic sage of the first century (see ch. 6). Also in the *Zohar* 1:15a. Also in *Eitz Chaim, Shaar Igulim VeYashar,* by Rabbi Chaim Vital, citing Rabbi Yitzchak Luria's teachings (see ch. 30).

force. Thus we cannot say that God moves, rests, or exists in a given place.... Very often, however, our holy Scriptures do speak of God in physical terms. Thus we find such concepts as walking, standing, sitting, hearing, seeing, and speaking used in relation to God. In all these cases, though, Scripture is only speaking in a figurative sense, expressing esoteric concepts in terms the human mind can grasp. Our Sages teach us, "*Dibberah Torah bilshon benei adam* – The Torah speaks the ordinary language of man" (*Berachos* 31b).

(*Rambam, Commentary on Sanhedrin 10:1*)

And so, when discussing the mystery of the *Sefiros*, we must bear in mind that all descriptions of conduits, emanations, radiations, and channels are only metaphors that express the means by which the Ein Sof (the Infinite One) makes His existence known. It is impossible to grasp the reality of the *Sefiros*, since, in essence, they are manifestations of divine attributes that are beyond human understanding.

Rabbi Moshe Cordovero,[1] in his *Pardes Rimonim*, in the chapter *Shaar HaTzinoros* (Gate of Conduits), presents a symbolic diagram that depicts the *Sefiros* in the shape of a human figure, wherein each of the major limbs and organs corresponds to one of the *Sefiros*. The following are the ten *Sefiros* in descending order.

1. *Keser* (Crown)
2. *Chochmah* (Wisdom)
3. *Binah* (Understanding)
4. *Chesed* (Kindness)
5. *Gevurah* (Power)
6. *Tiferes* (Beauty)

---

1   Rabbi Moshe ben Maimon (Maimonides), 1135–1204. He is revered as an illustrious halachic authority, codifier, philosopher, and physician. His commentary on the Mishnah and his great code *Mishneh Torah* are works of genius.
1   See ch. 29.

7. *Netzach* (Eternity)
8. *Hod* (Splendor)
9. *Yesod* (Foundation)
10. *Malchus* (Kingdom)

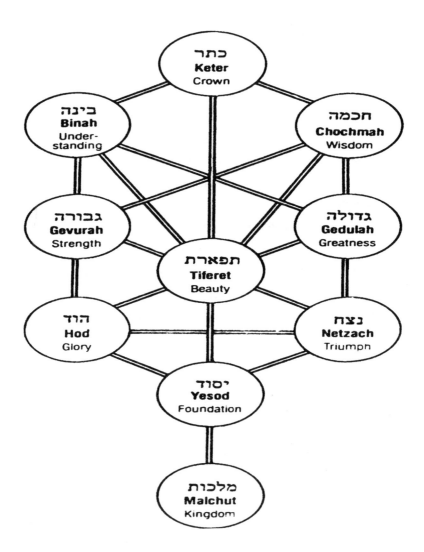

Representation of the ten *Sefiros*, based on the original illustration in *Pardes Rimonim* by Rabbi Moshe Cordovero.

Chapter 2
THE *SEFIROS*

Keser, *Chochmah*, and *Binah*, the Three Unfathomable *Sefiros*

Of the uppermost three *Sefiros* – *Keser* (Crown), *Chochmah* (Wisdom), and *Binah* (Understanding), the highest and holiest is *Keser*. It is the one nearest God, the manifestation of God's will. It is called *Keser* because a crown is worn above the head. *Keser* therefore refers to things that are above the human mind's ability to comprehend.

Taken together these three *Sefiros* are called *mochin*, which means "the brain." They are "the *Sefiros* of the head" and represent intelligence. In human terms, *Chochmah* can be described as the *Sefirah* of intuitive or direct knowledge, and *Binah* as the *Sefirah* of intellectual analysis, where intuition develops into actual thought.

The *mochin* (*Keser*, *Chochmah*, *Binah*) are also called *imos*, mothers, which is a fitting description because these three *Sefiros* of intelligence "give birth" to the seven lower *Sefiros*.

Keser, *Chochmah*, and *Binah* are also often referred to as *reisha delo isyada*, "the unknowable head." The relation between the three highest and the lower seven *Sefiros* is as man's soul to his body. Just as man's soul – his inner self — is hidden from others and becomes apparent only through his words and actions, so is the essence of God completely concealed and is manifest only in the *middos* (divine attributes), namely, the seven lower *Sefiros*.

Your Elusive "Self"

Taking this thought one step further, we can say that a person's inner self, his soul, is hidden, not only from others, but even from himself. Just as God is unknowable, so it is impossible for you to know your innermost self. It sounds bizarre, but you can easily prove it to yourself. As you read these lines, try to think about your conscious mind that is reflecting on the meaning of the words. Now try to detect the "I" that is doing the reading and thinking. As you think about your "self" you discover that there are really two "selfs" within you. There is the "active I" that is doing the thinking, and the "passive I" that is the object of your thinking.

Now, if you try to analyze this "active, thinking I" that is probing your "self," you find that there is yet a higher "I" that is thinking about your "thinking I." You suddenly realize that, no matter how high you reach in thinking about thinking about thinking...about yourself, your innermost "I" can never be apprehended. It is impossible to pinpoint your "real self" or to understand it, because your "I" is the divine spark within you. Like the Infinite, it is elusive, beyond your grasp. You have proved to yourself and know with absolute certainty that you are a thinking "I," but you cannot put your finger on it.

And so, by looking within yourself, groping for your hidden "I," you recognize your soul, your *cheilek Elokah mima'al*, "the small particle of God" in you. As Iyov put it, "In my flesh I see God" (*Iyov* 19:26). By contemplating my "self" I come to recognize God.

The "Lower" Seven *Sefiros*

The "lower" seven *Sefiros* (*Chesed, Gevurah, Tiferes, Netzach, Hod, Yesod, Malchus*) are the channels through which the world was created and is sustained. In *Sefer Yetzirah*[1] (1:5) they are called *middos*, divine attributes through which God administers the world; divine characteristics like kindness, strict justice, and mercy.

The word *middos* also means "measures." The term *measure* is highly appropriate because, in contrast to the three higher *Sefiros* which are infinite, the seven lower *Sefiros* are measured and restricted.

As we mentioned earlier, the three higher *Sefiros* are described both as *imos* (mothers) and as *mochin* (intelligence). The mother-child relationship between the three higher "*imos-mochin*" and the seven lower "*middos*" has a striking counterpart in man. Just as the *imos-mochin* give birth to the *middos*, so is man's intellect the source of his behavior, because all human qualities and emotions, such as love, fear, generosity, and pride, originate in his thinking process.[2]

The *Sefiros* can be seen as a configuration resembling an upright human figure, each of whose main limbs and organs corresponds to one of the *Sefiros*. The head represents the highest three *Sefiros*. The group of three *Sefiros* below the head corresponds to the heart and the two arms. The next three *Sefiros* match the parts of the body that sustain life: the two legs and the reproductive organ, while the tenth *Sefirah*, *Malchus*, is where the Divine Light reaches its destination in our world.[3]

As shown in the diagram on page 6, the *Sefiros* are arranged in sets of three. The two *Sefiros* on the right side represent *chesed* (kindness), the two on the left represent *din* (strictness). The third *Sefirah*, in the center, reconciles the two opposing extremes.

---

1 See ch. 5.
2 *Likutei Amarim* (*Tanya*), ch. 3, by Rabbi Shneur Zalman of Liadi. See ch. 46 in this book.
3 *Malchus*, the lowest *Sefirah*, is usually considered the female part to the male. Occasionally, this lowest *Sefirah* is considered part of the male body, specifically the crown of the male reproductive organ.

The *Sefiros* on one side balance those on the other. Thus, *Chochmah*, which is intuitive knowledge, is balanced by *Binah*, which is intellectual analysis. Similarly, *Chesed*, the *Sefirah* of limitless, unrestricted love, is kept in check by *Gevurah*, the *Sefirah* of restraint, fear, and awe.

Chesed, the Fourth *Sefirah*

Chesed (Kindness) is the trait of benevolence, bestowing boundless love and kindness on others, whether they deserve kindness or not. It is the cornerstone of this world, as it says, "*Olam chesed yibaneh* — The world is built on *chesed*" (*Tehillim* 89:3). God continuously showers His kindness on the world, nourishing and sustaining all His creatures. But the greatest act of divine kindness is that He gives of Himself, implanting in each of us a part of Himself, our soul.

Man, who has a spark of the Divine Essence and exemplifies the *Sefiros*, is urged to emulate the divine attributes in the phrase *hiddabeik biderachav*, "cling to His ways" (Rashi on *Devarim* 13:5; *Sotah* 14a). How can you make the *Sefirah* of *Chesed* a reality in your life? By loving God with all your heart and soul and by loving your fellowman, treating him with goodness and kindness. The *Sefirah* of *Chesed* is the right arm of the human body in the *Sefirah* diagram, symbolic of the helpful arm that is extended in welcome, friendship, and aid. Avraham exemplified the quality of *chesed* and became the personification of the *Sefirah* of *Chesed*.

Gevurah, the Fifth *Sefirah*

Gevurah (Power), the opposite of *Chesed*, is the trait of restraint, fear, and awe. It means a limited, controlled form of giving. On the human level it involves fearing God and shuddering at the very thought of transgressing His mitzvos.

The *Sefirah* of *Gevurah* is symbolized by Yitzchak, who at the *akeidah* (the binding of Yitzchak) allowed himself to be bound on the altar, ready to offer his life in fulfillment of God's command.

The *Sefirah* of *Gevurah* is depicted as the left arm of the symbolic human body.

Tiferes, the Sixth *Sefirah*

Tiferes (Beauty), the *Sefirah* of compassion, mediates the conflict between *Chesed* and *Gevurah*. The essence of beauty is harmony in nature, music, and other art forms. Thus *Tiferes* is the dimension that creates harmony between the love of *Chesed* on the one hand and the stern justice of *Gevurah* on the other.

In human terms, *Tiferes* means following the middle road, the path of moderation, and shunning the extremes on either side.

The prototype of the *Sefirah* of *Tiferes* is Yaakov, the *bechir ha'avos*, "the favorite patriarch," for he symbolizes truth, as it says, "Grant truth to Yaakov" (*Michah* 7:20). Truth implies the proper mix of opposing attributes. Since *Tiferes* stands for the perfect blend of *Chesed* and *Gevurah*, it is fitting that Yaakov is associated with this *Sefirah*.

In the symbolic human body, *Tiferes* corresponds to the heart. Just as *Tiferes* creates unity and harmony out of the divergent forces of *Chesed* and *Gevurah*, so does the heart unify and harmonize the varied functions of all parts of the body.

Netzach and *Hod*, the Seventh and Eighth *Sefiros*

Netzach (Eternity) and *Hod* (Splendor) are compared to "the two kidneys that give counsel." How is this to be understood? Having passed through the *Sefirah* of *Tiferes*, the Infinite Light is ready to penetrate the lower *Sefiros*. Before this can come about, advice must be sought as to how best to convey the flow of abundance. It can be compared to a teacher who wants to teach a difficult lesson. If he presents the lesson in its full complexity, the student will not be able to grasp it. Seeking advice on how best to explain the knotty problem, the teacher is told to impart the lesson in the way of a funnel. He should narrow down the subject matter and present it in small doses. Giving advice and counsel on how best to proceed is the function of the *Sefiros* of *Netzach* and *Hod*.

The word *Netzach* denotes triumph as well as eternity. Both meanings apply to this *Sefirah*, because one who triumphs over adversity can endure.

In man, the *Sefirah* of *Netzach* signifies the triumph over all obstacles that stand in your way of serving God, whether external or internal. *Hod* stands for gratitude, thanking God for all His kindness.

Moshe is the epitome of *Netzach*; Aharon exemplifies *Hod*. In the model of the human body, *Netzach* and *Hod* are represented as *trein shokin*, "the two thighs," and together they are described as *trei palgei gufa*, "the two halves of the body." In Kabbalistic writings, the thighs, which are the underpinnings of the body, are the reflection of *emunah*, faith, which is the foundation of Judaism.

Yesod, the Ninth *Sefirah*

Just as *Tiferes* mediates between *Chesed* and *Gevurah*, so does *Yesod* (Foundation) create a synthesis between the two opposing *Sefiros* of *Netzach* and *Hod*. *Yesod* is the *Sefirah* that channels the flow of divine abundance to *Malchus*, the lowest of the *Sefiros*, and through which souls are routed to the physical world. In other words, *Yesod* is the link that connects the giver and the receiver.

From the human perspective, the *Sefirah* of *Yesod* involves being bound and attached to God in thought, feeling, and deed. As a corollary, *Yesod* expresses the idea that all Jews should be bound together in unity and harmony with the intention of serving God.

In the *Sefirah* model of the human body, *Yesod* is symbolized as the male reproductive function, the organ that gives. Therefore, man's obligation not to abuse this function and the severity attached to the transgression of this obligation are related to this *Sefirah*. By extension, *Yesod* is associated with *bris*, the covenant of circumcision.

The sages of Kabbalah connect the *Sefirah* of *Yesod* with the quintessential tzaddik. He is considered the foundation of the world, as it says, "*Tzaddik yesod olam* — The righteous man is the foundation of the world" (*Mishlei* 10:25).

Yesod, the *Sefirah* of giving and the reproductive organ, is closely linked to Yosef, who is generally referred to as Yosef HaTzaddik. It is he who supplied his brothers with food during the seven years of famine in Egypt. It was he who provided grain for the Egyptian people, saying, "Take seed for yourselves" (*Bereishis* 47:23).

Yosef's righteousness became evident when he spurned the seductive advances of his master's wife (*Bereishis* 39) and did not tarnish the covenant of circumcision. As a result, Yosef the tzaddik is the embodiment of the *Sefirah* of *Yesod*.

Malchus, the Tenth *Sefirah*

Malchus (Kingdom) is the final *Sefirah*. It receives the flow of abundance from *Yesod* but does not pass it on. Therefore, this *Sefirah* is generally associated with the woman who receives the seed.[1] The *Zohar* often identifies *Malchus* with the moon, which represents the female, personified by Chavah.[2] For, like the female who receives the seed, the moon receives its light from the sun. Of course, there is an obvious connection between the monthly lunar cycle of waxing and waning and the menstrual cycle of a woman.

King David is the prototype of the *Sefirah* of *Malchus*. Just as the moon is reborn after a period of decline and total eclipse, so too, the Davidic dynasty endures and will rise again with the coming of Mashiach. Confident of the restoration of the messianic monarchy, we say every month in *Kiddush Levanah* (the Sanctification of the New Moon), "David, Melech Yisrael, chai

---

1   *Zohar Chadash, Yisro* 40b.
2   *Zohar, Noach* 16b.

vekayam — David, King of Israel, is alive and enduring."

Malchus, the *Sefirah* that only receives, is represented by the mouth, the organ through which man receives nourishment. *Malchus* has the further connotation of the oral Torah, as it says in *Patach Eliyahu*, "*Malchus* is the mouth, that is called *Torah shebe'al peh*, the oral Torah" (Introduction to *Tikkunei Zohar*).

Malchus, the seventh of the lower *Sefiros*, is the emanation where the Infinite Light reaches its destination and where the divine flow of abundance is spread throughout our world. The seventh *Sefirah* is closely linked to Shabbos, for analogously, Shabbos is the seventh day of Creation, the day "on which God ceased from all the work He had been creating" (*Bereishis* 2:3), the time when God's glory becomes visible on earth.

The analogy can be extended to include King David. The *Zohar* speaks of the Seven Shepherds who epitomize the seven *Sefiros*. They are the personalities who guided and shaped Israel's destiny: Avraham, Yitzchak, Yaakov, Moshe, Aharon, Yosef, and David. The seventh Shepherd is David, who stands for *Malchus*, and who as King of Israel represents God's majesty on earth.[1]

---

1   *Zohar, Emor* 103b.

Chapter 3
SHEVIRAS HAKEILIM

The *Zohar*[1] teaches that in the process of creation, only the three higher *Sefiros* (*Keser, Chochmah, Binah*) could contain the resplendent Light of God flowing through them. The lower *Sefiros* could not hold the Light. As a result of Adam's sin, a cosmic cataclysm occurred, and these vessels shattered (*sheviras hakeilim*), spilling sparks of holiness (*nitzotzos hakedushah*) all over the world. These holy sparks became trapped in shells (*klippos*) of impurity.

The reason why the vessels were originally created without the ability to hold the Light is so that evil should come into being. If the vessels had remained whole, the world would have been perfect, man would be like an angel, and the choice between good and evil, between mitzvah and *aveirah*, would not exist, but neither could there be reward and punishment. Through *sheviras hakeilim*, man has the opportunity to attain perfection by freely choosing good and spurning evil, and thereby earn the reward God has in store for the righteous.

It is the mission of the Jewish people to redeem these trapped sparks. By performing mitzvos and living a life of holiness, we transform even the most mundane acts, like eating and drinking, into a service of God. We thereby re-

---

1   *Zohar, Bereishis* 4a.

lease the trapped sparks contained in the food we eat and elevate the sparks back to their source. Kabbalah teaches that the Jewish people have been sent into exile in order to free the captive sparks all over the world. When that comes to pass, the final redemption will arrive.

Partzufim

Rabbi Yitzchak Luria, the Ari HaKadosh, teaches that in the wake of *sheviras hakeilim*, the five *partzufim* (Faces) formed.

1. The *Sefirah* of *Keser* became *Arich Anpin* (the "Long Face").
2. *Chochmah* became *Abba* ("Father").
3. *Binah* became *Imma* ("Mother").
4. The first six lower *Sefiros* became *Ze'ir Anpin* (the "Short Face").
5. *Malchus* became the female of *Ze'ir Anpin*.

The Four Worlds

Kabbalah teaches that the totality of existence is composed of four worlds. In descending order they are:

1. Atzilus (Emanation)
2. Beri'ah (Creation)
3. Yetzirah (Formation)
4. Asiyah (Action)

In Kabbalistic literature the four worlds are generally referred to by the acronym "Abiyah." These worlds can exist only because God has made "room" for them. This was necessary, for when the divine radiance shines in unrestricted brilliance, nothing else can exist. And so, God has withdrawn and hidden His all-pervasive Self, allowing the physical universe to come into being.

Descending from the higher to the lower worlds, God's concealment gradually increases. His radiance is most evident in the World of Emanation, and it is almost completely obscured in the World of Action, which is our world. This means that the creatures of the higher world – angels like *ofanim, serafim,* and *chayos* – are more God-like and closer to God. They more clearly perceive the Divine Light. By contrast, the inhabitants of the World of Action, meaning man, are separated from God by a massive barrier of corporeality. This barrier effectively shuts out the divine radiance and leads many people to doubt or even deny the existence of a Creator. They delude themselves into thinking that they are the masters of the world. They take their cue from Pharaoh, the archetypical atheist, who proclaimed, "My Nile is my own; I made it myself" (*Yechezkel* 29:3).

Only when disaster struck in the form of the ten plagues did Pharaoh "see the light." At last he declared to Moshe, "God is just! It is I and my people who are wrong. Pray to God" (*Shemos* 9:27–28).

Part II
THE EARLIEST KABBALISTIC WORKS

Introduction
THE EARLIEST KABBALISTIC WORKS

Kabbalah is the oral heritage that was communicated by God to Adam and Moshe. Its teachings, which attempt to fathom the mysteries of God and Creation, were zealously guarded and transmitted from generation to generation by devout teachers of utmost scholarship who instructed a few mature and worthy disciples. This was done in order to avoid the dangers of misinterpretations by unscrupulous people who would mislead the Jewish masses, as happened in the case of the false *mashiach* Shabsai Tzvi.

The earliest Kabbalistic text is *Raziel HaMalach*, attributed to Adam HaRishon. Another early Kabbalistic book is *Sefer Yetzirah*, attributed to Avraham Avinu, which explains Creation as a process involving the ten *Sefiros* and the twenty-two letters of the *alef beis*. One of the earliest commentators on *Sefer Yetzirah* is Rabbi Shabsai Donnolo.

A very important early work is *Sefer HaBahir*, written by the *tanna* Rabbi Nechunya ben HaKanah (first century C.E.), which introduces the concept of *gilgul* (transmigration of souls). Perhaps the most important of the early works of Kabbalah is the *Zohar*, written by Rabbi Shimon bar Yochai (second century C.E.). It is the primary book on Kabbalah and all later works are based on its teachings. In its running commentary on the Torah, it deals with the *Sefiros*, the sources of good and evil, and the soul. Every word and letter of the Torah is given a Kabbalistic explanation. Because of its great sancitity, it is often referred to as the *Zohar HaKadosh*, the holy *Zohar*.

Chapter 4
RAZIEL HAMALACH

Attributed to Adam HaRishon

Raziel HaMalach was first printed in Amsterdam in 1701. Since then the book has seen numerous editions, mainly because of the widespread belief that keeping a copy of the book protects one's home from fire and other disasters.

The earliest mention of the angel Raziel is found in the apocryphal book of *Chanoch*.[1] Another early reference to Raziel is in the ancient Targum interpretive translation of *Koheles* 10:20, where it says, "The angel Raziel makes daily announcements on Mount Chorev." Rabbi Avraham ibn Ezra, the great Torah commentator,[2] mentions *Raziel HaMalach* in his commentary to *Shemos* 14:19, in connection with the seventy-two-letter Divine Name.

The esoteric text of *Raziel HaMalach* deals with the attributes and the holy names of God and names of angels, *Sefiros*, Kabbalistic mysteries inherent in the letters of the Divine Name, the signs of the zodiac, and the texts of

---

1 Apocrypha, in Hebrew called *sefarim chitzonim* or *kesuvim acharonim*, are books that were written during the time of the Second Temple but were not included in *Tanach*. They include, among others, the books of *Ben Sira* (which is mentioned in the Gemara, *Bava Kama* 92b and *Sanhedrin* 100b), *Chashmonaim*, *Yehudis*, and *Chanoch*.
2 1089–1164.

various amulets. The title page of the book reads, "This is the book of Adam, the first man. It was given to him by the angel Raziel. Keeping this awesome holy book in your house — even if you do not study it — is an excellent aid for raising intelligent and wise children, for success and blessing. It affords protection against fire and other accidents and wards off demons and calamities."

Selections from *Raziel HaMalach*

[Note: Most of the contents of *Raziel HaMalach* are extremely abstruse and do not lend themselves to translation. The following selections are exceptions and do not represent the deeply mystical tenor of the book.]

Adam's Prayer

This is the prayer Adam said when he was banished from Gan Eden:

"Eternal God, You created the world according to Your will.... Nothing is hidden from You. You put me in charge of Your handiwork, and made me ruler over all Your creatures. But the cursed and cunning serpent seduced me [to eat from] the Tree of Lust and Desire. What's more, my wife tempted me and did not tell me what the consequences would be for me, my children, and future generations....

"I realize that I have sinned, and because of my transgression I was banished [from Gan Eden] today. I now must work the ground from which I was taken. The animals of the earth are not afraid of me anymore, because since I ate from the Tree of Knowledge, I lost my superior wisdom. I became a boor and a fool, and I have no idea what is to become of me. Please, merciful and gracious God, have compassion on me, Your creation.... Do not ignore my supplication. Forgive me, and let me know what will happen to me, to my offspring, and to the coming generations, every day and every month, and do not withhold from me the wisdom of Your angels."

From the opening paragraph

The Angel Raziel Appears to Adam

Sitting by the river that flowed out of Gan Eden, Adam continued praying and pleading for three days. At high noon, on the third day, the angel Raziel appeared to him, carrying a book. Said the angel, "Adam, why are you distraught? Your prayers have been accepted, and I have come to make you understand the great wisdom you will find in this holy book. From this book you will learn what will happen to you until the day you die. And whichever of your descendants will humbly do what is written in this book, he too will discover what the future holds for him, each and every day and month. He will know whether there will be bad times, famine, or wild animals; whether or not the rains will come, whether the crops will be plentiful or sparse, whether evil tyrants will rule, whether disease, war, bloodshed, and suffering will prevail, or favorable decrees will emanate from heaven. Come closer, Adam. Let me show you the holy contents of this book."

When Raziel HaMalach began to read from the book, Adam fell to the ground, overcome with awe. Said the angel, "Adam, stand up. Don't be afraid. Take this book and take good care of it, because it will make you wise." The moment Adam took hold of the book, a flame flared up from the river, and the angel rose toward heaven in a roaring blaze. Seeing this, Adam realized that [the man who had spoken to him] was a heavenly angel, and that the book had been sent to him by God Almighty. So he safeguarded the book in holiness and purity.

Raziel HaMalach, p. 2

Chanoch Finds the Book

[Note: The ten generations from Adam to Noach (enumerated in *Bereishis*, ch. 5) rebelled against God.[1] The lone exception was Chanoch (Enoch), a righteous man "who walked with God" (*Bereishis* 5:22). According to tradition, he entered Gan Eden without dying.]

---

1   See *Avos* 5:2.

Four generations after Adam,[1] Chanoch ben Yared appeared on the scene. A God-fearing man, he regularly immersed in a *mikveh* and prayed to the Creator. God appeared to him in a dream and told him where the Book was hidden and that he should treat the Book with great reverence. Early in the morning Chanoch went to the cave [where the Book was hidden]. He stayed there until noon, pretending to relax, lest the local idolatrous people realize [that he was looking for a precious book and harass him]. He prayed and implored God, invoking His holy Name, [asking for guidance].

[As he studied the Book] he learned about the seasons, constellations, the signs of the zodiac, the names of the angels that are assigned to the four seasons. He understood more of all fields of wisdom than Adam ever did. When Chanoch realized that the coming generations were not strong enough to absorb the awesome knowledge contained in this Book, he hid it. Since he understood the Book, he lived by its teachings to the point that he became an otherworldly holy man. "Then he was no more, for God had taken him" (*Bereishis* 5:24) [he did not die, but rose alive to heaven].

Raziel HaMalach, p. 2

The Vast Benefits of the Book *Raziel HaMalach*

[In Noach's days, the world was corrupt, and only Noach found favor in the eyes of God.] When Noach was five hundred years old, the angel Refael was sent to entrust the holy Book to him.... During his stay in the Ark, Noach transmitted the Book to his son Shem, who transmitted it to Avraham; from Avraham it went to Yitzchak and on to Yaakov, to Levi, to Moshe and Aharon, to Pinchas who handed it to his son, and so on, generation after generation....

When you possess this Book and observe the Torah in purity, you will never be disgraced. You will be protected from all adversity and live a

---

1   Actually, seven generations.

happy life. You will be well-liked and favored by God and man.... You will be successful in all your undertakings, and all your enemies will be afraid of you....

Raziel HaMalach, p. 4

Heart and Mind

[Note: *Nefesh* is the animal life-force that man has in common with animals.]

When a person eats and drinks to his heart's content, his veins expand and his organs warm up. The food is thereby digested, the nutrients enter the bloodstream, and the warmth of the blood sustains life. That is implied by the verse, "The life-force of all flesh is in its blood" (*Vayikra* 17:14).

The "life-force" is made up of three parts: an inner, an intermediate, and an outer part. The inner part is the heart. It is the seat of desire. When the heart craves something and its master can fulfill its wish, the heart is overjoyed. But if the master is unable to satisfy the heart's lust, it is angry and can think of nothing but the unfulfilled desire.

The heart is the seat of love and hate, and all wisdom, knowledge, planning, and thought spring from the heart. Now you understand that the heart holds sway over the mind. It quietly sits back and governs the mind. The heart uses the ingenuity and intellect of the mind to reach its goals. [Proof of this is the fact that] when a person is tired and exhausted, he immediately falls asleep [and his mind becomes dormant], but his heart evokes such vivid dreams that he does not know whether he is awake or asleep. [In other words, your thoughts are influenced by your desire.]

The intermediate part of the life-force is the tongue, while the external part consists of the hands, the voice, and speech. The inner part of the soul never sleeps, although [in your sleep] the life-force departs temporarily. When a person sleeps and is rudely awakened, he jumps up and his heart flutters like a little bird. That is the life-force suddenly coming back. But if a person wakes up naturally early in the morning, the life-force gently slides back into its habitat, and the intellect is back in operation.

Raziel HaMalach, p. 24

Bereishis, in the Beginning

The opening words of the Torah are "*Bereishis* – In the beginning God created" (*Bereishis* 1:1). The Torah starts with the letter *beis* [whose numeric value is 2], to indicate that God created two worlds with two letters of His name. The two letters are *yud* and *hei*, as it says, "For *Kah* [*Yud-Hei*] Hashem is the Rock of the universe" (*Yeshayah* 26:4). The two worlds God created are this world and the World to Come. This world was created with the letter *hei*[1] and the World to Come with the *yud*. [In the *alef beis*, the *hei* comes before the *yud*. But] in the divine Name *Kah* [with which God created the two worlds], the *yud* precedes the *hei*, because God had in mind to create the World to Come [*yud*] before bringing this world [*hei*] into existence.

Raziel HaMalach, p. 30

The Signs of the Zodiac[2]

The Holy One, blessed be He, created the twelve constellations of the zodiac and set them in the firmament. These are: T'leh (Ram), Shor (Bull), Te'omim (Twins), Sartan (Crab), Aryeh (Lion), Besulah (Virgin), Moznayim (Balance), Akrav (Scorpion), Keshes (Archer), Gedi (Goat), Deli (Water-Bearer), Dagim (Fish). [In English: Aries, Taurus, Gemini,

---

1   This is derived from the verse, "These are the chronicles of heaven and earth, *behibare'am*, when they were created" (*Bereishis* 2:4). The word *behibare'am*, "when they were created," is read as *b'hei bare'am*, meaning, "He created them with the letter *hei*." As further proof that this world is the one created with the *hei*, we are taught that just as the *hei* is open at the bottom, so is this world open for penitents to do *teshuvah* (*Menachos* 29b).

2   The zodiac is an imaginary belt around the heavens. It is divided into twelve parts, called signs of the zodiac.

Cancer, Leo, Virgo, Libra, Scorpio, Sagittarius, Capricorn, Aquarius, Pisces.] God arranged them to rule over the twelve months of the year. Their light shines day and night, but during the day they are not visible because the light of the sun outshines them.

[As they move along the night sky,] six of them alternately are visible in the sky while six are covered. When T'leh begins to set, Moznayim ascends. When Moznayim sets, T'leh rises, and so on. When one sign of the zodiac rises, its counterpart in the zodiac sets. One constellation does not encroach on the next. The constellation that dominates the planting season does not govern the harvest season, and vice versa.... And the Holy One, blessed be He, leads them in His wisdom.

Raziel HaMalach, p. 56

Man Is a Microcosm

> Realize it today and ponder it in your heart: God is the Supreme Being in heaven above and on earth beneath — there is no other.
> <div align="right">(<i>Devarim</i> 4:39)</div>

All thoughts originate in the heart. Without the heart there is no wisdom That is why the heart is called *leiv* [spelled *lamed-beis*], to tell you: Ponder [the Torah] which begins with the letter *beis* [of *Bereishis*] and ends with the *lamed* [of *Yisrael*]. It is for this reason that the first paragraph of *Sefer Yetzirah* begins with the words, "With thirty-two wondrous paths of wisdom He created the world." [The numeric value of *leiv* is thirty-two.]

The heart thinks: The Holy One, blessed be He, created me, and formed from a drop of semen a body that contains ten [physical] elements: skin, flesh, veins, bones, hair, blood, ... nails, the black and white of the eyes. Correspondingly, God gave ten [spiritual] elements of Himself: the soul, facial features, the sense of hearing, seeing, smell, the speech of the lips, the movement of the tongue, the use of hands and feet, wisdom, and understanding.

Man's spirit encircles his body, as the air surrounds the world. This tells you that man is a small-scale world. That's why you should think: How fortunate am I to have been created in the image and form of God who gave me the power of speech to serve Him. He gave a soul that He guards while I am asleep; and if He so desires He takes it from me. So how can I transgress? I will serve Him with joy and delight and set aside the pleasures of this world in favor of the happiness that awaits me in the World to Come.

Raziel HaMalach, p. 27

Chapter 5

SEFER YETZIRAH

Attributed to Avraham Avinu

Sefer Yetzirah (the Book of Creation) is the oldest and one of the most important books of Kabbalah. According to Rabbi Moshe Cordovero,[1] it was written by the Patriarch Avraham. Others maintain that Rabbi Akiva was the author and that he recorded in *Sefer Yetzirah* the teachings that originated from Avraham and were transmitted to him.

Sefer Yetzirah deals with the age-old question of how God, who is completely One, created a universe of infinite diversity; how God, who is spiritual, brought into being a world that is physical and tangible. *Sefer Yetzirah* teaches that God created the cosmos with the twenty-two letters of the *alef beis* and the ten *Sefiros*. Taken together they make up the thirty-two pathways of wisdom. Furthermore, the *Sefiros* and the letters of the Hebrew alphabet have their counterparts in the parts of the human body. This means that man is a small-scale replica of the universe and a microcosm of the spiritual world.

If the notion that God created the world by combining letters sounds bizarre, you should bear in mind that, unlike the secular alphabet, the letters of the Hebrew *alef beis* are not arbitrary characters. The letters of the Torah

---

1 In his work *Pardes Rimonim*. See ch. 29 in this book.

are a reflection of the spiritual alphabet and language that God utilized to create the universe. So, when the Torah says, "God said, 'Let there be light,' " it was not a physical voice speaking, but rather God combining the letters and words of this spiritual *alef beis* to create light. Thus the Midrash says, "God peered into the Torah and created the world" (*Bereishis Rabbah* 1:2). So you can say that the Torah is the blueprint of the universe, and the letters of the Torah the building blocks of the world.

The creative power inherent in the letters of the *alef beis* is mentioned in the Talmud. The Gemara (*Sanhedrin* 65b, 67b) relates that Rabbah created a man by combining the letters of the Divine name as set forth in *Sefer Yetzirah*. We also are told that Rabbi Chanina and Rabbi Oshayah, applying the mystic teachings of *Sefer Yetzirah*, created a plump calf every Friday which they then ate at their Shabbos meal (ibid.).

As another example of the application of the spiritual dimension of the *alef beis*, the Gemara tells us that Betzalel, the builder of the Tabernacle, was able to construct the Tabernacle and its holy vessels because "he knew how to combine the letters by which heaven and earth were created" (*Berachos* 55a).

But Kabbalah is not meant to be studied by everyone. The Talmud says that Kabbalah should only be taught through hints and allusions, and this is the course followed by the author of *Sefer Yetzirah*. Indeed, all major Kabbalah texts were written in cryptic phrases that could only be understood by a closed group of the initiated. In fact, the word *Kabbalah* means received teachings, implying that the mysteries embodied in Kabbalah were discreetly transmitted from master to a select circle of qualified disciples.

Sefer Yetzirah contains six short chapters which are subdivided into *mishnayos* (not to be confused with the *mishnayos* of the Talmud). Comprising fewer than two thousand words, *Sefer Yetzirah* is one of the most extraordinary works in Jewish literature. The concept of the ten *Sefiros*, mentioned here for the first time, has profoundly affected subsequent Kabbalistic thought. To this day, the mere mention of the title *Sefer Yetzirah* inspires people with a deep sense of awe and wonder.

Sefer Yetzirah was first printed in Mantua in 1562. More than fifty commentaries have been written on it, including commentaries by Rabbeinu Saadyah Gaon,[1] the Ramban,[2] the Ravad,[3] and Rabbi Eliyahu, the Vilna Gaon.[4] The book is written in an enigmatic style, and its meaning — despite the many commentaries — remains elusive.

It is important to remember that the *Sefiros* and other Kabbalistic concepts are figurative representations of lofty ideas that should not be taken literally.

Selections from Sefer Yetzirah with Commentary

The Thirty-Two Paths of Wisdom

> With thirty-two wondrous pathways of wisdom…He [God] created His world with three books, with *S'for* (number), *Sippur* (verbal instruction), and *Sefer* (book).
>
> Sefer Yetzirah 1:1

Rabbi Yehudah HaLevi explains in the *Kuzari*:

> *S'for* refers to the measuring and weighing of the physical creations. Before a builder builds a house, he first visualizes it in his mind [and calculates its measurements and the weight of the beams]. [*S'for* thus means that God envisioned Creation before implementing it.]
>
> *Sippur* [verbal instruction, literally, "story"] refers to God's speech and voice, [not a human speech and voice but rather] Divine speech. God's speech brings into being the structure and form of the object it describes. For example, it says, "God said, 'Let there be light'; and there was light."

---

1 882–942.
2 See ch. 12.
3 Rabbi Avraham ben David of Posquires, discussed in ch. 9. Others hold that it was a different Ravad.
4 See ch. 39.

Which means that light arose simultaneous with God's verbal instruction.

Sefer refers to writing, and God's writing is the objects He created. [Heaven and earth and everything in it are God's writing.]

S'for, Sippur, and *Sefer* are interrelated, since God's speech is His writing, and God's measurement is His speech. With God they are one, whereas with man they are three distinct entities. For man first maps things out in his mind, then articulates his thoughts with his mouth, and then carries out with his hands that which he said. These three acts are therefore meant to describe the one act that occurs when God creates. God's mental measurements and His speech *are* the object itself, which is synonymous with His writing.

Figure, if you will, a weaver of ornate clothing who simply has to imagine his work and the silk is made by itself; it takes on the texture he has imagined and the patterns he desires. We would then say that the garment was made with the weaver's mental measurements and writing.

The "thirty-two wondrous pathways of wisdom" mentioned in the paragraph are the ten *Sefiros* plus the twenty-two letters of the *alef beis*. These are allusions to how all things came into existence and how they are fixed by their measure and their substance.

(Kuzari 4:25)

Infinity

Ten *Sefiros* of nothing, they look like lightning and their end is infinite. His word in them is running and returning, and to His word they hurry like a storm, and before His throne they bow.

Sefer Yetzirah 1:6

The paragraph compares the *Sefiros* to lightning, as if to say: Be careful not to delve too deeply into the mysteries of Creation, for you may get burned. The danger of probing the celestial realm is illustrated in the *gemara* that tells about four Sages who entered Pardes, the higher levels of the spiritual world: Ben Azzai, Ben Zoma, Acher, and Rabbi Akiva. Ben Azzai looked and died, Ben Zoma looked and lost his mind, Acher became an apostate. Only Rabbi Akiva "entered whole and came out whole" (*Chagigah* 14b).

This paragraph introduces the phenomenon of *ratzo vashov*, "run and return," that is apparent in all of existence. For example, we see a manifestation of the "run" in the Divine Light that brought Creation into being and the "return" in God withdrawing from Creation to make "room" for the universe.

To illustrate the principle of "run and return," think of a father who teaches his child to walk. He begins by holding and supporting him, yet as soon as the child takes his first hesitant steps he moves away and encourages the child to come closer. As the child moves nearer, the father steps back and withdraws more and more.

The masters of Kabbalah find an allusion to the concept of "run and return" in *Maaseh Merkavah*, Yechezkel's vision of the Divine Chariot (*Yechezkel* 1). In his prophecy he saw that "the *chayos* [the highest category of angels] ran and returned, dashing to and fro like a flash of lightning" (*Yechezkel* 1:14).

Our paragraph says, "To His word they hurry like a storm," which means that the *Sefiros* obey God's orders. It continues, "Before His throne they bow." The *Pri Yitzchak*[1] comments that *Keser* is the first *Sefirah* beneath the Infinite (*Ein Sof*). It is considered God's throne. Thus, that which is "before the throne" is God Himself. In other words, the *Sefiros* bow before God.

The Three Groups of Letters

Twenty-two letters of foundation, three mothers, seven doubles, and twelve regulars. Three mothers, *emesh* [*alef*, *mem*, *shin*]; their foundation is the Scale of Merit and the Scale of Guilt, and the tongue of decree.

Sefer Yetzirah 2:1

---

1   By Rabbi Yitzchak Eizik of Mohalov; Horodno, 1798.

Rabbi Yehudah HaLevi explains in the *Kuzari*:

> All creations differ from each other because they are made of different substances. The twenty-two letters of the *alef beis* [which are source of these differences] are divided into three groups: three mothers, seven doubles, and twelve regular letters.
>
> The "three mothers" refers to the letters ***alef, mem, shin***, making up the acronym *emesh*. It is a great mystery how from these three letters there emerged wind (***a**vir*), water (***m**ayim*), and fire (*ei**sh***). Everything is created from wind, water, and fire, and *emesh* is also the source of all the letters of the *alef beis*. [That is why these three letters are called "mothers."]
>
> ["Doubles" are letters that are pronounced two ways. When a letter has a *dagesh* (dot) in the center, it is pronounced "hard"; a letter without a *dagesh* it is pronounced "soft." For example, we say "***b**erachah*" when the letter *beis* has a *dagesh*, and "*u**v**erachah*," when it has no *dagesh*.]
>
> The "seven double letters" are *beis, gimmel, dalet, kaf, pei, reish,*[1] *tav*.
>
> The "twelve regulars" are the letters *hei, vav, zayin, ches, tes, yud, lamed, nun, samach, ayin,* and *kuf*.
>
> (Kuzari 4:25)

The paragraph speaks of the two pans of the Scale of Justice and mentions the "tongue of decree." The "tongue of decree" refers to the vertical rod in the middle of the scale. It mediates and decides the case. The *Pri Yitzchak* explains that in man the tongue is the mediator between the palate and the throat. In the world of the *Sefiros*, the palate and the throat represent the two extremes of *Chochmah* and *Binah*, while *Daas* (Knowledge) mediates between *Chochmah* and *Binah*.

Space, Time, and the Soul

He made the letter *tav* king and tied a crown to it. With it He formed the

---

1 In conventional Hebrew grammar *reish* never has a *dagesh*.

moon in the universe, Shabbos in the year, and the mouth in the soul.

Sefer Yetzirah 4:11

In a figurative way, the author refers to the *Sefirah* of *Malchus*, the last of the seven lower *Sefiros*. It is in *Malchus* — the physical world — that the Infinite Light reaches its destination. The *Sefirah* of *Malchus* receives the Infinite Light from the *Sefirah* of *Yesod*, but the flow of Light stops in *Malchus*.

The human counterpart of *Malchus* is the female who receives the seed. The letter *tav* mentioned in the mishnah is indicative of the female, because in Hebrew grammar, *tav* is a feminine ending. Also, the letter *tav* symbolizes *Malchus*, since *Malchus* is the last of the *Sefiros*, and *tav* is the last letter of the *alef beis*.

The paragraph mentions three things: the moon, Shabbos, and the mouth. All three closely resemble *Malchus*, the *Sefirah* that receives the Light but does not convey it further. The moon parallels *Malchus* in that it receives its light from the sun. The mouth, too, corresponds to *Malchus*, since the mouth is the organ that receives the food. Shabbos, the seventh day of Creation, symbolizes *Malchus*, the seventh of the lower *Sefiros*. Just as the six upper *Sefiros* reach their goal in the creation of the universe, so is Shabbos the culmination of the six days of work in the material world.

The paragraph says that with the *Sefirah* of *Malchus* God formed the world (*olam*), the year (*shanah*), and the soul (*nefesh*). These are the three dimensions of the corporeal world. For in this world, man operates within the limits of space (*olam*) and time (*shanah*), and he is bound by the laws of morality (*nefesh*). Ashan, the term formed from the initial letters of *olam*, *shanah*, and *nefesh*, is a recurring theme in Kabbalistic writings.

Letters and Words

How were the seven double letters[1] combined? Two stones build two houses; four stones build twenty-four houses; five stones build 120

---

1   As explained above, these are the letters that have two different pronunciations.

houses; six stones build 720 houses; seven stones build 5,040 houses. From here on go and calculate that which the mouth is unable to utter and the ear cannot hear....

Sefer Yetzirah 4:12

A stone, in the idiom of *Sefer Yetzirah*, is a letter; a house is a word or phrase, a specific combination of letters. The Vilna Gaon[1] explains that "four stones build twenty-four houses" means that with four letters you can make twenty-four different combinations, and the seven double letters yield 5,040 possible letter combinations. (From all twenty-two letters of the *alef beis* you can form the astronomical number of $22 \times 21 \times 20 \times 19...^{50}$ combinations.)

The Ravad[2] explains: "The letters are called stones because, just as a stone is cut from a rock, so are the letters cut and carved from the name of God, as it says, 'God is my Rock' (*Tehillim* 18:3). Since houses are built from stones, buildings of stones are called houses.... All creatures are like houses, since a person's walls are his ribs, and his insides are like empty rooms.... This is the gate to [understanding] *shemittos* (seven-year cycles) and *yovelos* (Jubilees) as well as the secret of the seven weeks that make up the forty-nine days between Pesach and Shavuos, and the seven months beween Pesach and Sukkos."

God's Covenant with Avraham

When Avraham, may he rest in peace, observed, looked, saw, investigated, understood, engraved, hewed, combined, formed, and was successful [in knowing God clearly], then the Master of all, blessed be He, revealed Himself to him. He sat [Avraham] on His lap and kissed him on his head and called him, "He who loved Me" (*Yeshayah* 41:8). He made a covenant with him between the ten toes of his feet, which is the covenant

---

1 Commentary on *Sefer Yetzirah*.
2 Commentary on *Sefer Yetzirah*.

of circumcision [the male organ is situated between the legs]. He also made a covenant between the ten fingers of his hands, which is the covenant of the tongue [the tongue is midway between the two hands]. He tied twenty-two letters in his tongue and revealed to him their foundation. He pulled them in water, He burned them in fire, He made them turbulent in the wind, He ignited them, and led them in the twelve constellations [of the zodiac].

Sefer Yetzirah 6:4

Rabbi Moshe Botarel explains that the ten verbs mentioned in this paragraph, "Avraham observed, looked, saw, investigated...," allude to the fact that Avraham, the author of *Sefer Yetzirah*, was the first to recognize God and the first to discover the existence of the ten *Sefiros*. The ten *Sefiros* are hinted at by the covenant of circumcision, for the male organ lies between the ten toes, five on each foot. Similarly, the ten *Sefiros* are reflected in the covenant of the tongue, since the tongue is situated between the ten fingers, five on each hand.

"He tied twenty-two letters in his tongue and revealed to him their foundation." The *Pri Yitzchak* explains this to mean that God taught Avraham the secret of how to combine the letters of His name. With this knowledge he was able to create new beings.

Commenting on the verse, "[Avraham] took cream and milk and the calf which he had prepared, and placed these before [the three angels]" (*Bereishis* 18:8), the Malbim[1] asks: How could Avraham serve the angels meat and dairy together? He answers: He created the calf with his knowledge of *Sefer Yetzirah*, and the meat of such a "man-made" calf legally is not considered meat. Therefore, he could serve the angels this "meat" together with milk.

---

1   Famous Torah commentator, 1809–1879.

Chapter 6

SEFER HABAHIR

Attributed to Rabbi Nechunya ben HaKanah

Sefer HaBahir (referred to as "the *Bahir*"), one of the early classical works on Kabbalah, has had a profound and lasting influence on the development of Jewish mysticism. The book gets its title, *Sefer HaBahir* (Book of Brightness), from the verse, "Now then, one cannot see light; it is bright (*bahir*) in the heavens" (*Iyov* 37:21).

The *Bahir* deals extensively with the ten *Sefiros*, the system that explains the creation and continued existence of the universe. It clarifies a number of concepts from *Sefer Yetzirah*, such as the thirty-two pathways of wisdom and the idea that the ten fingers allude to the ten *Sefiros*. It expounds on a number of themes in the Torah, ranging from the mitzvos of tefillin, tzitzis, *lulav*, and *esrog* to the snake's seduction of Chavah.

The *Bahir* is the first book in Kabbalist literature to mention *tzimtzum*, the idea that God withdrew into Himself to make "room" for the cosmos.[1] It is also the first book to bring up the concept of *gilgul*, transmigration of souls, which means rebirth of the soul in successive bodies. This concept is further developed in the teachings of Rabbi Yitzchak Luria (the Ari)[2] in *Sefer HaGilgulim*.

---

1 See ch. 1.
2 See ch. 30.

The *Bahir* is attributed to Rabbi Nechunya ben HaKanah, a *tanna* (Talmudic sage) who lived in the first century C.E., during the period of the destruction of the second Temple. A student of Rabbi Yochanan ben Zakkai, he is the author of the prayer *Ana BeKoach*, which has deep mystical significance. His disciple, Rabbi Yishmael ben Elisha, who served as *kohein gadol* shortly before the destruction of the Temple, had a vision of "God sitting on a high and exalted throne" (*Berachos* 7a). In the *Heichalos*,[1] we are told that when there was a decree to execute the sages, it was Rabbi Nechunya ben HaKanah who ascended to heaven to ascertain the reason (*Heichalos Rabbasi* 2:8, 15:1). He lived to a ripe old age, and when his students asked him for the reason, he replied, "In all my life I never derived honor from the shame of my fellow, I never went to bed before appeasing those who were angry with me, and I was generous with my money" (*Megillah* 28a).

The *Bahir* was first published around 1176 by the Provence[2] school of Kabbalists. The first printed edition appeared in Amsterdam, 1651. Most recently it was published in Jerusalem, 1951. Commentaries include *Or HaGanuz* by Rabbi Meir ben Shalom Abi Sahula (a student of the Rashba),[3] *Peirush HaGra* by the Vilna Gaon, and *Or Bahir* by Rabbi Reuven Margolies.

Selections from Sefer HaBahir with Commentary

Tzimtzum

[There are two verses that contradict each other.] One verse says, "Now then, one cannot see light; it is bright in the heavens.... There is an awesome splendor around God" (*Iyov* 37:21-22). [In other words, God is surrounded by bright light.]

By contrast, another verse says, "He made darkness His hiding place" (*Tehillim* 18:12). And it says [in the same vein], "Cloud and dense dark-

---

1   A Kabbalistic work attributed to Rabbi Yishmael ben Elisha; Shklov, 1745.
2   Southern France.
3   Rabbi Shlomo ben Aderes, 1235-1310.

ness surround Him" (ibid. 97:2), [implying that God is enclosed in darkness].

But then there is a third passage that reconciles the two. For it says, "Darkness is not dark for You, and night is as light as day; darkness and light are the same" (ibid. 139:12).

Bahir 1

This paragraph deals with the concept of *tzimtzum* (stricture): God's Infinite Light pervaded all of existence, leaving no room for creation to take place. Creation was accomplished by the process of *tzimtzum*, the withdrawal of God into Himself, whereby God made "room" for the universe to come into being.

"Now then, one cannot see the light" – the light in this passage refers to God's essence. Since God has withdrawn through *tzimtzum*, we – from our human vantage point – cannot see His Light. To us His Light is concealed by a mantle of physicality. But God, whose essence fills all existence, sees Himself surrounded by brightness and awesome splendor, since for God, even this darkness is really light.

The Letter *Beis*

Why does the Torah begin with the letter *beis*? In order that it should begin with a blessing (*berachah*). How do we know that the Torah is called a blessing? Because it says, "Filled with God's blessing, possessing the sea and the south" (*Devarim* 33:23). And the sea stands for the Torah, for it says, "[The Torah] is wider than the sea" (*Iyov* 11:9).

What is the meaning of the verse "Filled with God's blessing"? It means that wherever we find the letter *beis*, it denotes blessing.

Bahir 3

The first letter of the Torah is the *beis* of *bereishis*; *beis* is also the first letter of *berachah* (blessing). Whenever God reveals His essence in anything, we say that He blesses that thing. That is why it says, "Filled with God's blessing." The channel for this blessing is the Torah. God's Light descends to our world by way of the ten *Sefiros*, the highest of which is *Keser*. Just as a crown is set above the head, so is *Keser* above our comprehension. *Chochmah*, the second *Sefirah*, is the first thing the mind can grasp. That is why *Chochmah* is called "beginning." Since *Chochmah* is the second *Sefirah*, it is associated with the second letter of the *alef beis*, namely the letter *beis*.

The Hands of the *Kohanim*

Why do [the *kohanim*] lift their hands when they bless the people? It is because the hands have ten fingers, alluding to the ten *Sefiros* with which heaven and earth were sealed. The [ten fingers] correspond to the Ten Commandments. The Ten Commandments comprise the 613 mitzvos [of the Torah]. If you count the letters in the Ten Commandments, you find that there are 613 letters.

The Ten Commandments contain all twenty-two letters [of the *alef beis*] except *tes*, which is missing. What is the reason for that? It teaches us that *tes* is the belly — and it is not included among the *Sefiros*.

Bahir 126

There are 613 commandments in the Torah, 248 positive commandments and 365 negative commandments. If you count them, you find that there are really 620 letters in the Ten Commandments, but the last seven letters represent the seven Rabbinical commandments. The *tes* is shaped like a belly, which denotes physicality and concealment of spirituality. The Ten Commandments and the ten *Sefiros*, on the other hand, are meant to bring the divine light into the world.

The Meaning of the Word *Sefirah*

Why are they called *Sefiros*? Because it says, "The heavens declare [*mesapperim*] the glory of God" (*Tehillim* 19:2).

Bahir 125

The words *Sefirah* and *mesapperim* have the same root, *safar*, which means "to declare" or "to tell." Thus, the *Sefiros* declare and make known God's glory here on earth.

The Four Species

What is the thing that is holy? It is the *esrog*, which is the [species the Torah calls] *hadar* (beautiful).[1] Why is it called *hadar*? Do not read *hadar* but *hador*, "which dwells" [a reference to the *Shechinah*, which dwells in the *Sefirah* of *Malchus*, exemplified by the *esrog*].

This refers to the *esrog*, which is not bound together with the *lulav*. Yet without the *esrog*, the mitzvah of waving the *lulav* cannot be fulfilled. The *esrog* is [held alongside and together] with [the three species in the *lulav* bundle]. It is with each of them and is unified with all of them.

Bahir 175

The four species taken on Sukkos consist of the *esrog* (citron), the *lulav* (palm frond), three *hadassim* (myrtle twigs), and two *aravos* (willow branches). The latter three species are bound together to form a single bundle which is held in the right hand, while the *esrog* is held in the left. The *Or HaGanuz* teaches that the *esrog* represents *Malchus*; the *lulav* represents *Yesod*; the three *hadassim* represent *Chesed*, *Gevurah*, and *Tiferes*; and the two *aravos* are *Netzach* and *Hod*. Thus the right hand grasps the male *Sefiros*, while the left grasps the female, *Malchus*. In order to fulfill the mitzvah, the *lulav* and the *esrog* must be held together.

---

1   *Vayikra* 19:40.

The *Lulav*

What does the *lulav* exemplify? It represents the spinal cord. As it says, "You must take for yourselves...a palm frond, myrtle branches, and willows" (*Vayikra* 23:40).

The leaves of the myrtle must cover the majority of the stem. If the leaves do not cover its majority, [and most of the myrtle stem is bare,] it is invalid.

Why? You can compare it to a man. A man has arms, and with them he protects his head. His two arms and his head make three. The *lulav* bundle has three myrtle branches and two willow twigs. The myrtles are on the right and the willows are on the left, and the "tree" is in the center.

Bahir 176

Just as the spinal cord originates in man's brain and extends to the sexual organ, so is the *lulav* the conduit that connects the three upper *Sefiros* [the *mochin*], *Keser*, *Chochmah*, and *Binah*, to *Yesod*, the ninth *Sefirah*. Since *Yesod* signifies the reproductive organ, the implication is that the sexual impulse travels from the brain through the spinal cord to the male organ.

Gilgul, Transmigration of Souls

[Rabbi Rechuma'i's colleagues asked him:] "Why is it that one righteous person enjoys good fortune, and another righteous person suffers?"

[He replied] "Because the righteous person who suffers used to be wicked; that's why he is punished."

"But is a person punished for offenses he committed during his youth? Did not Rabbi Shimon say that the Heavenly Tribunal inflicts no punishment until a person is twenty years or older?"[1]

He replied, "I am not speaking about his present life. I am speaking about sins he committed in a previous existence."

---

1   *Shabbos* 89b.

His colleagues said to him, "How long will you speak to us in mystical phrases?"

He said, "Compare it to the case of a person who planted a vineyard hoping that it would grow good grapes, but instead sour grapes grew. Realizing that he had failed, he tore out the bad vines and planted again. Again he did not succeed. After clearing the bad vines, he planted again. When he failed again, he once more removed the bad vines and tried again."

[His colleagues asked,] "How long does this go on?"

He said, "For a thousand generations, as it says, 'The word He commanded for a thousand generations' (*Tehillim* 105:8)." [Meaning: a soul is reincarnated over and over again, until all its transgressions have been rectified.]

Bahir 195

Chapter 7
SEFER HAZOHAR

Attributed to Rabbi Shimon bar Yochai

The *Zohar*, the foremost book of Kabbalah, was compiled by Rabbi Shimon bar Yochai, a disciple of Rabbi Akiva. Condemned to death by the Romans, Rabbi Shimon bar Yochai escaped, and, together with his son Rabbi Eliezer, hid in a cave in the Galilee. Miraculously, a carob tree and a well of water were created to sustain them. They stayed there for thirteen years, studying Torah the entire time (*Shabbos* 33b).

During his years of seclusion Rabbi Shimon bar Yochai wrote the holy *Zohar*, which forms the basis of Kabbalah. This great body of mystical knowledge was revealed by God to Moshe on Mount Sinai. Its mystical teachings were transmitted orally to a small group of saintly people in every generation, until Rabbi Shimon bar Yochai recorded them in the *Zohar*. According to the Ari HaKadosh,[1] Rabbi Shimon was granted permission to write the *Zohar* because, more than any of his predecessors, he had the ability to conceal and protect its mystical teachings. The *Zohar* has enriched Jewish spiritual life immeasurably. In the words of Rabbi Moshe Chaim Luzzatto,[2] "After the thirteen years he spent in the cave, the Gates of

---
1   See ch. 30.
2   See ch. 38.

Wisdom were opened for him in order to provide light for all Israel, until the end of time" (*Adir BaMarom*, Introduction). After being hidden for many years, a *Zohar* manuscript was discovered and copied by Rabbi Moshe de Leon, a scribe and Kabbalist who lived in Spain.[1]

The *Zohar* offers profound Kabbalistic interpretations of Torah verses, arranged according to the weekly Torah portions. It addresses the problems of creation, the purpose of human existence, the origin of evil, the suffering of the righteous, the role of the Jewish people, the end of days, transmigration of souls, and many other fundamental themes.

Revered as the major work of Jewish mysticism, it is often called *Zohar HaKadosh*, the "Holy *Zohar*." Its teachings have made a decisive impact on the chassidic movement, and many chassidic masters were great Kabbalists.

The first editions of the *Zohar* appeared in Mantua and Cremona, Italy in 1558 and 1560. Later editions were published in Lublin in 1623 and Sulzbach in 1684. It has been printed more than sixty-five times, mostly in Poland and Russia. The many commentators on the *Zohar* include Rabbi Moshe Cordovero, the Maggid of Koznitz, Rabbi Dov Ber Schneersohn of Lubavitch, and Rabbi Tzadok HaKohen. More recently, the cryptic Aramaic of the *Zohar* has been explained and translated into Hebrew by Rabbi Yehudah Leib Ashlag.[2]

Rabbi Shimon bar Yochai died on 18 Iyar, Lag BaOmer, and was buried in Meron, in the north of Eretz Yisrael. Every year on Lag BaOmer thousands of people gather at his gravesite for prayer and rejoicing.

Selections from the Zohar

Noach's Age at the Time of the Flood

> Noach was six hundred years old when the flood occurred; water on the earth.
>
> *(Bereishis 7:6)*

---

1 See ch. 15.
2 See ch. 54.

Why does it say here [in an offhand remark] that Noach was six hundred years old? [His age is mentioned officially in verse 11, where the Torah ties the onset of the flood to Noach's age.] The number six hundred alludes to the *Sefirah* of *Yesod*, the sixth of the lower seven *Sefiros*. Noach's age of six hundred makes him the symbol of *Yesod*, the *Sefirah* that leads into *Malchus* [the seventh *Sefirah*].

If Noach had not been six hundred years old, he would not have represented *Yesod*, so he could not have entered the Ark. For the Ark represents *Malchus*, the seventh of the lower *Sefiros* which is the physical world. Once he reached the age of six hundred years old, he was fit to unite with *Malchus* [and enter the Ark]. But Noach was only 480 years old when his generation had degenerated to the point where they deserved destruction. So God kept His anger bottled up for 120 years, waiting for Noach to reach the age of 600. Through his good deeds, Noach by then had become "a faultless tzaddik" (*Bereishis* 6:9) and was a worthy bearer of the *Sefirah* of *Yesod*.[1] Thereupon he entered the Ark to unite with *Malchus*.

Zohar, Noach 65b

Avraham and Lot

God said to Avram, "Go away from your land...." Avram went as God had directed him, and Lot [his nephew] went with him.
(Bereishis 12:1, 4)

What is the mystical meaning of "Avram went as God had directed him"? [The soul is called "Avram." And the verse tells us that] as soon as a soul [Avram] goes down to this world, Lot accompanies it on its journey. Lot personifies the Serpent that was cursed and the whole world along with it, and the Serpent is the *yetzer hara* (the evil impulse). But why is the *yetzer hara* synonymous with Lot? Because the name *Lot* is cognate to *letuta*, Aramaic for "curse" [and the *yetzer hara* brings a curse on a person]. For the

---

[1] It should be noted that *Yesod* is the *Sefirah* of Yosef, the *tzaddik yesod olam*, the tzaddik who is the foundation of the world.

evil impulse is standing at the door, ready to pounce. This means that as soon as a child is born, the *yetzer hara* is waiting to lead its soul away from the Torah. As it says, "Sin is crouching at the entrance [of the womb]" (*Bereishis* 4:7).

Zohar, Lech Lecha 78a

Avraham's Descent to Egypt

> There was famine in the land. Avram headed south to Egypt to stay there for a while, since the famine had grown very severe in the land.
>
> (*Bereishis* 12:10)

Rabbi Shimon said: Let me show you [the mystical reason why Avraham had to go down to Egypt]. If Avraham had not gone down to Egypt and would not have been purified there [from evil influences], he would not have been able to come close to the Holy One, blessed be He. The same thing happened to his children. God wanted to make them one perfect nation that is close to Him. But if they had not first gone down to Egypt and had not been purified there in the iron crucible, they never would have become His select nation. The same is true of Eretz Yisrael. If the Holy Land would not have been under Canaanite domination, it would not have been God's portion. It is all part of the same mystery.

Zohar, Lech Lecha 83a

Rabbi Moshe Cordovero explains: First there is the dominion of evil and darkness; only then comes the reign of light and holiness. This thought is reflected in the verse, "These are the kings that ruled in the land of Edom before any king reigned over Israel" (*Bereishis* 36:31). [Edom is synonymous with Esav (*Bereishis* 25:30).] And that's why Esav (the personification of evil) emerged from his mother's womb before Yaakov.

The reason the Jews had to be enslaved in Egypt is that sparks of evil[1] had infiltrated among the Jewish people, and in Egypt they were purged of those evil sparks. The same way, Eretz Yisrael under the Canaanites was filled with sparks of evil, but when the children of Israel came and destroyed the seven Caananite nations, the sparks of evil were completely obliterated.

Lot's Two Daughters

> [After the destruction of Sedom, Lot lived in a cave alone with his two daughters.] The older girl said to the younger, "...Come, let's get our father drunk with wine and sleep with him. We will then survive through children from our father." That night they got their father drunk, and the older girl went and slept with her father.... Lot's two daughters became pregnant from their father.
> *(Bereishis 19:31-33)*

Rabbi Yehudah said: Man's soul consists of three faculties: 1) His intellect, which stems from man's holy soul (*neshamah*) [and by which he overcomes his *yetzer hara* (evil impulse)]; 2) his instinct of self-preservation (*ruach*), which prompts him to take care of his bodily functions; 3) his animal instinct, which stimulates his physical desires and is rooted in his sensual soul (*nefesh habehamis*).

The *yetzer hara* holds sway over the last two of them [i.e., *ruach* and *nefesh*], but it cannot control man's holy soul (*neshamah*). The sensual soul is forever chasing after the *yetzer hara*, to satisfy its lust. This is the mystical meaning of the verse, "[Lot's] older daughter said to the younger one." Lot's older daughter [i.e., the sensual soul] speaks to the younger one [i.e., the soul of bodily functions] and entices it to embrace the *yetzer hara* [and indulge in sensual delights]. It says, "Let's get our father drunk with wine" [let's arouse our *yetzer hara* with wine]; "and sleep with him,"

---

1 As discussed above (ch. 3), after Adam's sin, the vessels that conveyed the Divine Light down to this world shattered, spreading sparks (*nitzotzos*) all over the world, where they were clothed in husks of good and evil. By doing mitzvos we release the sparks from their husks and elevate them back to their source. When the Jews left Egypt, they released all the sparks that were trapped there. This is implied in the verse, "[The Israelites] emptied Egypt" (*Shemos* 12:36).

as if to say, "There is no reward in the World to Come [for the body and the sensual soul]. So let's live it up in this world!" And what do these two souls do? They both agree to team up with the *yetzer hara*. And so it says, "That night, they got their father drunk." [Lot symbolizes the *yetzer hara*.] Meaning, they decided to arouse the *yetzer hara* by indulging in feasting and drinking.

"And the older girl went and slept with her father" — When a person is asleep, the sensual soul stimulates the *yetzer hara*, and the person is filled with bad notions to the point that the sensual soul is overcome by desire. [But at that point the desire is still only potential; it is not actualized.] So the sensual soul awakens the soul of bodily functions, and thereby the evil is accomplished. That is the mystical meaning of "Lot's two daughters became pregnant from their father."

Zohar, Vayeira 109b

When the Soul Departs

> God appeared to [Avraham] in the Plains of Mamrei while he was sitting at the entrance of the tent in the heat of the day. He lifted his eyes and saw three men [i.e., angels] standing over him.
> *(Bereishis 18:1–2)*

The Rabbis explain that this verse alludes to the end of a person's life. For Rabbi Yehudah said: When a person passes away and his soul leaves his body, it is the Great Judgment Day for him. The moment before death sets in, he sees the *Shechinah*. And so it says, "For no human can see My face and stay alive" (*Shemos* 33:20), [which implies that in his final moment one does see the *Shechinah*, and then he dies]. The *Shechinah* is escorted by three angels to receive the soul of the tzaddik. For it says, "God appeared to him" [meaning, the *Shechinah* appears to a person on his deathbed].

"In the heat of the day" — The day of death, when the soul is instructed to separate from the body, is a person's torrid Judgment Day. The verse continues, "He lifted his eyes and saw three men." This refers to the three angels that accompany the *Shechinah* to receive the dying person's soul. They review everything he did during his lifetime, and he affirms all they say.

When the soul sees [that the body is being judged for all its deeds], it gradually moves out of the body but stops at the throat [as it says, "at the entrance of the tent," and the throat is the entrance of the body]. The soul remains standing at the throat until the person confesses everything the body has done to the soul in this world [and then the soul departs]. At that moment, the soul of a tzaddik rejoices over the [good] things he has done in this world. The soul is happy to return unblemished to its source. Rabbi Yitzchak said: The soul of a tzaddik yearns for the moment it leaves this world of futility; it looks forward to the delights of the World to Come.

Zohar, Vayeira 98a

The Three Levels of the Soul

> Then Yehudah approached [Yosef] and said....
> (Bereishis 44:18)

When God created Adam, He gathered dust from the four corners of the earth. He formed him on the site of the Beis HaMikdash down below [on earth], and He drew into him a soul from the heavenly Beis HaMikdash [originating in the *Sefirah* of *Binah*]. The soul is composed of three levels: *nefesh*, *ruach*, and *neshamah*. *Nefesh* is the lowest of the three. [It is the primitive animal soul that originates in the *Sefirah* of *Malchus*, the lowest of the *Sefiros*.] *Ruach*, the soul that sustains life, is above *nefesh* and controls *nefesh*. *Ruach* stems from *Ze'ir Anpin* [i.e., the set of six *Sefiros* — *Chesed*, *Gevurah*, *Tiferes*, *Netzach*, *Hod*, *Yesod* — that lead into *Malchus*]. *Neshamah* is above the two lower levels [since it comes from *Binah*, which is higher than the six *Sefiros* of *Ze'ir Anpin*]. *Neshamah* is the soul in its most perfect state of holiness.

A person is born with *nefesh* [the basic life force]. If he grows spiritually, he rises to the level of *ruach*. If he ascends above *nefesh* and *ruach* by serving God perfectly, he reaches the level of *neshamah*.

[In a mystical sense] the phrase, "Then Yehudah approached [Yosef]" implies the union of the lower physical world with the spiritual world. [The physical world is represented by *Malchus*, the female, which is the level of *nefesh*, personified by Yehudah. When Yehudah approached Yosef, the world of *Malchus* united with higher world of *Yesod*, which is the level of *ruach*, personified by Yosef, the symbol of the male organ, the organ that gives.] Yehudah was a king [King David descended from Yehudah], and Yosef, too, was a king [in Egypt].

Thus, when Yehudah approached Yosef, the *Sefiros* of *Malchus* and *Yesod* united and became one.

Zohar, Vayigash 82b

Resurrection of the Dead

God said to Moshe and Aharon,... "You [Moshe] must tell Aharon, 'Take your staff and throw it down before Pharaoh — it will become a snake.'"

(Shemos 7:8–9)

Aharon's staff was a piece of dry wood, yet God used it for His first sign in Egypt. He performed two miracles with it: [When Aharon threw it down before Pharaoh, it turned into a snake,] and then it swallowed up the snakes [of the Egyptian sorcerers]. So for a time Aharon's staff became a living being.

A curse on those who say that the Holy One will not raise the dead, because it seems to them an impossibility! Let those fools who are far from the Torah and from God think a little. Aharon was holding in his hand a staff made of dry wood, and, for a short time, God turned it into a living creature with spirit and a body; don't you think that at the time when He will gladden the world, He will resurrect bodies that once had spirit and a holy souls in them, bodies that kept mitzvos and studied the Torah day and night, bodies He had hidden in the earth temporarily?

Said Rabbi Chiya: What's more, the words, "Your dead ones will live" (*Yeshayah* 26:19) prove that not only will there be a new creation, but the very bodies which were dead will rise again. For there is one bone in the body that remains intact and does not decompose in the earth, and on the Day of Resurrection God will soften it and make it like leaven in dough. It will rise and expand on all sides, and the whole body and all its parts will be formed from it, and then the Holy One will put His spirit into it.[1]

Zohar, Va'eira 28a–b

The Three Shabbos Meals

By [partaking of] the three meals of Shabbos the Jewish people are marked as the King's sons, as belonging to the palace, as sons of faith. If a person skips one of these meals, he causes a defect in the higher worlds. Such a person thereby shows that he is not one of the King's sons, not of the palace, not of the holy seed of Israel, and, [accordingly] he will be made to suffer a threefold punishment in Gehinnom.

Please notice. On all the festivals a person must rejoice himself and give to the poor. If he eats by himself and does not share his meals with the poor, his punishment will be great.... However, this applies only on the festivals, not on Shabbos. [If he enjoys his Shabbos meal alone, he is not punished, because on Shabbos God is the host, and He invites and gives joy to whomever He wishes, whereas at the *yom tov* meals we are the hosts who invite guests.]

The unique character of Shabbos is manifest in the words, "Between Me and the children of Israel [Shabbos] is a sign forever" (*Shemos* 31:17). And because the faith is centered in Shabbos, a Jew is given an additional,

---

1   The bone is called *luz*. It is a vertebra at the end of the spinal column and resembles an almond (*Vayikra Rabbah* 18:1).

higher soul [*neshamah yeseirah*]. This additional soul [which is rooted in the three highest *Sefiros*] is complete perfection. [He receives this additional soul in order to delight in the Shabbos] which is a semblance of the World to Come. [The additional soul of *yom tov* comes from the lower *Sefiros*].

Zohar, Yisro 88b

The Ten Commandments

We have learned that the first five commandments [of the Ten Commandments] include [by implication] the other five as well. How so? Take the first commandment, "I am the God, your Lord" (*Shemos* 20:2). Doesn't it include the first of the second five [i.e., "Do not commit murder" (ibid., 13)]? Indeed it does. [Since man is made in the image of God,] the murderer diminishes the likeness and image of God.

The second commandment, "Do not have any other gods before Me" (ibid., 3) is opposite the seventh, "Do not commit adultery" (ibid., 13). For the adulterer renounces the Name of God which is impressed on the [circumcised organ] of man. As it says, "They betrayed God, for they begat alien children" (*Hoshea* 5:7).

The third commandment, "Do not take the name of God, your Lord, in vain" (*Shemos* 20:7), is the counterpart of the eighth commandment, "Do not steal" (ibid., 13). For a thief is bound to swear falsely [when he is brought to justice].

The fourth commandment, "Remember the Sabbath to keep it holy" (ibid., 8) matches the ninth, "Do not testify as a false witness against your neighbor" (ibid., 13). For as Rabbi Yosei said, Shabbos is called a witness to God's creative activity, and a Jew is required to testify to the fact that "in six days God made heaven and earth" (ibid., 11). And he who bears false witness to his neighbor denies Shabbos — the witness of truth.

The fifth commandment, "Honor your father and mother" (ibid., 12), parallels the tenth, "Do not be envious of your neighbor's wife" (ibid., 14). For if someone covets his neighbor's wife and fathers a son by her, this son will honor someone who is not his father. [He will honor his mother's husband, thinking that he is his father.]

Zohar, Yisro 90a

The Power of *Teshuvah*

If [the Hebrew slave] was unmarried, he shall leave by himself. But if he was a married man, his wife shall leave with him.
(Shemos 21:3)

"If he was unmarried, he shall leave by himself." [On a spiritual level] this refers to a man who refused to get married and have children. But "if he was a married man," that is to say, if he had a wife but was not blessed with children, then he is not driven out [to the realm of the unclean shells, as the fellow who refused to get married]. For the Holy One does not let any creature go unrewarded. [Therefore, even though they did not have children,] since they tried, "His wife shall leave with him" — husband and wife both are reincarnated and unite again as they did before. Such a man marries the woman who was previously his wife but did not bear him children, in order that now both gain merit by [having children and] making good their insufficiency.

But the man who "went out" without a wife [that is, he never married at all],... [after he received his punishment for not getting married and repented,] the Master of the whole earth will have pity on him and bring him back to this world by himself, as he was, and give him a divorced woman as a wife. Then they unite, and she will bear him sons and daughters. For, since he repented of his former lapse, he is received by God, who restores him to the position intended for him. For *baalei teshuvah* (returnees to Torah) can enter the place where even the perfectly righteous are not admitted (*Berachos* 34b).

There is no obstacle in the world that can stand in the way of *teshuvah*.

For sure, the Holy One accepts every sinner who turns to Him. Such a person is set on the way of Life, in spite of his former stain. Everything is put right and restored to its former position. Even when God has solemnly decreed against a person, He forgives completely when there is perfect repentance.... Repentance annuls all decrees and judgments and breaks the numerous iron chains [by which sinners are fettered]. There is nothing that can stand against *teshuvah*.... Even when sinners intentionally commit sins, following the desires of their own hearts and not heeding the warnings of others, even for such people, when they repent and begin to walk in the way of righteousness, healing is prepared.

Zohar, Mishpatim 106a

The Souls of Converts

The number of souls that are created through the union of the souls [of tzaddikim] in the higher world exceeds by far the number of children that issue from the union of husband and wife in this world. In the higher world, when souls join together they produce souls that radiate light, as it says, "A man's soul is the lamp of God" (*Mishlei* 20:27). These divine lamps become souls of converts. They enter the first palace in the lower Gan Eden [the place where the souls of future converts are stored].

When a non-Jew converts to Judaism, a soul from this palace takes wing and soars aloft to a place beneath the wings of the *Shechinah*. The *Shechinah* kisses it lovingly because it is the offspring of the souls of tzaddikim. The *Shechinah* then sends this soul down to reside in the body of the convert. At that moment he becomes a *ger tzedek* (righteous convert).

This is the mystery contained in the verse, "The fruit of a righteous one is a tree of life" (*Mishlei* 11:30). Just as the Tree of Life, which is the *Ze'ir Anpin*,[1] brings forth souls, so does the soul of the tzaddik beget souls.

Zohar, Shelach 168a

The Sign of Og, King of Bashan

> God said to Moshe, "Do not be afraid of him [Og]. I have given him, along with all his people and territory, into your hand."
>
> *(Bemidbar 22:34)*

"Do not be afraid of him [*oso*]." The word *oso*, "him," also translates as "his sign." [Thus the passage can be rendered, "Do not be afraid of his sign."] What does this mean?

You should know that Og[1] had attached himself to Avraham and was a member of his household. And when Avraham was circumcised, Og, too, was circumcised by Avraham, as it says, "all the men of [Avraham's] household...were circumcised with him" (*Bereishis* 17:27). When Og saw that the children of Israel were approaching, he said, "[The Jews are victorious in the merit of the covenant of circumcision.] But I was circumcised before Yitzchak. This merit will help me [in my battle against them]."

Moshe was afraid of that, wondering, "How can I do away with the sign that Avraham placed on him?"

The Holy One immediately told him, "*Al tira oso* — Do not be afraid of his sign [*oso*]." His *milah* (circumcison) will not do him any good, because he has contaminated his sign of *milah* [with all kinds of depravity and promiscuity]. And whoever tarnishes this sign will be removed from the world.

That is why Og was blotted out from this world, even though he was a mighty giant. He wanted to destroy the Jewish people, but he was defeated and wiped out by Moshe.

Zohar, Chukas 184a

---

1   *Ze'ir Anpin* refers to the group of six *Sefiros*: *Chesed, Gevurah, Tiferes, Netzach, Hod,* and *Yesod*.

1   *Devarim* 1:4, 3:11. Rashi comments on "Then the fugitive came and brought the news [of Lot's capture] to Avram" (*Bereishis* 14:13) that the fugitive was Og.

Why Were the Children So Brilliant?

Rabbi Abba said to Rabbi Elazar: "I am surprised to see how advanced the children of our generation are in their Torah studies. Their [reasoning is solid] like a rock [you cannot argue against it]."

[Rabbi Moshe Cordovero explains: These children were reincarnations of the souls of children who were killed during the destruction of the Beis HaMikdash and did not live out their lives. God saw that in Rabbi Shimon bar Yochai's merit his entire generation would be granted life in the World to Come. That's why He brought these children back to life in Rabbi Shimon's generation. It was because of their lofty souls that they were familiar with the great mysteries of Kabbalah.]

Replied Rabbi Elazar: "My father, Rabbi Shimon bar Yochai, the leading sage of his generation, is fortunate that God wanted to rectify His two chambers in Gan Eden, [the upper chamber for the souls, and the lower chamber for the spirits. God reincarnated these souls so that through them the two chambers of Gan Eden should be a fitting residence for the holy souls]. There will never be another generation as exalted as this one until the coming of King Mashiach."

Zohar, Balak 206a

The God-like Aspect of the Human Soul

God created the human soul in His image. Just as God is not restricted to a specific name or to a specific place, rather, His dominion extends all over, so too, the soul cannot be defined by a specific name or place, for its dominion extends throughout the body; not one part of the body is devoid of the soul. This is not to say that the essence of the soul is comparable to God, for God created it. However, the soul is God-like only in the sense that it prevails over the entire body, just as God rules over the entire universe.

Zohar, Pinchas 312b

Part III
THE KABBALISTS OF SPAIN, ITALY, AND PROVENCE

Introduction

THE KABBALISTS OF SPAIN, ITALY, AND PROVENCE

In the twelfth century Spain became a flourishing center of Kabbalah study. An early great Kabbalist of this era was Rabbi Avraham ben David of Posquieres (Ravad III), who received instruction from Eliyahu HaNavi. His son, Rabbi Yitzchak Sagi Nahor (the Blind), was called "the father of Kabbalah of Provence and Spain."

The Kabbalist influence spread south from Provence to Catalonia (northern Spain), where a major center of Kabbalistic study arose in Gerona, early in the thirteenth century. The leading figures of the Gerona circle were Rabbi Azriel and Rabbi Ezra of Gerona and the Ramban, who expounds on Kabbalistic thought in his celebrated Torah commentary. Rabbi Yitzchak Sagi Nahor was also an important member of the Gerona school of Kabbalists.

Other important Kabbalists of Spain are Rabbi Yosef Gikatilla, who wrote the seminal *Shaarei Orah*; Rabbeinu Bachya, whose famous Torah commentary contains many Kabbalistic interpretations; and Rabbi Moshe de Leon, who discovered an ancient manuscript of the *Zohar* and introduced it to the Spanish Kabbalists.

The flourishing Torah center of Spain came to a tragic close with the expulsion of the Jews in 1492. The anguish of that catastrophe is embodied in the person of the great Kabbalist Rabbi Shlomo Molcho, who gave his life *al kiddush haShem* and was burned at the stake by the infamous priests of the Spanish Inquisition.

Chapter 8
RABBI SHABSAI DONNOLO

born: Oria, southern Italy, 913
died: after 982

Rabbi Shabsai Donnolo was a Kabbalist, physician, astrologer, and astronomer. When he was twelve years old, he and his entire family were taken prisoner by Arabs who captured his hometown. In this raid the Arab marauders killed ten rabbis and leaders of the community. Shabsai was ransomed by relatives in Otranto, Italy, while the rest of the family was carried off to Palermo and North Africa. Despite the hardship he suffered, he had an insatiable thirst for Torah and secular knowledge. He wandered about in search of someone to teach him "the wisdom of Greece, Arabia, Babylonia, and India. I did not rest until I copied all their books," as he puts it in his introduction to his work *Chachmuni*. He found a teacher, an Arab by the name of Bagdash, who was willing to instruct him for a hefty fee.

Rabbi Shabsai gained fame as a physician and was consulted by the Byzantine ruler of Calabria.[1] He wrote a medical treatise entitled *Sefer HaYekar*, one of the oldest pharmacological books in existence, in which he describes 120 different medications, drugs, remedies, and potions and the ways to prepare and apply them.

---

1   The "toe" of the Italian peninsula.

His main contribution is his commentary to *Sefer Yetzirah*, titled *Chachmuni*,[1] which combines Kabbalah with astronomy and astrology. This work is cited by Rashi in *Eiruvin* 56a in a complex commentary on the duration of the seasons. Says Rashi: "Rabbi Shabsai the doctor explains very well in his book *Chachmuni* why the stars are arranged in this pattern...."

Rabbi Shabsai opens *Chachmuni* by quoting the verse "God said, 'Let us make man'" (*Bereishis* 1:26), and develops the idea that man is a microcosm, a small-scale replica of the world at large, encompassing in his limited confines the vast universe in its infinite variety. This work is one of the oldest commentaries on *Sefer Yetzirah*.

His *Sefer HaYekar* and his other writings on medicine were published under the title *Kisvei HaRefuah LeRav Shabsai Donnolo*.[2]

Selections from the Writings of Rabbi Shabsai Donnolo

Teshuvah — Repentance

[Note: Astrology deals with understanding the influence of the planets and stars on earthly affairs in order to predict the destinies of individuals, groups, or nations. In Rabbi Donnolo's time astrology was considered an exact science and was studied widely. The *Zohar* mentions astrological concepts,[3] and *Sefer Yetzirah* speaks of astrological ideas in chapters 4, 5, and 6.[4] The problem arises as to how to reconcile predestination dictated by the stars with man's free choice. If all your actions are preordained by your horoscope, how can God hold you responsible for your deeds? This question is touched on by Rabbi Shabsai Donnolo in the following piece.]

God began by calculating the positions of the planets and the constella-

---

1   Leipzig, 1854.
2   Jerusalem, 1949.
3   For example, in *Ki Seitzei* 281.
4   Other Jewish thinkers who believed in astrology were the Ravad, the Ramban, the Rashba, Rabbeinu Bachya, Rabbi Yitzchak Abohab, Don Yitzchak Abarbanel, Rabbi Moshe Alshich, the Maharal of Prague, Rabbi Yonasan Eibeschutz, the Vilna Gaon, and others.

tions in their cycles and in their orbits even before He created them. Looking upon His calculations, He knew and saw the fate of all the generations that were to arise, from their beginning to their end, as it says, "Who brought about and accomplished [this]? He who proclaimed the generations from the beginning" (*Yeshayah* 41:4). Thus He knew each person's actions, his righteousness or his wickedness, and He knew what His judgment on each and every one would be, according to the good or evil deeds each would do. All this God did in His knowledge and understanding before the creation of the world; as it says, "God founded the earth with wisdom" (*Mishlei* 3:19).

Yet, although He fixed and appointed each person's planet and constellation according to each person's future actions, the Holy One, blessed be He, did not give the planets and constellations any power for good or evil because He saw that man, when created, would not be able to live without a free will. But it says, "Every plan devised by man's mind was nothing but evil all the time" (*Bereishis* 6:5). That's why God, who is a gracious and merciful God, slow to anger and abundant in kindness, with compassion on the wicked, also gave repentance its proper place before the creation of the world. As it says, "Before the mountains were born, and You had not yet fashioned the earth and the inhabited land, from the remotest past and to the most distant future, You are God. You reduce man to pulp, and You say, 'Repent, O sons of man' " (*Tehillim* 90:2–3).

For the evil impulse causes man to sin, yet if he repents before his Creator, if he forsakes his wicked deeds, asking pardon and forgiveness, if he then acts rightly, doing good in the eyes of God, then the Holy One, blessed be He, will have mercy on him, and his evil star will be turned into a lucky star.

Introduction to Chachmuni

Man Is a Microcosm

Just as God placed the two luminaries [the sun and the moon] and the five planets in the firmament of heaven, so He created in man's head two eyes, a left and a right eye. The right eye is like the sun, and the left eye is like the moon. The right nostril is like Mercury, the left nostril like Mars. Tongue, mouth, and lips correspond to Jupiter, the right ear is like Venus, and the left ear is like Saturn.

Chachmuni, Sefer Yetzirah 4:12

Analogies with the Human Anatomy

Just as God created man and beast and every living thing to dwell on the earth, so did God create the heart on the membrane of flesh which is over the liver and caused to dwell in the heart the breath of life. Just as He made beneath the earth the deep, mire, and mud, so He made in man the intestines which receive food and drink. And just as God made for the universe a reservoir of the seas, so He made for man a reservoir for his urine: a sack which is the bladder. Just as God made stones beneath the earth, so He made the backbone with its bones and its thighs on each side, a foundation for the structure of the whole body. Just as He made moisture-covered stones sunk in the deep where the water issues from between them, so He made the two kidneys, that the seed may issue from between them to the genitals, to the sexual organs....

And just as in the universe there are clear waters and clouded, sweet waters and those that are bitter and salty, so are there in man. From his eyes come salty waters, from his nostrils cold, from his mouth sweet, from his throat warm, and from his ears bitter, while the waters of his urine are both bitter and foul-smelling. In the universe there are both cold and warm winds; so with man. When he opens his mouth and blows, his breath is warm. When he closes his mouth and blows, his breath is cold. The universe has its thunders, man has his voice. The universe has its lightning, man's face lights up like lightning.

Chachmuni, ch. 1

Foretelling the Future

The universe has its signs of the zodiac, and those who observe the stars know how to predict future events. Similarly, man has signs, and experts in astrology can tell his future by it. They can tell his future by his build and by the look of his face. The wise men of old knew this science, but it has been forgotten in recent times. What's more, wise men could tell the future from trees and grasses. They said about Rabbi Yochanan ben Zakkai that he understood the speech of palm trees (*Sukkos* 28a). This means that he knew how to look at the movement of palm trees and from it foretell the future....

Just as God created in the universe stones and rocks, firm and hard, so He created in man teeth and jaws harder than any bone or iron. Just as He created in the world solid, hard earth and soft, moist earth, so He created in man flesh and skin: flesh like the soft earth, skin like the hard and solid earth. Just as He created in the world trees and grasses that produce fruit or seed, and also those that produce neither, so He created men who beget and those who do not beget. Just as trees grow old, so does man. Then, just as God causes grass and trees of the forest to spring forth from the earth, so in man He causes to spring forth the hair of the head, the beard, and the body.

Chachmuni, ch. 4

Chapter 9
RABBI AVRAHAM BEN DAVID OF POSQUIERES
(Ravad III)

born: Narbonne, Provence, c. 1120
died: Posquieres, Provence, 1198

One of the foremost Talmudic scholars of all time, Ravad was also a towering Kabbalist, revered by his contemporaries for his incredible range and depth of knowledge. He studied under Rabbi Moshe ben Yosef Halevi and Ravad II, who subsequently became his father-in-law. At a young age, Ravad became one of the leading rabbinical authorities of Provence (southern France) and headed a Talmudical academy in Nimes, which became the primary yeshivah in Provence. He later opened a yeshivah in Posquieres and personally paid for the support of his needy students.

An independent thinker, Ravad paved a new path in Talmudic analysis. Although extremely wealthy, he shied away from all luxuries, maintaining a pious and ascetic lifestyle. His wealth became a source of great anguish. Envious of Ravad's fortune, the Lord of Posquieres denounced him to the government and had him incarcerated. Count Roger of Carcassonne obtained his release and had the Lord of Posquieres banished to Carcassonne.

A prolific writer, Ravad started out by recording the teachings of his masters. But being an strong-minded scholar, he wrote his own novel insights to a number of tractates.

Ravad is best known for his sharply critical glosses on the Rambam's *Mishneh Torah*, the collection of all halachic material found in Talmudic literature. He disapproved of the Rambam's failure to list the sources on which he based his decisions. Notwithstanding his often caustic remarks, Ravad expressed his admiration for the Rambam "for producing an impressive work in compiling the material from the Gemara, *Yerushalmi*, and *Tosefta*" (*Hilchos Kelayim* 6:2). For his part, Rambam held Ravad in high esteem, bowing to his criticism. Ravad's critical notes have been incorporated as glosses into the standard text of all full editions of the Rambam as *Hasagos HaRavad*. In his later years Ravad wrote *Baalei Nefesh*,[1] a compendium of the laws of family purity, including the laws of *mikveh*.

Ravad was also a famous Kabbalist. He studied Kabbalah under his father-in-law, Ravad II, and reached such high levels of *ruach hakodesh* (divine inspiration) as to merit having Eliyahu HaNavi appear to him.[2] He mentions that "for many years *ruach hakodesh* has appeared in our *beis midrash* (house of study)" (*Hasagos, Hilchos Lulav* 8:5). In another place he says, "This was revealed to me [from heaven], as it says, 'The secret of God [is revealed] to those who fear Him' (*Tehillim* 25:14)" (*Beis HaBechirah* 6:4). A commentary on *Sefer Yetzirah* is attributed to him.

He instructed both his sons, Rabbi Yitzchak Sagi Nahor and Rabbi David, in Kabbalah. They became great Kabbalists and gathered around them a circle of students. Thus, they contributed greatly to the spread of Kabbalah in later generations.

Because Ravad's Kabbalistic writings exist only in manuscript, they could not be excerpted here.

---

1 Venice, 1602.
2 Recanati, *Naso*.

Chapter 10
RABBI YITZCHAK SAGI NAHOR

born: Posquieres, Provence, 1160?
died: Posquieres, Provence, 1234?

Rabbi Yitzchak Sagi Nahor was the son of Rabbi Avraham of Posquieres, the great halachist and Kabbalist, better known as Ravad III. Because he was born blind, he was called "Sagi Nahor" ("full of light," a euphemism for sightlessness).

In spite of his handicap, Rabbi Yitzchak was the foremost Kabbalist in Provence (southern France) and Spain. Rabbeinu Bachya (in his commentary on *Vayeishev*) called him "the father of Kabbalah." Until his time, Kabbalah was taught orally from teacher to chosen disciple, with one link being added to the chain each generation. Rabbi Yitzchak revealed these secrets to his entire group of students. They, in turn, expanded and publicized their master's teachings to a wider circle of scholars.

Very little is known about Rabbi Yitzchak's life; even his place of birth is in doubt. A saintly person, he lived in Gerona, Spain, leading a life of fasting and mortification, depriving himself of worldly pleasures. Rabbi Menachem Recanati (in his commentary on *Naso, Birkas Kohanim*) relates that Eliyahu HaNavi appeared to Rabbi Yitzchak and revealed to him many hidden mystical teachings.

His students recorded his commentary to *Sefer Yetzirah* in a style of writing that is cryptic and extremely difficult to understand.

Rabbi Yitzchak stressed the importance of *kavanah* (concentration of thought) as the means to achieving *deveikus* (attachment to God), which is the ultimate goal a person can aspire to. He taught that the divine emanations relate to the physical world as a burning flame hovering over the coal, establishing the continuity between spirit and matter. By gazing in the Torah, God created the physical world. Hence the spirit of the Torah is the blueprint of the universe.

Rabbi Yitzchak Sagi Nahor's method of understanding Kabbalah was disseminated in Spain by his disciples Rabbi Ezra, Rabbi Azriel, and Rabbi Menachem of Gerona.

Chapter 11
RABBI AZRIEL OF GERONA

born: Gerona, Spain, c. 1160
died: Gerona, Spain, c. 1238

Rabbi Azriel, together with his elder colleague, Rabbi Ezra of Gerona, led a group of Kabbalists in Gerona which included the Ramban, Rabbi Yaakov ben Asher, and other great mystics. Both Rabbi Azriel and Rabbi Ezra were students of Rabbi Yitzchak Sagi Nahor (the Blind). Very little is known about Rabbi Azriel's personal life, other than that he devoted himself to spreading Kabbalah in Spain. Unlike Rabbi Ezra, who taught only things he had heard from his masters, Rabbi Azriel's works show him to be an independent thinker and an innovator who opposed the study of philosophy. The poet Rabbi Meshullam de Piera of Gerona praises both Rabbi Azriel and Rabbi Ezra in one of his poems, "They are my priests who illuminate my altar; they are the stars of my night that are not blackened...."[1]

Rabbi Azriel wrote *Peirush Eser Sefiros*,[2] an explanation of the ten *Sefiros* in question-and-answer form. In this work he coined the term *Ein Sof*, "the Infinite," as an appellation of God, stating, "That which has no limit is called *Ein Sof*." It was printed as an introduction to Rabbi Meir ibn Gabbai's *Derech*

---

1   From *Yoel* 2:10.
2   Berlin, 1850, with *Derech Emunah*.

Emunah. He wrote also a commentary to *Sefer Yetzirah* and a commentary on the Aggados of the Talmud[1] which is one of the most important works to emerge from the Gerona circle of Kabbalists.

Selections from the Writings of Rabbi Azriel

God's Judgment of the Nations

> I will gather all of the nations and bring them down to the Valley of Yehoshafat, and I will contend with them there concerning My people and My possession, Israel, that they dispersed among the nations, and they divided up My land.
>
> (*Yoel* 4:2)

Rabbi Yishmael said: Let me show you how severe will be the judgment that God renders on the nations in the Valley of Yoshafat. [You can infer it from the sentence that is passed on a Torah scholar on Judgment Day.] When a Torah scholar comes before God [to be judged], God asks him, "My son, did you engross yourself in Torah study?"

"Yes," replies the Torah scholar.

"If so, tell some of the Torah and the Mishnah you learned," says God.

The Sages derive from this dialogue that you should memorize the portions of the Torah and the Mishnah you learned, so that you should not be embarrassed on Judgment Day. Rabbi Yishmael exclaimed about this humiliation: Woe for such shame! Woe for such disgrace!

If a person has studied only Torah but not Mishnah, the Holy One, blessed be He, turns away from him, and the guards of Gehinnom pounce on him like wild wolves and grab him and throw him in.

If someone has studied two or three orders of the Mishnah, the Holy One, blessed be He, says, "My son, why didn't you learn all six orders of the Mishnah?" If God then says, "Leave him alone," all is well, otherwise,

---

1 Jerusalem, 1943.

the guards of Gehinnom grab him as they did with the first fellow....

If someone has learned the five books of the Torah, the Holy One, blessed be He says, "My son, why didn't you learn Aggadah [the ethical and inspirational portions of the Talmud]? [And learning Aggadah is extremely important,] for when a rabbi teaches Aggadah, I forgive the sins of all Israel. What's more, when a person answers [in the Kaddish], 'Amen, May His great Name be blessed forever and ever' I forgive him, even if an evil verdict has been decreed on him...."

On the basis of this, Rabbi Yishmael said: How fortunate is a Torah scholar who retains what he has learned, so that he can answer his Creator on Judgment Day, as it says, "To hear discipline is a path to life" (*Mishlei* 10:17). But if he turned his back on his studies and stopped learning, he will be utterly shamed on Judgment Day, as the verse continues, "But one who abandons reproof goes astray" (ibid.). [If the judgment of a Torah scholar is so strict, how much more rigorous will be the punishment of the nations that persecute the Jewish people.]

Peirush HaAggados LeRabbi Azriel, p. 62

Resurrection

It says, "For with You is the source of light; by Your light may we see light" (*Tehillim* 36:10). The phrase "Your light" in this verse refers to the light of Mashiach. It teaches us that the Holy One, blessed be He, looked into the future and saw Mashiach and his generation. He stored him up beneath His Divine Throne of Glory. Mashiach then accepted suffering to atone for the sins of his generation, provided that God would bring back to life the people who died in his lifetime as well as all the people who died from Adam's time until his days. But that's not all, God was to revive also all those who were killed by wolves and lions, and those that drowned in lakes and rivers. What's more, God would return to life even aborted fetuses, and even all those whom God intended to create but did not actually bring to life. When God accepted Mashiach's conditions, he immediately and with love took the suffering upon himself.

Peirush HaAggados LeRabbi Azriel, p. 112

Moshe's Ascent to Heaven

The Midrash says: When Moshe rose to heaven to bring down the Torah to Israel, a cloud appeared and lay down before him. Moshe wavered whether he should ride on it or take hold of it. [Seeing Moshe's hesitation,] the cloud immediately opened its mouth, and Moshe entered into it as if he were walking on earth. There he met the angel Kemuel, who is in charge of twelve thousand destructive angels that are stationed at the gate of heaven.

Kemuel angrily scolded Moshe, saying, "What are you doing in this holy place! Coming from a place of filth and squalor, how dare you come into this pure place? You, man born of woman, are walking in a place of [holy] fire; you, man of flesh and blood, are intruding in a place of [divine] hail!"

Retorted Moshe, "I have come to receive the Torah for Israel."

When Moshe saw that the angel did not desist, he struck him on his face and obliterated him. Moshe kept walking in the cloud until he encountered [the angel] Hadarniel.

Now the Sages tell us that Hadarniel is six hundred thousand parsangs taller than the other angels, and every word he utters is accompanied by twelve thousand flashes of white lightning. When he saw Moshe he rebuked him, "Son of Amram, what business do you have coming into this place of lofty holy beings?"

When Moshe heard Hadarniel's voice, he quivered and shuddered. Tears welled from his eyes, and he wanted to jump out of the cloud.

At that moment the Holy One, blessed be He, took pity on Moshe. A heavenly Voice rang out, telling Hadarniel, "Listen, Hadarniel! Since the day I created you angels, you have been quarrelsome. When I wanted to create man, you protested, telling Me, 'What is frail man that You should remember him, and the son of mortal man that You should be mindful of him?' (*Tehillim* 8:5). You did not let Me create him until I burned a multitude of you. And now you are again resisting Me, and you are not letting Me give the Torah to Israel. If Israel does not accept the Torah, you have no dwelling in heaven."

When Hadarniel heard this, he began to plead before God, "Master of the universe, You know full well that I was not aware that Moshe came with your permission. Now [that I know this] I will be his messenger. I will walk in front of him as disciple before his master...."

Peirush HaAggados LeRabbi Azriel, p. 63

Chapter 12
RABBI MOSHE BEN NACHMAN
(Ramban)

born: Gerona, Spain, 1194
died: Eretz Yisrael, 1270

The Ramban, one of the most famous Torah scholars in the generation after the Rambam, was a Talmudist, Kabbalist, and commentator of Torah and Talmud. He lived in Gerona, where his synagogue in the Call, the ancient Jewish quarter, has been turned into a museum. A descendant of a long line of famous rabbis, he was related to Rabbeinu Yonah of Gerona[1] and was a student of Rabbi Yehudah ben Yakar. His knowledge of Kabbalah he received from Rabbi Ezra and Rabbi Azriel, both of Gerona. A physician by profession, he dedicated his life to teaching Torah to his numerous students. He personifies the best and noblest in Spanish Jewry, and as the foremost halachic authority in all of Spain he wielded great influence in the Spanish community.

In the controversy regarding the writings of the Rambam (Maimonides), the Ramban tried to quell the fury of the Rambam's opponents, trying to convince them that the Rambam's *Moreh Nevuchim* (Guide for the Per-

---
1 Author of the famous classic *Shaarei Teshuvah*.

plexed) was not meant for public use, but only for those who had been led astray by philosophy.

In 1263, King James of Aragon forced the Ramban to hold a public religious debate in Barcelona with a Jewish apostate Pablo Christiani, hoping to prove the superiority of the Catholic religion. In the presence of King James and many dignitaries and clerics, the Ramban completely demolished Pablo with the logic of his arguments. He conclusively proved the falseness of the Christian interpretations of Biblical passages that were cited by the ignorant Pablo.

In admiration, the king rewarded the Ramban with a gift of three hundred gold coins. However, the perfidious Dominican priests claimed that their side had won the dispute, whereupon the Ramban wrote *Sefer HaVikuach*, a detailed account of the questions and his answers. Claiming that the Ramban had vilified the Catholic religion, the Dominican priests prevailed upon Pope Clemens IV to have the Ramban banished from Aragon.

For three years, the Ramban stayed in Castille, where he wrote his monumental Torah commentary. In his commentary he sometimes disagrees with Rashi's interpretations, and often inserts very concise Kabbalistic insights. In a few cryptic words he hides profound Kabbalistic concepts which he refers to as *sod* (secret, mystery). He usually closes his Kabbalistic comments with *vehamaskil yavin*, "those who know Kabbalah will understand." The great Kabbalist Rabbi Yitzchak Luria (the Ari) praises the depth and reliability of the mystical portions of the Ramban's commentary.

In 1267, at the age of seventy-two, the Ramban settled in Eretz Yisrael. Finding Yerushalayim in utter desolation in the wake of the outrages of the marauding crusaders, he began to rebuild the devastated Jewish community. He wrote to his son, "Eretz Yisrael lies in ruin, and the holier the place the greater the destruction. The most desolate place of all is Yerushalayim." In all of Yerushalayim there were only two Jews, and not one *sefer Torah*. The Ramban converted a ruined old building into a synagogue, organized Jews to come back to Yerushalayim, and brought in a *sefer Torah* all the way from

Shechem. His synagogue is still in use, more than seven hundred years later.[1] He established a yeshivah in Akko which became a flourishing Torah center.

The Ramban's novellae on the Talmud had a lasting impact on the study of Gemara. His commentary on the Torah is his crowning achievement. Indispensable for a clear understanding of the Torah text, it is studied widely, and it is printed in all editions of the Chumash Mikra'os Gedolos.[2]

The Ramban died at the age of seventy-six. Strangely, the site of his grave is unknown. According to one version he is buried in Chaifah. According to another, his tomb is next to Me'aras HaMachpeilah in Chevron. No matter which is correct, it is certainly true that the Ramban's resting place is in the minds and hearts of his countless students, to whom his commentaries are part of Chumash and Talmud.

Selections from Kabbalistic Portions of the Ramban's Torah Commentary

The Lofty Source of Man's Soul

> God, the Lord, formed man out of the dust of the ground and breathed into his nostrils the soul of life; man thus became a living being.
>
> (Bereishis 2:7)

The fact that the text uses the full Divine name ["God, the Lord"] gives you an indication of the greatness and the mystery of the human soul. The phrase "He breathed into his nostrils the soul of life" implies that the human soul comes from a higher source than the life force of animals. It evolves from a source that is higher than the angels. The human soul is the spirit of God Himself, for when a person blows his breath into some-

---

[1] The Ramban Synagogue in the Old City of Jerusalem was rebuilt after the Six Day War in 1967. It serves as a shul and houses a yeshivah.

[2] Mossad Harav Kook published a Hebrew annotated edition in 1967.

one else, he infuses part of his soul into him [and God breathes the soul of life into man's nostrils]. That is the deeper meaning of the verse, "It is the soul of the Almighty that gives them understanding [*tevineim*, from the root *Binah*]" (*Iyov* 32:8). [The human soul originates in the *Sefirah* of *Keser* and comes down to man by way of *Binah* and *Tiferes*.] *Vehamaskil yavin* – he who knows [Kabbalah] will understand.

Gan Eden in Heaven and on Earth

> God said, "Man has now become like one of us in knowing good and evil...." God banished man from the Garden of Eden, to work the ground from which he was taken.
>
> (*Bereishis* 3:22-23)

You should know and believe that Gan Eden, the Tree of Life, and the Tree of Knowledge all exist here on earth. The river that flowed out of Eden divided into four major rivers (*Bereishis* 2:10), which are tangible waterways on earth. But you should also know that the physical things that exist on earth exist also in heaven. The heavenly Gan Eden with its trees has a counterpart on earth. This concept is alluded to in the verse, "The King brought me into His chambers" (*Shir HaShirim* 1:4). The Sages interpret this passage to mean that in time to come the Holy One, blessed be He, will show Israel the treasuries on High and the chambers of Heaven [where the counterparts of the treasures on earth are stored].

Alternately the passage, "The King brought me into His chambers," refers to the chambers of Gan Eden. The four rivers [that flowed out of Gan Eden] correspond to the four camps of the *Shechinah* in Heaven that give strength to the kingdoms of the earth. As it says, "[God] will deal with the hosts of heaven in heaven, and with the kings of earth on earth" (*Yeshayah* 24:21). [For every nation on earth has a guardian angel in heaven that protects it and promotes its interests.]

Yaakov's Eternal Struggle with Esav

> A man [the guardian angel of Esav] wrestled with Yaakov until the break of dawn. When he saw that he could not defeat him, he struck the upper joint of Yaakov's thigh; so Yaakov's hip socket was dislocated as he wrestled with him.
> *(Bereishis 32:25-26)*

This verse brings to mind the passage, "Bless God, O His angels; the strong warriors who do His bidding, to obey the voice of His word" (*Tehillim* 103:20). [Meaning: Esav's guardian angel – the strong warrior – could have defeated Yaakov, but he had to do God's bidding, and he had permission only to dislocate Yaakov's hip joint.] The Midrash (*Bereishis Rabbah* 77:4) says that the angel disabled [not only Yaakov but] all the righteous men and women who descended from him, specifically the generation that was forced [by the Romans[1]] to abandon the Torah.

The struggle with Esav's guardian angel foreshadowed a time when the offspring of Esav would vanquish the descendants of Yaakov to the point of virtual annihilation. This happened, for example, in the generation of Rabbi Yehudah ben Bava and his colleagues (see *Sanhedrin* 13b).... What did the Romans [who are the descendants of Esav] do? They took iron balls which they heated until they were white-hot. They then placed them in the armpits of their victims until they expired. In later generations Esav's offspring inflicted similar tortures and did other things that were even much worse than that [such as the Spanish Inquisition, the massacres of the crusaders, the murderous Chmielnicki hordes, and worst of all the unspeakable horrors of the Holocaust, perpetrated by the Germans, the most recent incarnation of Esav's offspring].

Yaakov Did Not Die

> Yaakov finished instructing his sons. He drew his feet back into

---

[1] Rome is synonymous with Edom, which is another name for Esav (*Bereishis* 36:1).

the bed, breathed his last, and was brought back to his people.
(*Bereishis* 49:33)

Rashi is struck by the wording, "he breathed his last," and notes that "the word *death* is not mentioned regarding Yaakov." Rashi then quotes the Midrash that says: "Yaakov our father did not die." The garment hovers over his soul all the time. That is the meaning of the Midrash: "Yaakov our father did not die."

The underlying idea of this *midrash* is that the souls of the righteous are bound in the Bond of Life, but Yaakov's soul hovers over his body all the time, ready to put on its physical garment.

[Explanation: All souls remain in their intangible spiritual state and cannot clothe themselves in an earthly garment whenever they wish to make an appearance in the physical world. Only when God wants to send the soul of a tzaddik down to earth to perform a mission his soul is garbed in tangible clothes. This happened, for example, in the case of the spirit of Navos the Yizraelite who came down to earth to lure Achav into fighting a war in which he would be killed (*Sanhedrin* 102a). As soon as the mission is accomplished, the soul sheds its corporeal garment and returns to its undraped spiritual state. However, the soul of Yaakov and those of other tzaddikim like him are so holy that they do not remain unclothed even for a minute. They are ready to go on a mission on earth at a moment's notice, any time they wish.] For example, after his death, Rabbi Yehudah HaNasi would appear in his house every Friday night dressed in his Shabbos suit to recite the Kiddush for his family (*Kesubos* 103a). Another example is found in the Gemara where it says that diggers were digging up Rabbi Nachman's land. Rabbi Achai bar Yoshiah, who was buried there (unbeknownst to the diggers), growled when the diggers disturbed his body (*Shabbos* 152b).]

The Names of God

According to Kabbalistic tradition, the entire Torah is made up of mystical names of the Holy One, blessed be He. For this reason, if a scribe by mistake added or omitted even one letter in the Torah text, that Torah scroll is invalid. Even if a letter *vav* is missing in the word *osam* [they, them], which occurs thirty-nine times in the Torah in its "full" spelling [with a *vav*; all other times it is spelled without a *vav*], the *sefer Torah* is invalid. The same is true if a *vav* is added in a case where *osam* should be written without a *vav*. This applies to all similar cases, even when the added or omitted letter does not affect the meaning of the word.

That is why the Masoretic scholars counted all the letters in the Torah and the other Scriptures. Ezra the Scribe worked very hard on this, as it says, "They read in the scroll, in God's Torah, clearly, with the application of wisdom, and they helped [the people] understand the reading" (*Nechemyah* 8:8). The Gemara expounds: "They read in the scroll, in God's Torah" refers to the Torah text; "clearly" refers to the Targum [translation];[1] "with the application of wisdom" refers to the division between the verses [since the Torah is written without punctuation marks]; "and they helped the people understand the reading" refers to the cantillation signs; other say, it refers to the Masorah [the traditional spelling of the words].

It seems that in God's original Torah in heaven, which was written with black fire on white fire, the letters were written in an unbroken sequence, without spaces between the words. That way it is possible to combine groups of consecutive letters to form names of God.[2] Or the Torah can be read as we know it, where the letters are grouped to form the familiar text.

[In each of the higher worlds, the letters of the Torah are grouped in a different way; and our Torah has the letter grouping that applies to our lower world.] It was given to Moshe in letter groupings of words that express the mitzvos. However, Moshe was given orally the letter combina-

---

1   Targum Onkelos, the Aramaic interpretive translation of the Torah.
2   The great Kabbalist Rabbi Meir ibn Gabbai says that the Torah is called "God's Torah" because it literally is made up of divine Names (*Avodas HaKodesh, Chelek HaYichud*, ch. 21).

tions that show the Divine names. For example, there is the great Divine name of forty-two letters that is contained in the first two verses of *Bereishis*,[1] where it is written as one uninterrupted series of letters, as is known to the masters of Kabbalah.

From the Introduction to the Ramban's Torah Commentary

---

1 See *Tosafos, Chagigah* 11b, s.v. *ein.*

Chapter 13
RABBI AVRAHAM ABULAFIA

born: Saragossa, Spain, 1240
died: Greece, after 1291

Rabbi Avraham Abulafia, the noted Spanish Kabbalist, was a colorful and adventurous personality. His father, who taught him Torah and Talmud, died when he was eighteen years old. Two years later Avraham set out on a journey to Eretz Yisrael in search of the river Sambatyon and the ten lost tribes dwelling on its banks. On his way there he passed through Greece, where he got married, but that did not dampen his wanderlust. When, on landing in the port of Akko (Acre), he found Eretz Yisrael mired in the turmoil of the marauding crusaders, he decided to return to Spain.

On his way home he spent some time in Capua, Italy, studying philosophy under a doctor named Rabbi Hillel (perhaps of Verona), particularly the Rambam's *Moreh Nevuchim*. Wrestling for clarity, his mind was in constant agitation. It became apparent to him that the Rambam's rationalist philosophy offered no certainty and therefore no satisfaction to his mind, thirsting after truth. He started looking for answers in the books of Kabbalah instead.

Delving into Practical Kabbalah

Returning to Spain in 1271, Rabbi Avraham settled in Barcelona and began to delve into the mysteries of *Sefer Yetzirah* and its numerous commentaries. However, the abstract doctrine of the *Sefiros* did not satisfy his soul. He found something better in the commentary of Rabbi Elazar of Worms, the author of *Sefer HaRokeach*, whose teachings of practical Kabbalah fascinated him. He learned that by applying this system a person could attain *ruach hakodesh*, prophetic insight, and closeness to God. To reach this lofty plateau a person had to be able to combine the letters of the divine Name, to transpose the component parts of a word in all possible permutations, and to use letters as numbers (*gematria*) as taught by Rabbi Elazar of Worms.

But it takes more than that. He learned that in order to be worthy of a prophetic revelation, one has to adopt an ascetic way of life of fasting, remove himself from the turmoil of the world, shut himself up in a quiet chamber, free his soul from worldly cares, clothe himself in white garments, put on tallis and tefillin, and prepare his soul for an encounter with God. One has to pronounce certain incantations, contort his body, bending forward until the mind becomes dazed and the heart is filled with glow. Then he will go into a trance and feel as though his soul were released from the body. After a while, divine grace is poured into his soul, and the prophetic revelation follows quite naturally.

Rabbi Avraham himself practiced this system of working oneself up into a state of ecstasy and taught it to his adherents. He considered this approach to Kabbalah to be prophetic inspiration and the only method by which one can penetrate the secrets of the Torah. To him, the plain meaning of the Torah text was merely for simple people, "like milk for children," as he put it. "*Yod'ei chein* [i.e., Kabbalists], on the other hand, find higher wisdom in the numerical value of the letters and in the permutations of the words." By employing this knowledge a person can perform miracles and discover mystical secrets.

Rabbi Avraham taught this form of Kabbalah in Barcelona, Burgos, and

Medina-Celi, attracting numerous devoted disciples, most notable among them Rabbi Yosef Gikatilla, author of *Shaarei Orah*. At one point, after much fasting and mortifying himself, he believed that he had reached his goal. He describes his spiritual elevation as follows: "My spirit came to life, and a sense of holiness sparked within me.... I had visions.... For fifteen years I felt like a blind man groping at noontime, while Satan was standing on my right to accuse me."

An Audacious Idea

Rabbi Avraham Abulafia left Spain a second time, traveling to Italy. While there, he conceived an idea that only a man with his wild imagination could have envisioned. He journeyed to Rome with the announced mission of persuading Pope Nicholas III to convert to Judaism. He paid dearly for the attempt. The pope, who was vacationing in Suriano, heard of his plan and issued orders to arrest the radical Jew and burn him alive as soon as he arrived. Although a huge stake was prepared outside of Rome, Rabbi Avraham continued on his way. Upon reaching Suriano he learned that the pope had succumbed to a stroke the night before. He was arrested two days later in Rome, and after languishing in prison for twenty-eight days he was released.

Castigated by Rashba

He then went to Sicily, settling in Messina, where he was welcomed by the community. He gathered a number of followers and announced the end of the *galus* and the imminent coming of Mashiach, which he said would occur in the year 1290. Rabbi Avraham Abulafia's strict moral conduct, ascetic life, and charismatic personality convinced many Jews in Sicily to believe in him and to make preparations for returning to Eretz Yisrael. Others were confused and turned for guidance to Rabbi Shlomo ben Aderes (Rashba) of Barcelona,[1] the leading Torah authority of that time.

---
1   1235–1310.

The Rashba sharply rebuked Abulafia and warned the community not to follow him. In the wake of the Rashba's severe criticism, Rabbi Avraham Abulafia was harassed so much in Sicily that he had to leave the island and went to Greece, where he wrote *VeZos LeYehudah* and *Sheva Nesivos HaTorah*, defending himself against the Rashba's denunciation, claiming that the Rashba did not know him personally and judged him on the basis of hearsay. Rabbi Chaim Vital quotes Rabbi Avraham extensively in *Shaarei Kedushah*.[1]

His Legacy

Rabbi Avraham Abulafia wrote altogether twenty-six books, as well as twenty-two works in which he describes his visions. Most of these books are still in manuscript. *Imrei Shefer*, written in 1291, is a commentary on the story of Creation. The place and time of Rabbi Avraham's death are unknown. He made a lasting imprint on the development of Kabbalah, centuries after his death. His influence is particularly evident in the works of the later Kabbalists of Tzefas, particularly the Ari and his disciples.

---

1 Amsterdam, 1715.

Chapter 14
RABBI YOSEF GIKATILLA

born: Castile, Spain, 1248
died: Penafiel, Spain, c. 1310

Rabbi Yosef Gikatilla, a Kabbalist and liturgical poet, was known as a holy man and was often called "Baal HaNissim" ("master of miracles"). He studied Kabbalah under Rabbi Avraham Abulafia,[1] a towering Kabbalist, under whose influence he abandoned his earlier leaning toward philosophy to devote himself completely to Kabbalah.

At the age of twenty-four he wrote *Ginas Egoz* (Orchard of the Walnut),[2] a Kabbalistic work dealing with the Names of God and the combinations of the letters and vowels of the Divine Name, whereby each vowel corresponds to one of the ten *Sefiros*. *Ginas Egoz* was published many times. Its Berlin, 1803, edition carries a commentary by Rabbi Elyakim of London.

His most famous work, *Shaarei Orah*,[3] greatly influenced later Kabbalists, who cite this seminal work with deep reverence. The Arizal[4] describes the book as "a key to understanding the mystical teachings." It

---

1 See ch. 13.
2 Hanau, 1615. The title is taken from *Shir HaShirim* 6:11.
3 Riva di Trento, 1559.
4 See ch. 30.

stresses knowledge of God through His Creation, rather than through linguistics, and it discusses the definitions and descriptions of the ten *Sefiros*. It has been translated into Latin, and Rabbi Mattisyahu Delacrut, a Polish Kabbalist who studied in Italy, wrote a commentary on it.

Rabbi Yosef Gikatilla also wrote *Shaarei Tzedek*[1] on the ten *Sefiros*, a commentary on *Moreh Nevuchim*,[2] and a number of other Kabbalistic works. In addition to a halachic work, *Sefer HaMitzvos*, he wrote several liturgical poems, including a *kinah* (elegy) for Tishah B'Av that begins with the words "*Yerushalayim hane'ehavah*, Yerushalayim, the Beloved."

Selections from Shaarei Orah

[Note: The chapters of the book are arranged in the order of the *Sefiros*, starting with the tenth *Sefirah*.]

Berachah – Blessing

[The Divine Name] *Ado-nai* contains all the treasures of the King and all His bounty; the *Sefiros* are concealed with Him, and it is from there that they will disperse and fulfill the needs of all Creation, like a pool from which the river draws its water to irrigate the garden and provide water to drink. Another Name for *Ado-nai* is *Berachah* (blessing), which comes from the word *bereichah* (pool).

[*Berachah*] is the divine Name that Yaakov Avinu used to bless his sons. He inherited [that Name] from Yitzchak Avinu who, in turn, inherited it from Avraham, to whom it was imparted by God Himself. And God gave it to Avraham for the purpose of opening the gates to *Ado-nai* and to give him and the rest of the world everything they need. This, therefore, is the underlying thought of the verse [where God speaks to Avraham, saying,] "...I will bless you and make you great. You shall become a *berachah*"

---

1   Riva di Trento, 1561.
2   Venice, 1574.

(*Bereishis* 12:2).... The Divine Name *Ado-nai* is like a storehouse of all the *berachos* (blessings) and other *Sefiros*.

Shaarei Orah, "The Tenth Sefirah"

Explanation: The Four-Letter Name of God is rooted in *Keser*, the highest of the ten *Sefiros*. The divine Name *Ado-nai* is associated with *Malchus*, the tenth and lowest *Sefirah*, which is our physical world. Having passed through the ten *Sefiros*, the flow of divine *berachah* reaches its destination in *Malchus*, the tangible universe.

Thus, the above-qutoed phrase, "[The Name] *Ado-nai* contains all the treasures of the King and all His bounty" means that God's bounty becomes manifest in the *Sefirah* of *Malchus* — the cosmos.

The passage, "The divine Name *Ado-nai* is like a storehouse of all the *berachos* and other *Sefiros*," implies that our material world receives all the *berachos* from the higher *Sefiros*. Thus, our world is like a *bereichah* that holds the *berachah* flowing into it from Above. And Avraham, Yitzchak, and Yaakov are the channels through which the *berachah* spreads to the entire world.

A Hundred Sockets of the Mishkan

[Note: The walls of the Sanctuary consisted of rows of wooden beams covered with gold. Two pegs were carved out at the bottom of each beam. These pegs were inserted into silver sockets, two sockets to each beam. Altogether there were fifty beams and a hundred sockets (*Shemos* 26:15–25). A socket is called *aden*; in plural, *adanim*; *adnei* in the construct form.]

Adnei kesef, the term for the silver sockets, has the same root the Divine Name *Ado-nai*, as it says, "The hundred talents of silver were used to cast the *adanim* (sockets) of the Sanctuary, [one talent for each socket]" (*Shemos* 38:27).

The hundred *adanim* that were used for the sockets are similar to the hundred *bereichos* (pools) which are filled from the great pool of *Ado-nai* [the flow of abundance that comes down to the world]. This is why you have to say a hundred *berachos* each day, so that you may draw from each of the hundred pools. If a person says fewer than a hundred *berachos*, he will bring a blemish on his soul.

The essence of the way the hundred blessings relate to the soul of Israel can be found in the letters *alef, yud, kuf*. The letter that follows *alef* is *beis*. The letter that follows *yud* is *kaf*, and the letter that follows *kuf* is *reish*. [Notice, by rearranging the letters *beis, kaf*, and *reish*, you obtain *barach*, the root of *berachah*.]

[The numeric value of] *kuf* is 100, for a Jew must give the Levi *maaser* (tithe), ten measures for every hundred. *Yud* is ten, for the Levi must give *maaser* to the *kohein*, one measure for every ten. The *alef* stands for the one measure the *kohein* receives. So the letters *alef, yud, kuf* symbolize the entirety of the Jewish people, which is the combined essence of the lower soul (*nefesh*), the spirit (*ruach*), and the higher soul (*neshamah*).

Shaarei Orah, "The Tenth Sefirah"

Shalom – Peace

> [Note: The Divine Name *Yud-Hei-Vav-Hei* is above *Keser*, the highest *Sefirah*. It is completely beyond human comprehension. The Divine Name *Ado-nai* is associated with *Malchus*, the tenth and last *Sefirah*, which is the physical world.]

When Israel is righteous and good, then the attribute *Ado-nai* [i.e., the physical world] is filled with completeness and with a vast flow of blessing. If, God forbid, Israel disregards what God desires, then the attribute of mercy, which is called *Yud-Hei-Vav-Hei*, removes itself from the realm of *Ado-nai* [this world], leaving it empty. When the tzaddik arouses the world to do *teshuvah*, the attribute called "*Shalom*" mediates effectively between *Yud-Hei-Vav-Hei* and *Ado-nai*. *Shalom* is the one that makes peace [between the Names *Yud-Hei-Vav-Hei* and *Ado-nai*], unifies them and brings them to dwell together without separation in the world. When this happens *Yud-Hei-Vav-Hei* will be One. You should know and believe that it is impossible to bring blessing to the world except through the attribute of *Shalom*. As it says, "Hashem blesses His people with *shalom*" (*Tehillim* 29:11).

The Rabbis have said: The only vessel that can hold blessing is *shalom* (*Uktzin* 3:11).

You have to realize that *shalom* is the lowest of the six lower *Sefiros* [i.e., *Yesod*]. It is the one that empties out blessing into the name of *Ado-nai* [into *Malchus*, i.e., this world]. That's why the word *shalom* is placed [in the *Shemoneh Esrei*] specifically at the end of the priestly blessing and at the end of the final *berachah* of the *Shemoneh Esrei*.[1] The reason for this is that it is only through *Shalom*'s command that all who leave and all who come are connected to the uppermost light, which is life in the World to Come.

I must make you aware of the deeper meaning [of this idea]. Remember that the Rabbis taught (*Shabbos* 89a):

"When Moshe went up to heaven, the Holy One, blessed be He, said to him, 'Moshe, don't they give greetings of '*shalom*' in your town?' Moshe replied, 'Is it respectful for a servant say "*shalom*" to his master?' Replied God, '[Instead of saying nothing], you should have helped Me [by wishing Me success in My work].' The next time Moshe spoke to God he said, 'And now, let the power of God be great, as You have said' (*Bemidbar* 14:17)." [So you see, even God needs *Shalom*.]

The underlying meaning of this is that the attribute *shalom* [i.e., the *Sefirah* of *Yesod*] empties life into the attribute *Ado-nai* [*Malchus*, i.e., this world] when they are fused into one. For great is the power of peace, since even the upper worlds need it, as it says, "He makes *shalom* in the heavens…" (*Iyov* 25:2).

When you hook up with the Torah and the mitzvos, it is as if you bring

---

1 Both *Birkas Kohanim* (the Priestly Blessing) and *Shemoneh Esrei* end with the word *shalom*.

shalom to the heavenly household, which is the real meaning of the verse, "If Israel would grasp My stronghold [i.e., if only Israel would hold fast to My Torah], then [Israel] would make peace with Me, peace would he make with Me" (*Yeshayah* 27:5).

Shaarei Orah, "The Ninth Sefirah"

The Three Patriarchs

[Note: This segment teaches that Avraham represents the *Sefirah* of *Chesed*; Yitzchak symbolizes the *Sefirah* of *Gevurah*, in addition to *pachad* (fear) and *din* (strict judgment); and Yaakov exemplifies *Tiferes*, the *Sefirah* that mediates between *Chesed* and *Gevurah*. Yaakov is also the symbol of *emes* (truth)].

> Give truth to Yaakov, *chesed* to Avraham.
> (*Michah* 7:20)

The meaning of this verse is this: You should know that Avraham Avinu, peace be with him, served God through the attribute of *Chesed* without the benefit of a teacher or a father or the appearance of a Divine prophet who offers rebuke and warning. It was he alone who saw, delved, and perceived until he came to know the kingdom of God, may He be blessed. For just as God created the world through the attribute of *Chesed*, so too Avraham came to know his Creator through the attribute of *Chesed*. Yaakov, however, did not know his Creator through *Chesed*, but through the attribute of *emes*.

Avraham came and proclaimed the attribute of *Chesed*, but how? He announced to the world God's abundant *chesed* and mercy for all His works, by which He created and sustained them. And all was done through the attribute of *Chesed*, and from this perspective it is fitting for all humans to serve God and accept the yoke of His kingdom, for we are all obliged to do this.

Then Yitzchak came and proclaimed the attribute of [*Gevurah*] which implies *Pachad*. For if you do not serve God, He will punish you like a servant who rebels against his master, and He will instill terror and fear among the created.... Thus Yitzchak warned mankind and admonished them, for he inherited the attribute of *pachad*. He warned them to be in awe of the Great Judge who judges the wicked with the attribute of *Pachad* which is known for the punishments of Gehinnom, as it says, "Sinners were afraid [*pachadu*] in Zion" (*Yeshayah* 33:14).

In light of this, you find that Avraham admonishes mankind with the attribute of *chesed*, while Yitzchak rebukes mankind with the attribute of *pachad*. Each one urges the community in accordance with his attribute: one through the attribute of *chesed* and reward, the other through *pachad* and punishment; one through the positive commandments, the other through the negative commandments. When Yaakov Avinu came, there was no third attribute for him to cling to, so he attached himself to both the attributes of Avraham and Yitzchak, *Chesed* and *Pachad*, and he announced to the world the significance of their truth, and never veered to the right or the left. [Therefore, Yaakov is the embodiment of *emes*.]

Yaakov was the middle line, and he exemplifies the central branch of the *lulav* [the date palm frond waved on Sukkos] which is connected in the middle between the attribute of Avraham – *Chesed*, the positive commandments – and the attribute of Yitzchak – *pachad*, the negative commandments [i.e., prohibitions], not veering right or left. That is why Yaakov is called a man of truth, for he acted in truth with the two attributes of his ancestors. This comes to the fore in the verse, "Yaakov was a perfect man, a dweller of tents" (*Bereishis* 25:27). It does not say a "tent dweller" but rather a "dweller of tents" [plural]. This refers to the "tent of Avraham," which is *Chesed*, and the "tent of Yitzchak," which is *Pachad*.

Shaarei Orah, "The Fourth Sefirah"

Blessings Flow from *Binah* to Our World

[Note: The *Sefiros* of *Binah* and *Malchus* are often juxtaposed and seen as facing each other. For example, *Binah* is frequently called "the upper Gan

Eden," while *Malchus* is called "the lower Gan Eden." The feminine aspect of both these *Sefiros* is often stressed. They are both represented in God's Four-Letter Name — *Binah* by the first *hei*, *Malchus* by the second *hei*. Sometimes the name *Leah* is associated with *Binah* and the name *Rachel* with *Malchus*. Rabbi Meir ibn Gabbai, in his book *Avodas HaKodesh*,[1] gives the following interpretive quote from *Shaarei Orah*, which is easier to understand than the original.]

The great Kabbalist Rabbi Yosef Gikatilla in his book *Shaarei Orah* in the chapter "The Third *Sefirah*" writes: You should know and believe that the *Sefiros* of *Binah* and *Malchus* face each other. For when the *Sefirah* of *Malchus* is set right through Israel's observance of the Torah and the mitzvos, the *Sefirah* of *Binah* pours out abundant blessing through the [spiritual] channels, until the *Sefirah* of *Malchus* is filled with blessing. Then all mankind will live in peace and tranquility. The blessing is sent [in the form of abundant] food, and there is blessing upon the land. This is affirmed in the verse, "If you follow My laws and are careful to keep My commandments, I will provide you with rain at the right time, so that the land will bear its crops and the trees of the field will provide fruit" (*Vayikra* 26:3-4).

Avodas HaKodesh 18

---

1 See ch. 18.

Chapter 15
RABBI MOSHE DE LEON

born: Leon, Spain, 1250
died: Avila, Spain, 1305

Rabbi Moshe de Leon, one of the early Spanish Kabbalists, was a scribe and copyist of old manuscripts, which he distributed. He was very close to Rabbi Yosef Gikatilla and the Kabbalists of Gerona. Traveling from city to city in search of manuscripts, he discovered an ancient manuscript of the *Zohar*, written by the *tanna* Rabbi Shimon bar Yochai, which he then copied. According to an old tradition, it was the Ramban who unearthed the manuscript of the *Zohar* hidden in a cave in Eretz Yisrael. He sent it to Catalonia, Spain; from there it found its way to Aragon (northeast Spain), where it was found by Rabbi Moshe de Leon.

People began to surmise that Rabbi Moshe de Leon himself had written the *Zohar*. In an attempt to establish the authentic authorship of the *Zohar*, Rabbi Yitzchak of Akko questioned Rabbi Moshe de Leon about this when they happened to meet on the road one day. Rabbi Moshe assured him that the original ancient *Zohar* manuscript which he had copied was locked away in his house in Avila, adding, "When you come to visit me, I will show it to you." Shortly after their chance meeting Rabbi Moshe passed away. When Rabbi Yitzchak of Akko came to Avila and asked Rabbi Moshe's widow to sell him the manuscript, offering her a large sum of money, she did not know anything about it.

The theory that Rabbi Moshe de Leon was the author of the *Zohar* has been conclusively discredited. Scholars have shown that the Kabbalistic views Rabbi Moshe set forth in his own books differ markedly from the *Zohar*'s ideology. Furthermore, it was shown that Rabbi Moshe de Leon's Kabbalistic terminology does not match the expressions commonly used in the *Zohar*.

Rabbi Moshe did write *Sefer HaRimon* (in manuscript) which deals with the mystical reasons for the mitzvos. In *Nefesh HaChochmah*[1] he discusses the divine nature of the soul and the resurrection of the dead. He also wrote a commentary on *Maaseh Merkavah* (the account of the Divine Chariot); *Shekel HaKodesh*[2] on a number of Kabbalistic themes; and *Sefer Hashem*,[3] dealing with the ten *Sefiros* and the thirteen attributes of mercy; and numerous other works, all in manuscript.

Selections from the Writings of Rabbi Moshe de Leon

Why He Wrote the Commentary on *Maaseh Merkavah*

It happened in the thirteenth year, in the fourth month, on the fifth of the month, as I was among the exiles by the river Kevar; the heavens opened and I saw visions of God.

(*Yechezkel* 1:1)

[This is the opening verse of *Maaseh Merkavah*, "The account of the Divine Chariot," Yechezkel's mystical vision of the Divine Throne.]

You should know that not everybody is qualified to delve into the mysteries of Kabbalah, even if he is wise and can figure out things by himself. [The Gemara says:] "A person should not study the account of the Divine

---

1 Basel, 1608.
2 London, 1921.
3 Venice, 1605.

Chariot by himself" (*Chagigah* 11b), much less speak about these profound mysteries. But since it came to my attention that there are a number of people who have the audacity to write commentaries [on Kabbalistic books] and dream up things that have no basis in fact, I feel that I must take a stand in defense of the truth and explain the concepts the way the Sages interpreted them, which is the true approach.

Yechezkel had the vision of the *Merkavah* (the Divine Chariot) in a prophetic revelation, even though he was outside Eretz Yisrael. [He was in Babylonia, which is problematic because we have a tradition that prophetic visions occur only in Eretz Yisrael.] At that time [in the Babylonian exile] there was an urgent need for Yechezkel's prophecy. The Sages explain: The Jewish people were driven into exile, the Temple was destroyed, its former glory shattered. "The heavens were clothed in darkness, and their garments were sackcloth" (*Yeshayah* 50:3). Suffering the hardship of the exile, the people felt forlorn and were deeply distressed. At a time like this, an exception was made with Yechezkel's prophecy [since it was needed to inspire the people and give them hope for a better future].

I undertake the project of writing a commentary [on *Maaseh Merkavah*] "to enlighten the wise" [an allusion to *Daniel* 12:3] and to silence the fools who live in darkness. May God favor me by teaching me His ways and remove the stumbling blocks from my path. By the name of God Almighty I appeal to anyone who understands these matters to keep them to himself and not add outlandish and false ideas to them. May God approve of my work, for "A man may arrange his thoughts, but what he says depends on God" (*Mishlei* 16:1).

Chapter 16
RABBI BACHYA BEN ASHER
(Rabbeinu Bachya)

died: Saragossa, Spain, c. 1340

Rabbi Bachya ben Asher, popularly known as Rabbeinu Bachya or Bechaya, was a student of the Rashba[1] and served as *dayan* (rabbinical judge) in Saragossa, Spain. He gained immortal fame through his Torah commentary *Midrash Rabbeinu Bachya*,[2] which is studied and quoted widely to this day. Its popularity is evident by the fact that it has been reprinted more than twenty-five times. At least ten commentaries have been written on his work, most recently a commentary by Rabbi Chaim Dov Chavel.[3]

Rabbeinu Bachya introduces the weekly Torah portions with a discourse on ethics, based on a verse from *Mishlei*. He then expounds the text according to the four methods of interpretation: *peshat*, the plain, rational meaning; *derash*, midrashic, homiletic exegesis; *remez*, philosophic allusions; and *sod*, Kabbalistic interpretation. In his profound Kabbalistic insights he often quotes the Ramban and the *Zohar*.

Rabbeinu Bachya also wrote *Kad HaKemach*[4] on ethics, faith, and the ob-

---

1 Rabbi Shlomo ben Aderes, 1235–1310.
2 Naples, 1492.
3 Mossad HaRav Kook, Jerusalem, 1982.
4 Constantinople, 1513.

servance of the mitzvos. A great Kabbalist, he wrote *Ohel Moed*, a penetrating commentary on *Sefer Yetzirah*.

Selections from Kabbalistic Portions of Rabbeinu Bachya's Torah Commentary

Why Do People Hate Snakes?

> God said to the serpent, ... "I will plant hatred between you and the woman...."
> *(Bereishis 3:15)*

Why do people loathe snakes more than they detest other reptiles? In the above verse Scripture is hinting at the mystical idea that the body of the cunning snake was the instrument that brought punishment on man. The snake has the tendency to infect people with its innate [satanic] power. That's how it provoked Chavah to sin, and because of that, death was decreed on her offspring. That is the source of the hatred between the snake and Chavah's descendants.

And that is the reason why the snake is called *saraf*, "the fiery serpent,"[1] as it says, "[When the people in the wilderness spoke out against God,] God sent the fiery serpents, [and they bit the people]" (*Bemidbar* 21:6). These snakes were offshoots of the primeval serpent [in Gan Eden].

This explains why God said to the serpent, "Man will pound your head, and you will bite his heel" (*Bereishis* 3:15). Man should be quick to overcome his innate "serpent" [i.e., his *yetzer hara*] and crush it; otherwise, "you will bite his heel." If man does not squash his *yetzer hara*, it will strike him in the heel and kill him. The heel [the end of the foot] is a metaphor for death [the end of life]. You surely know that our Sages say that the serpent, Satan, the *yetzer hara*, and the Angel of Death are one and the same (*Bava Basra* 16a).

---

1   The verb *saraf* means "to burn."

The Mitzvah of Circumcision

My covenant shall be in your flesh for an everlasting covenant.
(Bereishis 17:13)

The deeper meaning is that "My covenant in your flesh" shall be an embodiment of the everlasting covenant [of the *Sefirah* of *Yesod*,[1] which is the sixth of the seven lower *Sefiros*]. The *Sefirah* of *Yesod* is associated with the verse, "A tzaddik is the foundation [*yesod*] of the world" (*Mishlei* 10:25).

It is also described as "an eternal salt-like covenant" (*Bemidbar* 18:19), for [just as salt preserves food], this covenant sustains the world.

It could have said, "My covenant shall be in your flesh forever." Instead it says, "for an everlasting covenant." This "everlasting covenant" refers to the mystical covenant [*Yesod*, symbolized by the male organ] which is situated between the thighs, namely, the two *Sefiros*: *Netzach* and *Hod*. [In the human body, the male organ is the symbol of *Yesod*.] The Kabbalists find an allusion to *Yesod* in the verse, "He did not remember the *hadom* of His feet on the day of His wrath" (*Eichah* 2:1). They say that *hadom* [usually translated "footstool"] refers to the [*Sefirah* of *Yesod*, the male organ] that is between the feet. [The letters of *hadom*: *hei*, *dalet*, *vav*, and *mem* can be rearranged to read *middah vav*, "the sixth *Sefirah*," i.e., *Yesod*.[2]]

Yesod is directly above *Malchus*. In man, the counterparts of *Yesod* and *Malchus* [i.e., the male and female organ] are separated by the *periah* membrane.[3] For that reason the halachah rules: If the *milah* (circumcision) was performed without removing the *periah* membrane, the *milah* is invalid (*Shabbos* 137b). The right way to perform the mitzvah of *milah* is to re-

---

1   *Yesod* is the *Sefirah* through which the upper *Sefiros* and *Malchus* mate. It therefore exemplifies the male organ.
2   *Toras Chaim*, a commentary on *Midrash Rabbeinu Bachya*, written by Rabbi Chaim HaKohen (Livorno, 1894).
3   The preputial membrane, called *or haperiah*, that covers the tip of the male organ. In *milah*, after the foreskin is removed (*chittuch*), the corona (*atarah*) is uncovered by removing the *or haperiah* that covers it. Failure to remove the *or haperiah* makes the *milah* invalid.

move both [the foreskin and the *periah* membrane], for thereby the complete union [between *Yesod* and *Malchus*] is achieved.

Wine Is the Root of Evil

> [Note: After the destruction of Sedom and Amorah, Lot and his two daughters escaped to Tzo'an, where they lived in a cave.]

> [Believing that no man was left in the world, the older girl said to the younger,] "Let's get our father drunk with wine and sleep with him. We will then survive through children from our father."
> *(Bereishis 19:32)*

[The Midrash says that the Tree of Knowledge was a grapevine, and that Chavah pressed grapes and offered the wine to Adam.] The two girls followed in the footsteps of their ancestress Chavah, who made Adam sin [by giving him wine to drink]. [Since wine looks like blood,] Chavah was punished with the menstrual flow of blood, and also in that her husband keeps apart from her during her period. As a matter of fact, there are cases where Scripture plainly associates wine with blood, as in, "They drank the blood of grapes like delicious wine" (*Devarim* 32:14), and "He will launder his garments in wine and his robe in the blood of grapes" (*Bereishis* 49:11).

The sins of Chavah and Lot's daughters were one and the same in that they came about through wine. And wine is the cause of evil. Perhaps by repeating the phrase "our father" in the present verse the girls implied, "Not only our father Lot [was made drunk by a woman], but our primeval father [Adam] was also given wine by a woman."

Yaakov, the Man of Truth

> The boys grew up. Esav became a skilled trapper, a man of the field. Yaakov was a single-minded man, dwelling in tents.
> *(Bereishis 25:27)*

When you think about it, the passage should have characterized Yaakov as "a man of truth" [rather than as an *ish tam*, "a single-minded man"] because Yaakov exemplifies truth, as it says, "Grant truth to Yaakov" (*Michah* 7:2). The word *tam* denotes more than simple truth. It tells us that Yaakov [who represents *Tiferes*] mediates [between *Chesed* on the right and *Gevurah* on the left]. The word *tam* is from the same root as *teyomes*, which is the spine of the *lulav*, standing between the leaves on the right and the left. [Thus, the word *tam* most fittingly depicts Yaakov's character in this world and the spiritual realm.]

The verse describes Yaakov also as "dwelling in tents." In a Kabbalistic sense, this means that he dwelled in the tent of the higher [spiritual] world and in the tent of the lower [physical] world. It is a well-known fact that the image of Yaakov is engraved in the Divine Throne. Indeed, you can say that "dwelling in tents – *yoshev ohalim*" corresponds to "sitting on the Throne – *yoshev hakisei*" [the words *ohalim* (tents) and *hakisei* (the Throne) both have the numeric value of 86].

Kings of Edom

> These are the kings who ruled in the land of Edom before a king reigned over the children of Israel.
>
> (*Bereishis* 36:31)

[*Bereishis*, ch. 36, offers a detailed list of the generations of Esav as well as the names of the chiefs and kings that descended from him. At first glance this seems to be of no consequence, but Rabbeinu Bachya explains the Kabbalistic meaning behind these genealogies.]

This verse alludes to the worlds that God created with the attribute of Justice before He created this world, and before His sovereignty was revealed in this world. That is the Kabbalistic meaning of "[the kings that ruled] before a king reigned over the children of Israel." The verse suggests that God built many worlds [with the attribute of Justice] and destroyed them.¹ Only then did He create this world by combining His attributes of Justice and Mercy.² I cannot explain this because these things are exalted beyond human comprehension.

Let me make it clear that in the Torah there is no difference between the Shema and [the seemingly irrelevant verse,] "Timna became the concubine of Esav" (*Bereishis* 36:12). And there is no difference between [the seemingly unimportant,] "His wife's name was Meheitavel" (*Bereishis* 36:39) and the Ten Commandments. Every letter and every word in the Torah is tied to mystical concepts.

If you count them, you find that this chapter lists eight kings. And if you include the woman Meheitavel (*Bereishis* 36:40), you have nine. Now you may wonder why she is the only queen mentioned in this chapter. Anyway, who was she, for this is the only place we find her name in the Torah. And what is the purpose of mentioning her name in the first place?

Let me point out to you that this chapter mentions two kings, one named Hadad [ben Bedad], the other Hadar (*Bereishis* 36:35, 39). Their names are cognate to *hod* (glory) and *hadar* (splendor), which are Divine attributes. The name Hadad ben Bedad alludes to the thirteen Divine attributes³ that are drawn from the ten *Sefiros*. [The numeric value of *Hadad* (*hei, dalet, dalet* = 5 + 4 + 4) is 13. The numeric value of *Bedad* (*beis, dalet, dalet* = 2 + 4 + 4) is 10. Thus "Hadad son of Bedad" means: the thirteen attributes that emanate from the ten *Sefiros*.] You know that God conducts the affairs of this lowly world with the thirteen Divine attributes. That's why it says that the city of Hadad ben Bedad [i.e., the thirteen attributes] was named Avis (*Bereishis* 36:35). For this lowly world is the domain of the *yetzer hara* who distorts [*me'aveis*, related to Avis] a person's righteous ways.... Hadar's wife was Meheitavel [which translates: "the goodness of God"], for she represents the goodness of God saying to Moshe, "I shall make My goodness pass before you" (*Shemos* 33:19).

1 See *Bereishis Rabbah* 3:9–12.
2 See *Rashi* on *Bereishis* 1:1.
3 See *Shemos* 34:6–7.

The Ten Martyrs

[When Yosef's silver goblet was found in Binyamin's sack, the ten brothers offered to become Yosef's slaves, to which Yosef replied,] "Heaven forbid that I do that. The one in whose possession the goblet was found, only he shall be my slave. [The rest of you] go up in peace to your father."

(Bereishis 44:12)

[Note: Ten great *tannaim* were brutally murdered by the Romans. Their agony is recalled in the prayer *Eileh Ezkera* recited on Yom Kippur in the *mussaf* service. The Gemara (*Pesachim* 50a) says that the martyrdom of the ten *tannaim* was an atonement for the ten brothers' sin of selling Yosef into slavery.]

"Rabbi Yishmael said: How did God react [when the ten martyrs were brutally murdered by the Romans]? He decreed dreadful punishments on the evil Roman empire. He said: 'Rome will be stricken with boils, blisters, and leprous plagues. There will come a time that a person will say to his friend, "You can have Rome and all that's in it for a dime," and his friend will say, "I don't want it" ' " (*Pirkei Heichalos* 8).

[Before the brothers left with the grain they had bought, Yosef instructed the overseer,] "Put each man's silver [money] in the mouth of his sack" (*Bereishis* 44:1). The soul is compared to pure silver and the body to a sack that encloses the soul.

The parashah ends with Yosef saying to his brothers, "Go up in peace to your father" (*Bereishis* 44:17). It could have said, "Go in peace to your father." Why does it say, "Go up in peace"? In its plain meaning this chapter refers to Yosef and his brothers. But on a Kabbalistic level it hints at the ten martyrs, who went up in peace to their Father in Heaven, after being purified of the sin of [selling] Yosef. Indeed the Gemara relates that the *tanna* Rabbi Yosef once experienced a heavenly vision, and he heard them say [in heaven]: "No one can stand within the confines of the ten martyrs; [that's how saintly they are]" (*Pesachim* 50a).

Kil'ayim, Forbidden Mixtures

> Keep My decrees: Do not crossbreed your livestock with other species. Do not plant your field with different species of seeds. Do not wear a garment that contains a forbidden mixture of fabrics (*shaatnez*).
>
> (*Vayikra* 19:19)

This commandment falls under the category of *chukim*. *Chukim* are laws that cannot be explained in terms of physical reality; they have to do with heavenly beings. [You must realize that] every creature in our world has a guardian angel in the heavenly realm that makes it grow and keeps it alive. The Sages put it succinctly: "Every blade of grass has a guardian angel in heaven that taps it lightly and says, 'Start growing!' " (*Bereishis Rabbah* 10:7).

You should know that the guardian angels need to have peace [in order to do their job], as it says, "He makes peace in His heights" (*Iyov* 25:2). When they have peace they are able to carry out their specific mission. Therefore, when you plant or grow species according to their own kind down in this world, you enable the guardian angels to function properly, and you bring about peace Above. But if a person here on earth raises mixed breeds, he causes discord in heaven, because he mixes up the guardian angels and foils their mission. This is evident in the word *kil'ayim* (forbidden mixtures), which is cognate to *keleh*, "prison," for a prisoner is unable to work at his regular job....

Shaatnez (wearing a garment made of a mixture of wool and linen) is forbidden because Kayin and Hevel both brought an offering. Kayin brought some of his crops [including flax from which linen is made], and Hevel offered sheep that produce wool. This brought about conflict among the heavenly beings and strife here on earth, to the point that Kayin killed his brother Hevel, so that both of them perished [Hevel physically, Kayin spiritually].

Chapter 17
RABBI MENACHEM RECANATI

Italy, late thirteenth–early fourteenth century

Rabbi Menachem Recanati, commonly called "the Ricanti," one of the first Italian Kabbalists, wrote several books on Kabbalah. His commentaries are strongly influenced by the outlook of the *chassidei Ashkenaz* (the rabbis in Germany), mainly by Rabbi Yehudah HeChassid, author of *Sefer Chassidim*, and Rabbi Elazar Rokeach of Worms, author of *Sefer HaRokeach*. But he also was greatly inspired by Rabbi Ezra of Gerona and the Ramban, both of whom he frequently quotes. He always refers to the Ramban simply "the Rav."

The Ricanti was a serious student of philosophy, since he considered it an important aid toward understanding Kabbalistic ideology, and he avidly studied the philosophical writings of the Rambam, particularly *Moreh Nevuchim*. The Ricanti's main Kabbalistic work is his commentary on the Torah.[1] Its profound and novel ideas greatly influenced the Kabbalists of succeeding generations. Filled with mysteries and visions, it has been translated into Latin by the Italian humanist Pico della Mirandola, who learned Hebrew from Jewish teachers. Rabbi Mordechai Yaffe (the Levush) thought so highly of this volume that he composed a running commentary, *Levush*

---
1   Venice, 1523.

Even Yekarah, to clarify the Ricanti's terminology and logic.

Rabbi Menachem Recanati also wrote *Taamei HaMitzvos*[1] on the Kabbalistic reasons for the mitzvos and Kabbalistic interpretations of the prayers.

---

1   Constantinople, 1544.

Chapter 18
RABBI MEIR IBN GABBAI

born: Spain, c. 1480
died: Eretz Yisrael, c. 1540

A native of Spain at the time of the expulsion, Rabbi Meir ibn Gabbai and his family found refuge in Turkey (some say in Egypt), where he spent the rest of his days. Nothing is known about his personal life. He wrote three popular Kabbalistic works, in which he deals with the main ideas of Kabbalah: *Tolaas Yaakov*,[1] a Kabbalistic interpretation of the prayers, which he wrote at the age of twenty-six; *Derech Emunah*,[2] a treatise written in dialogue form in response to questions by his disciple, Rabbi Yosef HaLevi, on the concept of the ten *Sefiros*; and *Avodas HaKodesh*,[3] an introduction to Kabbalah in four volumes, dealing with God's Oneness, service of God, the purpose of man in this world, and an elucidation of the secrets of the Torah. *Avodas HaKodesh* was the most recognized work on the fundamentals of Kabbalah before the advent of the Ari.

---

1   Constantinople, 1560.
2   Constantinople, 1560.
3   Mantua, 1545.

Selections from the Writings of Rabbi Meir ibn Gabbai

Prenatal Knowledge

> Unveil my eyes that I may perceive wonders from Your Torah.
> *(Tehillim 119:18)*

Before a soul comes down to this world it apprehends wisdom and perceives and recognizes the Oneness of God with extraordinary clarity. As the Gemara says: "A lamp burns above the head [of the fetus], and by its light it can see from one end of the world to the other" (*Niddah* 30b). The lamp symbolizes the sublime light by which the soul fathoms the unity of God and grasps the secrets of the Torah and their underlying rationale. The Gemara continues: "They teach [the embryo] the entire Torah. But when the baby emerges from the womb, an angel comes and taps him lightly on his mouth, making him forget all he learned." That is why the psalmist says, "Unveil my eyes that I may perceive wonders from Your Torah" — uncover my eyes which were prevented from seeing the wonders I apprehended [before I was born].

Avodas HaKodesh, Introduction

The Four Worlds

[Note: The *Zohar* speaks of four worlds, ranging from the spiritual realm down to the physical: 1) Atzilus, "the World of Emanations," depicted as bordering on the divine; 2) Beri'ah, "the World of Creation," described as the world of the Holy Throne; 3) Yetzirah, "The World of Formation," the world of the angels; and 4) Asiyah, "The World of Action." This is the physical world with the earth at its center. Rabbi Meir Gabbai in *Avodas HaKodesh* states that there are actually forty *Sefiros*, ten in each of the four worlds.]

All the worlds are patterned after man. Just as man's body is the vessel that holds his soul, so too, in the hierarchy of the four worlds, the lower world is the body, and the world that ranks above it is the spirit of the lower one. This higher world, in turn, is the body for the world above it, which is its soul. In other words, every lower world is the body for the one above it, and every higher world is the soul of the one below it. This process continues in ascending order until Atzilus, the World of Emanations. And Atzilus is like the body or vessel for the *Ein Sof*, the Infinite, and the *Ein Sof* is the soul of Atzilus. Be sure to understand that when we speak in terms of "body" or "vessels" it is meant in a figurative sense. It is not to be taken literally, as a physical body, God forbid.

Derech Emunah 6

Built-in Blessings

The Kabbalist Rabbi Yosef Gikatilla in his *Shaarei Orah* [in the chapter "The Third *Sefirah*"] writes: "You should know and believe that the *Sefirah* of *Binah* and the *Sefirah* of *Malchus* face each other. For when the *Sefirah* of *Malchus* [i.e., our physical world] is repaired through Israel's observance of the Torah and the mitzvos, the *Sefirah* of *Binah* pours out an abundance of blessings through the [spiritual] channels, until the *Sefirah* of *Malchus* is filled with blessing. Then all mankind lives in peace and tranquility. The blessing is sent [in the form of an abundance of] all kinds of food, and there is blessing upon the land. This is stated in the verse, 'If you follow My laws and are careful to keep My commandments, I will provide you with rain at the right time, so that the land will bear its crops and the trees of the field will provide fruit' (*Vayikra* 26:3-4)."

Tikkun (cosmic rectification) is achieved when Jews keep the Torah and the mitzvos. An outpouring of blessings follows in the wake of the *tikkun*. These blessings need not be especially ordained by God. They are the natural consequence of our virtuous conduct. Keeping the Torah leads to blessings as a matter of cause and effect. Reward is inherent in the observance of the Torah. It requires no special divine directive to be activated. Keeping the Torah and the mitzvos is the key to all good things. The passage, "If you follow My laws...I will provide you with rain" tells you that fulfillment of the mitzvos has blessing built into it as a fact of nature. No specific divine decree is needed to make the blessing happen.

Avodas HaKodesh 18

The Soul Ascends Step-by-Step

God intended for Adam to live forever. That's why Adam was placed in the most precious habitat on this lowly earth.... But when he strayed by following the advice of the serpent, he was driven out of Gan Eden. He forfeited his pure [spiritual] garments. The glory and splendor that hovered over him faded away. He was lonely and desolate, for he had brought death on himself.

It is impossible for man to regain Adam's former lofty status until he divests himself of his body, and his soul departs from this world. And when the soul is full of good deeds and faithful service of God, it is worthy to reach the glorious level of the earthly Gan Eden where Adam dwelled before he sinned. From there a person's soul rises to the spiritual heights of the heavenly Gan Eden....

But the soul does not ascend straight to the heavenly Gan Eden at the first try. Since it is accustomed to living in the darkness of the physical body, it cannot endure the immense brilliance of the Divine Light. It gradually has to get used to this light by staying in the lower Gan Eden, which is the mediator between the physical and the spiritual worlds.

Something similar happened to Moshe, the greatest prophet who ever lived. Initially, at the burning bush, he did not attain the highest and clearest form of prophecy. It says there, "God's angel appeared to Moshe in the flame of a fire, in the middle of a thorn bush" (*Shemos* 3:2) [an angel, not God Himself]. But after he became accustomed to prophetic revelations, he gradually became the greatest prophet that ever lived.

The same thing happens to the pure soul. It is not launched right away from the pitch darkness of this world into the blazing radiance of the World to Come. In order to get accustomed to that brilliant light the soul has to spend some time in a place that is in between the two worlds, namely in the earthly Gan Eden. When it is time for the soul to come and prostrate itself before the Divine King, it ascends to the Bond of Life [to be bound together in everlasting life with the souls of the *avos* and *imahos* and the tzaddikim], which is the heavenly Gan Eden.

Avodas HaKodesh 27

When Will Mashiach Come?

[Note: The Kabbalistic doctrine of *gilgul* (reincarnation) teaches that the souls of sinners are reborn and return to this world, where they have the opportunity to make amends for their transgressions in a previous existence. A soul may be sent back numerous times. When all the souls have been set right, Mashiach will come.]

The Sages revealed a deep secret as to why the coming of Mashiach has been delayed for so long. Rav Assi said: "The son of David [i.e., Mashiach] will come only when all the souls destined to [inhabit earthly] bodies will have been born in this world. As it says, '[For not forever will I contend, nor will I be eternally wrathful,] when the spirit that is from Me *yaatof* [is delayed], and I made the souls' (*Yeshayah* 57:16)" (*Yevamos* 62a, and other places). The teachers of Kabbalah received the tradition that all souls have to be born into earthly bodies before Mashiach comes. Only then will new souls be created.

The Sages interpret the verse, "For not forever will I contend" — with Israel, "nor will I be eternally wrathful" — by delaying their redemption. And what prevents Me from redeeming Israel? The souls that still need to be reincarnated. These souls are holding up the redemption. The Sages interpret *yaatof* as "hold up, postpone," as derived from *atufim*, "the late ones" (*Bereishis* 30:42).

But when all souls have been placed into earthly bodies, then "the [new] souls that I made" will emerge, and Mashiach will be one of them.

It says in the *Bahir*: "When the Jewish people are virtuous the [new] souls deserve to come down to this world, but if they are not righteous, the [new] souls do not emerge. We therefore say, 'The son of David will not come until all the souls in the *Guf* [the treasury of unborn souls] are disposed of.' Mashiach will then be born, since his soul will emerge among the other new souls" (*Bahir* 1:184).

Avodas HaKodesh 37

Circumcision of the Heart

> Even if your dispersed will be at the ends of heaven, from there God, your Lord, will gather you in, and from there He will take you.... He will bring you to the land your forefathers possessed.... God, your Lord, will circumcise your heart....
> *(Devarim 30:4-6)*

The *yetzer hara* incites a person to sin. The *yetzer hara* is the "foreskin" that dulls the heart and makes it unfeeling, so that a person cannot see things in their true light. But in time to come the Holy One, blessed be He, will remove this "foreskin of the heart," when "He swallows up death forever" (*Yeshayah* 25:8).

God pledges, "I will remove the heart of stone from your flesh and give you a heart of flesh" (*Yechezkel* 36:26). God promises that our hearts will not be drawn toward evil anymore, but do only what the mind dictates according to the Torah. The world will then return its primordial state, to the way it was before Adam's transgression, the time of absolute perfection. When evil is no more, death — which resulted from evil — will cease to exist. It will be a time of life without death, of goodness without evil.

"God will then direct all these curses against your enemies and against the foes who pursued you" (*Devarim* 30:5). The curses follow in the wake of sin, and sin is caused by the "foreskin of the heart" [callousness due to the *yetzer hara*]. God promises to remove the "foreskin that covers the heart." So the curses will not apply to us anymore, because we will not transgress anymore. Instead they will come upon those whose hearts are uncircumcised, namely "our enemies and foes who pursued us."

Avodas HaKodesh 36

Chapter 19
RABBI SHLOMO MOLCHO

born: Portugal, 1500
died: Mantua, Italy, 1532

Shlomo Molcho, a child prodigy, was a descendant of a Marrano family.[1] Growing up as a Catholic under the name Diego Perez, he was only twenty years old when he was appointed to serve as secretary at the royal court of King Manuel I, in Lisbon, Portugal.

His life underwent a radical change in 1525, when he met a mysterious half-mystic adventurer named David Reuveni. This bizarre figure created a stir among the Jews of his time, claiming to be the commander of an army of the lost Ten Tribes that would free the Holy Land from the ruling Moslem Turks. Reuveni was cordially received by Pope Clement VII, and his proposal was given serious consideration. When he reached Portugal he was received with high honors at the royal court, to the glee and cheers of the local Marrano community, who thought that he was the forerunner of Mashiach.

Unfulfilled in Christianity, Diego Perez began to search for his Jewish roots. He knew Hebrew well and taught himself Talmud and Kabbalah.

---

1   Marranos, also called conversos or *anusim,* are the Spanish and Portuguese Jews who were forced to accept Christianity, but continued to observe the Torah in secret. When discovered by the Inquisition, they were brutally tortured and then burned at the stake in a public ceremony called an "auto-da-fé."

Deeply inspired by David Reuveni's passionate oratory, he decided to return to the Jewish fold and circumcised himself by his own hand. He now called himself Shlomo Molcho and taught Torah to others.

Fearing the wrath of the Inquisition, he secretly left Portugal and went to Salonica, then under Turkish rule. In Salonica, Rabbi Shlomo became acquainted with Rabbi Yosef Taitatzak and Rabbi Yosef Karo, under whose guidance he studied Kabbalah. Amazingly, in just a short time Shlomo Molcho was able to master this extremely difficult facet of Torah to the extent that people flocked to hear his lectures. He then moved on to Tzefas, the center of Kabbalists, where he became engaged to be married. In 1530 he arrived in Italy where he traveled from town to town, preaching to enthralled crowds about the coming redemption. Even high-ranking members of the Catholic clergy were inspired by his fiery sermons, in which he prophesied that the Tiber River would overflow its banks and that an earthquake would shake Portugal.

On October 8, 1530, the Tiber actually did overflow, causing great havoc in Rome, and on January 26, 1531, Portugal was shaken by an earthquake as he had foretold. Disguised as a beggar, Rabbi Shlomo Molcho went to Rome and managed to see Pope Clement VII, who was impressed by the visionary and granted him complete safety in Rome. When it became known that he was a Christian who had converted to Judaism, he was immediately incarcerated by the Inquisition, but the pope helped him escape.

Rabbi Shlomo then made his way to Ratisbon (now Regensburg, Germany), where he had an audience with Charles V, Emperor of the so-called Holy Roman Empire, to plead the cause of the Jews. Some say that he even tried to convert the emperor to Judaism. Angrily, the emperor had Rabbi Shlomo Molcho put in chains and transferred him to Mantua, where he was condemned to death. A gag was placed in his mouth, since his eloquence was so persuasive that the emperor feared that he might sway the crowd. Facing the flames, he was given the choice of returning to Catholicism or facing death. He answered that he bitterly regretted having spent his youth as a Christian and that he was now prepared to return his soul to his Maker as a proud Jew. He sanctified God's name and was burned at the stake.

Rabbi Shlomo Molcho was not only a martyr, but he also became the symbol of Jewish martyrdom of his age. Rabbi Yosef Karo in his diary *Maggid Meisharim*[1] expresses his wish to die by sanctifying God's name "as did the holy Shlomo Molcho." Two of Rabbi Shlomo's Kabbalistic works have been published: *Sefer HaMefo'ar*[2] and *Chayas Kaneh*,[3] both containing sermons and visions of the Redemption.

---

1 Amsterdam, 1654.
2 Salonica, 1529.
3 Amsterdam, 1660.

Part IV
THE MEDIEVAL EUROPEAN KABBALISTS

Introduction

THE MEDIEVAL EUROPEAN KABBALISTS

In the Middle Ages the movement of the Chassidei Ashkenaz[1] (the devout men of Germany) emerged. Although the movement flourished for only one century, from 1150–1250, it struck deep roots in the hearts of the Jews of Germany. The mindset of extreme piety of the Chassidei Ashkenaz is exemplified in the classic work *Sefer Chassidim* by Rabbi Yehudah HeChassid, who inherited his vast Kabbalistic knowledge from his father, Rabbi Shmuel HeChassid. A colorful book, *Sefer Chassidim* has become a classic.

In contrast to the mystics of Spain who studied the abstract and theoretical aspects of Kabbalah, Rabbi Yehudah HeChassid taught practical Kabbalah, paying much attention to the strict observance of mitzvos and to concentration in the prayer service. Included in the book are a number of instructions based strictly on Kabbalah rather than halachah. Rabbi Yehudah HeChassid transmitted the Kabbalistic teachings to Rabbi Elazar of Worms, who wrote *Sefer HaRokeach* and a commentary on *Sefer Yetzirah*.

A number of towering Kabbalists flourished in eastern Europe during the sixteenth century. In Prague, the legendary Rabbi Yehudah Loeve

---

1 Not to be confused with the present-day Chassidic Movement that was founded by the Baal Shem Tov in eastern Europe in the eighteenth century.

(Maharal of Prague) wrote a number of important books based on Kabbalistic thought without using the esoteric Kabbalistic terminology, thereby making them accessible to a wider circle of Torah students. He stressed the fact that the anecdotes of the *Aggados* contain profound wisdom and deep mysteries and should not be dismissed as legends and quaint folk tales.

In Italy the leading Kabbalist was Rabbi Menachem Azaryah of Fano (Rama of Fano), a prolific writer who spread the teachings of the Ari throughout Italy, stirring a keen interest in Kabbalah among Torah scholars of his own time and those of subsequent generations. In Prague we find Rabbi Yeshayah Horowitz (the Shelah), author of the monumental *Shenei Luchos HaBris*, which summarizes laws and *minhagim* for the whole year and gives basic instruction in Kabbalah. This *sefer* gained widespread popularity. It can be found on the shelves of virtually every Torah library in yeshivos, *shuls*, and private homes.

Chapter 20
RABBI YEHUDAH HECHASSID

born: Speyer, Germany, c. 1150
died: Regensburg, Germany, 1217

Rabbi Yehudah HeChassid, the foremost Kabbalist of German Jewry, received his knowledge of Kabbalah from his father, Rabbi Shmuel ben Kalonymos, who led a famous yeshivah in Speyer, Germany. He also studied under the Ri (Rabbi Yitzchak Dampierre), a famous Tosafist whose name is mentioned in the *Tosafos* on most pages of the Talmud. Rabbi Yehudah HeChassid himself is mentioned in *Tosafos* on *Bava Metzia* 5b.

Rabbi Yehudah HeChassid is the most prominent of the Chassidei Ashkenaz, the devout men of Germany, a movement that stressed strong and simple faith. Their mystical practices and beliefs provided a means of consolation from the dreadful massacres and persecutions at the hands of the crusaders and other German mobs that plagued the Rhineland during the twelfth and thirteenth centuries. Although the movement flourished for only one century, from 1150–1250, it struck deep roots in the hearts and minds of the Jews of Germany, molded their character and customs, and sustained them in all their dreadful ordeals down to the present.

Rabbi Yehudah HeChassid, who was a *rishon* (one of the early rabbinic authorities who flourished from the tenth to fifteenth centuries) emphasized piety, humility, and the mystical meaning of prayer. He led a life of self-denial and fasted nearly every day, eating only at night. *Sefer Chassidim*,[1] a work of sublime nobility, radiates the author's piety, warmth, and kindheartedness. The purpose of the book is to guide a Jew to a life of devoutness and love of God. It teaches him how to resist temptation and endure insults and shame.

Capturing the reader's attention with parables and thought-provoking anecdotes taken from daily life, the author imparts the most profound concepts of Kabbalah, ethics, and impassioned prayer. He discusses philosophical themes such as reward and punishment and divine justice, and gives practical advice for day-to-day living. Unlike most Kabbalistic works, which deal with the mysteries of God, the *Sefiros*, and Creation, *Sefer Chassidim* does not delve into abstract and esoteric themes, although it does probe a number of Kabbalistic subjects such as revival of the dead, *Maaseh Merkavah* (Yechezkel's vision of the Divine Chariot), death and afterlife, and the meaning of dreams. Here and there we find instructions based on practical Kabbalah, rather than on halachah, that have gained acceptance, such as the custom to refrain from marrying a woman with the same name as one's mother.

The Chida (Rabbi Chaim Yosef David Azulai)[2] wrote a commentary on *Sefer Chassidim*. Another commentary, *Mekor Chesed*, was written by Rabbi Reuven Margaliot. Rabbi Yehudah HeChassid wrote a number of Kabbalistic works, and a commentary on *Sefer Yetzirah* is attributed to him. He also wrote the famous liturgical poem *Anim Zemiros* which closes the Shabbos morning service. Among his many disciples were Rabbi Elazar Rokeach,[3] Rabbi Yitzchak, author of *Or Zarua*,[4] and Rabbi Yehudah ben Klonymos.

---

1 Bologna, 1538. *Sefer Chassidim* was translated by the author of this work and published by Jason Aronson, Inc. (Northvale, NJ, 1955).
2 See ch. 35.
3 See ch. 21.
4 Zhitomir, 1862.

Selections from the Writings of Rabbi Yehudah HeChassid

Life after Death

After death, the soul continues to exist as it did in life. And so, the Sages said, "He who has intercourse with a gentile woman, [after death] his foreskin is drawn so that he appears uncircumcised" (*Eiruvin* 19a). [The *Mekor Chesed* explains (based on the *Chiddushei HaRan* on *Mo'ed Katan* 24b) that the *Zohar* states that the angels circumcise babies who died before undergoing *milah* and place their foreskins on the male organ of apostates, so that the apostates look like uncircumcised gentiles.] So, you see, in Gehinnom they are like in life.... If the dead want to appear to the living, they are given permission to do so. And even though they were buried in shrouds, they can appear to their children in the clothes they used to wear.

We read in the Scripture that when the sorceress of Ein-Dor conjured up the spirit of Shmuel from the dead, Shaul asked her, "What does he look like?" "It is an old man coming up," she said, "and he is wrapped in a robe" (*Shmuel* I 28:14). In the same vein, the Gemara (*Kesubos* 103a) relates that after his death, Rabbeinu HaKadosh [Rabbi Yehudah HaNasi][1] used to visit his earthly home at twilight every Shabbos eve. He appeared in his best clothes, the ones he used to wear on Shabbos, and not in death shrouds, to show his family that he still had his strength. He recited Kiddush for them, like a living person — unlike the dead who are exempt from all mitzvos. This is in line with the saying, "In their death, the righteous are called living" (*Berachos* 18a).

Sefer Chassidim 1129

In Gan Eden

[In Gan Eden] the righteous are sitting clothed in splendid [spiritual] gar-

---

1 The compiler of the Mishnah. He died around 219 C.E.

ments enjoying many [spiritual] delights. The wicked are standing outside, looking at them for afar. Unmitigated evildoers are not allowed to come close and have direct knowledge [of the delights of Gan Eden]. They only learn [about Gan Eden] from hearsay. Occasionally, they receive permission to surround the tzaddikim and peek at them through holes and cracks, as it says, "The wicked roam on all sides" (*Tehillim* 12:9). And the tzaddikim look at the wicked.

If it would be painful for a tzaddik to see his son, brother, or other relative in Gehinnom, the tzaddik may not come close to look at him. But there are tzaddikim who are unaffected if they see their father, son, or brother in Gehinnom, if those relatives had converted to Christianity, because they rightfully belonged there. These tzaddikim may view their apostate relatives, as long as they are not saddened by what they see, because in Gan Eden there can be no anguish.

Sefer Chassidim 1130

An Out-of-Body Experience[1]

It happened that a non-Jewish noblewoman died, and just as she was about to be placed in the grave she came back to life. She said, "I was in a different world where I saw princes and kings in Gehinnom." She then foretold the day that certain people in the audience would die and predicted that they would wind up in Gehinnom.

"But I saw Jews in Gan Eden," she continued, "and there was one Jewish woman I knew. I noticed that her sleeve was stained with wax. I asked her,

---

1   Out-of-body experience, called OBE for short, is a rare but medically documented phenomenon whereby the soul leaves the body and can actually view its own lifeless body from a vantage point on the ceiling. The subject usually catches a fleeting glimpse of the beyond and perceives a dazzling light accompanied by a flow of sublime love. As one person describes it, "It attracted me like a magnet with the power of its goodness. But I asked to be returned to my body.... My soul returned to my body. I had made it back. Before I knew it I had slipped back" (Rachel Noam, *The View from Above*, translated by Avraham Yaakov Finkel [Lakewood, NJ: CIS Publishers, 1992], 96–97).

'Why is it that you look different from all the other women?' The woman replied, 'I once lit a lamp on the Sabbath.'[1] That's why I have to suffer the disgrace that my sleeve is soiled with wax.' "

Sefer Chassidim 270

He Cheated His Servant

It happened that a man's sons and daughters all died after they were married. He told his rabbi, "I had a non-Jewish servant, and after he died all my sons and daughters passed away." He added, "As long as this servant was alive, I was successful in all my enterprises."

Replied the rabbi, "Could it be that you earned your money by dishonest means?"

"I never hurt anybody, except for this servant. I cheated him and treated him unfairly," the man replied.

Retorted the rabbi, "You see, when your servant died, his guardian angel revealed to him [how you deceived him]. He complained about it to God, and the Holy One, blessed be He, renders justice for the exploited, Jew and non-Jew alike."

Therefore, a Jew should not steal, neither from a Jew nor from a non-Jew, so that he should not desecrate the name of God.[2]

Sefer Chassidim 661

Theodicy

Sometimes you find that miracles happen both to good and bad people. The reason that miracles happen to bad people is that they had ancestors who were good people. For example, King Uziyah and King Yosam were upright men[3] who merited that their offspring should live long; but

---

1 Lighting a fire is forbidden on the Sabbath; see *Shemos* 35:5.
2 See *Bava Kama* 113a.
3 *Melachim* II 15:34 and *Sukkah* 45b.

Achaz, son of King Yosam, was corrupt, and he and his children deserved to die. So the Holy One, blessed be He, said, "Although Achaz deserves death, how can I destroy him? I will remember the good things his ancestors did."

Sometimes God performs miracles because of an event that will happen in the future. For example, a good and a bad man grew up together; they went to the same school and studied under the same teacher. One day an epidemic broke out. All the children died, except for these two. They grew faint, they became very sick, their skin peeled, and they lost hair, but both survived. One grew up to be a learned tzaddik who never listened to gossip or slander. The other became an ignorant scoundrel and an informer who hounded the tzaddik's children and all the other people.

Now, if you say that a miracle was performed for the tzaddik because he was going to do good deeds in his life, the obvious question is: Why was the scoundrel also saved through a miracle? The answer is: God said, "I will keep this scoundrel alive in order that he will harass the children of the tzaddik if they fall into sin...." or perhaps God saved him because He foresaw that many years hence one of the scoundrel's descendants would save the life of a tzaddik.[1]

Therefore, if you see things that seem inscrutable to you, don't question God's fairness. Think that perhaps God did this because of some future event, or because of the merit of a person's ancestors. We must accept the fact that it is not in our power to explain either the tranquility of the wicked or the suffering of the righteous (*Avos* 4:19).

Therefore I am writing about a few of the ways of the Holy One, blessed be He. If you ponder this problem, and you attribute God's action to one cause or another, think of Iyov.[2] Was there ever a greater tzaddik than

---

1. The Gemara (*Bava Kama* 38a) explains that the Israelites were forbidden to attack the Moabites and make war against them (*Devarim* 2:9) because of Rus the Moabitess, who was to be born three hundred years later.
2. The Chida in *Bris Olam*, his commentary to *Sefer Chasidim*, answers the question

Iyov? Scripture describes him, "There is none like him on earth, a blameless and upright man who fears God and shuns evil" (*Iyov* 1:8). Now Iyov questioned God's justness, and he said, "I will challenge God in a court of law." God replied, "By wanting to charge Me with unjustness, you demeaned My wisdom, because you implied that I do not have enough knowledge to win the case."

As soon as God spoke to Iyov, he was put to silence, and he said at once, "I cannot fathom Your wisdom or understand why You did this." God did not bring this agony on Iyov because of any sin he had committed — rather, in order to test him. And when God said that Iyov's suffering was meant to be a test, Iyov admitted that God was just.

That is the reason why *Sefer Iyov* was written. It teaches a person who is stricken with misfortune to say to himself: "Iyov certainly was a righteous man. When a series of dreadful calamities befell him, he questioned God's equity, and he even wanted to challenge God in court. But as soon as he faced God in the tribunal, he instantly admitted that God was right." Let that person consider, "Maybe I committed a sin?" If he cannot find any sin that he is guilty of, let him think, "Perhaps God is putting me to the test to determine if I will keep my integrity; for Avraham, too, was tested, as it says, 'God tested Avraham' (*Bereishis* 22:1).[1]

Sefer Chassidim 549

A Miracle Worker

A rabbi was asked the following question: A man who has knowledge of the Kabbalistic mysteries inherent in God's Name, and with this knowl-

---

of why the righteous suffer and evildoers prosper by pointing out that according to the *Zohar* and *Sefer HaGilgulim* by the Arizal, most present-day people are reincarnations of earlier generations. The suffering that people endure or the well-being they enjoy in the present incarnation are compensation for the deeds they did in their previous lives. He comments that Iyov was made to suffer because he was the reincarnation of Terach, the idolatrous father of Avraham.

[1] At the *akeidah*, the binding of Yitzchak, when God asked Avraham to bring Yitzchak as an offering.

edge is able to destroy the enemies of the Jewish people and transform the community into God-fearing Jews, [is he permitted to use his mystical power]? Replied the rabbi, "He is allowed to kill the enemy only if he knows with certainty that not one of this enemy's descendants will be a righteous person — as Moshe did when he killed the Egyptian. For it says, '[Moshe] looked all around and, seeing no one about [meaning, seeing that no righteous man would issue from him],[1] he killed the Egyptian' (*Shemos* 2:12)."

Sefer Chassidim 484

Amulets Are Worthless

If a non-Jewish or Jewish scholar says to you, "Let me write an amulet for you that will make you popular or persuasive," or he says, "I'll give you a charm that will make you rich if you wear it" — needless to say, you may not wear it on Shabbos, because carrying on Shabbos is forbidden.[2] [Wearing jewelry is permitted, but an amulet is not an ornament — only a worthless trinket.] But you should not even wear an amulet on weekdays because by wearing it you indicate that that you believe in such nonsense. It says, "You must remain totally faithful to God, your Lord" (*Devarim* 18:13). If you want to be faithful to God, don't consult the practitioners of the occult who are mentioned in the preceding verse: a person who practices witchcraft, uses incantations, consults mediums and oracles, or who communicates with the dead. Put your faith in God and pray to Him.

Sefer Chassidim 269

Don't Engage in Occult Practices

Don't engage in witchcraft, astrology, the writing of amulets, or dream interpretation. Don't say that you are doing these things to save a life be-

---

1   *Shemos Rabbah* 81, *Rashi* to *Shemos* 2:12.
2   *Shabbos* 60a. On Shabbos it is forbidden to carry an object from a house into a public domain.

cause there is no wisdom in these occult practices. They shorten one's life and one's children's lives, and we don't save one life at the expense of another life. The Torah says, "You must remain totally faithful to God, your Lord" (*Devarim* 18:13).[1] You should pray only to God for relief from every plague, illness, trouble, and distress.

Sefer Chassidim 469

Ecstatic Love of God

If, while praying, a person is suddenly overcome by a feeling of joyous love of God, that is a sign that God wants to fulfill his desire. And so it says, "If you delight in God, He will grant you the desires of your heart" (*Tehillim* 37:4). If this sense of ecstasy arises during the *berachah* of *Shema Koleinu*, "Hear Our Voice" [in the *Shemoneh Esrei*], he should say the following prayer: "May it be Your will that this love may forever be embedded in my heart and the hearts of all my children."

If this joyful rapture stirred in him at any time of the day or night while he was not praying, then as long as he is entranced by this joyous fervor he should not speak to anyone until the feeling subsides.

When the biblical prophets were seized by a surge of overpowering love of God, they felt as though they had been catapulted out of this world. [This is illustrated by the following: The prophet Elisha sent a disciple to anoint the army commander Yeihu as king over Israel.] Yeihu's fellow commander asked him, "What did that madman come to you for?" Yeihu replied, "You know the man and his rantings!" (*Melachim* II 9:11). [According to *Vayikra Rabbah*, when a prophet would prophesy his face "lit up like a torch."]

Sefer Chassidim 773

---

1 Rashi explains, "Walk with Him wholeheartedly and hope in Him. Do not pry into the veiled future, but accept whatever lot befalls you. Then you will be His people and His portion."

A Visit to Gan Eden

There once was a pious man who used to mortify himself. In the summer he would lie down on the earth and allow himself to be bitten by fleas. In the winter he would immerse his feet in a pail of cold water until the water froze and his feet stuck in the ice. Said his student, "Why do you do such things? Don't you know that it says, 'Of the blood of your own lives I will demand an account' (*Bereishis* 9:5)? [This is the commandment against suicide.] Why do you endanger your life?"

Replied the pious man, "Although I have not committed any grave sins, it is impossible that I have not stumbled on any of the minor transgressions. It is true that for these minor transgressions I don't have to inflict such dreadful pain on myself. But we know that Mashiach and the perfect tzaddikim suffer because of the sins of the Jewish people. Well, I don't want anyone to suffer for my sins but myself."

Once the student witnessed his master searing himself with a burning torch. He said, "I'm afraid that you will be punished for mortifying yourself."

When afterwards the pious man was bedridden, the student said to him, "You are neglecting your Torah studies, and that is a sin."

When the pious man died, the student thought that perhaps his death was caused by his agony. He was distressed, wondering whether in the hereafter this self-inflicted torture was considered a sin. He then prostrated himself on the pious man's grave and asked him to reveal to him in a dream whether he was being punished or rewarded. Appearing in a dream, the pious man said, "Come, I'll show you." With that he brought him to Gan Eden.

The student asked, "Where is my future place in Gan Eden?"

"Over here," replied the master. "And if you gain more merits you will attain a higher spot."

"And where is your place?" the student asked.

"Yonder on that high elevation," replied the master.

"Please take me there," asked the student.

"Not yet. You haven't done enough good deeds to be able to see my place," came the answer. Meanwhile, the student relished the magnificent luminescence that pervaded Gan Eden, but he was not worthy to see his master's place.

Sefer Chassidim 528

The Wagon Train of the Dead

It happened one night, a man was riding alone through the desert by the pale light of the moon, when suddenly he caught sight of a bizarre spectacle. On the horizon there appeared a long wagon train. Sitting in the wagons were what seemed to be human beings, and the wagons were pulled by human beings. Approaching them, he recognized that all these were people who had died.

He asked them, "What is the meaning of this? Why are some of you sitting in the wagons and others pulling the wagons?"

They replied, "This is the punishment for our sins. When we were alive, we used to flirt with women and girls, and now we have to pull these wagons until we are exhausted. Then those inside the wagons take over, and we get to rest up until they are worn out and it is our turn again to pull."

That is what the prophet had in mind when he said, "Woe, I will slow your movements as a wagon is slowed" (*Amos* 2:13), and "Woe, those who haul sin with cords of falsehood and iniquity as with cart ropes!" (*Yeshayah* 5:18). If a person behaved like an animal during his lifetime, he is put to work like an animal in the hereafter. If a person oppressed or tyrannized people or tormented animals, he will be put to work like an animal in the hereafter.

Sefer Chassidim 169

Cruelty to Animals

If a person needlessly hurt an animal by overloading it and hitting it when it cannot go, he will be judged for it in the hereafter. The same goes for people who pull a cat's ears just to make it scream. The Sages interpret the verse, "On that day — says God — I will strike every horse with confusion and its rider with madness" (*Zecharyah* 12:4) to mean that in the hereafter God will take to task the riders who pierce their horses with their spurs.

Sefer Chassidim 66

Be Fruitful and Multiply

Adam HaRishon's height extended from one end of the earth to the other.[1] When the ministering angels saw him filling the earth, they wanted to exclaim, "Holy, holy, holy." [But when he sinned], the Holy One, blessed be He, diminished him and took a few pieces of his limbs and placed the pieces of flesh around him. Said Adam to God, "Master of the Universe, why do you rob me? 'Does it befit You to defraud, to despise the toil of Your hands?' (*Iyov* 10:3)."

Replied God, "I shall return them to you. 'Be fertile and increase, and fill the earth' (*Bereishis* 1:28). Take these pieces and scatter them throughout the world. Wherever you deposit them, they will return to dust, and in those places your offspring will settle. Any land that you decree should be inhabited by your Jewish offspring will inhabited by Jews, and land that you assign to your gentile offspring will inhabited by gentiles" (*Berachos* 31a). This is alluded to in the verse, "A land no man has traversed, where no human being has dwelled" (*Yirmiyah* 2:6) — because Adam did not plant any pieces of his flesh there.

Sefer Chassidim 500

---

[1] Lying down, he stretched from east to west (*Chagigah* 12a).

Excerpts from Rabbi Yehudah HeChassid's Ethical Will[1]

12. Don't visit a grave twice on the same day.

15. Don't weep excessively for a deceased person. There are three days for weeping, seven days for eulogizing, thirty days for mourning...beyond that God says, "Don't be more merciful than I am."

23. A person should not marry a woman if her name is the same as that of his mother, or if his name is the same as that of her father. If he does marry her, the name of one of them should be changed; then there may be hope [for a happy marriage].[2]

26. A person should not marry his deceased wife's sister, unless he has small children and she has pity on them.

30. Don't celebrate the weddings of two of your children on the same day.

35. You should not designate the same person as *sandek* for more than one of your children. [The *sandek* holds the infant on his lap for circumcision.]

45. Don't cut down a fruit tree.

47. You should not inscribe a book, "This book belongs to ———." Just write your name [because everything belongs to God].

Excerpts from *Anim Zemiros* – Song of Glory

> [*Anim Zemiros* has been ascribed to Rabbi Yehudah HeChassid. It is recited at the end of the Shabbos and *yom tov* services. Due to the song's great holiness, the Ark is opened when it is recited.]

---

1   Printed in the beginning of *Sefer Chassidim*.
2   The phrase "there may be hope" refers to the case where they were married before the name was changed. All later authorities agree that before the engagement, there is no question that the name may be changed. For example, the illustrious Rabbi Moshe Sofer, known as the Chasam Sofer, took as a son-in-law a young man named Moshe and suggested that he change his name to Moshe Tuvyah.

I shall compose pleasing songs and hymns,
Because my soul yearns for You.
My soul desired the shelter of Your hands,
To grase every mystery of Your secrets.
As I speak of Your honor,
My heart pines for Your love.
Therefore I shall speak Your grandeur,
And venerate Your name with songs of love.

Chapter 21
RABBI ELAZAR ROKEACH OF WORMS

born: Mainz, Germany, 1160
died: Worms, Germany, 1238

Rabbi Elazar Rokeach of Worms, a great Talmudic scholar and an eminent Kabbalist, became the father of the Chassidei Ashkenaz, who studied Kabbalah from a practical aspect.

Rabbi Elazar's forebear, Rabbi Klonymos, was brought to Mainz from Lucca, Italy, by the great French king Charlemagne to strengthen that ancient Jewish community. Rabbi Elazar studied under his father, Rabbi Yehudah ben Klonymos of Speyer, and Rabbi Eliezer of Metz. He received his instruction in Kabbalah from his father and from Rabbi Yehudah HeChassid, author of *Sefer Chassidim*.[1]

Rabbi Elazar's life is a long chain of torment and misfortune. He relates: "On Friday, 28 Shevat, 1188, they entered the Jewish ghetto [of Mainz], but God helped us and we were saved" (from his commentary on the prayers, Paris manuscript). A month later, the Jews of Mainz, including Rabbi Elazar, had to flee the city. They found refuge in the fortified city of Munzenberg,

---

1   See ch. 20.

but shortly thereafter Rabbi Elazar settled in Worms.

Eight years later, in 1196, disaster struck. While he was engrossed in his studies, a savage mob of crusaders broke into his house and brutally murdered his wife, Dolca, and his two daughters before his very eyes and ruthlessly beat him and his son Yaakov. The pain of this tragic loss never subsided. He wrote a moving elegy memorializing his martyred wife and daughters. Yet, in spite of his agonized and turbulent life, his works reflect an aura of inner peace and love. From 1201 on he served as rabbi of Worms.

Rabbi Elazar had a large number of disciples. Foremost among these are Rabbi Moshe of Vienna, author of *Or Zarua*, and Rabbi Menachem Ashkenazi, who bridged the gap between the German and the Spanish approaches of Kabbalah. The German Kabbalists engaged in practical Kabbalah, letter permutations, and *gematria*, by which they hoped to achieve closeness to God and bring about the ultimate redemption. The Spanish approach was reflective, designed to counteract the prevalent trend of philosophical inquiry. One of the principles of the German trend of practical Kabbalah as taught by Rabbi Elazar of Worms is that a sinner who wants to do *teshuvah* has to take on himself *teshuvas hamishkal*, mortify himself for each sin he committed to offset the enjoyment he derived from that sin.

He wrote many books on halachah, Kabbalah, and *mussar* (ethics), but he is best known for his *Sefer HaRokeach*,[1] a Kabbalistic guide to ethics and halachah. He wrote a commentary on *Sefer Yetzirah*[2] that appears in most editions; a commentary on the prayers, *Sodei Razya*;[3] *Sefer Hashem*; *Yein HaRokeach*;[4] seventy liturgical poems; and many unpublished writings.

---

1 Fano, 1505. The word *rokeach* (perfumer) has the same *gematria* as *Elazar*, 308.
2 Mantua, 1562.
3 Bilgoray, 1936.
4 Lublin, 1608.

Selections from the Writings of Rabbi Elazar

Symbolism of the Nut

> I went down to the nut grove.
> (*Shir HaShirim* 6:11)

A walnut has four segments and a ridge at its center. The same way, there are four camps in Israel [the camps of the *Shechinah*, *kohanim*, Levi'im, and Yisraelim, and one camp of the mixed multitude (*eirev rav*), compared to the ridge]. Just as the nut has an outer bitter shell surrounding it, so did the Torah and the sword come down from heaven wrapped together [as if to say: If you keep the Torah, you will be saved from the sword, otherwise you will be slain by the sword].

Beneath the bitter shell there are two other shells dry as wood. Similarly, two brothers, Moshe and Aharon, guard Israel and act as its guides. Beneath those shells there is a soft husk in the center of the kernel divided in four directions, corresponding to the leaders of thousands, hundreds, fifties, and tens, who judge Israel at all times.[1] Finally, there is a shell which clothes the kernel, to match the clouds of glory and the Levi'im and the *kohanim*. The kernel is shaped like four double corner posts to parallel the four camps...and the uppermost bitter shell corresponds to heaven, which encompasses everything.

Yein HaRokeach, "Chochmas HaEgoz"

The Letter *Alef*

The letter *alef* represents the Holy One, blessed be He. He is the First and the Last, King of the universe, and there is none like Him. Just as the *alef* is the head of all the letters [of the *alef beis*], so is the Holy One, blessed be He, King of all kings. And consider this: *Alef* is one, the smallest number, and there is nothing less than it. The word *ribo* [literally "ten thousand,"

---

1   *Devarim* 1:15.

and written *reish, yud, beis, alef*] represents infinity, as it says, "Myriad (*ribo*) myriads were standing before Him" (*Daniel* 7:10). And *ribo* ends in an *alef*. So you see, *alef* is the first letter of *echad*, "one" [written *alef, ches, dalet*] and *alef* is the last letter of *ribo*, "infinity." This tells you that God is One and there is no unity like His Oneness, He is First and He is Last, as the *alef* is the first and the last of the [infinite] number line.

Now, consider the letter *alef* [written *alef, lamed, pei*]. The guttural sound of the letter *alef* is produced by the throat. The *lamed* is pronounced by pressing the tip of the tongue against the roof of the mouth (the palate), while the *pei* is pronounced with the lips. [Thus *alef* gives the following progression:] First the throat, then the tongue and the palate, and last the lips, to tell you that God is One, He is First, Middle, and Last.

Sodei Razya, "Os Alef"

Chapter 22

RABBI YEHUDAH LOEVE
(Maharal of Prague)

born: Posen, Poland, c. 1526
died: Prague, Czechoslovakia, 1609

The Maharal, a scion of a great rabbinic family, was a giant of Jewish scholarship, an original thinker, a prolific author, and a great leader. His works, which are heavily Kabbalistic in outlook without using Kabbalistic terminology, became the basis of many chassidic works. It is said that the Baal HaTanya[1] based his work on the ideas expounded by Maharal. The Maharal's teachings also were the cornerstone of the ideology of the *Mussar* Movement[2] of the nineteenth and twentieth centuries.

In 1553, the Maharal was elected rabbi of Nikolsburg and the province of Moravia, where he remained for twenty years. In 1573, he moved to Prague, where he opened a yeshivah and taught many outstanding disciples, including the famous Rabbi Yom Tov Lipman Heller, author of *Tosafos Yom Tov* on the Mishnah. In 1592 the Maharal accepted the position of rabbi of Posen. He returned to Prague in 1598 to serve as its chief rabbi.

He wrote numerous works, including *Tiferes Yisrael*[3] on the greatness of Torah and mitzvos; *Nesivos Olam*[4] on ethics; *Be'er HaGolah*,[5] a commentary

---

1   Rabbi Shneur Zalman of Liadi, founder of the Chabad chassidic movement. See ch. 46.

on Aggadic passages of the Talmud; *Netzach Yisrael*,[1] about the rewards of the World to Come and the Messianic era; *Gevuros Hashem*,[2] on the Exodus; and many others. The Maharal's works reflect his illustrious personality and reveal him as a profound thinker who penetrates the mysteries of Creation and metaphysics, clothing Kabbalistic themes in a philosophic garment.

A staunch leader of his community, he became the hero of many legends in which he appears as the defender of Prague Jewry against all its enemies. He was assisted in his exploits by the *golem*, a robot he made and gave life to by placing Kabbalistic formulas in its mouth. He had an original outlook on Jewish education, expressing reservations to the practice of teaching young children Talmud. His suggestion: a child should begin by studying Scriptures at five years of age; in his tenth year he should be introduced to the Mishnah; and only in his fifteenth year should a boy begin to study the Talmud.

The Maharal's synagogue, the Altneu Schul, still exists today and is preserved as a shrine by the Prague municipal authorities, who in 1917 erected a statue in his honor. The Maharal lives on in his writings, which are an enduring source of wisdom and inspiration.

Selections from the Writings of the Maharal

The Numbers Seven and Eight

The mitzvos of the Torah are the tools by which you can attain perfection. Since your soul is divine, you cannot reach perfection through earthly,

---

2   The movement of ethical revival founded by Rabbi Yisrael Lipkin of Salant, better known as Rabbi Yisrael Salanter, 1810–1883.
3   Prague, 1593.
4   Prague, 1596.
5   Prague, 1598.
1   Prague, 1599.
2   Cracow, 1582.

physical means — it takes Torah and mitzvos, which are of a spiritual nature, to achieve wholeness. [This idea is reflected in Psalm 19.] The first seven verses of Psalm 19 describe the marvels of nature, beginning with, "The heavens declare the glory of God, and the firmament tells of His handiwork." From the eighth verse on the text relates the greatness of the Torah, "The Torah of God is perfect, restoring the soul" (*Tehillim* 19:8). Nature is praised in seven verses because nature came into being during the seven days of Creation. The Torah — which transcends nature — is praised in the eighth verse.

The idea that eight suggests the supernatural is evident in Psalm 119. This psalm glorifies the Torah and the mitzvos [which are symbolized by the number eight]. The psalm begins, "Praiseworthy are those whose way is perfect, who walk with the Torah of God." Significantly, the verses of this psalm are arranged in groups of eight, according to the *alef beis*: each of the first eight verses begins with an *alef*, followed by eight verses beginning with *beis*, then eight beginning with *gimmel*, and so on. This gives you a clear indication that the Torah [eight] transcends nature [seven].

The same way, things that rise above nature and are designed to correct an imperfection in nature come after the number seven. For example, take *milah* (circumcision). By the laws of nature [symbolized by seven], man is created uncircumcised; but [for a Jew] the foreskin is considered an flaw of nature. Since *milah* corrects this defect of nature, it is performed on the eighth day. Now you understand that by doing mitzvos you arrive at a level that surpasses nature.

Tiferes Yisrael, ch. 2

Only Man Has the Potential to Grow

Among all beings — from angels above to animals below — man is unique in that he has not yet fulfilled his purpose in life. He does have the potential to reach the level of a heavenly being and the capacity to reach lofty heights, but as things stand he has not accomplished his goal. Therein lies the difference between man, on the one hand, and the lower and higher beings, on the other.

The higher beings — angels — exist in a state of perfection. They don't have to struggle to attain perfection; they are perfect already. Earthly creatures [like animals, plants, and minerals] don't have the potential for advancement either. They are what they are and will remain so. They never change and have no capacity [for spiritual growth]. Only man has the potential to develop spiritually, and only man has the makings to bring his potential to fruition.

The word *adam* (man) points to his unique station among God's creatures. He is called *adam* because he is made from the dust of the *adamah* (earth).

Now you may ask: Don't all creatures come from the earth? Why is man singled out to be called *adam*, implying that only he is made from the dust of the earth? The answer is that man has more in common with the earth than any other creature. For the earth is unique in that it has the potential to bring forth the things that grow in it: herbs, plants, and trees. And growth is the factor man has in common with the earth. For man, like the earth, has the power to grow and reach perfection.

For that reason Scripture characterizes man's perfection as "fruit," as it says, "Tell each righteous man that [his deeds] are good, for they shall eat the fruit of their deeds" (*Yeshayah* 3:10). So you see, perfection is called "fruit," and the title *adam* is a very fitting designation for man.

Tiferes Yisrael, ch. 3

Torah Study Elevates You

The Torah can be understood on three levels. First there is the plain meaning; it is obvious, everyone can understand it. The second level takes in the hidden, Kabbalistic meaning of the Torah. Only a wise and insightful person can grasp that. Then there is the third level. It deals with the

World to Come. These are things nobody can comprehend, as it says, "People had never heard, never observed, no eye has ever seen...except for You..." (*Yeshayah* 64:3)....

The three levels are also present in man. First there is the human body which is plainly visible. Then there is the soul which is hidden from view. The third level can be found in a person who is destined for the World to Come.... At any rate, you can understand that the Torah is infinitely exalted; it consists of level upon level [of meaning] and reaches all the way to the World to Come. You realize that, although the stories of the Torah seem to be involved mainly with physical things, their meaning reaches upward all the way to the World to Come.

There is an interesting correlation between the Torah and man. Man, who is flesh and blood, living in this physical earthly world, can earn a place in the higher world, which is nonphysical. So too, by learning Torah and studying Torah laws relating to tangible mitzvos, you can reach the loftiest spiritual heights and penetrate the deepest mysteries of the Torah. And even when you study such earthly laws as the case of the ox that gored a cow, or the case of a man who fell into a pit that negligently was left uncovered, things which on the surface do not have any bearing on mystical points, your soul is connected to the uppermost spiritual worlds and ties in with the deepest mysteries of the Torah.

Tiferes Yisrael, ch. 13

The Nonphysical Desert

> Moshe tended the sheep of his father-in-law Yisro, prince of Midyan. He led the flock to the edge of the desert, and he came to God's mountain, in the Chorev area.
>
> (*Shemos* 3:1)

"Rabbi Yehoshua asked: Why did Moshe take [the flock] to the desert? Because he foresaw that Israel was destined to rise to eminence in the desert.

For it was in the desert that Israel received the manna, the quail, Miriam's well, the Torah, the Tabernacle, the *Shechinah*, priesthood, kingship, and the Clouds of Glory" (*Shemos Rabbah*).

Everything in this world has a place. Towns and cities are the places designed for physical things [like buildings, furnishings, appliances, transportation], all of which are needed for city life. Supernatural things, like the Torah, the Tabernacle, the *Shechinah*, and the Clouds of Glory, have no place in a built-up city. Spirituality and physicality are opposites; they cannot coexist. That's why the spiritual gifts [of the Torah, the Tabernacle, the Clouds of Glory] were not given to the children of Israel in a settled and established environment [but in a barren desert].

The same way, the mind is the opposite of the body; the mind is spiritual, the body physical. For this reason, only in the desert [wasteland, devoid of physical amenities] could Israel rise to spiritual supremacy. This is indicated in the verse, "[The nations have asked:] Who is she that comes up from the desert, her way secured and smoothed by pillars of smoke, in clouds of myrrh and frankincense, of all the perfumer's powders?" (*Shir HaShirim* 3:6). [Israel became a nation in the desert, a place far removed from any form of materialism.]

Gevuros Hashem, ch. 22

The Seven Noachide Commandments

Originally [at Creation], the *Shechinah* dwelled here on earth. When Adam transgressed, the *Shechinah* withdrew to the first heaven. When Kayin sinned, the *Shechinah* withdrew to the second heaven; when the generation of Enosh sinned,[1] It withdrew to the third heaven. At the sin of the generation of the Flood, It withdrew to the fourth heaven. The sin of the generation of the Dispersion[2] caused It to draw back to the fifth heaven. When the people of Sedom sinned, It withdrew to the sixth heaven. When

---

1   *Bereishis* 4:26.
2   The generation that built the Tower of Bavel (*Bereishis* 11:1–9).

the Egyptians sinned in the days of Avraham, the *Shechinah* retreated to the seventh heaven.

But then seven tzaddikim appeared on the scene who brought the *Shechinah* back to earth. They were: Avraham, Yitzchak, Yaakov, Levi, Kehas, Amram, and Moshe. And so it says, "The righteous will inherit the earth and dwell [*yishkenu*] forever upon it" (*Tehillim* 37:29). [*Yishkenu*, "they will dwell" can be read as *yashkinu*, "they cause to dwell."] What the verse means is that the righteous will cause the *Shechinah* to dwell [*yashkinu*] upon the earth.

The seven generations that sinned transgressed the seven commandments that were given to all mankind at the time of Creation. They are the prohibitions against eating a limb torn from a live animal, blasphemy, idolatry, adultery, robbery, murder, and the commandment to establish courts of justice. God gave these commandments to regulate man's conduct toward God and toward his fellowman. Three of the seven mitzvos are meant to put man right with God, namely, the prohibitions against immorality, blasphemy, and idolatry. Three of the mitzvos pertain to man's relations with his fellowman, namely, robbery, murder, and the establishment of a court system. The seventh mitzvah, which forbids eating a limb torn of a live animal, is the root of the other six. This seventh mitzvah is designed to suppress the *yetzer hara* (the lustful impulse). It tells a person to control his unbridled desire for food which prods him to sever a limb from an animal before it has died. [In a broader sense] this mitzvah teaches a person not to give in to his base instincts. For if a person yields to his *yetzer hara* [and commits one transgression], he will end up transgressing all the commandments.

Gevuros Hashem, ch. 66

Time, Motion, and Matter

Time and matter are two concepts that are closely linked. Time is essentially motion. [Before the universe was created, matter did not exist. Since nothing moved, nothing changed, thus time had no meaning. That's why the first word of the Torah is *bereishis*, "in the beginning." For when matter was created, change came into being, and time is determined by the motion of the planets or movement of the hands of the clock. Since motion is a function of matter, we can say that time, motion, and matter are an integral whole.]

Matter — i.e., a physical object — can be defined in terms of its six surfaces: top, bottom, right, left, front, and back. There is, however, a seventh dimension — the center inside the object. It bears no relation to any of the six surfaces. It is an intangible, incorporeal entity, a point without dimensions. Time, which as we have said is an integral component of matter, is measured by the six weekdays. The seventh day is the holy Shabbos. The six weekdays correspond to the six sides of a material object, while Shabbos represents the incorporeal center.

Gevuros Hashem, ch. 46

"Five," the Symbol of Redemption

[The Midrash asks:] Why did God appear to Moshe in a thorn bush? [The Midrash answers:] Just as a thorn bush has five leaves, so was Israel redeemed because of [five tzaddikim]: Avraham, Yitzchak, Yaakov, Moshe, and Aharon. What does this meean?

When the Jews are in *galus* (exile) they are dispersed all over the world. They are not united. Redemption — the opposite of exile — is the ingathering and reunification of the scattered exiles. The number four symbolizes *galus*, because "four" suggests the four directions and the four corners of the world where the Jews are dispersed. On the other hand, the number five is associated with redemption. The reason is this: The four angles [of a rectangle] come together in one central point where the connecting diagonals intersect. This central point is the fifth point that unites the four angles. For this reason five is the mystery of the redemption, and that is why in the merit of the five tzaddikim the dispersed Jews will be reunited.

Let me prove to you that five means unity. The numeric value of the letter *hei* is five. Unlike all other letters, *hei* cannot be divided. [When you pronounce the letter *hei*, you say or write only *hei*, whereas when you say the words *alef, beis, gimmel, dalet, vav, zayin,* etc., you articulate more than one letter.] This points to the fact that five is the mystery of the Redemption and unification which will come about in the merit of the five tzaddikim.

Gevuros Hashem, ch. 23

Chapter 23
RABBI MENACHEM AZARYAH OF FANO
(Rama of Fano)

born: Fano, Italy, 1548
died: Mantua, Italy, 1620

Rabbi Menachem Azaryah of Fano, referred to as "Rama of Fano," one of the leading Kabbalists of Italy, inherited great wealth from his parents. Besides generously dispensing alms to the needy, he also used his fortune to buy rare manuscripts, some of which he published. While still a young man, he was known far and wide as a Torah scholar and big-hearted philanthropist. Rabbi Yosef Karo sent him the manuscript of his work *Kesef Mishneh*,[1] which Rama then published at his own expense.

Rama of Fano, a fervent Kabbalist, was a great admirer of Rabbi Moshe Cordovero, and when the latter completed his Kabbalistic classic *Pardes Rimonim* he sent a copy to Rama, who gave him a generous donation. After Rabbi Moshe Cordovero's death, Rama paid one thousand ducats to his widow for the right to copy the manuscript of Rabbi Moshe's comprehensive commentary on the *Zohar*, *Or Yakar*.

Later on, he was greatly influenced by Rabbi Yisrael Seruk, a student of

---

1 Venice, 1574. A commentary on the Rambam's *Yad HaChazakah*.

the Ari, who traveled all over Europe after the Ari's death, spreading the Ari's teachings. Rama of Fano committed himself to disseminating these teachings in the communities of Ferrara, Venice, Reggio, and Mantua, attracting students from all over Italy and Germany. His disciples were completely under the spell of his charismatic and saintly personality. He is described as having the appearance of an angel, and it is said that he was visited by a *maggid*, a heavenly messenger, who revealed to him hidden mysteries of the Torah.

A prolific author, he wrote numerous works on Kabbalistic themes. Best known are *Asarah Maamaros*[1] and *Amaros Tehoros*,[2] a compendium of five essays. He also wrote *Ayin-beis Yedios*,[3] introductory rules to the study of Kabbalah; *Gilgulei Neshamos*,[4] on reincarnation of souls; *Maamar Chikur Din*; *Maamar HaNefesh*;[5] and many more.

Selections from the Writings of Rama of Fano

Judgment of the Soul

On the day a person leaves this world he is judged by God, and the decision is rendered whether his soul will enter Gan Eden or Gehinnom, and how he is to be punished or what delights are in store for him. It is also decided whether his soul will remain at rest or must return to this world in reincarnation. This Judgment Day is described in *Koheles* in the verses, "Remember your Creator in the days of your youth before the evil days come...and the wheel is smashed at the pit" (*Koheles* 12:1-6)....

The Mishnah says in this regard: "Akavya ben Mehalalel said: Consider

---

1 Venice, 1600.
2 Frankfurt am Main, 1688.
3 Lemberg, 1867.
4 Prague, 1688.
5 Pietrkow, 1903.

three things and you will not come into the grip of sin. Know from where you came, where you are going, and before whom you will give justification and reckoning. From where you came — from a putrid drop; where you are going — to a place of dust, worms, and maggots; and before whom you will give justification and reckoning — before the King who reigns over kings, the Holy One, blessed be He" (*Avos* 3:1). Akavya cautions a person not to treat the soul with disdain, for the soul is a princess, the daughter of the King in Heaven [for the soul is a portion of God].

Maamar Chikur Din 3:1

The Court Case of the Future

> Come, now, let us reason together, says God. If your sins are like scarlet they will become white as snow; if they have become red as crimson, they will become [white] as wool.
>
> (*Yeshayah* 1:18)

The phrase "let us reason together" means "let us settle our differences [in court]." [Regarding a court case,] it says in the chapter "Laws of Judges": If a poor and a rich man bring a case to court, we tell the rich man: Either you dress like the poor man, or have the poor man dressed in the same fine clothes you are wearing [so as not to prejudice the judges] (*Mishneh Torah, Hilchos Sanhedrin* 21:2). At the beginning of the court case of the future, God will apply to Himself the first part of the ruling [that the rich man has to dress like the poor man, and so it says, "Who is coming from Edom with sullied garments? ... He who is majestic in His raiment ..." (*Yeshayah* 63:1)]. But at the end of the court case God will clothe Israel [in His divine kind of garment, for Israel says]: "I will rejoice...for He has dressed me in the raiment of salvation, in a robe of righteousness" (ibid. 61:10).

Maamar Chikur Din 1:2

Chapter 24

RABBI SHABSAI SHEFTL HOROWITZ
(Shefa Tal)

born: 1565
died: Prague, Czechoslovakia, 1619

Rabbi Shabsai Sheftl, a nephew of the Shelah, was a Kabbalist and a medical doctor. He wrote the very popular Kabbalistic work *Shefa Tal*,[1] which follows the ideology of the Remak, whom he considered his master. *Shefa Tal* is an introduction to the fundamentals of Kabbalah, and its simple style of writing makes it accessible to a wide circle of students of Kabbalah. He also wrote a Kabbalistic discourse on the nature of the soul titled *Nishmas Shabsai HaLevi* and a commentary on *Moreh Nevuchim*, which is still in manuscript.

Selections from Shefa Tal

A Particle of God

It is a well-known fact that the souls of the Jewish people are a part of God. This is hinted at in the verse, "[The Jewish] people is a portion of God"

---

1 Hanau, 1612. The title *Shefa Tal* ("Abundant Dew") is a play on the author's name *Sheftl*.

(*Devarim* 32:9), which is to be taken in a literal sense. Now, a part of an object contains all the elements of that object [a small chip of a big rock has all the components of that rock], the only difference is that since the object is the whole thing it is larger than the part, but the particle has the same [chemical] composition as the object from which it came. The same way, there is no essential difference between the soul of a man and the blessed Creator, except for the fact that the Creator is the totality of existence, the all-embracing Infinite Light, and the soul is a tiny particle of that great Light.

As Shlomo put it, "A man's soul is the lamp of God" (*Mishlei* 20:27). He means to say that the soul is a spark and a lamp of the Divine Light. Shlomo makes it a point to describe the soul in terms of a "a lamp [*ner*] of God" rather than "the light of God." By using the word *ner*, he hints at the fact that the three levels of the soul — *nefesh, ruach, neshamah* — are all a part and a spark of the Divine Light. For *ner* [written *nun, reish*] is an acronym of the initials of *nefesh, ruach* and *neshamah*. In other words, all three — *nefesh, ruach,* and *neshamah* — are holy sparks, minute fragments of the Divine Light, as the passage says, "A man's soul is the *ner* [lamp] of God."

Introduction to Shefa Tal

The Mystery of Twenty-eight

When you count the small bones in your fingers [phalanges] you find that there are fourteen of them in each hand, and twenty-eight in the two hands taken together. The number twenty-eight in Hebrew is *kaf ches*, which spells *ko'ach*, "strength." Indeed, the hands are the instruments of man's strength, the tools with which he performs all his tasks.

The divine Name *Yud-Hei-Vav-Hei* [when written in full] is also made up of twenty-eight letters [this will be explained in the next paragraph], corresponding to the twenty-eight spiritual parts of the divine hands[1] that ema-

---

1 When the text mentions divine hands, we must remember that this is meant in a figurative sense.

nate from the holy source of *Yud-Hei-Vav-Hei*. The divine right hand is the hand of mercy, whereas the divine left hand is the hand of strict justice. When God's right hand of mercy overcomes the left hand of justice, then the left hand is transformed and becomes also a hand of mercy. As Rashi interprets the verse, "Your right hand, God, is adorned with strength (*ko'ach*); Your right hand, God, smashes the enemy" (*Shemos* 15:6). Rashi asks: Why does the verse repeat the phrase, "Your right hand"? [Rashi answers:] When Israel fulfills God's will, God's left hand of justice is turned into God's right hand of mercy, so that the twenty-eight parts of the two divine hands become "fingers of mercy."

Now let me show you how the divine Name *Yud-Hei-Vav-Hei* of mercy adds up to twenty-eight letters corresponding to the twenty-eight parts of the "fingers of the hands of mercy." The full spelling of the letters *yud, hei, vav, hei* is יוד הא ואו הא [ten Hebrew letters]. And if you write the full spelling of these ten letters you obtain twenty-eight letters: *yud* [יוד ואו דלת = 9 letters]; *hei* [הא אלף = 5 letters]; *vav* [ואו אלף ואו = 9 letters]; *hei* [הא אלף = 5 letters]; for a total of twenty-eight letters, corresponding to the Light emanating from the twenty-eight parts of the divine hands.

Introduction to Shefa Tal

God's Name Intertwined with the 613 Mitzvos

> This is My name forever, and this is My remembrance from generation to generation.
>
> (*Shemos* 3:15)

Kabbalah teaches that God's Name is the source of the 248 positive commandments and the 365 prohibitions. There is an allusion to this in the verse, "This is My name [*shemi*] forever, and this is My remembrance [*zichri*] from generation to generation." [There are two parts to the divine Name *Yud-Hei-Vav-Hei*, namely *Yud-hei* (whose *gematria* is 15) and *Vav-hei* (whose *gematria* is 11). The numeric value of *shemi* is 350 (*shin*=300, *mem*=40, *yud*=10) and that of *zichri* is 237 (*zayin*=7, *chaf*=20, *reish*=200, *yud* =10).] Now if you combine the value of *shemi* (350) with the value of *Yud-hei* (15) you get 365, which is the number of prohibitions. If you add the numeric value of *zichri* (237) to the value of *Vav-hei* (11), you get 248, which is the number of positive commandments. So you see that in a metaphoric sense God's Name *Yud-Hei-Vav-Hei* includes all 613 mitzvos (365+248).

[The verse begins, "This is My name forever [*le'olam*]."] Since the world *le'olam* in this passage is written without the usual *vav*, it can be read *le'alem*, "to be hidden." This tells us that the 613 mitzvos that are included in the divine Name are spiritual mitzvos whose essence is completely hidden and beyond human understanding. They are intangible and have no corporeality. They are infinitely far removed from the lowly physicality of this world. [The essence of the spiritual mitzvos that are included in God's Name is *le'alem*, completely concealed and incomprehensible to the human mind.]

Introduction to Shefa Tal

Chapter 25
RABBI YESHAYAH HOROWITZ
(Shelah HaKadosh)

born: Prague, Czechoslovakia, 1565
died: Teveriah, 1630

In his youth, Rabbi Yeshayah studied under his father, Rabbi Avraham, a noted scholar and a disciple of Rabbi Moshe Isserles, the Rema. Later he studied under the Maharam Lublin and Rabbi Yehoshua Falk in Lemberg, where he gained a reputation as an outstanding scholar.

Reb Yeshayah's rabbinical career took him to posts in the important Torah centers of Dubno, Ostroh, Posen, and Cracow. In 1606 he was called to serve in the rich and flourishing community of Frankfurt am Main. In the wake of the attack on the Jewish ghetto by the Fettmilch mob in 1614, Reb Yeshayah returned to Prague, where he was appointed as rabbi.

In 1620, after the death of his wife, he resigned his post in Prague and emigrated to Eretz Yisrael, where he accepted the offer to be rabbi and *rosh yeshivah* of the Ashkenazim in Yerushalayim, without a salary. It was there that he completed his monumental work, *Shenei Luchos HaBris*,[1] called "the *Shelah*" for short. It deals with the fundamentals of the Jewish faith, mitzvos, education, and ethical values.

Since many of Reb Yeshayah's commentaries on the Torah are of a very

---

1 Amsterdam, 1649.

exalted Kabbalistic nature, the work became known as the *Shelah HaKadosh*, the "holy Shelah," an accolade it shares with only three other works: the *Zohar HaKadosh*, the *Alshich HaKadosh*, and the *Or HaChaim HaKadosh*. The work became extremely popular, and it has left its mark on Jewish thought. Reb Yeshayah's other works include *Shaar HaShamayim*,[1] a Kabbalistic commentary on the siddur, and *Bigdei Yesha*, a halachic commentary.

In 1625, during the Shabbos morning service, the Shelah and fourteen other rabbis were arrested and held for ransom. After his release he fled to Teveriah, where he spent his final days. He was buried near the tomb of the Rambam.

Selections from the Shelah HaKadosh

The Letters Beis and Lamed

The letter *beis* is made up of two parallel horizontal lines and a vertical line connecting them. The two parallel lines of the *beis* are at odds with each other, going their separate ways, never converging [this is reflected in the numeric value of *beis*, which is two, suggesting the breakup of unity]. Indeed, on the second day of Creation separation came into the world [for on the second day, "God made the firmament, and it separated between the water below the firmament from the water above the firmament" (*Bereishis* 1:7)].

There was no alternative; peace had to be made between the two feuding lines of the *beis*, and that's why the connecting line had to be created, for without peace you have nothing.

Now consider the letter *lamed*. It consists of a base of two lines that are connected [a horizontal line forming an acute angle with a slanted line]; there is no separation between the two. On top of this acute angle base

---

1   Amsterdam, 1717.

there is a *vav*, pointing upward. Like a rocket, the *vav* lifts its base into space. The two legs of the base of the *lamed* symbolize a dispute for the sake of Heaven.[1] Although each of the disputants defends his own view, their aim is to arrive at the truth. Both break through the gravity barrier [of physicality] to rise aloft aboard the *vav* that carries them to the celestial heights.

That's why the *lamed*, aside from being the name of a letter, also carries the meaning of "to learn." For you only learn something when you debate for the sake of Heaven, and your aim is to seek the truth.

That explains why the Torah starts with the letter *beis* [of *Bereishis*] and ends with a *lamed* [of *Yisrael*]. For the *beis* represents this world, *olam ha'asiyah*, the world of action, a world of conflict and continual change. In contrast, the *lamed* denotes the World to Come, the world of peace and unity. [Between those two letters lies the entire Torah, as if to say:] If in this world you live by the laws of the Torah, you will reap your reward in the World to Come.

Shelah, Lech Lecha

Adam Guilty of Murder

> If one person strikes another and [the victim] dies, [the murderer] must be put to death. If he did not plan to kill [his victim] but God caused it so to happen, then I will provide a place where [the killer] can find refuge.
>
> *(Shemos 21:13–14)*

This law is rooted in the mystery of Adam's expulsion from Gan Eden (*Bereishis* 3:23). Let me explain: When Adam sinned at the instigaton of the primeval serpent, he brought death into the world. For that he was judged as a murderer. That is the mystical meaning of the phrase, "If one person strikes another [and the victim] dies, [the murderer] shall be put to death."

---

1   See *Avos* 5:17.

But Adam caused yet another form of death, indicated in the verse, "You are dust, and to dust you shall return" (*Bereishis* 3:10), for Adam's sin caused *gilgul* (reincarnation, rebirth of the soul), whereby a person revolves from dust to dust, that is, his soul moves from one body to another, dying over and over again. This is alluded to in our verse, "*mos yumas* – he must be put to death" [literally: "die he shall die," i.e., die repeatedly].

However, although Adam was a murderer, he did not die right away. In fact, he lived almost for one thousand years.[1] Why? Since the serpent had led him on, he was considered an unintentional murderer and was banished from Gan Eden. Thereby he set a precedent for the law whereby an unintentional murderer is to be exiled [to one of the cities of refuge].[2] But an intentional murderer is put to death immediately, as it says, "If a person...kills intentionally, you must even take him from My altar to put him to death" (*Shemos* 21:14).[3]

Shelah, Mishpatim

Hevel's Reincarnations

> If [two] men fight, and one hits the other with a stone or with [his] fist, and [the victim] does not die but becomes bedridden, and then gets up and can walk with his cane, the one who struck him shall be acquitted. Only for his lost time shall he pay, and he shall provide for healing.
>
> (*Shemos* 21:18-19)

In a Kabbalistic sense this verse alludes to the fight between Kayin and Hevel. It tells us that although Kayin killed Hevel, he did not totally kill him, for Hevel would come back to life in a different incarnation. This is implied by, "He gets up and can walk with his cane." For Hevel was rein-

---

1 He lived 930 years (*Bereishis* 5:5).
2 *Devarim* 4:41-43.
3 Even if the murderer is a priest who is in the act of offering a sacrifice in the Temple, he must be removed from the altar (*Rashi*).

carnated as Moshe, and the cane refers to the staff of Moshe. The phrase, "Only for his lost time shall he pay, and he shall provide for healing" intimates that Kayin has to wait a long time until his soul will be redeemed.

Hevel's final incarnation was Korach [who rebelled against Moshe and was swallowed by the earth alive[1]]. But in time to come Korach will rise up, as Chanah prophesied, "God brings death and gives life, He lowers to the grave and raises up" (*Shmuel* I 2:6). This is hinted at in the verse, "*Tzaddik katamar yifrach* – A righteous man will flourish like a date palm" (*Tehillim* 92:13), for the acronym of the last letters of *tzaddik katamar yifrach* – *kuf, reish, ches* – forms the name *Korach*. That is the underlying meaning of the phrase in our verse, "[God] shall provide healing."

Shelah, Mishpatim

Binyamin's Distinction

> Then the handmaids came forward – they and their children, and they bowed down [before Esav]. Leah, too, came forward with her children, and they bowed down; and afterwards Yosef and Rachel came forward and bowed down.
>
> (*Bereishis* 33:6–7)

Binyamin had a higher degree of holiness than his brothers. His brothers all bowed down to Esav – the personification of evil. Binyamin was the only brother who did not bow down to him since he was not yet born at that time.... That's why the Beis HaMikdash was built in the territory of Binyamin.

It is interesting to note that after the Beis HaMikdash was destroyed and the Jews lived in exile in Persia, Mordechai – a descendant of Binyamin – "would not bow down or prostrate himself [before Haman]" (*Esther* 3:2). As a result, Mordechai was indirectly responsible for the rebuilding of the second Beis HaMikdash, for Mordechai reared Esther. And Esther had a son [by King Achashveirosh], namely, Koreish, King of the

---

1   *Bemidbar*, ch. 16.

Persia. Now Koreish was the king who ordered the rebuilding of the second Beis HaMikdash[1] in the territory of Binyamin. Thus history came full circle.

Shelah, Vayishlach

The *Alef* of Adam's Name

> Yisrael loved Yosef more than any of his other sons.... He made Yosef a colorful garment (*kesones passim*).
>
> (*Bereishis* 37:3)

[Note: After Adam sinned, "God made for Adam and his wife garments of leather (*or*), and He clothed them" (*Bereishis* 3:21). *Or* when written with an *alef* means "light"; when written with an *ayin*, it means "leather." Originally they wore garments of *or*, Divine Light, but after they sinned, God made for them physical garments of *or*, leather.]

Yaakov and Yosef represent the *alef* of the *or* (light) in *kosnos or* (garments of Divine Light). Therein lies the mystery of the *kesones passim* [the colorful garment that Yaakov made for Yosef. Note the similarity between *kosnos* and *kesones*].

This is what happened: When the serpent caused Adam to sin, the *alef* was removed from Adam's name [written *alef, dalet, mem*]. The remaining letters [are]: *dalet, mem* [which spells *dam*, "blood"]. The *dam* of Adam's name tells you that as a result of his sin, death came into the world, and blood was spilled.

Continuing this train of thought: When the *alef* was removed from Adam, it was also taken away from his original garment of *or*. The *alef* of *or* was replaced with an *ayin*, so that Adam's garment became a garment of *or* [meaning "leather"].

Like Adam, Yosef's brothers also sinned [by selling him into slavery]. Their sin began when they stripped Yosef of his *kesones passim* (colorful coat).[2] By sending Yosef on a path of pain and misery, they severed his

---

1 *Ezra* 1:1.

great attachment to God [because you must serve God with gladness].[1] Similarly, when Adam sinned, his close attachment to God was broken, and the *alef* [one, symbol of God's Oneness] was removed from his name. Thus, the sin of the brothers recalls the *dam* that was left from Adam [after the *alef* was removed].

This idea takes on a tangible form in the fact that the brothers slaughtered a goat and "dipped [Yosef's] garment in the *dam*, blood" (*Bereishis* 37:31). By showing the blood-stained garment to their father, they caused the *Shechinah* [i.e., the *alef*, the One and Only] to leave Yaakov. The *Shechinah* did not return to Yaakov until he learned that Yosef was alive. As it says, "The spirit of their father was then revived" (*Bereishis* 45:27).

Shelah, Vayeishev

God's Name Imprinted on the Human Body

God's Four-Letter Name, *Yud-Hei-Vav-Hei*, is imprinted on the human body from above to below and from below to above. The round head resembles the letter *yud*, the elongated body is shaped like the letter *vav*. The five fingers of each hand correspond to the letter *hei* [whose numeric value is five], and similarly, the five toes on each foot correspond to the two letters *hei* in the divine Name. The male organ resembles the letter *vav*, and its crown is shaped like a *yud*. The eyes are shaped like a *yud*, and the nose has the configuration of a *vav*. The ten fingers represent the ten *Sefiros*.

The three parts of the soul — *nefesh*, *ruach*, and *neshamah* — are seated in three different organs of the body.

The *nefesh* [the elementary animal life-force] resides in the liver, which is the seat of life. It harbors the natural instinct which gives sustenance to all parts of the body in accordance with their needs. The *nefesh* holds the power of growth and reproduction and the five senses — hearing, seeing, tasting, smelling, and touching.

---

2 See *Bereishis* 37 for the story of the sale of Yosef.
1 See *Tehillim* 100:2.

The *ruach* [the higher part of the soul] is seated in the heart, which is the will that guides its forces, like a king who rules his people whichever way he wishes. The *neshamah* [the spiritual part of the soul] is located in the brain. It is the element of pure intelligence and rules over everything. This is how it works: Before the heart wills anything, it communicates with the brain. After due deliberation a particular action is decided on and instructions are given to the appropriate organs which carry out the directive.

Shelah, Shoftim

Chapter 26
RABBI NASSAN NATA SHAPIRA
(Megaleh Amukos)

born: Poland, 1585
died: Cracow, Poland, 1633

Born into a distinguished rabbinical family, Rabbi Nassan Nata was educated in both religious and secular studies from early youth. A Talmudic scholar of eminent stature, he had mastery in philosophy, science, and Hebrew grammar. But his primary interest was the study of Kabbalah, particularly the works of the Ari (Rabbi Yitzchak Luria).

From 1617 until his death, Reb Nassan Nata served as rabbi and *rosh yeshivah* in Cracow. Through his books and discourses he spread the teachings of the Ari among the learned people of his community. One of his outstanding disciples was the Shach.[1]

Reb Nassan Nata was universally regarded as a holy man. Every midnight he used to recite *Tikkun Chatzos*, a lament over the destruction of the Temple, praying for its restoration with a plaintive chant. It is said Eliyahu HaNavi once appeared to him and told him that the angels bemoan the de-

---
1   Rabbi Shabsai HaKohen (1622–1663), celebrated halachist, author of the authoritative commentary on the *Shulchan Aruch, Choshen Mishpat* (Amsterdam, 1653).

struction of the Temple to the tune of Reb Nassan Nata's sorrowful *niggun* (melody).

His most most famous work is *Megaleh Amukos*, a profound Kabbalistic Torah commentary[1] in which he offers a variety of alternate interpretations of the verses. In fact, he expounds the word *va'eschanan*, "I implored" (*Devarim* 3:23), no less than 252 different ways. The title *Megaleh Amukos* means "Revealing the Depths." A new edition of the work was published recently together with a commentary, *Perishas Shalom*.[2]

Rabbi Nassan Nata Shapira died at the young age of forty-eight. The inscription on his tombstone characterizes him as "a Godly and saintly man, like one of the early Sages, one who revealed deep and precious secrets, and to whom Eliyahu appeared regularly."

Selections from Megaleh Amukos

Yaakov Rectified Adam's Sin

> [After being warned by his mother that Esav planned to kill him,] Yaakov left Be'er Sheva and headed toward Charan. He encountered the place and spent the night there because it was past sunset.
> (*Bereishis* 28:10–11)

[A Kabbalistic interpretation of this verse is:] Yaakov left Be'er Sheva in order to put right Adam's sin of eating from the [forbidden] tree. That tree is called *shu'ach* (a fig tree). The name *shu'ach* is alluded to in the initials of [the phrase in our verse,] "*Be'er Sheva vayeilech Charanah*" [Yaakov left Beer Sheva and headed toward Charan — *shin, vav, ches* spells *shu'ach*].

In the same vein, it says, "Yitzchak went out to pray [*lasu'ach*] in the field" (ibid. 24:63). Yitzchak, too, went to rectify [Adam's sin of eating from] the *shu'ach* tree [*lasu'ach* is seen as related to *shu'ach*].

---

1   Cracow, 1637.
2   By Rabbi Shalom Weis, New York, 1984.

"He encountered [*vayifga*] the place." [What place?] The place where Adam was punished [*vayifga* means both to encounter and to be punished].

"Because it was past sunset" – [The word *sunset*] brings to mind the verse, "If you take your fellow's garment as a security, until *sunset* shall you return it to him" (*Shemos* 22:25). The "garment" that should be returned at "sunset" hints at Adam's precious [spiritual] garment that Yaakov inherited. [After Adam sinned, he was unworthy to wear the precious garment, and Yaakov fell heir to it. By rectifying Adam's sin, Yaakov was returning the precious garment to Adam.]

The ladder that Yaakov saw in his dream [and that was standing on the ground, reaching toward heaven, was a sign that] Adam's sin was rectified. [The ladder alludes to Adam], because [before he sinned] Adam's height reached from earth all the way to heaven [like the ladder].[1]

Three Times "the Place"

> He encountered the place and spent the night there because the sun had set; he took from the stones of the place which he arranged around his head, and lay down in that place.
>
> (*Bereishis* 28:11)

Three times "the place" is mentioned in this verse: "he encountered the place," "he took from the stones of the place," and "he lay down in that place." [The place was the site where the Beis HaMikdash was later to be built.] The Sages say [that the threefold mention of "the place" implies] that God showed Yaakov the Beis HaMikdash standing, destroyed, and rebuilt (*Bereishis Rabbah* 69:6).

Alternately, the threefold mention of "the place" refers to the three worlds: Beri'ah (the world of creation), Yetzirah (the world of formation), and Asiyah (the world of action).[2]

---

1   This is a metaphor that means that before Adam sinned his intellect was so perceptive that he understood all the mysteries of heaven and earth.

"He lay down in that place" — The Hebrew word for "he lay down" is *vayishkav*. And *vayishkav* can be read as *veyesh kaf-beis*, meaning "there are twenty-two," an allusion to the twenty-two letters of the *alef-beis* with which the Torah is written. [Note: The word *sulam* (ladder) has the same numeric value as Sinai, the mountain where the Torah was given, both adding up to 130. Thus, the dream of the ladder foreshadows the giving of the Torah.]

Yaakov's Dream

[Note: Kabbalah teaches that the soul has five levels. In ascending order they are: *nefesh, ruach, neshamah, chayah,* and *yechidah*. Of these, only the lower three enter into man's being. The higher two, *chayah* and *yechidah*, do not directly affect man.]

> He had a vision in a dream. A ladder was standing on the ground, and its top reached up toward heaven. God's angels were going up and down on it. Suddenly he saw God standing over him.
> *(Bereishis 28:12-13)*

Man is like a ladder. Just as a ladder has two side pieces, so too, man has two sides. In a ladder the rungs connect the two side pieces; in man, the Torah and the mitzvos link his two sides [i.e., they unite his physical and spiritual elements]. Man, a composite of body and soul, stands on the ground, while his head [i.e., his intellect] reaches toward heaven. His *ruach* and *neshamah* [the two higher parts of his soul] unite his physical and spiritual parts.

The Refining Process

[Note: *Be'er Sheva* is translated here as "Well of the Seven." The conventional meaning is "Well of the Oath," because Avraham and Avimelech took an oath there (*Bereishis* 21:31).]

---

2 See ch. 3 for an explanation of these concepts.

> Yaakov left Be'er Sheva and headed toward Charan.
> *(Bereishis 28:10)*

In a Kabbalistic sense, the word *sheva* alludes to the fact that Yaakov was the seventh person to try and wash away [the sin of Adam]. They were: Adam, Sheis, Noach, Shem, Avraham, Yitzchak, and Yaakov.

[Before going to Eretz Yisrael, Avraham lived in Charan (*Bereishis* 11:31).] While there he tried to rectify the souls of the twenty generations that preceded him. [There were twenty generations from Adam until Avraham.] These souls are reincarnated in all the converts that will arise until the days of Mashiach. Similarly, Yitzchak settled in [the Philistine city] Gerar (*Bereishis* 26:1) in order to convert the people of Gerar. Yaakov went to Charan to rectify the souls that were stashed away there.

[As a result of these efforts,] Adam's soul was [partially] cleansed by Avraham, who refined it to the level of silver. [Since Adam's soul was not yet completely purified,] Avraham had a son Yishmael whose soul came from the [unclean] leftovers of the refining process. Adam's soul was then further purified by Yitzchak to the level of gold, and the residue of that refining process was the source of the soul of [the impure] Esav, son of Yitzchak. Yaakov completed the refining process and removed every last trace of pollution [from Adam's soul], as it says, "The false gods will perish completely" (*Yeshayah* 2:18). [That's why there were no flawed leftovers,] and all of Yaakov's sons were perfect [in their closeness to God, and not one of them deviated from the Torah].

The Offspring of the Childless

> After Rachel had given birth to Yosef, Yaakov said to Lavan, "Let me leave. I would like to go home to my own land."
> *(Bereishis 30:23)*

The Kabbalistic sages tell us that when the righteous are barren [and have no children], they beget souls. That's why it says that although Avraham and Sarah were barren, when they left Charan "they took along the souls they made in Charan" (*Bereishis* 12:5). These were the souls of [future] converts. The same is true for Yitzchak. He got married at forty years of age, and his son Yaakov was born when Yitzchak was sixty years old. During the intervening twenty years, Yitzchak begat souls of [future] converts. It was the same with Rachel. All the years that she was childless, she gave birth to souls in heaven [of future converts]. Therefore, when Rachel said to Yaakov, "Give me children! If not, let me die" (*Bereishis* 30:1), he became furious, saying, "You should be satisfied giving birth to divine souls! Since you don't have children in this world, surely our marriage has a higher purpose that rises up to God's [Throne], and God has chosen you to bring into being exalted souls."

Therefore, "after Rachel had given birth to Yosef, Yaakov said to Lavan, 'Let me leave. I would like to go home to my own land' " (*Bereishis* 30:25). Yaakov reasoned: Avraham generated souls of converts during the forty-eight years he lived in Charan [before coming to Eretz Yisrael]. Yaakov then thought that as for himself, his seed did not go to waste, although Rachel was childless in Charan in Lavan's house. Like Avraham's seed, Yaakov's seed produced souls of converts. But now that Rachel had given birth to Yosef, Yaakov's seed had brought forth offspring here in this world, too. [Therefore, he did not want to stay in Charan where his seed had produced souls, but wished to return to Eretz Yisrael.]

A Well in the Field

> [Yaakov came to a place] where he saw a well in the field. Three flocks of sheep were lying beside it.... The top of the well was covered with a large stone. When all the flocks would be assembled there they would roll the stone from the mouth of the well and water the sheep....
>
> (*Bereishis* 29:2–3)

[The mystical meaning is:] The well refers to Adam, for he is the wellspring of all generations until the end of time. The three flocks of sheep are the three patriarchs, Avraham, Yitzchak, and Yaakov, who rectified Adam's soul: Avraham mended Adam's *nefesh*; Yitzchak remedied Adam's *ruach*, Yaakov set right Adam's *neshamah*.

The large stone on top of the well represents the soul of Moshe, since all the generations draw nourishment from the wellspring of the Torah through Moshe.

Alternately, the well in the field stands for the Jewish people in the exile of Esav [our current exile], for Esav is described as "a man of the field" (*Bereishis* 25:27). The large stone on top of the well symbolizes Eliyahu, who will come "before the coming of the great and awesome day of God [the day of the final redemption]" (*Malachi* 3:23).

Ready-made Bread and Clothes

> Yaakov made a vow, "If God will be with me," he said, "if He will protect me on the journey that I am taking, if He gives me bread to eat and clothing to wear.... Of all that You give me, I will set aside a tenth to You."
>
> (*Bereishis* 28:20–22)

"If He gives me bread to eat" — Before Adam sinned, the earth of Eretz Yisrael produced ready-made cakes and ready-made clothes (*Shabbos* 31b; *Toras Kohanim, Bechukosai*). That's why Yaakov said, "If He gives me bread to eat and clothing to wear" — meaning, "If he gives me ready-made bread and ready-made clothes [as before Adam's sin], so that I don't have to work hard [and can spend my time learning Torah]."

Yaakov continued, "Of all that You give me, I will set aside a tenth for You." He meant to say: "If you give me ready-made bread, so that I don't have to do the ten labors [of bread-making] — beginning with plowing, ending with baking — that are involved in the production of a loaf of bread...."

[Calling to mind these ten labors,] we place our ten fingers on the bread when reciting the *berachah* before eating it: "*Baruch Atah Hashem Elokeinu melech ha'olam, hamotzi lechem min ha'aretz* — Blessed are You, Hashem, our God, King of the universe, who brings forth bread from the earth." And for this reason the *berachah* of *HaMotzi* has ten words.

Part V
THE KABBALISTS OF ERETZ YISRAEL

Introduction
THE KABBALISTS OF ERETZ YISRAEL

The expulsion of the Spanish Jews spurred a great wave of immigration to Eretz Yisrael. A sizable community of Spanish exiles settled in Tzefas (Safed), which became the dominant center for the study of Kabbalah. It counted among its residents such masters of Kabbalah as Rabbi Shlomo Alkabetz (author of *Lechah Dodi*), Rabbi Moshe Cordovero, Rabbi Moshe Alshich, and Rabbi Yosef Karo (author of the *Shulchan Aruch*).

In 1570, Rabbi Yitzchak Luria, the Ari HaKadosh, left Egypt to be near Rabbi Moshe Cordovero and join the other Kabbalists of Safed. The Ari soon was recognized as the foremost Kabbalist of his generation. He had the power to perform miracles, read a person's thoughts, and predict the future. Eliyahu HaNavi revealed to him previously unknown mysteries.

The Ari developed his own Kabbalistic system and greatly influenced the spiritual atmosphere of Tzefas. His doctrines were recorded by his pupil Rabbi Chaim Vital under the title *Eitz Chaim* and became the foundation of all later Kabbalistic writings. It is the most significant work on Kabbalah since the appearance of the *Zohar*.

Among other prominent Kabbalists in Eretz Yisrael are counted Rabbi Avraham Azulai and his illustrious grandson Rabbi Chaim Yosef David

Azulai, known as the Chida, author of *Shem HaGedolim*. His contemporary, Rabbi Shalom Sharabi, known as Rashash, is a revered Kabbalist, especially in the Sefardic communities. A great eighteenth century master in Eretz Yisrael is Rabbi Chaim ibn Attar, author of the Torah commentary *Or HaChaim*.

Chapter 27
RABBI SHLOMO ALKABETZ

born: Salonica, Turkey (now Greece), c. 1505
died: Tzefas, c. 1584

Rabbi Shlomo Alkabetz, one of the great Kabbalists of Tzefas, studied in the yeshivah of Rabbi Yosef Taitatzak. In 1529 he married the daughter of Rabbi Yitzchak Cohen, one of the wealthiest men in Salonica. As *mishlo'ach manos* (Purim gift) he sent his father-in-law his latest book *Manos HaLevi*,[1] a commentary on the Book of Esther. The father-in-law thanked him, saying, "I appreciate this *sefer* far more than any gift of gold or expensive jewelry."

Rabbi Shlomo wanted to settle in Eretz Yisrael, which he considered "the source of *kedushah*, the place ideally suited to learning Kabbalah." On the way to the Holy Land he stopped off in Adrianople, where he met Rabbi Yosef Karo, the author of the *Shulchan Aruch*,[2] who taught him Kabbalah. It was there that he wrote *Beis Hashem* and *Avosos Ahuvim*, which remain in manuscript, and began *Ayeles Ahuvim*,[3] a commentary on *Shir HaShirim*. Legend has it that once, on the night of Shavuos, while Rabbi Shlomo was

---

1   Venice, 1585.
2   The Code of Jewish Law, Venice, 1564.
3   Venice, 1552.

studying Kabbalah with Rabbi Yosef Karo, they both experienced divine visions. In Adrianople Rabbi Shlomo also wrote *Bris HaLevi*,[1] a Kabbalistic commentary on the Haggadah.

Around 1535 he moved to Eretz Yisrael and made his home in Tzefas, the city of Kabbalists. It was not long before he became a leading figure among the group of Tzefas Kabbalists, which included the Ari and Rabbi Yosef Karo. Among his many disciples was his brother-in-law Rabbi Moshe Cordovero, who was married to his wife's sister.

Rabbi Shlomo Alkabetz used to take his disciples on walks through the gently rolling hills of the northern Galilee to visit the graves of the tzaddikim in nearby Meron. The deep mystical talks he gave on these walks are recorded in *Sefer Gerushin*.[2]

In all of his numerous books, Rabbi Shlomo Alkabetz expresses his love of Eretz Yisrael and his yearning for the *geulah*, the ultimate redemption. Without a doubt, his most famous creation is the inspiring hymn *Lechah Dodi*,[3] which ushers in Shabbat and is chanted on Friday night in all communities. The Ari highly praised *Lechah Dodi*, because, as he said, "Its words are in tune with Kabbalah." The song is based on the Talmud's description of the way the Sages joyously greeted Shabbat (*Shabbos* 119a).

Selections from the Writings of Rabbi Shlomo Alkabetz

Excerpts from Lechah Dodi

[The Jewish nation says to God:]
Come, my Beloved [God], to welcome the Bride [the *Shechinah*],
Let us usher in the presence of Shabbos!
Come let us go to salute the Shabbos,

---

1 Lemberg, 1863.
2 Venice, 1602.
3 First printed in a Sefardi *siddur* in Venice, 1584.

For it is the wellspring of blessing;
From time immemorial she was acclaimed,
Last in deed, but first in thought.
Don't be ashamed, don't be embarrassed,
Why are you distraught? Why are you doleful?
In you my people's downtrodden will find refuge
As the City is rebuilt on its hilltop.
May those who preyed on you be despoiled,
And those who devoured you be repelled.
Your God will rejoice over you,
Like a groom rejoices over his bride.
Enter in peace, you, crown of her husband,
In joy and in elation,
Among the faithful of the treasured nation.
Enter, dear bride! Enter, dear bride!

Chapter 28
RABBI MOSHE ALSHICH

born: Adrianople, Turkey, 1508
died: Tzefas, 1593

Rabbi Moshe was born in Adrianople into a family of Spanish exiles. He studied in the yeshivah of Rabbi Yosef Karo and under the Kabbalist Rabbi Yosef Taitatzak in Salonica. As a young man he moved to Eretz Yisrael, settling in Tzefas. It was there that he was ordained by Rabbi Yosef Karo and served as *dayan*. He had a large number of disciples, including Rabbi Chaim Vital, who became the main disseminator of the Kabbalistic teachings of the Ari. Although not a disciple of the Ari, Rabbi Moshe is considered one of the great Kabbalists. He wanted very much to study Kabbalah under the Ari, but the Ari discouraged him, telling him that he had come into this world to be a preacher. Nevertheless, he explored Kabbalistic teachings all his life, especially in his later years.

An eloquent speaker, his sermons drew large and enthusiastic crowds. These sermons were compiled in his highly respected work *Toras Moshe*,[1] popularly known as *Alshich HaKadosh* ("the holy Alshich"). It comprises his commentary on *Bereishis* and *Shemos*. The other volumes were published by his son Rabbi Chaim.[2]

---

1   Constantinople, 1595.

Although he follows mainly a homiletic approach, extracting from the text lessons on ethics, morality, and piety, many of his commentaries are based on Kabbalistic themes. Although written in a very lucid style, the sheer length of his comments make them inaccessible to the average person. Rabbis find his work a rich source of material for their sermons. It has seen many editions and is readily available today.

In 1590, the eighty-two-year-old Rabbi Moshe left Eretz Yisrael to raise funds for the impoverished Jewish community of Tzefas. He died shortly after his return to Tzefas in 1593. According to other sources, he died in Damascus in 1593.

Selections from Toras Moshe

The Heavenly Source of the Soul

> God formed man out of dust of the ground and breathed into his nostrils a breath of life. Man [thus] became a living creature.
> *(Bereishis 2:7)*

The soul is a spiritual light that emanates from the *Shechinah*. When it goes forth from its source to be clothed inside a person's body, it is not completely disconnected from its root. In the physical world, when you draw a pail of water from the sea or you dig up a clod of earth out of the ground, you separate the part from the whole. But in the spiritual realm the soul is not severed from its heavenly root but remains connected to it.

It is the same with the angels. Michael, Gavriel, and Rafael are called the "feet of the Divine Chariot." When Gavriel was sent to destroy Sedom, and Rafael to save Lot,[1] and when Gavriel slew the Assyrian army on the night of Pesach in the days of Chizkiyah,[2] do you think that one of "the feet of

---

2   Venice, 1601.
1   See *Bereishis*, ch. 19.
2   See *Melachim* II 19:35.

the Divine Chariot" was missing? Of course not. These angels remained connected to their heavenly base.

Or take Eliyahu HaNavi. He is present at every *bris milah* that takes place anywhere in the world. What is he to do, since there are Jews living all over the world, and there are many *brisos* at the same time? The answer is that the spiritual realm extends without limit; there is no separation [for angels and souls], much less with regard to the *Shechinah*. Consequently, when a soul is sent down to this world it is not cut off from its source beneath the wings of the *Shechinah*. The soul that enters the human body is an extension [of the heavenly soul].

But when a person transgresses, the connection of the soul to its root in the *Shechinah* is broken, as it says, "Your iniquities have been a barrier between you and your God" (*Yeshayah* 59:2). And that's why a wicked person whose sins outweigh his good deeds is considered as dead, for the lifeline that connects his soul to God is severed. But as long as the majorty of a person's deeds are virtuous, he is alive, his lifeline is still intact, and he is considered a tzaddik.

The Trees of Gan Eden

> God made grow out of the ground every tree that is pleasant to look at and good to eat, including the Tree of Life in the middle of the garden, and the Tree of Knowledge of good and evil.
> (*Bereishis* 2:9)

[Since Gan Eden is a spiritual place] it is inconceivable that trees and flowers should flourish there as in an earthly garden. After all, we have a basic rule that the reward for a mitzvah is of a spiritual nature [and Gan Eden is the reward for the righteous]. On the other hand, regarding the passage, "The dove came back [to Noach] toward evening, and there was a freshly plucked olive leaf in its beak" (ibid. 8:11), the Kabbalists comment that the dove brought the leaf from Gan Eden, and they say also that the vineyard that Noach planted (ibid. 9:20) came from a branch of Gan Eden [proof that Gan Eden is here on earth].

The contradiction may be resolved as follows: The material world in which we live has a spiritual counterpart in a higher world. Consequently, just as there is a Gan Eden above, so is there a Gan Eden in this world. And the Gan Eden above has numerous counterparts in higher worlds, one above the other, in as many worlds as there are in the realms of Atzilus, Beri'ah, Yetzirah, and Asiyah, as the Kabbalistic sages know.

You can compare it to a ladder where the lowest rung is Gan Eden here on earth, reaching higher and higher. That's why it is not inconceivable for angels, which are spiritual beings, to come down to this world clothed in an earthly garment and appear as men. This was the case when Avraham was visited by three angels in the guise of Arab wayfarers (*Bereishis* 18:2) and Lot welcomed the two angels into his house (ibid. 19:2). Although the earthly Gan Eden is essentially supernatural, its trees look like tangible trees as long as they are in their place in Gan Eden. But once a branch or a leaf is taken out of Gan Eden, its quality "thickens" to the point that it becomes a regular earthly branch or leaf, as was the case with the leaf of Noach's dove and the branch of Noach's vineyard.

Why Was He Called Yaakov?

> After [Esav was born] his brother emerged, and his hand was grasping Esav's heel [*akeiv*]. [Therefore, Yitzchak] called him Yaakov. Yitzchak was sixty years old when [Rivkah] gave birth to them.
>
> *(Bereishis 25:26)*

It is strange that for a detail as trivial as grasping Esav's heel [*akeiv*] he was named Yaakov. And why is the Torah mentioning this minor point in the first place? And what is the relevance of Yitzchak's age of sixty years?

Notice that Yitzchak called him *Yaakov* [meaning, "he will grasp"], which is in the future tense, rather than *Akav* ["he grasped"] in the past tense. Why? The Torah wants to tell us the reason why Esav and not

Yaakov was born first. It has to do with the fact that this world precedes the World to Come. And that's why it says [in the story of Creation], "It was evening and it was morning" (ibid. 1:5) [evening before morning], indicating that this world comes before the World to Come.

Thus Esav [who came first] was allotted this world, and Yaakov [who came second] was assigned the World to Come. This is hinted at in the phrase, "his hand was grasping Esav's heel" [the heel is the end of the foot], to tell you that Yaakov's share and abundant reward comes at the end, whereas Esav's success and affluence is in this world. And that's why he was called Yaakov in the future tense to indicate that his reward awaits him in the future.

Now you may ask: How did Yitzchak know all that? That's why it says, "Yitzchak was sixty years old when [Rivkah] gave birth to them," implying that his mental faculties were at their peak, that he had the prophetic spirit to tell which son was going to grow up to be a tzaddik, and which son an evildoer.

Why Didn't Yosef Communicate with His Father?

> Yosef named the firstborn Menashe, for "God has made me forget [*nashani*] all my troubles and my father's house."
> (Bereishis 41:51)

How can we explain that Yosef did not send a letter or a message to his father while he was a servant in Potifar's house, during the twelve years he was in the dungeon, and during seven years of abundance and two years of famine [when he was viceroy of Egypt]? Why didn't he let his father know that he was alive?

When Yosef realized that "God was with him" (ibid. 39:2), he concluded that he had been sent to Egypt for a purpose. He understood that he was meant to be the chariot for the *Shechinah*, and that it was his mission in life to pave the way for the *Shechinah* to come to Egypt. He reasoned that when his father would find out that he was in bondage in

Egypt, he would redeem him immediately. And for this reason he sent no message.

You would think that at least when he was in the dungeon he would have written to his father [to ask for help]. But with all his might he forced himself to suppress his desire to tell his father. For that reason he named his firstborn Menashe ["for God has made me forget my father's house"] to thank God for giving him the strength to keep his whereabouts a secret. He reasoned that if he would let his father know, Yaakov would give all his resources to ransom him and bring him home. If that were to happen, God's plan of bringing the *Shechinah* to Egypt and making Yosef the chariot of the *Shechinah* would come to nothing. The Egyptian exile [which led to Jewish nationhood and culminated in the giving of the Torah] would never take place, and the destiny of the Jewish people would never be fulfilled.

Chapter 29
RABBI MOSHE CORDOVERO
(Remak)

born: 1522
died: Tzefas, 1570

Rabbi Moshe Cordovero's birthplace is unknown, but the name *Cordovero* suggests that his family originated in Cordova, Spain. They fled during the expulsion of 1492. The Remak (an acronym of his name) lived in Tzefas, studying under Rabbi Yosef Karo, the author of the *Shulchan Aruch*, and learning the *Zohar* with his brother-in-law, the famous Kabbalist and poet, Rabbi Shlomo Alkabetz, composer of *Lechah Dodi*. Rabbi Moshe Cordovero established a *beis midrash* for Kabbalah in Tzefas, where one of his students was Rabbi Chaim Vital.

Although the Remak studied philosophy as a young man, he rejected its analytical method of inquiry, because "philosophers are not versed in the Kabbalistic approach." He also was critical of people who interpret the Torah only in its literal sense and ascribe corporeality to God, ignoring the deeper Kabbalistic meanings.

The Remak considered the *Zohar* as the basic text of Kabbalah, essential for a true understanding of the Torah and for finding answers to all questions of faith. By formulating the concept of the *Sefiros*, Kabbalah succeeded in explaining how God — a completely spiritual Being — created and interacts with the physical world. The cornerstone of the Remak's doctrine is the Oneness of God. God is the Prime Cause, devoid of any physicality; He is above time and space. God withdrew His Infinite Light that filled all existence to make "room" for the *Sefiros* and for the universe.

According to Rabbi Moshe Cordovero, the *Sefiros* are the agents of God by which God brought the world into being, and by which He guides and supervises the world. Just as there is a stream of abundant light downward, so is there a flow of light from below upward. This is called *or chozeir*, "returning light." In simple terms, what this means is that before there can be an *isra'usa dele'eila*, "a stirring above," there has to be an *isra'usa deletata*, "a stirring below." In other words, before the flow of abundance from above comes down, there has to be a prior stimulus from below. If we take the first step, God responds by showering His abundant kindness on us. This idea points up the essential role man plays in the functioning of the world: when he is virtuous he brings blessings upon the world; conversely, when he transgresses, his sins block the Infinite Light that flows down through the *Sefiros*.

In *Pardes Rimonim*,[1] the Remak explains the system of the ten *Sefiros*. In his discourses he differs greatly from Rabbi Meir ibn Gabbai's belief as set forth in *Avodas Hakodesh*, despite the fact that both *Avodas HaKodesh* and *Pardes Rimonim* are based on the *Zohar*.

Considering the *Zohar* to be the bedrock of Kabbalah, the Remak dedicated his life to expounding its concepts. Legend has it that Eliyahu HaNavi appeared to him and revealed to him many Kabbalistic mysteries. His first major work, *Pardes Rimonim*, is a classic that explains the system of the *Sefiros*. *Or Yakar*, his commentary on the *Zohar*, is sixteen volumes long and exists only in manuscript form. He also wrote *Elimah Rabbasi*[2] on Kabbalistic terminology; *Tomer Devorah*,[3] a seminal work on ethics seen from a Kabbalistic aspect; and a commentary on *Sefer Yetzirah*, which was not published.

---

1   Salonica, c. 1580.
2   Brody, 1881.
3   Venice, 1588.

Rabbi Moshe Cordovero was the foremost Kabbalist of his era, revered for his superior knowledge, his piety, his pureness of heart, and his otherworldly saintliness. Rabbi Yitzchak Luria (the Ari), who was his student and great admirer, referred to him as *moreinu verabbeinu,* "our master and teacher." Until the emergence of the Ari, the Remak was considered the greatest Kabbalist of his day. However, the enormous popularity and widespread acceptance of the teachings of the Ari eclipsed all other Kabbalists, including the Remak. Rabbi Chaim Vital, Rama of Fano, and other prominent disciples of the Remak became ardent followers of the Ari's school. They spread the Ari's teachings and considered the Remak a forerunner of the Ari, who paved the way for the Ari's ideology.

Selections from the Writings of Rabbi Moshe Cordovero

The Ten *Sefiros*

Everyone knows that all Kabbalists unanimously agree that there are ten *Sefiros*. We know about the *Sefiros* from *Sefer Yetzirah*, attributed to Avraham Avinu. There are some who attribute it to Rabbi Akiva, but there is no consensus on that. The text of *Sefer Yetzirah* is highly esoteric and remains obscure in spite of the numerous commentaries that have been written on it. Nevertheless, I will try to explain its text as best I can with my limited knowledge.

It says in *Sefer Yetzirah* (1:3): "Ten *Sefiros* of nothing, the number of the ten fingers, five opposite five, and the single covenant is in between, as in the circumcision of the male organ and the circumcision of the tongue." ... The author begins by saying "ten *Sefiros*," implying that since they are numbered, they are subject to a certain degree of limitation and corporeality.

What is meant by "of nothing"? The author means that, in reality, the

Sefiros are intangible. Although we speak of them in terms of the number ten, we firmly believe that they are "of nothing," that is, they have no substance. Meaning, that the *Sefiros* have no essence that can be understood by the human mind because they are above physicality. And something that has no physicality can be perceived only by Jewish visionaries, like prophets.... The word *Sefiros* is related to *mispar* (number), to indicate that although they are "of nothing" [and intangible], nevertheless they can be counted.

To establish the fact that there are exactly ten *Sefiros*, the author says, "the number of ten fingers." [Everything in this world has its counterpart in the higher world. In the physical world there is man who has ten fingers, and his counterpart in the higher world is God, in whose image man was created.] Speaking of the Creator, Scripture says, "When I behold Your heavens, the work of Your fingers" (*Tehillim* 8:4). The passage implies that the creation of heaven and its legions of stars came about through God's "fingers," which is a metaphor for the *Sefiros*. Since man has ten fingers, it follows that God created the world through ten *Sefiros*....

Pardes Rimonim 1

The Scriptural Basis for the Ten *Sefiros*

Since we are convinced that there is a system of ten *Sefiros*, we really should investigate whether this principle stands the test of logic. We have come to the conclusion that there are several reasons why the concept of the *Sefiros* holds true and is rationally well grounded.

First: Since we believe that God exercises general supervision over the laws of nature [*hashgachah kelalis*] and even close supervision of each person's deeds [*hashgachah peratis*], we are compelled to say that He guides the world by means of the *Sefiros*. For God, the One and Only, the Prime Cause, Cause of all causes, is completely incorporeal and transcends all physicality. Then how can we say that He is involved with the material universe, unless we hold that His emanations give rise to the different divine attributes such as Justice and Compassion [with which He guides the world]? So, in order to avoid contradictions in our fundamental beliefs, we must believe in the principle of the *Sefiros*.

The commentators offer many more philosophical reasons, but I do not quote them because I don't want to go into philosophical speculation in this book. I do want to say that the idea of the ten *Sefiros* is based on scriptural sources.

The first three *Sefiros* [*Keser, Chochmah, Binah*] are mentioned in the verse, "*Veha***chochmah** *mei'***ayin** *timatzei, ve'ei zeh mekom* **binah**," (*Iyov* 28:12). Iyov is saying that the *Sefirah* of *Chochmah* emanates from the *Sefirah* of *Keser*, which is also called *ayin*, and that the *Sefirah* of *Binah* flows from *Chochmah*.

The seven lower *Sefiros* can be found in the words of David, "Yours, God, is the greatness, the strength, the splendor, the triumph, and the glory, even everything in heaven and earth. Yours, God, is the kingdom, and the sovereignty over every leader" (*Divrei HaYamim* I 29:11). "*Gedulah*," greatness, stands for *Chesed*, "strength" stands for *Gevurah*, followed by *Tiferes* (Splendor), *Netzach* (Triumph), and *Hod* (Glory). "Everything in heaven and earth" stands for *Yesod*. Then comes "*mamlachah*," kingdom, which represents *Malchus*.

Pardes Rimonim 8

Is Denying the *Sefiros* Considered Heresy?

The question arises: Should a person who denies the existence of the ten *Sefiros* be considered a heretic or not? If the denier's error stems from ignorance, because he is not familiar with this way of thinking, and he does not recognize the truth, he surely cannot be called a heretic or an unbeliever.

Proof of this is the Ravad's view regarding anthropomorphisms where Scripture speaks of God's hand, God's eyes and ears, God walking, sitting, and speaking. He says that if a person believes – on the basis of such anthropomorphistic passages – that God has physicality, but otherwise serves God faithfully and follows the laws of the Torah, such a person should not be considered a heretic. He is just ignorant, but he does not have bad intentions.

Pardes Rimonim 89

Emulating God's Attributes

In your effort to emulate your Creator in His mystical attribute of *Keser*, you must exhibit certain fundamental traits. The one all-encompassing trait is that of humility. It is rooted in the *Sefirah* of *Keser*, which descends and gazes downward.... Likewise, you should not arrogantly look skyward, but, imbued with a sense of inner shame, you should always keep your eyes downcast.

Generally, the trait of humility becomes manifest in the way a person holds his head. A head held high is the mark of an arrogant person, whereas a poor man always lowers his head. There is no one more humble and forbearing than God in His divine attribute of *Keser*, which is the essence of compassion.

You should always keep your ears open to listen to good things. False or disparaging remarks should never enter your ears. Emulating divine "hearing," you should listen only to favorable and beneficial things, but close your ears to tidings that provoke anger. Let your eyes never gaze on anything disgraceful, but keep them wide open, looking on the less fortunate with all the compassion you can muster. When you see a destitute person in distress, don't look away; have mercy on him.

Always keep smiling, and greet everyone with a cheerful face. Let only good tidings and Torah words emanate from your mouth. Never say anything shameful. Never let a curse, words of anger and resentment, or idle talk emerge from your mouth.

Tomer Devorah 2

Share Your Knowledge

How can you imitate the divine attribute of *Chochmah*? God's wisdom pervades all existence, as the psalmist says, "How great are Your works, God, You made them all with *Chochmah*" (*Tehillim* 104:24). The same way, you should make your wisdom available to all, by sharing your knowledge and insight with your fellowmen, teaching each individual according to his intelligence, letting nothing stand in your way....

And just as the attribute of *Chochmah* extends to each *Sefirah* according to its measure and needs, you should disseminate your *Chochmah* to each person in the measure his intellect can grasp, according to what is proper for him and as much as he needs. You should take care not to give more than the mind of the student can absorb, otherwise harm will result, for the higher *Sefirah* does not convey more light than the receiving *Sefirah* can hold.

Tomer Devorah 3

Adopting the Attribute of *Malchus*

[Note: *Malchus*, as the last of the ten *Sefiros*, receives the Infinite Light but does not transmit it further. In that sense it is comparable to a humble, poor man.]

How should you train yourself in the attribute of *Malchus*? To begin with, don't be proud of your possessions. Rather, you should always behave like a poor man, standing before your Maker like a pauper, begging and pleading. Even a rich man should adopt this attitude and imagine that none of his wealth belongs to him, and that he is forsaken and requires the constant mercies of his Creator, having nothing but the bread he eats. He should humble and afflict himself, especially at the time of prayer, for this is a very effective aid....

A second, extremely important method is explained in the *Zohar*. It says there that a man should go into exile, wandering from place to place for the sake of Heaven. He thereby becomes a vehicle for the exiled *Shechinah*. [Ever since the Beis HaMikdash was destroyed, the *Shechinah*, along with the Jewish people, is in exile.] He should think to himself: "Look, I am in exile, but at least I have all the vessels I need. But what about the honor of the Almighty, for the *Shechinah* is exiled without any vessels [the *aron*, the *mizbei'ach*, the *menorah*, the *shulchan*...], for they were lost as a result of the exile?" For this reason, he should make do with as little as possible, as it says, "Make for yourself implements of exile" (*Yechezkel* 12:3) — and let the exile humble his heart, while he binds himself to Torah. Then the *Shechinah* will be with him.

Tomer Devorah 9

Chapter 30
RABBI YITZCHAK LURIA ASHKENAZI
(Ari HaKadosh)

born: Yerushalayim, 1534
died: Tzefas, 1572

One of the most celebrated Kabbalists, Rabbi Yitzchak Luria created a new approach to Kabbalah known as *shittas haAri*, the doctrine that forms the basis for all later Kabbalistic writings. He descended from Ashkenazim, which is evident from his surname *Luria*, meaning "Lorraine" (a region in France) and the byname *Ashkenazi* attached to his name. His father died when young Yitzchak was still an infant, whereupon his mother moved from Yerushalayim to Cairo to live with her prosperous brother, Rabbi Mordechai Francis, who raised the young boy. He studied Torah and Kabbalah under Rabbi David ben Zimra, author of the famous responsa work *Teshuvos Radvaz*,[1] and Rabbi Betzalel Ashkenazi. Under their tutelage he became an accomplished Torah scholar.

After his marriage, the Ari studied for six years with Rabbi Betzalel Ashkenazi and collaborated with him in the compilation of *Shittah Mekubetzes*,[2]

---

1 Venice, 1749.
2 Metz, 1764.

a basic text for talmudic scholars. Fascinated by Kabbalah and inclined to piety and self-denial, the Ari went into seclusion in a house on the banks of the Nile, coming home only for Shabbos. In the tranquility of his retreat he immersed himself in the study of Kabbalah, attaining such spiritual heights that Eliyahu HaNavi would reveal to him previously unknown mysteries. It was Eliyahu who told him that he was to move to Eretz Yisrael and settle in Tzefas, the center of Kabbalistic study at that time.

The Ari arrived in Tzefas in 1570, where he wanted to study under the foremost Kabbalist, Rabbi Moshe Cordovero, the Remak. The Remak died shortly after meeting the Ari, who now attracted a circle of devoted disciples who considered him the successor of the Remak.

The Ari did not write down any of his teachings; they were recorded by his foremost student Rabbi Chaim Vital in his work *Eitz Chaim*.[1] The Ari's thoughts, as they emerge in *Eitz Chaim*, are based on the *Zohar* and deal with such esoteric topics as *tzimtzum*, *klippos*, and the four worlds (see Part I, "Concepts of Kabbalah"). A number of popular *zemiros* (songs for the Shabbos table) are attributed to the Ari: "*Azamer Bishvachin*," "*Asader Lis'udasa*," and "*B'nei Heichala*" in Aramaic, and "*Yom Zeh LeYisrael*" in Hebrew.

The Ari is buried in Tzefas in the upper Galilee. His tomb, his synagogue, and his *mikveh* are pilgrimage sites for thousands of visitors annually who come there from all over the world to pray and to be inspired by the *kedushah* that pervades these holy places.

Selections from Eitz Chaim

Tzimtzum

[Note: The following selection — the first paragraph of *Eitz Chaim* — contains one of the fundamental teachings of the Ari.]

---

1   Koretz, 1782.

Before Creation, the Exalted Light was simple. It filled all existence, so that there was no empty space. Everything was filled with the Infinite Light. The concepts of "beginning" and "end" did not exist. Everything was simply light, the Infinite Light.

When it was [God's] will to create all worlds, He constricted Himself at the central point [of His light]. And exactly in the middle He withdrew His Light and pulled it back to the sides around the central point. Thus, an empty space encircling that central point came into being. This *tzimtzum* (withdrawal process) was the same on all sides of the central point, so that the empty space [that was created] was a perfect circle — not a square — because the Infinite Light withdrew evenly [in all directions]. We know from mathematics that, unlike a square or a triangle, a circle is the most perfect of all forms....

After this *tzimtzum* took place, and the empty space came into being in the middle of the Infinite Light, there was a place in which all things could be created. [God] then drew from His Infinite Light one single straight line and brought it into that vacated space.... It was through that line that the Infinite Light was brought down below [to the physical universe].

Eitz Chaim 1:1

Bilam, the Reincarnation of Lavan

> [When Bilam's] donkey saw God's angel standing in the road with a drawn sword in his hand, the donkey went aside from the road into the field. Bilam beat the donkey to get it back on the road.
>
> (*Bemidbar* 22:23)

[Bilam was on his way to curse the Jewish people when the donkey he was riding saw an angel blocking his way.] Our Sages comment that [by pressing against the wall] the donkey was reminding Bilam of the oath that Lavan had given to Yaakov. [Lavan had pledged, "This mound (*gal*) shall be a witness...that I will not go beyond this mound...with bad intention" (*Bereishis* 31:52).] We explained earlier that Bilam was the reincarnation of Lavan, so that by preparing to curse the Jewish people Bilam was violating the oath he had made in his former incarnation [as Lavan]. For that reason Bilam did not live long. In fact, he was only thirty-three years old when Pinchas killed him (*Sanhedrin* 106b). [Note: Thirty-three is the numeric value of *gal*,[1] the mound that Lavan designated as witness to his oath not to harm the Jews, the vow he violated.] And so it says, "Men of bloodshed and deceit shall not live out half their days" (*Tehillim* 55:24) [half of the normal life span of seventy years].

Eitz Chaim, Shaar HaPesukim, Parashas Balak

Inanimate, Vegetative, Animal, and Man

Without a doubt, even inanimate matter like stone or metal contains a life-giving nucleus that keeps it in existence. We know that even inanimate things have an angel in heaven that instills vitality into them. Proof of this is the fact that earth is capable of making seeds and plants grow. Also, earth is thirsty for rain like a woman desires her husband.

Plants have more vitality and greater life force than inanimate minerals, for plants have the power to sprout, to absorb nutrients, to grow, and to propagate.

Animals have more spirit than plants, and man ranks highest of the four. For this reason you are capable of digesting elements of the three lower groupings. By ingesting the nutrients from inanimate and vegetative matter you elevate them to a [spiritual] level that is above your own status. For the food you eat becomes part of yourself. You absorb the nutrients it contains and expel the waste.

The wicked, on the other hand, spoil everything [they eat]. Because of their misdeeds, all the food they eat is reduced to the level of inanimate minerals. As a matter of fact, the evildoers themselves are reincarnated as animals. During their lifetime they behaved like animals, and now after death they are reincarnated as animals [or inanimate stone]. That is what

---

1   *Gimmel* (3) + *lamed* (30) = 33.

happened to the evil Naval. [When Naval found out that his wife Avigayil had given food and drink to the fugitive David and his cohorts,] "his heart died within him, and he turned to stone" (*Shmuel* I 25:37).

Eitz Chaim, Shaar HaMitzvos, Parashas Eikev

Finding Unknown Graves

[Note: The location of most of the graves of the *tannaim* and great tzaddikim in Eretz Yisrael were unknown until the Ari traversed the country and identified them through divine inspiration.]

[Rabbi Chaim Vital writes:] Now I will write about the gravesites of tzaddikim as I heard it from my master [the Ari]. The Ari had the power to gaze at souls of tzaddikim whenever and wherever he wished, and he certainly could see them when he visited their graves, since their souls linger there. Even from a distance he could perceive the soul of a tzaddik hovering over his grave. That's how he could pinpoint the location of the graves of all the tzaddikim. After researching and investigating the matter, I found his statements to be absolutely correct. I don't want to elaborate because these things are so awesome and wondrous that they cannot be put into words.

West of Tzefas [in the Galilee] there is a Jewish cemetery. In it there is a building with a tall dome. On the north side of that building there is a small opening that leads into a cave. People say that [the prophet] Hoshea ben Be'eri is buried there, but that is not so. Rather, it is the *tanna* Rabbi Yehoshua[1] who is enshrined there. People mistook the name *Yehoshua* for *Hoshea*.

When you get to a point below [the grave of Rabbi Chiya] and you continue on that road for a good distance, you find on the east side of the road one solitary straight rock. Underneath that rock is the grave of Rabbi Nechunya ben HaKanah [a *tanna* of the Mishnah; author of the revered Kabbalistic work, the *Bahir*].

1　A *tanna* of the second generation, student of Rabbi Yochanan ben Zakkai. He is mentioned 142 times in the Mishnah and numerous times in the Gemara.

North of Tzefas, if you take the road to the village of K'far Ein Ziton, you pass a carob tree. That is where Yeshu HaNotzri [the Nazarene][1] is buried. There are two roads that branch off from there. The one on the right leads to Ein Ziton, the other to Hakarael. At the intersection there is a valley crowded with olive trees.... Near the very last olive tree is the grave of the mother of Rabbi Kruspeda'i, who is mentioned in the *Zohar, parashas Shelach Lecha*.

Going south from Teveriah along Lake Kinneret (Sea of Galilee) to the hot springs of Teveriah, exactly midway on the lakeside, you come upon a large grove of date palms, opposite a castle on the mountaintop. That is the location of the Well of Miriam [which supplied water to the children of Israel on their forty-year wandering through the Sinai desert].[2]

Eitz Chaim, Shaar HaGilgulim, Hakdamah 37

The Song of Birds

[Rabbi Chaim Vital relates:] The Ari was able to understand the chirping of birds. Let me explain. You have to realize that on the day the Temple was destroyed, the secrets of the Torah were captured by the *klippos*.[3]

You should know that all creatures — even unclean animals, birds, and creeping things — have a guardian angel above. So, ever since the destruction of the Temple, the guardian angels of unclean animals know the mysteries of the Torah. And these guardian angels infuse profound secrets of the Torah into the chirpings of the birds. A person who understands bird chirpings can gather many secrets of the Torah by listening to their songs. In fact, I personally saw my master [the Ari] do that.

You also should realize that when a decree is made in heaven, it is pro-

---

1 He was a disciple of the *tanna* Rabbi Yehoshua ben Perachyah (*Sotah* 47a).
2 See Rashi, *Bemindbar* 20:2.
3 See ch. 3.

claimed in all the worlds. And whenever a person commits a transgression, the heavenly tribunal announces it in this world. But the density of the atmosphere forms a barrier that prevents the ethereal heavenly sound from coming through, so that it remains bogged down in the air. However, [there are two ways this sound can break out]. [There are birds that fly but do not chirp.] When such birds take flight into the air they crash this barrier, enabling the heavenly announcement to pass [through the opening]. That is the mystery behind the verse, "For a bird of the skies carries the sound" (*Koheles* 10:20). By soaring through the sky, the bird opens a path for the sound to traverse the opaque atmosphere. Other birds chirp. When they twitter, the trapped spiritual sound blends with their chirping, and together with the bird's song the heavenly sound becomes audible in this world. And so the verse ends, "And some winged creature may report the word."

Eitz Chaim, Shaar Ruach HaKodesh 5b–6a

Gilgul – Reincarnation

After death, the souls of the wicked are reincarnated in any of the four levels of creation: inanimate, vegetative, animal, man. Some evildoers come back one level below man, as an animal. Others come back as a plant; they have to rise two stages before they achieve *tikkun* (correction, restoration). Then there are those that are reincarnated as an inanimate mineral. They have to ascend three stages: from inanimate to vegetative, when they sprout from the earth and grow into plants. Then, when an animal eats that vegetation, they rise to the level of an animal. And when that animal is slaughtered and people eat it, they becomes part of a human being, and thereby they are repaired.

Sometimes they skip a stage. How so? If they were reincarnated as a vegetable, and a person eats this vegetable, they skip from the level of vegetable to that of man. Sometimes they skip from inanimate mineral to man. That happens when a grain of sand sticks to a salad, and a soul was reincarnated in that grain of sand. Then, when a person eats the salad [the soul imprisoned in the sand jumps from inanimate mineral to the level of man].

Eitz Chaim, Shaar HaGilgulim, Hakdamah 22

The Ten Martyrs

[Note: The Gemara relates that ten great *tannaim* were brutally killed by the Romans. Their martyrdom is recalled in the prayer *Eileh Ezkerah* that is recited on Yom Kippur during the *mussaf* service. One of the ten martyrs was Rabbi Akiva.]

> His eye saw every precious thing.
>
> (*Iyov* 28:10)

The Midrash (*Bemidbar Rabbah* 19) applies this verse to Rabbi Akiva, stating that Rabbi Akiva perceived visions that were more exalted than the revelation Moshe received on Mount Sinai.

The Kabbalistic interpretation of this passage is: The souls of Rabbi Akiva and the other nine martyrs were born of the ten drops [of semen] that came forth from Yosef. [When Potifar's wife tried to seduce Yosef, he subdued his passion by sticking his ten fingers into the ground, but ten drops were ejaculated (*Sotah* 36b).] The Gemara (ibid.) says that originally Yosef was worthy to have twelve tribes issue from him, just as his father Yaakov begat twelve tribes, but his procreative power was reduced [through the incident with Potifar's wife], and he had only two sons. [The ten drops were ejaculated when he gazed at Potifar's wife.] The Midrash (*Yalkut Shimoni, Vayeishev* 146) says that he did not want to look at her, but she forced him by pressing an iron bar on his throat. This is alluded to in the verse, "Yosef was sold as a slave...his soul came into irons" (*Tehillim* 105:17–18). When he glanced at her, the ten drops were discharged. These ten drops were incarnated as the Ten Martyrs....

Since Rabbi Akiva was the incarnation of one of Yosef's ten drops, his name was Akiva ben Yosef. Originally an ignorant shepherd, Rabbi Akiva was forty years old when he began to learn Torah and subsequently became the towering luminary Rabbi Akiva. Analogously, a *mikveh* must hold forty *se'ah* (a volume measurement) of water to purify a person from seminal emission.

Rabbi Akiva perceived more than Moshe, because Moshe attained forty-nine Gates of Wisdom, but Rabbi Akiva reached the fiftieth Gate of Wisdom.

Eitz Chaim, Shaar HaKavanos, Rosh HaShanah, p. 90

Don't Kill Animals Needlessly

The *Zohar* (*Parashas Yisro*) says that every animal was created for a purpose, and therefore, it is forbidden to kill a living creature needlessly. My master, the Ari, was careful not to kill even the tiniest insect, even if it annoyed him. The Sages say about the verse, "Even his foes will make peace with him" (*Mishlei* 16:7), that "his foes" refers to fleas.

Eitz Chaim, Shaar HaMitzvos, Parashas Noach

The Final Redemption

[The divine blessings in *Parashas Bechukosai* close with the words,] "You will eat very old grain and remove the old to make way for the new. I will place My sanctuary among you, and My Spirit will not reject you" (*Vayikra* 26:10).

This verse contains an allusion to the saying in the Gemara, "The son of David [Mashiach] will not come before all the [unborn] souls have passed through the life of this world" (*Yevamos* 63b).

Based on this Gemara, the *Zohar* (*Parashas Pekudei*, 253) says: Ever since the day the Beis HaMikdash was destroyed, no new souls have come into being. All existing souls are old souls that are being recycled until they have their *tikkun*. At that point Mashiach will come, and then new souls will come forth.

That idea is hinted at in the verse, "You will remove the old to make way for the new." The reference is to the old souls that existed before the new souls emerge. After the old souls have been repaired, Mashiach will come. That's why the verse continues, "I will place My sanctury among you," which means that [when the old souls have had their *tikkun*] the Beis HaMikdash will be rebuilt, may it happen speedily in our days. And that is when the new souls will enter into the world.

Eitz Chaim, Shaar HaPesukim, Parashas Bechukosai

The Greatness of the Ari HaKadosh

[Rabbi Chaim Vital relates:] The Ari HaKadosh told me that when he began to study Kabbalah he sometimes struggled for an entire week trying to understand one passage in the *Zohar*. He did not receive an answer from heaven because then it would not be his own Torah insight. So when he strained very hard to understand a difficult passage. All he was told from heaven was, "You pondered such-and-such problem, and your solution is correct. But you still have to dig a little deeper." Sometimes they would tell him from heaven, "You have made a mistake." He would then start all over again until he arrived at the truth.

The breadth and depth of his knowledge was limitless. He had the power to raise up before him the soul of a live or dead person of the early or later rabbinic sages. He would question it about future events and about secrets of the Torah. Eliyahu HaNavi would appear to him and would teach him. The Ari was able to tell by a person's face what was the root of his soul, and he could detect a mystical luminescence on a person's skin and hair. He could make sense of the chirping of birds and understood the meaning of the swishing sound of palm trees and rustling shrubs. He could even fathom the language of inanimate things and interpret the speech of a flame of a lamp or burning embers. He saw angels and spoke to them. He was an expert in the healing qualities of herbs and the remedies they afford. His prodigious greatness was sublime, and I am speaking from personal experience.

Eitz Chaim, Shaar Ruach HaKodesh 4b

Chapter 31
RABBI CHAIM VITAL

born: Tzefas, 1543
died: Damascus, Syria, 1620

Rabbi Chaim was the son of Rabbi Yosef Vital (Calabrisi), a highly respected *sofer* (scribe) in Tzefas, known for his great piety. Rabbi Chaim studied Talmud under Rabbi Moshe Alshich and learned Kabbalah from the prominent Kabbalist Rabbi Moshe Cordovero, the Remak. When Rabbi Yitzchak Luria, the Ari, arrived in Tzefas in 1570, Rabbi Chaim Vital became his foremost disciple and expounder of his school of thought, known as *shittas haAri*. The Ari selected him to record his profound mystical teachings, and when the Ari died in 1572 during an epidemic that ravaged Tzefas, Rabbi Chaim Vital was considered his successor and spiritual heir.

In 1576 Rabbi Chaim Vital began to lecture on Kabbalah to a large group of students. A saintly man, he gained the reputation of being a miracle worker. By applying practical Kabbalah, he cured many afflictions and exorcised spirits in Tzefas and during his travels through Syria and Egypt. He compiled the Ari's Kabbalistic teachings in *Eitz Chaim*.[1]

Among the other writings of Rabbi Chaim Vital are *Sefer HaGilgulim*,[2] on

---

1 Koretz, 1782; most recently, Tel Aviv, 1960.
2 Frankfurt am Main, 1684.

the transmigration of souls; *Shaarei Kedushah*,[1] on reward and punishment; *Likutei HaShas*,[2] a commentary on the Aggadic portions of the Talmud, and *Sefer HaLikutim*, an anthology of Torah thoughts. He was greatly admired by rabbis and Kabbalists alike but found a severe critic in Rabbi Yaakov Abulafia, the rabbi of Damascus (Reb Chaim lived in Damascus from 1594 until his death). In 1620, while preparing for his return to Tzefas, he fell ill and died.

Selections from the Writings of Rabbi Chaim Vital

[Note: Since Rabbi Chaim Vital's main work *Eitz Chaim* contains the teachings of his master, the Ari, the selections from *Eitz Chaim* are presented in the chapter of the Ari. A few personal notes of Rabbi Chaim Vital from *Sefer HaGilgulim* are offered here.]

Why the Ari Moved from Cairo to Tzefas

On Rosh Chodesh Adar, 1571, the Ari told me that while in Egypt he began to receive heavenly messages. He was told to move to Tzefas, because I, Chaim, was living there, and he was instructed to teach me [Kabbalah]. The Ari told me that he moved to Tzefas only because of me. What's more, he said that the main reason that his soul was reincarnated [and came down to this world] was for my sake, in order to make me perfect. He did not come into this world for his own benefit because he did not need to be reincarnated. He told me also that I was the only person he needed to teach, no one else. And since I was learning, it was not necessary for him to continue living in this world.[3]

Sefer HaGilgulim

---

1 Constantinople, 1734.
2 Livorno, 1784.
3 The Ari died at the young age of thirty-eight.

A Message from the Grave

The Ari told me also that my soul was on a higher level than that of many angels. On the first day of Chol HaMoed Pesach I went with him to the village Achbara. While there we entered the cave of Rabbi Yannai,[1] which is in an orchard. A spring flows from the narrow opening of the cave. The Ari told me, "The only one buried here is Rabbi Yannai; Rabbi Dusta'i and Rabbi Nehora'i, who are said to be buried here, are, in fact, not interred here."

The Ari's soul then attached itself to Rabbi Yannai's soul, and Rabbi Yannai told him: "I, Rabbi Yannai, am buried underneath this marker. You should know that the Holy One, blessed be He, told me: 'Tell Chaim Vital, the fellow who came along with you, that he should be careful not to engage in gossip or frivolous talk, and that he should be extremely humble. [If he does that,] I will be with him wherever he may be.'"

Sefer HaGilgulim, Shaar HaGilgulim, Hakdamah 38

Sleepless Nights over the *Zohar*

I once asked the Ari how he had attained his phenomenal Kabbalistic wisdom. He replied that he had worked very hard at it. I retorted: "But the Remak[2] and I myself have toiled very hard, too, [but we have not achieved your level of perfection]."

He answered: "True, you studied harder than anyone else in our time, but not as hard as I did. I spent many a sleepless night over just one paragraph in the *Zohar*. Sometimes I would seclude myself six nights in a row without sleep and immerse myself in one saying of the *Zohar*."

Sefer HaGilgulim, Shaar Ruach HaKodesh, 11b

---

1 Rabbi Yannai, an *amora* of the first generation, established a yeshivah in Achbara (*Berachos* 9a).
2 See ch. 29.

His Student in a Previous Existence

One day the Ari told me that I would attain lofty levels of Kabbalistic knowledge because I was eager to learn. He said that his soul would assist me, especially so since in a previous incarnation I also was his student. He added that I should always have him in mind, that this would help me a great deal.

Ibid.

A Drink from Miriam's Well

At first Rabbi Chaim Vital had difficulty understanding the intricate secrets the Ari revealed to him. Once, while the Ari and Rabbi Chaim Vital were in Teveriah, the Ari took Rabbi Chaim for a ride in a small boat. At a certain spot the Ari filled a cup with water and commanded Rabbi Chaim to drink. After he drank, the Ari assured him that from now on he would be able to absorb the sublime wisdom of Kabbalah, as the water he had given him to drink was from the biblical well of Miriam [which accompanied the Jewish people on their forty-year wandering through the Sinai Desert].

Ibid.

How the Hidden Manuscripts Were Published

Rabbi Chaim Vital kept his manuscripts tightly locked away, not allowing anyone to see them, as he feared that he would be punished — his life span shortened — for disseminating these "secrets of the Torah." Once, when he fell seriously ill, his brother, Rabbi Moshe, accepted five hundred gold coins from someone in return for the key to Rabbi Chaim's locked closet. Within three days about one hundred scribes copied most of the manuscripts, which were subsequently returned to their original place. That's how the Kabbalistic doctrine of the Ari began to circulate among the Kabbalists of Eretz Yisrael.

Even after he had put down the Ari's Kabbalah in writing, Rabbi Chaim still devoted considerable time and energy to explaining his master's teachings. He wrote explanations of difficult points, clarified concepts, and resolved contradictions in the Ari's system. Rabbi Chaim did not want these writings to be published and had them buried in a cemetery. However, a generation later, Rabbi Yaakov Tzemach and Rabbi Avraham Azulai received permission in a dream from Rabbi Chaim Vital to exhume the manuscripts, which they did. These manuscripts formed the nucleus of the many books of the Ari's Kabbalah, which were later published.

Ibid.

Study Torah and Talmud before Kabbalah

You should not say: I'd rather study Kabbalah than delve into the complexities of Torah, Mishnah, and Talmud. The Sages said about this: "You should not enter the orchard [of Kabbalah] before you filled your stomach with meat and wine [Torah and Talmud]." Learning Kabbalah without a thorough knowledge of Torah and Talmud is just like a soul without a body. A soul cannot act and earn a reward unless it is bound to a body and attains perfection by fulfilling the 613 mitzvos of the Torah. [Therefore, a thorough knowledge of the parameters of the mitzvos is required before engaging in the study of Kabbalah.]

Conversely, learning Mishnah and Talmud without devoting some time to the hidden facets of the Torah is comparable to a body steeped in darkness, without the light of a soul, "the lamp of God."

A Torah scholar should first engross himself in Torah, Mishnah, and Talmud, and only then should he get to know his Creator through the study of Kabbalah. That is what David told his son Shlomo, "Know the God of your father and serve Him with a perfect heart and a willing soul" (*Divrei HaYamim* I 28:9).

Introduction to Eitz Chaim

Chapter 32
RABBI AVRAHAM BEN MORDECHAI AZULAI

born: Fez, Morocco, 1570
died: Chevron, 1643

Rabbi Avraham Azulai, a Kabbalist and Talmudic scholar of note, was born to a family of Castilian refugees who had fled Spain in 1492 and settled in Morocco. Since his earliest youth he longed to travel to Eretz Yisrael in order to study Kabbalah under the disciples of the Ari and Rabbi Chaim Vital. His wish was not fulfilled until 1610, when he and his entire family sailed for Eretz Yisrael.

After a stormy journey, the flimsy ship docked at the port of Damietta in northeast Egypt, but hardly had the passengers disembarked when a sudden squall blew the ship out to sea, where it sank, taking all of Rabbi Avraham's possessions and books to the bottom of the Mediterranean. In recognition of the miracle of having escaped death, Rabbi Avraham's signature from that time on was in the form of a ship.

Eventually he settled in Chevron, but due to an epidemic he was forced to move to Yerushalayim in 1619. When the plague spread further he moved to Gaza, and when it abated he returned to Chevron.

Rabbi Avraham wrote a number of Kabbalistic works, including *Zoharei Chamah*[1] and *Or HaChamah*.[2] His *Chesed LeAvraham*,[3] fundamentals of Kabbalah according to the teachings of Rabbi Moshe Cordovero, became very popular. He had many distinguished descendants, but his most famous offspring is his great-great-grandson Rabbi Chaim Yosef David Azulai, the celebrated Kabbalist known as the "Chida."

Selections from the Writings of Rabbi Avraham Azulai

Satan Was Sidetracked

Our Sages tell us that for the first twelve months after a person's death, his soul periodically rises to heaven and returns to earth. At the end of twelve months, the soul ascends and does not come down anymore.

The secret is that since the soul was accustomed to living in the physical world, it is unable to soar and rise to Gan Eden immediately after death. You can compare it to what happens to small chicks. When they break through their egg shells [and emerge from their embryonic existence] they cannot fly at first, but gradually they learn to flutter and flap their wings. So, too, the soul. It takes twelve months [for it to shed its earthly habits] and gain the strength to rise to Gan Eden.

As long as Yosef was alive, his merit protected his brothers [in Egypt], and Satan was unable to lodge his accusations against them. But when Yosef died, and his soul was busy trying to ascend to Gan Eden, he could no longer protect the children of Israel. That gave Satan the opportunity to denounce the Jews. But God in His mercy diverted Satan and made him pounce on Iyov instead,[4] in order to save the Jews. As the Sages say: "You can compare it to a shepherd who was watching his flock when a wolf de-

---

1 Venice, 1655.
2 Pshemishl, 1896.
3 Amsterdam, 1685.

scended on his sheep. What did he do? He pushed one little goat to pacify the wolf and thereby saved the herd" (*Shemos Rabbah* 21:7).

Another reason [why Iyov was made to suffer] is that God wanted to try Iyov and see whether he would stand the test as Avraham did [at the *akeidah*]. But Iyov did not hold up, for he complained about his ordeal. However, Iyov agonized only for twelve months, [to keep Satan occupied] until Yosef's soul reached Gan Eden where he pleaded on behalf of the children of Israel. From that time on, Yosef protected Israel.

Chesed LeAvraham 50

Iyov Lived 210 Years

God does not let good deeds go unrewarded. [How was Iyov rewarded for his exemplary life?] ... He received his reward in this world. All his losses were restored to him twofold, and 140 years were added to his life. As it says, "After this, Iyov lived 140 years" (*Iyov* 12:16). This implies that up to this point he had lived seventy years, not counting the one year of his affliction which is not included, so that he actually lived a total of 211 years, but only the 210 good years count. Iyov died in the second year after the Exodus, around the time the spies were dispatched.[1] We know that the children of Israel were in Egypt for 210 years, and Iyov was born two years after they went down to into Egypt. Since he died two years after the Exodus, it follows that he lived 210 years.

Chesed LeAvraham 50

Closing the Eyes

> God said to Yaakov, "...Yosef will place his hands on your eyes."
> (*Bereishis 46:4*)

---

4   The book of *Iyov* relates that God gave permission to Satan to test the faith of the righteous Iyov by making him suffer a series of dreadful calamities.

1   For more on the identity of Iyov and when he lived, see *Bava Basra* 15a–b.

The portal to man's intellect are his eyes. The eyes see the physical form of things and convey the image to the brain by way of the optical nerve. So, when your eyes are open your brain perceives the things you are looking at. That's why it is a mitzvah to close your eyes when you pray, to shut out all physical impressions and focus your thoughts on abstract ideas.

Now, when a person dies, his connection to the physical world is cut off. During his life he enjoys serving God with tangible mitzvos, and when he dies his soul loses the benefit it derives from the tangible mitzvos of this world. But when a person leaves a decent and respectable son who fulfills the mitzvos in this world, the father above is crowned with the luminescence of the son's mitzvos, and through his son he derives the joy of the mitzvos. That is the deeper meaning of the phrase, "Yosef will place his hands on your eyes," meaning that in the World to Come Yaakov will derive spiritual delight from the mitzvos Yosef fulfills.

Chesed LeAvraham 51

The Small Bone that Lives On

The Midrash (*Vayikra Rabbah* 18:1) and the *Zohar* tell us that after a person dies the soul remains connected to the body. And even when the body is decomposed, this connection remains intact because of a small bone in the body that never disintegrates. This bone is like the yeast in the dough; it revives the body at the time of the resurrection. This bone, the size of a grain of barley, is round and situated beneath the brain inside the skull. It is not connected to any other bone, and it is covered with a network of little veins like a spider web. These tiny veins contain the genes of the five senses and the limbs, and from this bone the entire body is rebuilt. Through this indestructible bone the connection of the original body with its soul — its *kedushah* component — is reestablished. This is implied in the verse, "I will make your sanctuaries desolate" (*Vayikra* 26:31) — even though they are desolate, they still retain their sanctity.

When God created man, He did not mean for him to die. Man was intended to live forever. But when he sinned he brought death and nonbeing on himself. Nevertheless, death is not a permanent state, for man is destined to come back to life, as the Torah testifies in many places.[1] Therefore, death is not lasting, but rather a passing condition. Through this bone the powerful bond between body and soul remains intact until it returns to its original state, and therein lies the secret of resurrection.

Chesed LeAvraham 52

---

[1] For example, "I put to death and I revive" (*Devarim* 32:39).

Chapter 33
RABBI CHAIM IBN ATTAR
(Or HaChaim)

born: Sale, Morocco, 1696
died: Yerushalayim, 1743

Rabbi Chaim ibn Attar, the author of the Torah commentary *Or HaChaim*, was born into a wealthy family of descendants of Spanish exiles. He studied under his grandfather, an extremely pious man named also Rabbi Chaim ibn Attar (in line with the Sefardic custom of naming children after living relatives). Under his grandfather's tutelage he became a celebrated Kabbalist and halachist.

In the wake of persecutions, Rabbi Chaim was forced to wander from town to town until he decided to make his way to Yerushalayim, for, as he put it, "There is no place on earth that is really pure, except Eretz Yisrael." His travels brought him to Livorno, Italy, where he was received with great honor. Wherever he went he urged people to settle in Eretz Yisrael and "restore its ruins." There were many who heeded his call and migrated to Eretz Yisrael. In 1741, Rabbi Chaim himself embarked for Eretz Yisrael with a group of students and their families, altogether thirty people. This saintly scholar established Yeshivas Or HaChaim in Yerushalayim, which still exists today.

His commentary on the Torah, named *Or HaChaim*,[1] became enor-

---
1   First printed in Venice in 1742. Appears in all editions of *Chumash Mikraos*

mously popular and is studied avidly today, especially by chassidim. In this work he employs the four methods of exegesis: *peshat*, explaining the simple meaning; *derash*, homiletic interpretation; *remez*, allusion; and *sod*, the Kabbalistic, esoteric approach. Chassidim are wont to say that the Or HaChaim is a spark of the soul of Mashiach.

He is one of the four personalities that earned the title *hakadosh*, "the saintly," the other three being the Alshich HaKadosh, the Ari HaKadosh, and the Shelah HaKadosh.

The grave of the Or HaChaim on Har HaZeisim (the Mount of Olives) is visited by thousands every year.

Selections from the Kabbalistic Commentaries of Or HaChaim

Why Does the Torah Begin with the Letter *Beis*?

[Note: The letter *alef*, spelled *alef, lamed, pei*, can be read as *elef*, which means one thousand.]

In the beginning of God's creating heaven and earth, the earth was without form and empty....

(Bereishis 1:1)

It says in the *Zohar*[1] that [before God created the world] He created a thousand other worlds. The Sages call these worlds "Worlds of Yearning." The thousand worlds are hinted at in the verse, "*Ha'elef lecha Shlomo* — The thousand [worlds] are Yours, You to whom peace belongs" (*Shir HaShirim* 8:12).[2] Since the *alef* was already put to use when God created the *elef* (one thousand) worlds, the Torah begins with the letter *beis* of *bereishis*.

Alternately, God began the creation of this world with the letter *beis*

Gedolos, and printed separately and annotated by Or Bahir (Brooklyn, 1973).

1   Zohar Chadash, Bereishis 1:1, s.v. Tanu Rabbanan.
2   *Shir HaShirim* is a sublime allegory about the love between the Jewish people and God. The name *Shlomo* is symbolic of God, "the king to whom peace (*shalom*) belongs" (Rashi, *Shir HaShirim* 1:1).

[whose numeric value is two] because this world has two components: heaven and earth. [Since there existed a thousand worlds before this one], it does not say, "In the beginning God created"[1] because that would imply that this world was His first creation. And that is not so, because He created a thousand "Worlds of Yearning" before this world. Therefore it says, "In the beginning of God's creating heaven and earth" [but not in the beginning of *all* creations].

Avraham and the Three Angels

> [Avraham said to the three angels:] "Let some water be brought, and wash your feet. Rest under the tree. I will get a morsel of bread for you to refresh yourselves...."
>
> (Bereishis 18:4–5)

The *Zohar* says that the angels appeared in human form with bodies that God created by solidifying rarefied air.[2] When Avraham told them, "Let some water be brought," he meant water from the wellspring of the Torah. When he said, "Wash your feet," he hinted: Cleanse your physical body. With "rest under the tree" he had in mind the Torah, which is characterized as the "tree of life." That is why he said "*the* tree," meaning, "the specific tree" [i.e., the Torah]. By "a morsel of bread," he pointed to the mystical inner meaning of the Torah which he presented to them, "to refresh their spiritual essence." By emphasizing the "morsel of bread" he indicated that the bread he offered them [*lechem*] had a spiritual quality. For the numeric value of *lechem* is 78,[3] which is three times the numeric value of God's ineffable Name, Yud-Hei-Vav-Hei, [i.e., 26],[4] for 3 x 26 equals 78.

---

1   The conventional translation, "*In the beginning God created*," is problematic because the word *bereishis* is a *semichus* (construct) form and should be translated "In the beginning *of*."
2   *Zohar, Bereishis* 58a.
3   *Lamed* (30) + *ches* (8) + *mem* (40) = 78.
4   *Yud* (10) + *hei* (5) + *vav* (6) + *hei* (5) = 26.

Do Dreams Have Meaning?

> Two full years passed. Then Pharaoh had a dream. He was standing near the Nile....
>
> *(Bereishis 41:1)*

The phrase "Pharaoh had a dream" indicates that, while dreaming, Pharaoh realized that he was dreaming. Since he was seeing impossible things, he sensed [in his dream] that these creatures could not be factual, that it had to be a dream. Scripture tell us this in order to give us the sign by which to tell whether a dream contains a kernel of truth. The sign is this: If, while dreaming, you sense that you are clearheaded, and you are able to distinguish between fact and fiction, and you are aware that you are dreaming, that tells you that your dream is not an illusion or a mirage. Rather, you are being informed from Heaven about events that lie ahead.

Magnetized Sparks of Holiness

> [Moshe said to Pharaoh,] "Every firstborn in Egypt will die, from the firstborn of Pharaoh sitting on his throne to the firstborn of the slave girl behind the millstones. Every firstborn animal [will also die]."
>
> *(Shemos 11:5)*

> [Note: In this commentary the Or HaChaim touches on the subject of *nitzotzos hakedushah*, sparks of holiness. See ch. 3 for an explanation of this concept.]

The phrase "Every firstborn will die" suggests that they will die of natural causes. Why didn't God say, "I will slay every firstborn"?

You should know that every evil thing in this world must contain an ingredient that sustains it. For the essence of evil is death; therefore, without this life-giving nucleus, evil could not survive. What is this vitalizing ingredient? It is a minute particle of goodness that sustains even the worst evildoer. This will clarify a puzzling saying in the Gemara: "In the Messianic Age, the Holy One, blessed be He, will bring forth Satan and slaughter him in the presence of the righteous...." You may ask: How can an angel be slaughtered? The answer is: God slaughters Satan by removing his life-giving ingredient, the particle of goodness embedded in him.

There is something else you should know: Every source attracts its offshoots [and the Divine Light exerts a powerful pull on the imprisoned holy sparks that emanated from it]. That is the secret of how the sparks of holiness are freed [from the shells of impurity that enclose them]. The holy sparks are released by Jews studying the Torah. The great tzaddikim of old were able, just by looking at a wicked person, to extract his life-giving particle of goodness, so that he died on the spot.[1] The pure soul of the tzaddik acts as a magnet, pulling out the spark of goodness lodged in the soul of the evildoer, leaving him lifeless.

Now you can understand why God said, "Around midnight I will go out in the midst of Egypt. Every firstborn in Egypt will die." By the mere fact that God went out into Egypt, every firstborn automatically died, just as the evildoer perished when the tzaddik glanced at him. The life-giving particles of goodness were plucked out of the firstborn so that they died instantly.

Redeeming the Sparks of Holiness

> When the Ark would journey, Moshe said, "Arise, O God, and scatter Your enemies! Let Your foes flee before You!"
> *(Bemidbar 10:35)*

What enemies is Moshe referring to? It says (in *Eitz Chaim*[2] 1:332) that the reason the Jews had to wander in the desert for forty years was to seek out and set free the holy sparks that were imprisoned by the force of evil. Our verse tells us that when the Ark went forth it attracted [like a magnet] all the sparks of holiness. As soon as the sparks of holiness were released

---

1   See *Shabbos* 34a, where it says that Rabbi Yochanan ben Zakkai cast his eyes on an evil person and, as a result, he turned into a heap of bones.
2   The teachings of the Ari, recorded by his disciple, Rabbi Chaim Vital. See ch. 30.

from the shells [of evil that encased them], these shells exploded and disintegrated.

That is the deeper meaning of "Arise, O God, and scatter Your enemies!" The enemies are the shells of evil that attached themselves to the sparks of holiness [and when the sparks were set free, the shells crumbled]. Moshe said "Your enemies" in the plural, because the force of evil has many facets. The Gemara (*Yoma* 69b) says that there is a *yetzer hara* (evil impulse) of idol worship, of immorality....

[In a broader sense,] Moshe was asking God in this prayer to strengthen the power of *kedushah* in the Jewish people, and to enable them to overcome the force of evil and liberate [the sparks of *kedushah* wherever Jews happen to be].

Souls of Converts

> When you wage war against your enemies...you will take captives.
> If you see a beautiful woman among the prisoners and desire her,
> you may take her as a wife.
> (*Devarim* 21:10-11)

This chapter is hard to understand. Why did God allow a warrior to defile himself by marrying a heathen woman? This will only weaken our bond with God and cause God to despise us.

There is a mystical idea behind this, based on the *Zohar*.[1] It says there that when Adam sinned, many precious souls were captured by the *sitra achara*, the "other side" [i.e., the force of evil]. These souls are the souls of converts. You can tell that this is so when you realize how many towering Jewish luminaries are descendants of gentiles, such as Rus the Moabitess[2] Shemayah and Avtalyon,[3] and Onkelos the Convert,[4] and there are many more such great personalities.

---

1   *Zohar Chadash, Balak* 53.
2   The ancestress of David and Mashiach.

Let me reveal to you another secret. It happens sometimes that a pure soul becomes attached to an impure soul, and the pure soul is unable to rectify the impure soul. The pure soul then remains tied up until it is set free.

Sometimes a holy soul that is trapped among the unclean husks (*klippos*) convinces the heart in which it is held captive to do good and succeeds in driving out the evil element. Such souls are the souls of proselytes who feel an irresistible urge to convert, as Rus and Naamah.[1] And we see with our own eyes that there are many gentiles who have a strong impulse to convert to Judaism....

---

3   Teachers of Hillel, both were descendants of Sancheiriv, King of Ashur. Shemayah was *nasi* (leader or prince of the Jewish people) and Avtalyon was head of the *beis din* (rabbinical court).

4   Onkelos wrote the Aramaic [*Targum*] translation of the Torah that appears in the standard *chumashim*. He was a nephew of the Roman emperor Hadrian (*Avodah Zarah* 11a).

1   Naamah the Ammonite was the mother of King Rechavam (*Melachim* I 14:21).

Chapter 34
RABBI SHALOM MIZRACHI SHARABI
(Rashash)

born: Sharab, Yemen, 1720
died: Yerushalayim, 1782 (others say 1777)

Rabbi Shalom Mizrachi Sharabi, one of the outstanding Kabbalists of the Middle Eastern Sefardic communities, spent his early years in Sana, Yemen. As a young man he moved to Yerushalayim where he studied in the Kabbalist yeshivah Bet El.[1] Legend has it that he kept his phenomenal knowledge of Kabbalah a secret, working as caretaker of the yeshivah. When by accident his greatness in Torah and mysticism was discovered, he was immediately welcomed into the inner circle of the most advanced yeshivah students.

Before long Rabbi Shalom made a name for himself as a distinguished Kabbalist, and when the *rosh yeshivah*, Rabbi Gedalyah Chayon, passed away in 1751, Rabbi Shalom was appointed as his successor. His reputation as a divinely inspired person spread rapidly, and many tales about his miraculous cures and other marvels began making the rounds. In 1754, at thirty years of age, he was considered one of the leading rabbis of

---

1   Founded in 1737.

Yerushalayim, and his signature appears alongside that of Rabbi Chaim Yosef David Azulai (the Chida) on various official documents of the Yerushalayim community.

Under Rashash's leadership, the learning at the yeshivah Bet El focused exclusively on the teachings of the Ari, as recorded by Rabbi Chaim Vital. Rashash's books, which reflect his piety and erudition, greatly influenced the thinking of the scholars of his day and later generations. His *Emes VeShalom*[1] is a commentary on the Ari's *Eitz Chaim*; the second part, *Nehar Shalom*,[2] deals with the meditations that go with the various prayers.

It has become a custom for admirers of Rashash to assemble in Yeshivas Bet El on the tenth of Shevat, the anniversary of his passing, to study his works and sing a special song that was composed in his memory. His writings, which are very profound and esoteric, can be understood only by accomplished Kabbalists and cannot be translated.

A descendant of Rashash, also called Rabbi Shalom Sharabi, was a famous Kabbalist in Eretz Yisrael who passed away a few years ago.

---

1   Salonica, 1806.
2   Jerusalem, 1866/67.

Chapter 35
RABBI CHAIM YOSEF DAVID AZULAI
(Chida)

born: Yerushalayim, 1724
died: Livorno, Italy, 1806

Rabbi Chaim Yosef David Azulai, known by the acronym of his name, Chida, was the son of Rabbi Yitzchak Zerachyah Azulai and descendant of a line of famous rabbis of Castile, Spain. Studying under the great teachers of Yerushalayim — Rabbi Yonah Navon, Rabbi Yitzchak Rappaport, and the towering Kabbalist Rabbi Chaim ibn Attar (author of *Or HaChaim*) — he displayed early signs of genius and piety. Leading a life of self-denial, he ate sparingly and abstained from worldly delights. When he was only twenty years old, he was acclaimed as one of the foremost Torah scholars in Eretz Yisrael and was invited to serve as a member of the *beis din* of Rabbi Meyuchas in Yerushalayim.

Thirsting for knowledge of Kabbalah, he entered the yeshivah of the famous Kabbalist Rabbi Shalom Mizrachi Sharabi, where he soon made a name for himself as an outstanding Kabbalist.

In 1755, the leaders of the Yerushalayim community sent him to Europe on a fund-raising mission on behalf of the needy of Eretz Yisrael. On his travels through Italy, France, Germany, and the Netherlands, he gave rousing sermons and profound lectures in halachah. His successful first journey led to many similar missions. Everywhere he went he was received with great honor by communal leaders and rabbis who asked him their unresolved questions. Even princes, dukes, and ambassadors paid homage to him, asking for his blessings. He used his years of traveling to study ancient manuscripts and long-lost books which he discovered in various collections and libraries, including the Vatican library. The product of his research is the famous *Shem HaGedolim*,[1] an authoritative bibliography containing the combined biographies of all the prominent sages from the time of the *geonim* until his time.

A prolific author, the Chida wrote a large number of books on halachah, Aggadah, ethics, and Kabbalah. To name just a few titles: *Torah Or, Nachal Kedumim,*[2] *Chomas Anach,*[3] *Petach Einayim,*[4] and *P'nei David.*[5] His Torah commentary became a basic text for the interpretation of Torah, both in its plain meaning and through the prism of Kabbalistic thought. Popular tradition credits him with authoring eighty-three books, one for each year of his life. However, to date only half of his works have been published.

Selections from the Works of the Chida

The Reason for the Four Exiles[6]

> In the beginning God created heaven and earth.
> *(Bereishis 1:1)*

---

[1] Vilna, 1853, in three volumes, comprising the names of over 1,300 scholars and the titles of over 2,000 books.
[2] Livorno, 1795.
[3] Pisa, 1803
[4] Livorno, 1793, a commentary on *Ein Yaakov*.
[5] Livorno, 1792.
[6] The Babylonian, Persian, Greek, and Roman exiles.

Man cannot live without a soul. Neither can the physical world exist without the life force from the higher world. But how does this life force descend from heaven to earth? Through the creation of man. For man contains elements of the four worlds [Atzilus (Emanation), Beri'ah (Creation), Yetzirah (Formation), Asiyah (Action)]. When man fulfills the Creator's will, his soul is sanctified and becomes the pipeline through which God's abundant blessings flow down from heaven to the universe and keep it intact.

The Ari says that the reason for Israel's exile among the seventy nations of the world is so that the Jews should extricate the *nitzotzos hakedushah* (sparks of holiness) that mingled with the *klippos* (shells of impurity) after Adam's sin.[1] The Sages remark: If one Jew is captured by a nation, he alone is able to free all sparks locked up in the *klippos* [shells of impurity of that nation].

This ties in with the saying of the Sages [regarding the four exiles of the Jewish people]: " 'The earth was without form' alludes to [exile in the Kingdom of] Babylonia; 'and empty' alludes to [the exile in] Persia; 'and darkness' refers to the Greek exile; 'on the surface of the deep' hints at the [exile of the] evil Roman empire [i.e., our present exile]; 'and the Divine Presence hovered' points to the Messianic King" (*Bereishis Rabbah* 1:1). This means that the purpose of the four exiles is to enable the Jewish people by means of the Torah and the *Shechinah* to retrieve all the sparks that are imprisoned in the *klippos* of those nations. And when that task is completed, Mashiach will come.

Devarim Achadim 19

Noach's Two Reincarnations

These are the offspring of Noach. Noach was a righteous man, perfect in his generations....

(*Bereishis* 6:9)

---

[1] See ch. 3.

[The verse begins by stating that it is going to list the offspring of Noach. Instead, it proceeds to speak about Noach himself. Are we discussing Noach's offspring or his good deeds?]

The Ari says that a soul that returns to life in a new incarnation is called "father," and the person in whom this soul is reincarnated is called "son." The Ari further says that Noach was reincarnated twice: once as Yosef and again as Moshe. That's why the present passage mentions the name *Noach* twice in succession. Yosef is the epitome of a righteous man [and since Noach came back to life as Yosef, it says, "Noach was a righteous man"]. Moshe was the most perfect man who ever lived; [and since Noach became Moshe] our verse says that Noach was "perfect." The verse then says, "in his generations" (plural), implying that Noach was reincarnated in two different generations [as Yosef and as Moshe].

Nachal Kedumim, Parashas Noach

An Amazing *Gematria*

Lot looked up and saw that the entire Jordan Plain had plenty of water....

(*Bereishis* 13:10)

The Ari HaKadosh says that the good element of Adam's soul was reincarnated in Avraham, Yitzchak, and Yaakov. The evil part of his soul was reincarnated in Yishmael, Lot, and Esav. This is alluded to in the verse, "A man's stumbling [in sin] undermines [his] sanctity" (*Mishlei* 20:25). [The Hebrew word for "man" is *adam*; the Hebrew for "undermines" is *yala*, spelled *yud, lamed, ayin*.] Now *yud, lamed, ayin* is the acronym of the initials of Yishmael, Lot, and Esav. These three men undermine "the sanctity of *adam*," meaning, they constitute the bad part of Adam's soul.

This idea is supported by a striking *gematria*,[1] for the name *Lot* (*lamed* = 30, *vav* = 6, *tes* = 9) has the same numeric value as *Adam* (*alef* = 1, *dalet* = 4,

---

1 The method of using letters as numerals and converting words into their numeric value.

mem = 40), both amounting to 45. And remember, the Hebrew noun *lot* means "curse,"[1] curse alluding to the fact that Lot came from the bad side of Adam's soul.

But there is more: If you combine the last letters of Yishmael, Esav, and Lot [*lamed, vav, tes*] you obtain the name Lot!

Now consider the mysterious ways of God. Lot — the evil side of Adam's soul — was the ancestor of King David,[2] who descended from the good side of Adam's soul [i.e., Avraham]! This tells you that inside the very core of evil there resides a spark of good [that keeps the evil alive. Once the spark of good is removed, the evil shell collapses and disintegrates].

Chomas Anach, Parashas Lech Lecha

Eliezer's Test

> [Note: The *Sefirah* of *Gevurah* is personified by Yitzchak, who allowed himself to be bound on the altar of the *akeidah*. The antithesis of *Gevurah* is the *Sefirah* of *Chesed*, exemplified by Avraham. And remember, the *Sefirah* of *Malchus* symbolizes the woman.]

> [Eliezer, Avraham's servant, said,] "If I say to a girl, 'Tip over your jug, and let me have a drink,' and she replies, 'Drink, and I will also water your camels,' she will be the one whom You have designated for Your servant Yitzchak. [If there is such a girl] I will know that you have done a kindness [*chesed*] for my master."
>
> (*Bereishis* 24:14)

[Why did Eliezer devise this test?] Perhaps he knew that Yitzchak embodied the attribute of *Gevurah*. He knew also that, in general, women have an innate tendency toward stern justice. Now, if Yitzchak's future wife would

---

1   The Aramaic words *letat* and *letuta* from the root *lot* mean curse; see *Sanhedrin* 48b, *Berachos* 7a, and *Niddah* 13b.

2   As a result of an incestuous union with his daughter, Lot fathered a son, Moav, who was the progenitor of Rus the Moabitess. Rus, in turn, was the ancestress of David, who is the ancestor of Mashiach. This proves that hidden in the greatest depravity there is a kernel of *kedushah*.

be stern and unyielding by nature, she would not be a suitable match for Yitzchak, who is the pillar of strict justice. If they were to get married, their shared rigidity would grow exponentially. They would not get along with Avraham, the pillar of *chesed*. It would come to the point that they would have to part company with Avraham. On the other hand, it would be wonderful if the personality of Yitzchak's wife would be a blend of justice and kindness, if her character would be stringency "sweetened" with kindness.

With his test Eliezer wanted to determine whether the girl at the well was kind, gracious, and tenderhearted. If indeed that was her character, she would be a perfect match for Yitzchak.

P'nei David, Parashas Chayei Sarah

Mordechai Rectifies Yaakov's Shortcoming

[When Yaakov saw that Esav was coming] he went ahead of [his family] and bowed down seven times until he reached his brother.

(Bereishis 33:3)

It says in *Sefer HaKinuyim* that Mordechai was the reincarnation of Yaakov and Haman the reincarnation of Esav. Since Yaakov did wrong by bowing before Esav seven times, Mordechai came and repaired Yaakov's failing by refusing to bow down to Haman.[1]

The question is, how could Yaakov, the most perfect of the patriarchs, bow down to the wicked Esav? He surely knew that it is forbidden to greet an evildoer. [The answer is:] Yaakov did not do anything wrong. When he prostrated himself he was bowing down to the *Shechinah* that was coming to meet him.

---

1 This is supported by the fact that in *Megillas Esther*, it says seven times that Mordechai did not bow to Haman. "Mordechai would not bow (1) and would not prostrate (2) himself" (in 3:2 and again in 3:5, which makes 4); "Mordechai did not stand up (5) and did not stir (6) before [Haman]" (5:9); and "yet all this is worth nothing to me when I see Mordechai sitting [and not bowing down to me] at the king's gate (7)" (5:13) (Rabbi Dovid Rockove, Lakewood, N.J.).

[Then why is it counted as a failing that needs rectification?] Yaakov was guilty of giving a false impression to his wives and his children, causing them to think that he was bowing down to Esav. [Mordechai repaired this misstep by refusing to bow down to Haman.]

Midbar Kedeimos, Parashas Vayishlach

Yosef's Temptation

[Note: Yosef exemplifies the *Sefirah* of *Yesod*, the sixth of the lower *Sefiros*. *Yesod* channels the Divine Light to *Malchus*, the seventh and last *Sefirah*. Note also that *Yesod* is associated with the reproductive organ, "the organ that gives," since procreation is the foundation of the world. *Yesod* is also connected with *milah*, the holy sign of circumcision. *Malchus*, the *Sefirah* that receives the Light from *Yesod*, represents the female gender. Since Yosef repressed his *yetzer hara* and refused to be seduced, he is called *tzaddik yesod olam*, "the tzaddik who is foundation of the world."]

> After these events, his master's wife cast her eyes upon Yosef and she said, "Lie with me." But he adamantly refused.... He would not listen to her to be with her.
>
> *(Bereishis 39:7–10)*

The Midrash says that Potifar's wife danced, swayed, and spun around and went to great lengths to entice Yosef. Why did she try so hard?

The Ari HaKadosh says that the purpose of the Egyptian bondage was to enable the Jews to release the *nitzotzos hakedushah* that were embedded in Egypt. By bringing his father and his brothers to Egypt, Yosef paved the way for the Egyptian exile. Yosef, who represents the *Sefirah* of *Yesod*, was sold into slavery in Egypt, the land of the greatest depravity, the embodiment of the *sitra achara* ["the other side," i.e., the *yetzer hara*, Satan]. Had Yosef sinned [with Potifar's wife], the world would have been destroyed, because then the *sitra achara* would have defeated the holy *Yesod*, and the captive holy sparks could never be freed through the Egyptian bondage.

That's why the *sitra achara* took on the form of Potifar's wife and made every effort to seduce Yosef, for thereby the holy *Yesod* would be polluted in the Egyptian swamp of immorality. But Yosef subdued his *yetzer hara*. That's why he became the ruler over Egypt.

We know that Yosef was the reincarnation of Adam's soul. Menaced by the provocative allure of Potifar's wife, he sensed that the *sitra achara* was about to snare his soul along with Adam's soul. This is suggested by the cantillation mark *shalsheles*[1] (literally, "chain") on the word *vayima'ein*, "he adamantly refused." The chain-like chant of *shalsheles* implies that Yosef realized that to sin with this woman was not just a personal one-time lapse, but that it would touch off a chain reaction of far-reaching historic repercussions. By rejecting her advances, Yosef made it possible for the children of Israel to come to Egypt to retrieve the sparks that had fallen in the wake of Adam's sin. Thus Yosef repaired Adam's sin.

Now consider this: Adam sinned by yielding to the enticement of a woman [Chavah] who had been tricked by the serpent [i.e., the *sitra achara*]. By resolutely rebuffing the seduction of a woman who was the embodiment of the *sitra achara*, Yosef rectifed Adam's transgression.

P'nei David, Parashas Vayeishev

Adam's Unblemished Larynx

> The voice is Yaakov's voice, but the hands are the hands of Esav.
> *(Bereishis 27:22)*

It is very fitting that the voice should be associated with Yaakov. The author of *Kotnos Or* explains that Yaakov's soul stemmed from Adam's larynx. [Note: Many parts of Adam's body participated in the eating of the forbidden fruit: his hands, feet, mouth, and digestive system all took part in it.] But we know that Adam's respiratory system [his lungs, trachea (windpipe), and larynx (voice box)] did not savor the forbidden fruit [since food goes down the esophagus and bypasses the windpipe]. Therefore, Adam's larynx was not stained by sin. [Note: The larynx is seated at

---

[1] A drawn-out, rolling chant that occurs only four times in the Torah.

the top of the windpipe. Speech is caused by pushing air from the lungs through the windpipe and the larynx.]

Since Yaakov's voice came from Adam's larynx, it was pure and untarnished by sin. In light of this we can understand the importance of Torah study. As the Midrash puts it, "When Yaakov's voice is heard in the study halls, Esav's hands are powerless" (*Bereishis Rabbah* 68). Because when Jews are learning Torah they use their larynx, the organ that was not marred by Adam's transgression. That is also the reason why slander and gossip are such grave offenses, because the person who slanders defiles an unblemished organ. Therefore, in the merit of Torah study [and refraining from *lashon hara*], the Redemption will come.

P'nei David, Parashas Toldos

The Journey through the Wilderness

> These are the journeys of the children of Israel.... Moshe recorded their stops along the way at God's command.
>
> (*Bemidbar 33:1*)

It is a well-known fact that the reason for the forty-year wandering through the Sinai wilderness was to enable the Jews to extricate the *nitzotzos hakedushah* that were lodged there. Since the *klippos* that imprisoned the sparks were very strong, it took all 600,000 Jews, together with Moshe, Aharon, and the Aron to release the holy sparks. Therefore it says, "When the Aron went forth, Moshe said, 'Arise, O God, and scatter Your enemies! Let Your foes flee before You!' " (ibid. 10:35).

What enemies did God have in that desolate desert? Why did Moshe have to make this proclamation each time they moved on?

The enemies of God were none other than the *klippos* and the forces of impurity [that abounded in the desert]. And just as the Jews took all the holy sparks out of Egypt, they rectified the entire vast wilderness of Sinai.

It says that they traveled "at God's command," because only God knew how long it would take to restore the area at each stop along the way. In a related matter, Kabbalists say that when you read in the Torah, *Nevi'im*, or *Kesuvim* about a certain nation, you are releasing the holy sparks that are imprisoned there.

P'nei David, Parashas Massei

Why the Chida Became a Traveler

Three Kabbalists, the Chida, Rabbi Chaim de la Rosa, and their teacher Rabbi Shalom Mizrachi Sharabi (known as the Rashash), decided to make a supreme effort to bring an end to the *galus*. Thinking that the time was ripe, they went into seclusion and sanctified themselves through mortification and various ascetic disciplines. Then they fasted for three days straight during which time they prayed and meditated on the hidden mysteries of unifying God's name. Sadly, the generation was not worthy of the *geulah* (final redemption). At the end of the three days of fasting, to their great consternation, they suddenly heard a *bas kol* [heavenly voice] announcing, "Dear children, you are not allowed to hasten the end of the *galus* before its time. And since you are such a powerful spiritual threesome, you must break up, and one of you must leave Eretz Yisrael."

Since the *bas kol* did not specify who was to go into exile, they cast lots, and the lot fell on the Chida. Without a moment's hesitation, the Chida accepted the decision and immediately set out on his wanderings.

Introduction to Sefer Chida

Part VI
EUROPEAN KABBALISTS OF THE SEVENTEENTH AND EIGHTEENTH CENTURIES

Introduction
EUROPEAN KABBALISTS OF THE SEVENTEENTH AND EIGHTEENTH CENTURIES

In 1670, the false *mashiach* Shabsai Tzvi turned his back on Judaism and was exposed as an imposter. His pseudomessianic movement, based on fraudulent Kabbalistic interpretations, collapsed, causing bitter disillusionment among the Jewish masses. In the wake of the debacle, many leading rabbis opposed the public study of Kabbalah. Nevertheless, the seventeenth century produced a number of prodigious Kabbalists whose works made an enduring impact.

In western Europe we encounter the great Kabbalist Menashe ben Israel, rabbi of Amsterdam. In Hamburg, the eminent scholar and Kabbalist Rabbi Yonasan Eibeschutz was appointed rabbi of the community. The election of an outstanding Kabbalist greatly rankled the opponents of the study of Kabbalah. Rabbi Yonasan was persecuted and tormented by communal leaders who, in all sincerity, took a dim view of his practice of writing Kabbalistic amulets, suspecting him of being a closet follower of Shabsai Tzvi.

Around that time there lived in Italy the brilliant Rabbi Moshe Chaim

Luzzato (the Ramchal), who wrote a number of Kabbalistic treatises and whose *Mesillas Yesharim* has greatly influenced Jewish thought to this day. It is one of the basic texts of the *Mussar* Movement. In the aftermath of the Shabsai Tzvi excesses, the Ramchal, like Rabbi Yonasan Eibeschutz, was attacked for his love of Kabbalah and forced to leave his native Italy.

In eastern Europe there lived the foremost Kabbalist of the eighteenth and later centuries, the Gaon of Vilna. Although at that time many rabbis looked askance at the public study of Kabbalah, no one criticized the Gaon. Revered throughout the world for his piety and phenomenal knowledge in the revealed and mystical aspects of the Torah, he was the supreme scholar of his time, a man whose depth and breadth of knowledge seemed limitless.

His illustrious student, Rabbi Chaim of Volozhin, was the founder of the great Volozhiner Yeshivah. He wrote *Nefesh HaChaim*, a seminal work on basic Torah weltanschauung, interspersed with Kabbalistic interpretations.

Chapter 36
RABBI MENASHE BEN ISRAEL
(Nishmas Chaim)

born: Island of Madeira, Portugal, 1604
died: Middelburg, Holland, 1657

Rabbi Menashe ben Israel, the son of Marranos, was taken in infancy to Amsterdam, where many Marranos found refuge from the Spanish Inquisition. His father returned to Judaism, adopted the name Yosef ben Israel, and called his two sons Menashe and Efrayim.[1]

Young Menashe studied under Rabbi Yitzchak Uziel,[2] the chief rabbi of the Amsterdam Sefardic community. He excelled in his Talmudic studies, was proficient in science and philosophy, and fluent in ten languages. At the age of fifteen he gave a public lecture, and at the age of seventeen he wrote his first book, *Safah Berurah* on Hebrew grammar.

On the death of Rabbi Yitzchak Uziel in 1620, the eighteen-year-old Menashe was appointed to succeed him as rabbi of the Sefardic community, Neveh Shalom. In 1627 he established the first Jewish printing press in Holland and used it to print all the Jewish literature needed by the community. Admired by Jews and non-Jews alike, he communicated with many Christian theologians, and it is said that Cromwell was persuaded to recommend

---

1   The names of the Biblical Yosef's two sons.
2   1550–1622.

the readmission of Jews to England by Rabbi Menashe's work *Esperanca de Israel*.[1] In it Rabbi Menashe argued that the American Indians were the descendants of the ten lost tribes, and that, therefore, the New World was already inhabited by Jews. Among his non-Jewish friends was the famous Dutch painter Rembrandt van Rijn, who made an etching of Rabbi Menashe, and the Dutch jurist and statesman Hugo de Groot (Hugo Grotius).

In 1639 the three Sefardic communities in Amsterdam united and designated Rabbi Shaul Mortera as rabbi and Rabbi Yitzchak Abohab as his assistant. Rabbi Menashe was given a minor appointment, and he now found himself without an adequate income. He decided to move to Brazil, which had a large Jewish population. Just then the community in Brazil selected Rabbi Abohab as their rabbi, and the Amsterdam *kehillah* (community) chose Rabbi Menashe as their new assistant rabbi.

In 1644, the wealthy Pereira brothers founded a yeshivah and appointed Rabbi Menashe as its head. In 1655 Rabbi Menashe traveled to England to plead for the right of Jews to settle there. (Jews had been banished from England in 1290.) Oliver Cromwell granted him an audience, but stopped short of officially granting Rabbi Menashe's plea. He did agree to let Jews live in England and practice their religion on an informal basis. Only in 1753 were Jews granted English citizenship.

Soon after his return from England, in 1657, Rabbi Menashe ben Israel died, at the age of fifty-three. Almost all of his twenty-six works were written in Portuguese, Spanish, or Latin. One of his Hebrew books is *Nishmas Chaim*,[2] an important work that deals with Kabbalistic thoughts on the soul, afterlife, Gan Eden, and Gehinnom. The book reflects Rabbi Menashe's profound knowledge of the writings of the early and later Kabbalists. It gained wide acceptance in the entire Jewish world, especially among former Marranos, who were confused by the Christian theology that was instilled in them during their youth.

---

1   "*Hope of Israel*," Amsterdam, 1650, written in Latin.
2   Amsterdam, 1652.

Selections from Nishmas Chaim

Body and Soul

Although secular scholars believe that the soul is created together with the body, Jewish thinkers are firmly convinced that all souls were created during the six days of Creation. It says in *Midrash Tanchuma* (*Parashas Pekudei*): All souls, from Adam until the end of the world, were created during the six days of Creation. All of them were in Gan Eden, and all of them were present at the giving of the Torah. For it says, "I am making this covenant both with those who are standing here with us today...and with those who are not here with us today" (*Devarim* 29:14). Now how could God make a covenant with people who are nonexistent?

Here is what it means: Not only did God make His covenant with all the people who were standing at Mount Sinai with body and soul, but He made the covenant also with the souls that were created at Creation and that were present at Sinai without a body. These unborn souls also accepted the oath of Mount Sinai. That's why the word *standing* is mentioned in the present verse. It is used in [the sense of "existing in the heavenly realm"]. It has the same thrust in [the verse], "I will give you strides among those who are *standing* here" (*Zecharyah* 3:7), where "those who are standing" refers to the angels in the World to Come.

This is discussed at length in *Pardes Rimonim* 65a.[1] In the same vein, the Sages say: "[One of the seven heavens is called] 'Aravos.' It is the dwelling place of the souls of the righteous that will be created in time to come" (*Chagigah* 12b). And so it says: "The Son of David [Mashiach] will not come before all the souls in *Guf* [the heavenly treasure house inhabited by the souls of the unborn] will have been disposed of" (*Yevamos* 62a).

Nishmas Chaim 2:16

---

1 By Rabbi Moshe Cordovero (Remak); see ch. 29.

When Does the Soul Enter the Body?

All Jewish sages agree that the Divine soul enters the body in the earliest stages of gestation, well before birth. Proof of this is the *gemara* in *Niddah* 30b:

"Rabbi Simla'i lectured: What does an embryo look like in its mother's womb? It looks like a folded ledger. Its hands rest on its two temples, its two elbows on its two legs, and its two heels rest against its buttocks. Its head lies between its knees, its mouth is closed and its navel is open. It eats what its mother eats and drinks what its mother drinks, but it does not defecate, because that would kill the mother. But as soon as it is born, the closed organ [the mouth] opens, and the open one [the navel] closes, for if that would not happen, the infant could not live even one single hour. A lamp burns above [the embryo's] head, and it looks and sees from one end of the world to the other,[1] as it says, 'When His lamp would shine over my head, and I would walk in the dark by His light' (*Iyov* 29:3). This should not surprise you, for a person sleeping here [in Babylonia] might see Spain in his dream. And a person is never happier than in his prenatal existence.... The embryo is taught the entire Torah, ... and as soon as it enters the world, an angel comes, taps it gently on its mouth, and makes it forget all the Torah completely...."

The upshot of this is that God breathes the soul into man at conception. All Jewish sages are sure of this.

I know that there are people who have doubts about this and who think that the soul enters the body only at birth. They quote the following *beraisa* in support of their view:

"If a woman is in labor and her life is in danger, [then, if the fetus sticks out a limb,] it may be cut off because the fetus is considered a potential murderer [of the mother]. But once the baby's head has come out, he may

---

[1] While the embryo is in the womb, the *yetzer hara* has no power over it. Therefore it enjoys the pure primordial light that was set aside for tzaddim (*Anaf Yosef* on *Niddah* 30b).

not be harmed, because one life may not be taken to save another" (*Sanhedrin* 72b). [They cite the fact that the fetus that sticks out a limb may be killed as proof that before birth the fetus has no soul.]

In short, my answer is: The unborn fetus is considered part of the mother. For that reason a woman does not menstruate during pregnacy, because these fluids are nourishment for the embryo. For the same reason, if a pregnant woman is condemned to death, she is executed and her unborn child dies along with her. The gist of all this is that God gives man a pure soul at conception, and all Jewish sages believe this implicitly.

Nishmas Chaim 2:18

The Fire of Gehinnom

After death, the souls of evildoers are judged according to their deeds. That is what Yechezkel had in mind when he said, "Behold, all souls are Mine, like the soul of the father, so the soul of the son, they are Mine. The soul that sins – it shall die" (*Yechezkel* 18:4). But then he says, "As for the wicked man, if he repents of all the sins he committed, and he observes all My decrees, and practices justice and righteousness, he shall surely live, he shall not die" (*Yechezkel* 18:21).... Shlomo had this to say about Gehinnom, "Can a man walk on coals without his feet being scorched? So is one who consorts with his friend's wife, anyone who touches her will not go unpunished" (*Mishlei* 6:28–29). Which means: he will not go unpunished by the judgment of Gehinnom....

But you should know that even the wicked who go down into Gehinnom and do not come up enjoy a respite on Shabbos. That's why Shabbos is called a delight, for Shabbos brings contentment to souls in the higher realm and to the souls in the nether world. The Ramban[1] in *Shaar HaGemul* says that every Shabbos eve the angel that is in charge of the souls announces, "All the souls of the wicked may take a break!" And they are left alone the entire Shabbos. At the conclusion of Shabbos, as

---

1   Rabbi Moshe ben Nachman; see ch. 12.

soon as it gets dark, the angel who is in charge of the spirits shouts, "All evildoers, back into Gehinnom! Shabbos is over!" That's why we drag out the *maariv* (nighttime prayer) service of *motza'ei Shabbos* (Saturday nigiht) by saying *Vihi No'am*, and we say it very slowly [to give the evildoers a few more minutes of relief].

Nishmas Chaim 1:12, 14

The Soul of a Jew

Rabbi Shimon bar Yochai repeatedly says in the *Zohar* that the souls of Israel are on a higher level than the souls of other nations. He says in *Parashas Emor* (p. 223): "The Jewish people have the merit that God gave them souls that are holier and emanate from a holier place than the souls of all other nations. [God did this] in order that [the Jews] should keep His commandments."

The source for this can be found in the *Zohar*: "Rabbi Abba said: In the phrase 'Man became a living soul' (*Bereishis* 2:7), the words *nefesh chayah*, 'living soul,' refer to Israel, because they are the children of the Holy One, blessed be He, and their holy souls spring forth from Him. And where do the souls of the idolatrous nations come from? Rabbi Elazar said: From the left side [i.e., the *Sefirah* of the left side, *Gevurah*, the side that symbolizes strictness and harsh justice]" (*Zohar, Bereishis* 125).[1]

Rabbi Yehudah HaLevi in his *Kuzari* expresses the same idea. He says: "We are now in the year 4500 [from Creation].[2] The Torah records the lives of Adam, Sheis, Enosh, down to Noach, then Shem, and Ever, to Avraham, Yitzchak and Yaakov, and on to Moshe. These men were the elite and nobility of their generation. Though they had many children, most of [these children] resembled their fathers only outwardly, like shells of a fruit, lacking their fathers' Divine fervor" (*Kuzari* 1:47).

---

1   It cannot be stressed enough that these are metaphysical concepts and should not be taken literally.
2   This corresponds to the year 740 C.E.

The children were different because of their souls. That's why it says, "I have separated you out from among the nations to be Mine" (*Vayikra* 20:26). And, "You will be a kingdom of priests and a holy nation to Me" (*Shemos* 19:6). That is the deeper meaning of the saying: "Rabbi Shimon ben Yochai said: It says, 'Only you are called Adam' (*Yechezkel* 34:31), but the nations of the world are not called Adam" (*Yevamos* 61a; *Bava Metzia* 114b). Israel is called Adam because of the preciousness of their soul. The name Adam refers to the human soul, not to the flesh. As it says, "A man's [Adam] soul is the lamp of God" (*Mishlei* 20:27).

Nishmas Chaim 2:7

The Seven Days of Shivah

We have proof that Heaven demands that the dead should be mourned and eulogized for seven days, for it says in the Gemara: "Abaya and Rava eulogized Rabbah bar Nachmani for three days when a message came down from Heaven: 'Any person that leaves now will be put under a ban.' So they eulogized him for seven days. This time a message came down from heaven: 'Now you may go home in peace' " (*Bava Metzia* 86a).

But the clearest proof [for the seven-day mourning period] is found in the *Zohar*. It says there: "Rabbi Yehudah said: For seven days the soul [of the deceased] goes from its home to the grave and from the grave back to its home. It mourns its body, as it says, 'He [the deceased] feels only the pain of his flesh, and his soul will mourn over him' (*Iyov* 14:22). When the soul comes home it sees the mourners grieving and lamenting. After seven days, while the body is in its resting place, the soul ascends to the heavenly Me'aras HaMachpeilah (the Cave of Machpeilah).[1] There it is judged. It then goes up to the upper regions until it reaches its place in Gan Eden."

Nishmas Chaim 3:5

---

1   The burial place of Adam and Chavah, Avraham and Sarah, Yitzchak and Rivkah, Yaakov and Leah.

Chapter 37
RABBI YONASAN EIBESCHUTZ

born: Pintchov, Poland, 1690
died: Altona, Germany, 1764

Rabbi Yonasan Eibeschutz was born into a family of Kabbalists whose ancestry reaches back to Rabbi Nassan Nata Shapira, author of *Megaleh Amukos*, and the Ari. After the death of his father, Rabbi Nassan Nata, the Rabbi of Eibenschitz, Moravia, Yonasan was raised by Rabbi Meir Eisenstadt of Prosnitz, author of *Panim Meiros*.[1]

Endowed with a brilliant mind and a flawless memory, young Yonasan totally immersed himself in the study of Talmud, halachah, and Kabbalah. His mastery of Kabbalah was such that he knew by heart the entire *Zohar* and the writings of the Ari. In addition, he was an expert in the sciences, philosophy, medicine, and foreign languages. At eighteen years of age he was widely recognized as a *gaon* and was chosen to be the rabbi of Jungbunzlau, Bohemia.

At the age of twenty-one he settled in Prague, where he headed the great yeshivah. His profound Talmudic lectures and sparkling wit won the admiration of his thousands of students. An accomplished orator, he drew large crowds who came to listen to his inspiring sermons. Being good-hearted by

---
1 Amsterdam, 1715.

nature, he deeply involved himself in the needs and sorrows of the community.

Reb Yonasan maintained friendly relations with government officials and the Catholic clergy, often engaging them in debates about religion and philosophy in an effort to clear up their misconceptions about Judaism and avert perils that threatened the Jewish community. Due to his good connections with the Catholic clergy he frequently was able to save Jews from evictions, expulsions, and heavy fines. On one occasion he even traveled to Vienna, the capital of the Austrian empire, to plead for the lifting of expulsion decrees against Jewish communities in Bohemia and Moravia and succeeded in having the rulings rescinded. By the time he was thirty years old, he was regarded as a rabbinic authority not only in Prague but in the Jewish communities at large.

Amulets[1]

In 1741 Rabbi Yonasan Eibeschutz was appointed to the rabbinate of Metz, France. While leading the Metz community he continued to work for the welfare of the Jews of Bohemia and Moravia, who were threatened with expulsion. His efforts bore fruit, and the Austrian empress revoked the decree. His reputation as an illustrious scholar, Kabbalist, and miracle worker spread rapidly, and throngs of people flocked to him to receive his blessings and ask for amulets which he readily wrote and dispensed. These amulets were to become the source of endless grief and distress that pursued him all his life.

Bitter Strife

In 1750, Rabbi Yonasan Eibeschutz was chosen as chief rabbi of the

---

1 An amulet or *kamia* is a small slip of paper or parchment inscribed with a Kabbalistic formula or diagram that is worn for protection from harm, sickness, and demons, to find a match, for easy labor and childbirth, for a safe journey, and various other remedies.

three communities Altona, Hamburg, and Wandsbeck, known by the acronym "Ahu." This was one of the most prestigious rabbinical positions in all of Germany. At that time there lived in Altona a towering Torah scholar named Rabbi Yaakov Emden.[1] He had once served as the rabbi of Emden, Germany (from which he derived his surname), but because of his irascibility and strong-willed character he was forced to abandon this post. He settled in Altona, where he opened a Hebrew printing press. The appointment of Rabbi Yonasan Eibeschutz as chief rabbi of the "three communities" did not sit well with Rabbi Yaakov Emden. Although Rabbi Yonasan showed deep respect for Rabbi Yaakov Emden, the latter gave him the cold shoulder, and a painful conflict ensued that caused a rift in the community.

Around the time that Rabbi Yonasan assumed the position of rabbi of Ahu, a disease was raging in the area that was fatal to many pregnant women. Within the year sixteen Jewish women died in childbirth. The expectant mothers of the community were terrified. When word spread that the new rabbi was a noted Kabbalist and miracle worker, the panic-stricken women begged him to write a *kamia* (amulet) for them to ward off the dreaded disease. Filled with compassion, Rabbi Yonasan graciously wrote the amulets.

When an opponent of his read the text of one of these amulets, he claimed that they contained veiled references to the false messiah Shabsai Tzvi.[2] He showed the *kamia* to Rabbi Yaakov Emden, who promptly announced in his private synagogue that the author of the *kamia* was a follower of the discredited Shabsai Tzvi, and he called for the excommunication of the author without mentioning Rabbi Yonasan's name explicitly.

---

1   1698–1776.

2   Shabsai Tzvi (1626–1676) was a charismatic impostor who declared himself messiah in 1658. Many people were deluded by his rantings, including the Jews of Amsterdam, Hamburg, and Altona. In 1666 the hoax was exposed when self-styled "messiah" converted to Islam. In spite of his apostasy, Shabsai Tzvi still retained many supporters. In light of this, the rabbis were extremely suspicious of anything that smacked of the perfidious messianic movement.

The pronouncement ignited a quarrel in the community that spread like wildfire. It eventually involved rabbis and their communities throughout Europe. The hostility and rancor ultimately led to a decline of respect for Torah authorities and brought about a lamentable weakening of Torah observance in Germany.

In defense of their beloved Rabbi Yonasan, the leaders of the community closed down Rabbi Yaakov Emden's synagogue and printing press. Rabbi Yaakov Emden received the support of Rabbi Yaakov Yehoshua Falk (the Pnei Yehoshua), the rabbis of Frankfurt, Rabbi Shmuel Hellman of Metz, and his brother-in-law, Rabbi Aryeh Leib of Amsterdam. Rabbi Yonasan received the backing of such leading personalities as Rabbi Yechezkel Landau (the Noda BeYehudah) and the Vilna Gaon.

Rabbi Yonasan Innocent

At a dramatic meeting in his synagogue, Rabbi Yonasan, standing in front of the Ark, took a solemn oath, swearing that he did not believe in a single tenet of the Sabbatean heresy.

Meanwhile, other amulets were opened and read by long-time opponents of Rabbi Yonasan, who claimed that they included presumed allusions to Shabsai Tzvi. Rabbi Yonasan Eibeschutz declared that the text of the amulets was altered and forged and translated incorrectly. He proved that the so-called references to Shabsai Tzvi were in fact Kabbalistic divine Names. Two great Kabbalists of that time, Rabbi Shmuel Essingen of Munster and Rabbi Eliyahu Olianov, examined the amulets and agreed that the text was based on holy Kabbalistic concepts, intelligible only to Kabbalists.

Rabbi Yaakov Emden was forced to leave Altona, whereupon he moved in with his brother-in-law, the rabbi of Amsterdam. The acrimonious dispute spread beyond the local Jewish community to reach Emperor Frederick of Denmark under whose jurisdiction lay the city of Altona. The emperor ruled that Rabbi Yaakov Emden was justified in his accusations and removed Rabbi Yonasan Eibeschutz from his rabbinical post. However, after reconsidering the matter, the emperor reinstated him as rabbi of Altona in 1765.

Support from Leading Rabbis

It should be noted that the majority of the leading rabbis of Poland, Lithuania, Hungary, Bohemia, and Moravia supported Rabbi Yonasan. At a rabbinic conference in Mir, Poland, they decided to excommunicate anyone writing defamatory and abusive leaflets against Rabbi Yonasan Eibeschutz.

Throughout the controversy, Rabbi Yonasan never spoke out against his attackers or reviled them. However, he did write a book entitled *Luchos Eidus*[1] in which he published all the letters of support he had received from rabbis during the bitter controversy. In the introduction to the book he humbly defends himself in a factual and detached manner without denouncing his adversaries.

Both Rabbis Held in High Esteem

With the passing of time the conflict finally died down, and the rift was healed. Today Rabbi Yonasan Eibeschutz is universally revered as a legendary *gaon* and tzaddik, cleared of all the false accusations against him. He led the three communities of Ahu until his death on 21 Elul, 1764, disseminating Torah in his yeshivah to tens of thousands of devoted disciples. Rabbi Yaakov Emden, too, is esteemed in the Torah world of today as an illustrious Torah scholar. His responsa have been reprinted numerous times and the famous *Rabbi Yaakov Emden Siddur* can be found in many homes and synagogues. He died in 1776 on a Friday afternoon and was buried within hours in the Jewish cemetery in Hamburg. In the rush to conduct the funeral before Shabbos, he was buried in an already opened grave only a few spaces away from the tomb of Rabbi Yonasan Eibeschutz. The two great men who were so far apart in their lives were joined forever in death.

---

1 Altona, 1756.

Rabbi Yonasan's Writings

Rabbi Yonasan wrote a number of Kabbalistic treatises which are still in manuscript. His published works include the halachic *Kreisi U'Pleisi*,[1] *Urim VeTumim*,[2] and a number of other halachic commentaries. His most popular works are *Yaaros Devash*,[3] a collection of sermons and eulogies, and *Tiferes Yonasan*,[4] insights on the weekly Torah portions.

---

1   Altona, 1756.
2   Karlsruhe, 1775.
3   Karlsruhe, 1779.
4   Zalkava and Ostroh, 1825.

Chapter 38
RABBI MOSHE CHAIM LUZZATTO
(Ramchal)

born: Padua, Italy, 1707
died: Akko, 1747

Rabbi Moshe Chaim Luzzato — known by the acronym Ramchal — was a brilliant Talmudic scholar, ethicist, and Kabbalist. At an early age he showed signs of greatness in scholarship and piety. An original thinker of the highest order, he became an expert in Kabbalah while still a young man.

At the age of fourteen the Ramchal could faultlessly cite all the works of the Ari,[1] and at twenty years of age he understood the mystical combinations of sacred letters. At that time he received communications from a heavenly teacher, a *maggid*, who revealed to him Kabbalistic secrets and mystical insights. He secluded himself with three friends, and together they delved into the mysteries of Kabbalah and engrossed themselves in prayer and contemplation.

His ascetic way of life and fascination with Kabbalistic studies raised the suspicion of people committed to uproot the heresy of Shabsai Tzvi, the

---

1   Rabbi Yitzchak Luria Ashkenazi. See ch. 30.

false *mashiach* who duped the Jewish masses and caused havoc in seventeenth century. Ramchal's opponents, led by Rabbi Moshe Chagiz, forced him to leave Italy, although the leading rabbis of his time cleared him of Sabbatean tendencies.

He moved to Amsterdam, where he became an optical lens grinder and diamond polisher. It was in Amsterdam that he published the famous *Mesillas Yesharim*, "The Path of the Just," which became the classic text of the *Mussar* Movement.[1]

The Ramchal also wrote more than forty other books on philosophy, poetry, and Kabbalah, including the Kabbalistic works *Choker U'Mekabeil*[2] and *Adir BaMarom*.[3] In 1743 he moved to Eretz Yisrael, where, in 1747, he and his family perished in an epidemic that ravaged Akko.

Selections from the Kabbalistic Writings of the Ramchal

The 600,000 Jewish Souls

There are 600,000 souls in the heavenly realm; these souls are the roots of all the souls of Israel. Each soul is made up of two parts, that is, each soul has an upper part that stays in heaven while its counterpart down below [in this world] inhabits the human body. In the body it splits up into *nefesh* (the basic animal, lustful soul), *ruach* (the instinct of self-preservation), and *neshamah* (the holy, spiritual element). Collectively, all Jewish souls are included in 600,000 heavenly souls, although down below [in this world] the counterparts of these heavenly souls proliferate into much [more than 600,000 individual] parts. But the souls of all the Jews are rooted in the 600,000 heavenly souls. And when a soul returns

---

1 The movement of ethical rebirth, founded by Rabbi Yisrael (Lipkin) Salanter (1810–1883).
2 Shklov, 1785.
3 Warsaw, 1886.

to its place in Heaven, it finds its way to its root [among the 600,000 souls] and is integrated into it.

Adir BaMarom

After Adam's Sin

God told Adam, "On the day that you eat from [the Tree of Knowledge of Good and Evil] you will definitely die" (*Bereishis* 2:17). Thus, Adam really should have died on the very day [that he ate the forbidden fruit]. But God had mercy on Adam, and [instead of ending his life then and there] He demoted him from his high spiritual station. Had he remained on his high level, he could not have stayed alive, because his soul was tarnished with the evil that became part of him in the wake of his sin. But since he was downgraded [he was not the same Adam anymore], and he was able to live a long life.

Every day the *sitra achara* [the "other side," meaning the *yetzer hara*] tries to overpower a person and kill him, since by rights the person should not be alive at all. [If God had taken Adam's life when he sinned, he would not have had offspring, and mankind would never have emerged.] But God had pity on Adam [and mankind descended from him]. God has to repeat this act of compassion every day [for mankind to stay alive]. That is the intent of the verse, "Day by day He supports us, God of our salvation" (*Tehillim* 68:20).

That is the mystical reason why we have to recite a hundred *berachos* (blessings) each day. [Before Adam sinned, his height reached from earth all the way to heaven.] But when he sinned his height was reduced to one hundred cubits. As it says, "When Adam sinned, the Holy One, blessed be He, placed His hand on him and shrank his height to a hundred cubits."[1]

Thus, mankind exists only because God in His mercy reduced Adam's

---

1   The *Nefesh HaChaim* explains that this Aggadah means that originally Adam's intellect was so clear and all-encompassing that he could comprehend the actions and processes of the entire universe and the heavenly realm. When he sinned, his phenomenal intellect was diminished and his discernment faded.

height to a hundred cubits, and He renews this act of mercy each and every day. [The hundred cubits signify God's blessing to us.] Accordingly, we must thank Him for His mercy by reciting a hundred *berachos* each day.

Adir BaMarom

The Purpose of Creation

It says that on the first Shabbos of Creation, "God ceased from all the work which God created to continue to work" (*Bereishis* 2:3). On a spiritual level this means that God began Creation [but left it unfinished] in order that man eventually should bring it to completion. Thereby man would earn a reward for [perfecting Creation].

Although man was created in the image of God, he is not entirely Godlike until he reaches perfection by performing the mitzvos. That's why the 613 mitzvos correspond to the 613 parts of the human body [so that man with the 613 parts of his body attains perfection through the 613 mitzvos].

God left Creation unfinished for two reasons:

First, since evil exists, man is swayed by his evil impulse (*yetzer hara*). If God had brought Creation to full completion [the world would be absolutely perfect], and evil would not exist at all. In the absence of evil, man would not be tempted by the *yetzer hara* [and would not deserve a reward for choosing to do good]. But God wanted man — born with a *yetzer hara* — to rectify himself by observing the Torah and the mitzvos. That way he would become pure and unblemished.

Second, [God left Creation unfinished, because He] wanted to bestow a boundless stream of goodness on man. But He wanted man to earn this Divine abundance. Man deserves it [by subduing the *yetzer hara* and freely] choosing to do good. And when he has drawn down this abundance to all parts of the world, the purpose of Creation is fulfilled, and man's task in the world is completed.

To summarize, the two things needed to bring about man's perfection are doing away with evil and drawing down the flow of Divine abundance to the world. So you see, there really are two sets of 613. One set of 613 which God gave to man, namely his body that consists of 613 members; the other set of 613 entails man's mission in this world: to fulfill the 613 mitzvos.

Adir BaMarom

Gilgul — Transmigration of Souls

> [Note: Transmigration is the process by which a deceased person's soul is sent back to the world in order to atone for one or more sins he committed during his life.]

The human soul is made up of a number of elements: *nefesh, ruach, neshamah, chayah,* and *yechidah* [*nefesh* being the primitive animal life-force, the other elements constituting stages of increasingly greater spirituality and holiness]. These five elements again break down into many individual parts. Any one of these parts of the soul may be reincarnated a second, a third, or even numerous times [entering into a different body each time].

In most cases not all of the parts of a person's soul are reincarnated. Depending on a person's merits, some of the elements of his soul may have been rectified, so that they do not need to be reincarnated, and only the parts that were not corrected will be reborn. However, it makes no difference whether a person is reborn with six hundred or only two parts of [his previous] soul; his health and his intellect are not affected by that. A person who has six hundred parts [of his previous soul] will not be smarter than the one who has only two parts....

But aside from this, there is an altogether different kind of *gilgul*, whereby a human soul is reincarnated not as another human being, but as an animal, a plant, or as lifeless matter. In the case where the soul comes back in another person it functions as soul [and induces the person to be virtuous]. By contrast, the soul that is reincarnated as an animal is as though confined in a prison, because it is in an environment that is the antithesis of its own lofty nature. Since the essence of an animal is diametrically opposed to the lofty, thinking human *neshamah*, the soul imprisoned in an animal endures incredible anguish, and its torment atones for the person's sins [in his previous life]. The same is true for a *neshamah* that is reincarnated in a vegetable or mineral. But the pain erases its sin.

Ma'amar HaChochmah

Counting the Omer[1]

The deeper meaning of the counting of the Omer is this: There are fifty Gates of Wisdom in the world. Moshe attained the wisdom of forty-nine of these Gates, but the fiftieth Gate — that of infinte wisdom — was beyond his reach. In line with this, there are forty-nine days of counting the Omer, and on the fiftieth day [which is the holiday of Shavuos], the Torah was given. Just as there are forty-nine Gates of Wisdom and Holiness, so there are forty-nine Gates of Defilement, as it says, "God has made the one opposite the other" (*Koheles* 7:14). [Everything God has made has an opposite counterpart], thus there is a good and an evil inclination, and the forces of impurity counterbalance the forces of holiness.

When the children of Israel were in Egypt, they descended to the depth of the forty-ninth Gate of Defilement. [If they had sunk to the impurity of the fiftieth Gate, they would have been irretrievably lost.] They had to be taken out of this state. But God wanted to extract Israel from these forty-nine Gates of Defilement in stages, by illuminating on each day between Pesach and Shavuos the Gate of Holiness that is the counterpart of its op-

---

1   Beginning with the second night of Pesach and every night after that, it is a *mitzvah* to count the days for a period of seven full weeks (49 days) (*Vayikra* 23:21). The fiftieth day is Shavuos, when we commemorate the giving of the Torah, which occurred on that day.

posite Gate of Defilement. We relive this *tikkun* (rectification) each year in the counting of the Omer during the forty-nine days between Pesach, the day of the Exodus, and Shavuos, the day of the giving of the Torah. Shavuos represents the illumination of the fiftieth Gate of Wisdom and Holiness.

Choker U'Mekabeil

Silence Is Golden

"Rabbi Shimon ben Gamliel said: I found nothing better for a person than silence" (*Avos* 1:14).

You should be aware that the *yetzer hara* takes hold of a person's body. But it cannot invade the body until it receives permission to enter. It obtains permission when the person's mouth utters shameful things. Surely the mouth is the gateway to the body. It is the only way the *yetzer hara* can enter.

Adir BaMarom

From Adam until Avraham

Adam was created free of sensuality. All he was meant to do was to elevate the world to the highest spiritual level and thereby complete Creation. When this would be accomplished, the *yetzer hara* would be rectified, and all evil would turn into good. All Creation would be holy, without any contamination. That is the reason why Adam was not given the 613 mitzvos. The mitzvos are the way to serve God on a lower level, whereas Adam was to attain *kedushah* by allowing the Divine Light to flow into him, the same way as Shabbos [descends on the world]....

But when Adam transgressed he became tarnished with sensuality [and God's plan came to nothing]. Nevertheless, God wanted to set him right by having him go through a number of *gilgulim*. So the souls that were included in Adam's soul were reincarnated in the ten generations from

Adam to Noach. But God did not give them the Torah either. He wanted those souls to be rectified by *gilgul*, wandering from one body into another and suffering death, that thereby they would rid themselves of the sensuality that clung to them. That is why they lived so long. During their long lives they should have attained high levels of *kedushah*, and their souls should have been rectified.

In Noach the *gilgul* wanderings came to a close, and in the six hundred years of his life before the flood the world could have reached its *tikkun*, for during that time there was a great illumination of Divine Light. But the people did not want to mend their ways and persisted in their corrupt ways. Instead of the great illumination there was *sheviras hakeilim*. The spiritual channels [that conveyed the divine light down to this world] could not contain the splendor. As a result, they fell and broke [as happened in the wake of Adam's transgression]. That is the deeper meaning of the flood.

And so, Adam's sin was not rectified by the ten generations that followed. Even Noach was not fully rectified, for he failed by becoming drunk. God still wanted to mend the sins of Adam and Noach through another ten generations [from Noach to Avraham]. But that did not succeed either. A new way of *tikkun* was devised: the way of Avraham. Avraham's way [toward perfection] involves personal effort and exertion, in contrast to the divine illumination [which failed to rectify the twenty generations before Avraham].

So Avraham began by keeping the Torah (*Yoma* 28b). But he had a son Yishmael, and Yitzchak had a son Esav [both of whom drifted away from the Torah]. By having these sons, Avraham and Yitzchak removed all traces of sensuality [from their progeny]. The Jewish people spring from Yaakov. They had to go into exile in order to achieve *tikkun* on the lowest level, until the coming of Mashiach, when the whole world will have its *tikkun* and will be set right.

Adir BaMarom

Chapter 39
RABBI ELIYAHU OF VILNA
(The Vilna Gaon)

born: Vilna, Lithuania, 1720
died: Vilna, Lithuania, 1797

Popularly known as "the Vilna Gaon," "the Gaon," or "the Gra,"[1] Rabbi Eliyahu was the towering rabbinic authority of his time and of all generations that came after him. A child prodigy of unparalleled genius, he astounded the community when at seven years of age he gave a Talmudic discourse in the great synagogue of Vilna. With superhuman diligence he acquired an encyclopedic knowledge of all facets of the Torah, both in its plain and its mystical, Kabbalistic meanings. A man of surpassing piety, he donated to the poor one-fifth of his meager stipend. He was an expert in the sciences, mathematics, philosophy, music, and medicine, among other disciplines. To him, all fields of knowledge are included in the Torah and are helpful to a better understanding of the Talmud.

He was never a rabbi in any official capacity and never held public office or headed a yeshivah. After his marriage at a young age he secluded himself and studied Torah day and night in saintly devotion, wrapped in his tallis and wearing his tefillin, never sleeping more than two hours a night. In his thirties, for reasons known only to himself, he set out on a self-imposed ex-

---

1   An acronym of Ha**G**aon **R**abbi **E**liyahu.

ile. For five years he wandered westward from town to town in total anonymity, suffering the hardships of an itinerant wanderer. When he reached Germany his identity was discovered. Hailed as the great *gaon*, he quickly returned to Vilna.

When he reached the age of forty he began to teach a few outstanding scholars, who recorded his remarks and later published them, so that most of the Gaon's books are compilations of the notes of his students. The cleared a new path to Talmud study, focusing on gaining a clear understanding of the text through keen analysis of the principles and approaches of the early authorities. His methodology stood in sharp contrast to the *pilpul* system of the Polish scholars, an intricate way of creating a complex mental framework with which a series of questions are answered. He worked hard on emending the Talmudic and Midrashic texts, clearing them of copyists' and typographical errors. Subsequent discoveries of ancient manuscripts confirmed the soundness of his corrections, which appear in the Vilna edition of the Talmud (*Haga'os HaGra*).

His greatness in Kabbalah is evident in his commentary to *Sefer Yetzirah*,[1] which is indispensable to an understanding of this esoteric work. He is said to have authored thirty books of commentary on the *Zohar*, and many of his other writings are interspersed with Kabbalistic insights.

Stories abound about the Vilna Gaon's supernatural powers. It is said that before his bar mitzvah he tried to create a *golem* with the knowledge of *Sefer Yetzirah*, but he thought the better of it. Tradition has it that a *maggid*, a heavenly messenger, regularly appeared to him wishing to reveal to him answers to problematic passages, but he declined, preferring to find the solutions by his own effort.

All his life, the Gaon dreamed of going to Eretz Yisrael. He set out on a journey to the Holy Land, but when he reached Koenigsberg (the capital of East Prussia at that time) he decided to return home. Some say that the Gaon's soul was a spark of the soul of Moshe, who was not allowed to enter Eretz Yisrael.

---

1   Horodno, 1806.

He zealously opposed the Chassidic Movement, fearing that it might lead to another debacle like that brought on by the false messiah Shabsai Tzvi. His fears proved to be unfounded.

His works include a commentary on *Sifra DiTziniusa*,[1] a Kabbalistic work attributed to Yaakov Avinu; *Dikdukei Eliyahu*,[2] on Hebrew grammar; *Aderes Eliyahu*,[3] a commentary on the Torah; *Even Shlomo*,[4] a selection of comments; and many other works.

The Vilna Gaon was revered in Vilna and throughout the world for his phenomenal knowledge and saintly character. One of his most outstanding disciples was Rabbi Chaim of Volozhin, the founder of the yeshivah of Volozhin. Following the Gaon's approach to learning, his yeshivah spread Torah for more than a century. Today most yeshivos follow the study method of Volozhin, keeping alive the style of Torah learning pioneered by the great Vilna Gaon.

Selections from the Kabbalistic Commentaries of the Vilna Gaon

The Soul Returns to Earth

> [A brief synopsis of *Sefer Yonah*: God sent the prophet Yonah to Nineveh in Babylonia to tell its sinful inhabitants that their city would be destroyed unless they repented. Yonah fled God's command, sailing away aboard a ship, but God sent a mighty storm that threatened to break up the ship. When the sailors determined that the calamity was due to Yonah's transgression, they cast him overboard. God sent a great fish to swallow the drowning Yonah. Deeply distressed, Yonah prayed from the belly of the fish, and after three days the fish spewed him out to the shore. Now Yonah went to Nineveh and warned the inhabitants of their impending doom unless they mended their ways. Heeding Yonah's admonition, the people repented, and Nineveh was

---

1   Vilna, 1820.
2   Vilna, 1833.
3   Dubrovna, 1804.
4   Vilna, 1873, with a commentary by Rabbi Shmuel Maltzan.

spared. But in the aftermath Yonah was made to suffer a great deal.]

[In a Kabbalistic sense] Yonah personifies the soul of a deceased that is sent back to earth to rectify the world. However, instead of fulfilling its mission, the soul goes astray. So it is sent down in a second incarnation. This time it does carry its assigned task, but it has to endure great affliction.

"The word of God came to Yonah" (*Yonah* 1:1) — God sends the soul down to this world, telling it: "Enter the body of So-and-So, and do as I tell you."

"Arise and go to Nineveh" (ibid., 2) — Leave your place in Gan Eden. Go down to this world and turn things around.

"He went down to Yaffo" (ibid., 3) — [Yaffo is seen as related to *yafeh*, "beautiful."] The soul descends to this world, [but instead of fulfilling its mission] it pursues earthly delights [*yafeh*].

"He found a ship" (ibid.) — The soul finds a body [in which to be reincarnated]. This world is compared to the sea because people that go to sea do not stay there permanently; they sail to faraway shores to bring back valuable merchandise. The afflictions of this world are the waves of the sea; the human body is the ship that sails the sea. The World to Come is equated with dry land [for a person builds his permanent home on dry land, and the World to Come is man's permanent dwelling].

"The ship threatened to be broken up" (ibid., 4) — The body thinks that it is going to destroyed. While alive a person thinks he will never die, and now he realizes that he is facing death. But the soul, although it suffers agony because of its sins, is not lost forever; it will be set right in future reincarnations. But the body decomposes and perishes since it cannot be repaired through reincarnation.

"[The crewmen] said to one another, 'Come, let us cast lots that we may determine because of whom this calamity is upon us' " (ibid., 7) — The limbs want to find out which of them brought on this calamity, whether it was the tongue that sinned [by slandering] or the male organ [through immorality], or perhaps it was another part of the body.[1]

"So they cast lots, and the lot fell on Yonah" (ibid.) – The lot falls on the soul [it is the cause of the disaster]. For if the soul is good, it guides the person toward goodness, even if the body has a deep-seated tendency toward evil.

"God designated a large fish to swallow Yonah" (ibid. 2:1) – [The fish] represents the grave and symbolizes the angel called "Dumah" that is in charge of the dead. The angel of the dead is called "Dumah" (silence) because in the grave there is absolute silence. As it says, "Neither the dead can praise God, nor any who descend into *dumah* (silence)" (*Tehillim* 115:17).

"And Yonah remained in the fish's belly for three days and three nights" (ibid.) – For three days after his death a person's soul hovers over his grave wanting to return into his body. When it sees that the body's radiance has dimmed it leaves.

"Then God addressed the fish, and it spewed out Yonah onto dry land" (ibid., 11) – God tells the angel Dumah to return the soul to Him, so he brings it back to Gan Eden [symbolized by dry land].

"The word of God came to Yonah a second time" (ibid. 3:1) – God reincarnated Yonah's soul to redress his weakness [of running away from God's command].

Commentary to the Book of Yonah

Four Levels of Prophecy

There are four kinds of dreams: ordinary dreams, dream-like visions [of the minor] prophets, prophetic visions of the major prophets, and the prophecy of Moshe. An ordinary dream may need an interpretation, and

---

[1] The tongue and the male organ are the focus of Kabbalistic thought with regard to the ten *Sefiros*. The significance of the tongue and the male organ is seen in the fact that they are situated midway between the ten fingers and the ten toes (see *Sefer Yetzirah* 1:3).

the dreamer does not know its meaning. He just realizes that his dream has some significance. Pharaoh had a dream like that, as it says, "Pharaoh awoke, and behold! — it had been a dream" (*Bereishis* 41:7). But while he was asleep he had no idea that he was dreaming.

When a prophet has a dream-like vision, he is aware that he is having a vision in a dream, and while dreaming he knows the meaning of the vision. He either grasps it by himself or through an angel, as was the case when Zecharyah asked the angel, "What are the two clusters of olives that are next to the two golden presses?" (*Zecharyah* 4:12). Zecharyah knew that his vision had a deeper meaning, and the angel gave him the interpretation.

The same thing happened with [the minor prophet] Daniel who said, "I was watching in night visions.... The visions of my head bewildered me. I approached one of the standing ones [i.e., an angel], and I asked him for the truth concerning all this. So he spoke to me, making the interpretation of the matters known to me" (*Daniel* 7:13-16).

By contrast, the [early] prophets understood the meaning of their visions by themselves [without the help of an angel], even though the prophecy was conveyed to them in puzzling images. However, this was not the case with Moshe. God said about Moshe, "Mouth to mouth do I speak to him, in clear vision and not in riddles" (*Bemidbar* 12:8).

Heichalos, Pekudei 53

Moshe Admonishes Israel

> These are the words that Moshe spoke to all Israel, on the other side of the Jordan, concerning the wilderness, concerning the Aravah...opposite the Sea of Reeds [Suf]....
> (*Devarim* 1:1)

"On the other side of the Jordan" — This world is characterized as Jordan. So what is meant by "the other side [*eiver*] of the Jordan"? It tells you that man is only a passing traveler [*oveir*] in this world. Down here in this world the Jordan River is the border of Eretz Yisrael. Correspondingly, in the higher world the [fiery] stream Dinur[1] forms the boundary of Gan Eden, and it is impossible to enter Gan Eden without crossing the stream [of fire] of Dinur. [Everyone — even a perfect tzaddik — passes through the fires of Gehinnom before being admitted to Gan Eden.]

"Concerning the wilderness" — [Moshe hinted] that a person should not run after the pleasures of this world. Instead, he should be like the wilderness, spurning material pursuits and devoting himself to Torah study.

"Opposite the Sea of Reeds [Suf]" — [Moshe intimated] that a person should always have in mind the day of death and contemplate the end [*sof*].

Aderes Eliyahu

Eleven Journeys after Death

> Eleven days from Choreiv, by way of Mount Sei'ir to Kadesh Barnea.
>
> (*Devarim* 1:2)

"Eleven days" — After death, a person is required to make eleven journeys until he reaches his final resting place. These are: 1) the journey from his home to his grave, 2) from his grave to Gehinnom — for even a perfect tzaddik has to pass through Gehinnom, 3) from Gehinnom to Gan Eden... 10) from Gan Eden to the seven heavens, 11) from the seventh heaven to the Upper Gan Eden. And in each of these places he has to render an account of his actions.

Aderes Eliyahu

Tzaddikim in Gan Eden

The righteous can look forward to learning new Torah insights from the Teacher in the World to Come. And when a tzaddik comes to Gan Eden he

---

1   See *Chagigah* 13b.

is given 150 days in which to expound in public the Torah wisdom he learned in this world.

There were numerous steps in the earthly Beis HaMikdash: first you climbed the steps that led to the Temple Mount, then you mounted the steps to the *cheil* [a place within the fortifications of the Temple], then there were the steps to Women's Court. There are just as many steps in the world above. According to the number of good deeds a person has done in this world, he builds altars in each of the higher worlds, and on these altars the soul presents the gifts [of his good deeds].

Even Shlomo 10:29-30

Reincarnation

The Holy One, blessed be He, created man in order to bestow goodness on him. If a person transgressed, God sends him back to this world until he has repaired his shortcomings. He is placed in Gehinnom until he is cleansed and the filth has been removed. The difference is that if a person lived a good life the first time around, his body merits entry into the World to Come. If he did not live properly in his first incarnation, [his soul is sent back,] but the bodies in which he is reincarnated will cease to exist. But if he did not mend his failings in his fourth reincarnation, all hope is lost. [This is true only if he did not rectify any of his vices at all, but if he did correct them partially he will be given a chance in another incarnation.]

Even Shlomo 10:31

The Final Redemption

The Redemption is described as "morning." As it says, "Watchman, what of the night? The Watchman said, 'Morning is coming, but also night' " (*Yeshayah* 21:11-12). This means: Deliverance is at hand, but the night will continue for the wicked.] The Redemption is also described as "birth." As it says, "Has a nation ever been born at one time, as Zion went through her labor and gave birth to her children?" (ibid. 66:8). What is meant by the metaphors of "morning" and "birth"? Before the day begins to dawn, the night is at its darkest, and just before a woman gives birth, her labor pains are the most intense. Similarly, before the advent of the Redemption and the coming of Mashiach, the oppression of the exile will be more severe than ever before.

Even Shlomo 11:5

Changing Times

In every generation God guides the world with a different divine attribute. As a result, the world experiences climatic and environmental changes which bring about shifts in behavioral and cultural patterns and upheavals in economic conditions. The prevailing divine attribute hinges on the moral and ethical choices people are making. The resulting historic and cultural trends are all hinted at in the Torah. That is the meaning of the saying of the Sages: "God showed Adam all future generations and their teachers" (*Sanhedrin* 38b). In other words, Adam was able to elicit future developments from the Torah.

In each generation there are moments [when Mashiach could come], depending on the repentance and the particular merits of that generation. But the final Redemption is not contingent on the people's repentance but solely on God's kindness and the merit of the patriarchs. For God says, "For My sake, for My sake will I do it" (*Yeshayah* 48:11), and as we say [in the *Shemoneh Esrei*], "He recalls the kindnesses of the patriarchs and brings a redeemer to their children's children, for His Name's sake, with love." The time of the final Redemption was revealed only to the patriarchs, as it says: "I revealed it to My heart" which means, to the patriarchs and Moshe who are called "My heart."

Even Shlomo 11:9

Chapter 40
RABBI CHAIM BERLIN OF VOLOZHIN
(Reb Chaim Volozhiner)

born: Volozhin, Lithuania, 1749
died: Volozhin, Lithuania, 1821

As a youngster, Rabbi Chaim Berlin of Volozhin, known as "Reb Chaim Volozhiner," studied under Rabbi Refael Kohen of Minsk and under Rabbi Aryeh Leib Ginzburg, the famous rabbi of Volozhin, better known as the "Shaagas Aryeh." But his character and his approach to Torah study were decisively shaped by Rabbi Eliyahu, the illustrious Gaon of Vilna, his primary teacher for twenty years.

At the recommendation of Rabbi Refael Kohen, he was appointed as rabbi of Volozhin at twenty years of age, a post he held until his death. In 1802 he founded the Volozhin Yeshivah, which was destined to become the "mother" of all the yeshivos of the nineteenth century. Reb Chaim's methodology of Torah study, based on logical reasoning and intellectual honesty, became the hallmark of the Lithuanian way of study. It is the approach followed by most major yeshivos today.

Only a few of his writings survived the tragic fire that swept through

Volozhin in 1815. Of these, his Kabbalistic work *Nefesh HaChaim*,[1] a blend of Kabbalah and *mussar* (Torah ethics), gained universal acceptance. Unlike the Vilna Gaon, who opposed chassidism, Reb Chaim had a conciliatory attitude toward chassidim, and among the students of his yeshivah there were a number of chassidim. The spirit of the Volozhin Yeshivah lives on today in the multitude of yeshivah students in America, Israel, and all parts of the world.

Selections from Nefesh HaChaim

Your Actions Make an Impact in Heaven

You should never think: What am I? How can my insignificant actions make a difference in this world?

You should realize and etch it in your mind that the things you say or do are not irrelevant. On the contrary, your actions are very important. Every deed you do makes an impact in the loftiest heights and affects the brilliance of the lights above.

By the same token, a person should realize with a trembling heart that his missteps cause a devastation above that is far greater than the destruction [of the Beis HaMikdash] at the hands of Nevuchadnetzar and Titus.[2] After all, the actions of Nevuchadnetzar and Titus did not cause any damage in heaven. The souls of these fiends were not rooted in the higher worlds, so their actions did not affect those worlds at all. [The amount of damage that is caused above is according to the soul of the sinner. A small misdeed of a person with a lofty soul causes great damage in heaven; a serious crime by an inferior soul makes no impact at all above.][3]

---

1 Vilna, 1824.
2 Nevuchadnetzar destroyed the first Beis HaMikdash; Titus destroyed the second Beis HaMikdash.
3 *Ramchal, Da'as Tevunos* 126.

Due to our sins, the strength of God was diminished [so that His attribute of strict justice prevailed over His attribute of being slow to anger], and that is what gave Nevuchadnetzar and Titus the power to destroy the Beis HaMikdash here on earth. And the earthly Beis HaMikdash corresponds to the Beis HaMikdash in heaven, or, as the Sages put it, "[Titus] ground up fine flour" (*Eichah Rabbasi* 1:43). [Just as grinding fine flour is an pointless effort, so too, Titus's destruction of the Temple was a hollow achievement, because God wanted the Beis HaMikdash to be destroyed.] So you see, it was [not Titus, but] our sins that demolished the Beis HaMikdash above. Nevuchadnetzar and Titus destroyed only the Temple below [which was destined to be destroyed because of our sins].

Nefesh HaChaim 1:2

Is Man Greater than the Angels?

There is a dispute among the early rabbinic Sages whether man ranks higher than the angels or the angels rank higher than man. Each Sage cites proof texts to bolster his thesis. The truth is that both sides are right, depending on how you look at it.

No doubt, angels are greater than man in their essence, their holiness, and their marvelous perception. There's simply no comparison. As the *Zohar Chadash* says, commenting on the verse, "God named the light 'day' " (*Bereishis* 1:5): "The power of perception of angels is sublime...whereas man's power of perception is the lowest, third-rate kind of perception. It is rooted in the dust. But there is one aspect in which man ranks higher than angels. Man has the power to elevate the lower worlds to higher levels and connect them to one another. No angel can do that."

An angel cannot raise himself above his current status. He cannot connect to a higher world. That's why angels are portrayed as "standing," as it says, "*Seraphim* were standing" (*Yeshayah* 6:2), and "I will grant you strides [i.e., eternal life] among the angels who are standing here" (*Zecharyah* 3:7).

Only man can rise and interconnect the worlds. He does that by means of his actions [i.e., the performance of mitzvos]. The three elements of the human soul, *nefesh*, *ruach*, and *neshamah*,[1] do not have the power to elevate themselves until they descend to this world, the world of action, and inhabit a human body. And so it says, "He [God] breathed into his [Adam's] nostrils the soul of life" (*Bereishis* 2:7).

That is the idea behind the ladder in Yaakov's dream. The *Zohar* (*Naso*, 123b) connects the verses, "He breathed into his nostrils the soul of life" and, "He dreamed, and behold! A ladder" (*Bereishis* 28:12). Says the *Zohar*: "Surely the ladder stands for the soul of life. And that's why 'God's angels were going up and down on it,' meaning: when the soul of life is standing on the ground, its lower end enwraps itself with the human body." [Note: It does not say, "The ladder was set *on* the ground," but rather, "The ladder was set *toward* the ground." This means that its top was up in heaven and from there it gradually descended. The ladder is the *neshamah* that emanates from God's breath and gradually descends like a ladder and connects with the *ruach*, and the *ruach* with the *nefesh*, until it comes down to this world where it connects with the human body.]

Nefesh HaChaim 1:10

The Healing Power of the Torah

There is a well-known saying in the *Zohar* to the effect that the 613 mitzvos have their counterparts in the 613 limbs and sinews of the body. When a person does a mitzvah, the mitzvah sanctifies the limb [that performs the mitzvah] and energizes it. Or, if he has the opportunity to transgress but refrains from sinning, he receives the same reward as if he had done a mitzvah. And the limb that he restrained from committing the sin is sanctified and vitalized.

But when a person studies the Torah, all his limbs are made whole. Thus the Gemara (*Eiruvin* 54a) says, "If someone has a headache, he

---

1   *Nefesh*, animalistic; *ruach*, organic; *neshamah*, intellectual.

should engross himself in Torah study; if he has a sore throat, let him learn Torah; if he has a stomachache, let him study Torah; if he feels pain all over his body, let him study Torah, for it says, 'It is a healing for his whole body' (*Mishlei* 4:22)."

The reason is that by immersing yourself in Torah study all your limbs and sinews become sanctified and purified. That's why it says, "The study of Torah is equivalent to all the mitzvos" (*Shabbos* 127a).

The Gemara says: "What is the meaning of the verse, 'You have made man like the fish of the sea' (*Chavakuk* 1:14)? Why is man compared to the fish of the sea? To tell you that just as the fish of the sea die as soon as they come on dry land, so too, man perishes as soon as he abandons the Torah and mitzvos" (*Avodah Zarah* 3b).

[In the same vein] it says, "The Torah of God is perfect, restoring the soul" (*Tehillim* 19:8). This means that even if a person's soul has been cut off from its source and he has sunk to the bottom of the morass of evil, if he learns Torah, it will put him in order, release him from his fetters, and restore his previous bond with the Torah with greater illumination than he ever had before.

That's why the early Sages arranged the liturgy of *Vidui* on the order of the twenty-two letters of the *alef beis*, in order to awaken the heavenly root of the soul which is tied up with the Torah, to cleanse and purify the soul. [Every soul is rooted in one of the 600,000 letters of the Torah.] As long as a person is attached to the Torah, it will light up his life and protect him from the entrapments of the *yetzer hara*.

Nefesh HaChaim 4:29, 32

God Is the Place of the World

The deeper meaning of the metaphor "God is the Place of the world" touches on a fundamental concept. The idea that God is called "the Place of the world" has nothing to do with the conventional definition of "place" as the site that supports the object resting on it, because an object exists independent of its location. The place where it stands only prevents it from falling down and breaking. Similarly, the human body exists independently; it does not cease to exist even when the soul departs from it.

Not so the world. The only reason the world continues to exist from one moment to the next is because God wills it. If God were to rescind His will to sustain the world, it would instantly revert to nothingness.

No living person can understand that the entire universe is essentially without foundation and owes its continued existence to the will of God. That's why God is known by the appellation of "the Place." The name "the Place" suggests that just as an object shatters if the place on which it stands is taken away, how much more so would the universe cease to exist if the "Place" on which it stands [i.e., the Will of God] were removed.

Nefesh HaChaim 3:1

The Importance of Torah Study

At the time of Creation, the Torah was stored away in the higher worlds. It illuminated the universe from a remote distance to give it life and keep it going. The Torah's essence had not yet come down to this world for those who dwell below to engross themselves in it. The world was still shaky and not fixed in place. It remained unsettled until the giving of the Torah two thousand years later.[1] For the Gemara says that the Holy One, blessed be He, stipulated with the works of Creation: "If Israel accepts the Torah, you will continue to exist; if not, I will return you to primordial emptiness and void." And ever since the Torah came down to this world from its hidden wellspring, the continuing existence of the universe depends on the breath of our mouths [with which we expound the Torah] and our thoughts with which we ponder [its wisdom].

---

1   The revelation on Mount Sinai occurred in the year 2448 from Creation (1313 B.C.E.).

It is an undeniable fact that, God forbid, if there would be a split second when all around the globe no one was learning Torah, then all the worlds — upper and lower — would be annihilated and revert to nothingness.

Nefesh HaChaim 4:1

Man Holds the Key

The Gemara says: "The Holy One, blessed be He, affixed His Name to Israel [the divine Name *El* is part of *Yisrael*]. A parable: A king had a small key to unlock the door to his palace. He said to himself: 'If I keep it just as it is, it will surely get lost. I'll attach a chain to it, and that way it will not be misplaced.' And so the Holy One, blessed be He, said: 'If I leave the Jewish people to their own devices, they will vanish among the nations of the world [and lose their identity]. So I will attach My great Name to them' " (*Yerushalmi, Taanis* 2).

The parable of the key and the chain holds a deeper meaning. It applies to every single person. Man holds the key that unlocks and closes all the worlds, the palace above and the palace below. For man's actions stemming from his *nefesh* have a bearing on all the worlds.

God in His kindness watches over our well-being. He said: If I leave man alone, there will be no connection between the three levels of the soul [*nefesh, ruach, neshamah*]. Since there is no inherent connection between the three levels of the soul, if he becomes obsessed with the low *nefesh* aspect of his soul and sinks to the bottom of the swamp of evil, the higher *ruach* and *neshamah* levels of the soul cannot extricate him. He will remain there, lost forever.

That's why God created the "chain" connecting the three levels of the soul [*nefesh, ruach, neshamah*], linking the lower one to the one above it. That way, if the lower soul [the *nefesh*] is captured by the forces of impurity, it is set free and restored through its connection with the *ruach*. Similarly, if the *ruach* deteriorates, it will be rectified by the *neshamah*.

Nefesh HaChaim 1:19

Sound Advice

It's a good thing to learn the *Zohar* and along with it study *Shaarei Orah* in order to understand the meaning of the *Zohar* text. But don't study the commentary on *Shaarei Orah*, because it will only confuse you and lead you in the wrong direction.

Reb Chaim was wont to say: People say: Studying halachah rulings without the relevant Gemara is like eating fish without horseradish. But I say: On the contrary. Studying halachah without the related Gemara is like eating horseradish without fish.

Etz HaChaim 40[1]

The Repentant Priest

One day, an apostate who had become a Catholic priest visited Reb Chaim Volozhiner. Reb Chaim closeted himself with him in a private room, and expounded on the verse, "Their sorrows will multiply, those who rush after other [gods]" (*Tehillim* 16:4). Listening intently to Reb Chaim's comments, the apostate priest broke into tears. Remorseful and contrite, he repented and returned to the Torah way of life with perfect *teshuvah* (related by Rabbi Aharon Kotler, the revered founder and *rosh yeshivah* of the Lakewood Yeshivah).

Etz HaChaim 170

Forgiving Judges

Reb Chaim Volozhiner once said that the judges of the heavenly court are the tzaddikim of their generation. They will judge the people of their era, because angels cannot possibly understand how a person can commit a sin. Even a tzaddik of an earlier generation cannot favorably judge people of the generation after him (Rabbi Simchah Zissel of Kelm).

Etz HaChaim 150

---

1   *Etz HaChaim* is a compilation of Reb Chaim's teachings, written by his students and printed as an appendix to *Nefesh HaChaim*.

Don't Overeat

When you come to think of it, the whole concept of eating is really sickening. Imagine, a person ingests food that is physical, deposits it in his internal organs, and his life depends on that! His soul surely must find it repulsive.

But you have no choice; so don't disparage the inevitable. However, overeating is foolish and shameful. A wise man is happy to eat in moderation.

Etz HaChaim 118

Part VII
KABBALISTS OF THE CHASSIDIC WORLD

Introduction
KABBALISTS OF THE CHASSIDIC WORLD

Chassidism, or Chassidus, one of the great movements in Jewish history, emerged in eastern Europe during the middle of the eighteenth century in the aftermath of two disastrous events: first, the Chmielnicki massacres in 1648 and 1649, in which three hundred communities were destroyed with the slaughter of more than two hundred thousand Jews; and second, the dreadful disillusionment that followed in the wake of the collapse of the messianic movement of the impostor Shabsai Tzvi, in 1666. Deeply despondent, the Jews of eastern Europe fell into a spiritual stupor.

It was upon this dismal scene that the Baal Shem Tov burst forth like a shining meteor, offering the dejected Jews hope and consolation. His message of Chassidus, based on the bedrock of halachah and Kabbalah, lifted the Jews out of their gloom and despair into the sublime spiritual closeness to the Creator. It took old elements and transformed them through Kabbalistic ideas, infusing them with new meaning and vitality. Thus Kabbalah became one of the cornerstones of Chassidus, and every chassidic Rebbe weaves Kabbalistic concepts into his discourses and writings.[1]

Chassidus spread rapidly thanks to the efforts of a chain of talented and inspired disciples of the Baal Shem Tov. Prominent among these were Rabbi

Yaakov Yosef of Polnoye (author of *Toldos Yaakov Yosef*) and Rabbi Dov Ber of Mezritch, who became the Baal Shem Tov's successor. Rabbi Elimelech of Lizhensk wrote *No'am Elimelech*, one of the principal works on Chassidus, in which he stresses the important role of the Rebbe in the life of a chassid.

Rabbi Shneur Zalman of Liadi, the Baal HaTanya, one of the pillars of the Chassidic Movement, is the originator of Chabad Chassidus, also known as Lubavitch Chassidus. Its ideology seeks to create a synthesis between Chassidism and Torah scholarship and to establish a fusion of the mystical and revealed aspects of the Torah.

Rabbi Nachman of Breslov, a great-grandson of the Baal Shem Tov, was an innovator who roused his followers to ecstatic heights of *deveikus*, attachment to God, coupled with sublime joy.

One of the famous chassidic leaders of the nineteenth century was Rabbi Tzadok HaKohen of Lublin, a highly creative and original thinker. A master of Kabbalah, he integrated the teachings of the Maharal, Rabbi Nachman of Breslov, and the works of the early Kabbalists.

Since Kabbalah is an integral part of Chassidus, every chassidic rebbe and many chassidim are well-versed in the *Zohar* and the teachings of the Ari.

---

1   My books *The Great Chasidic Masters* and *Contemporary Sages*, published by Jason Aronson, Inc., offer biographical sketches of the main chassidic rebbes, along with selections of their works.

Chapter 41
RABBI YISRAEL BEN ELIEZER
(Baal Shem Tov)

born: Okop, Podolia, South Poland, 1698
died: Medzihbosh, South Poland, 1760

Rabbi Yisrael ben Eliezer, or the Baal Shem Tov ("Master of the Good Name"), the founder of the Chassidic Movement, could not claim notable ancestry. His early years are shrouded in mystery. All that is known is that he often went into seclusion in the Carpathian Mountains, immersing himself in prayer, contemplation, and the study of Torah and Kabbalah. He became known as a good-hearted rabbi who helped the sick and the downtrodden and was a miracle worker. In 1740 he settled in Medzhibosh, where he established a *beis midrash* that became the nucleus of his newly emerging Chassidic Movement.

The Baal Shem Tov taught that a Jew should strive to attain *deveikus*, attachment to God, not through fasting, penance, ascetic practices, mortification, and self-denial, but by joyful prayer, singing, and dancing in fellowship with chassidim. The essence of his message was: Don't fret about the sins of the past. Turn over a new leaf. Find strength, joy, and ecstasy in *ahavas Hashem*, the love of God, since He knows and delights in your good intentions and your happiness. God is everywhere – in every blade of grass, in every mighty mountain. Through prayer and the performance of mitzvos you are linked to Him.

Uplifted by the exhilarating message of Chassidism, the masses of simple, hardworking Jews joined the charismatic leader in creating a vibrant movement that spread rapidly through all of eastern Europe. The Baal Shem Tov did not commit his teachings to writing. His disciples, such as Rabbi Yaakov Yosef of Polnoye, often quoted his thoughts in their works. A compilation of his teachings, culled from authentic sources, was published under the title *Sefer Baal Shem Tov*.[1] It bears the approbations of such luminaries as the Gerrer Rebbe, the Sochatchover Rebbe, and the Boyaner Rebbe. An introductory chapter entitled *Me'iras Einayim* comprises eighty-seven tales about the life and miraculous deeds of the Baal Shem Tov.

With his teachings the Baal Shem Tov infused Judaism with new vitality, making Chassidism a creative force for the advancement of Torah — a force that is still growing, with flourishing chassidic communities in virtually every corner of the world.

Selections from the Teachings of and Anecdotes about the Baal Shem Tov

Let There Be Light

> [Note: Before Creation, God's Infinite Light filled all existence. In the presence of this Divine Light nothing else could exist. Therefore, before bringing the universe into being, God made "room" for it by yielding space in a process called *tzimtzum*, which means contraction or withdrawal of God's Infinite Light.]

God said, "There shall be light," and there was (*vayehi*) light.
(Bereishis 1:3)

The Gemara says: "Wherever Scripture uses the term *vayehi*, 'and there was,' it indicates pain and distress" (*Megillah* 10b). [Then why does it say

---

1   Lodz, 1938.

vayehi or, "and there was light"? What is painful about God creating light?] God's Infinite Light restricted Itself in order for the world to receive His goodness and splendor [for the world could not endure the unrestricted radiance of the Divine Light. The contraction of the Divine Light is the distress implied in the word *vayehi*].

Whenever the word *vayehi*, "and there was," occurs in the story of Creation, it denotes *tzimtzum*, contraction of God's Infinite Light. So don't say that the phrase "*vayehi or* — and there was light" tells you that light came into being. That is not what it means. Rather, *vayehi or* is part of God's decree. God proclaimed [the entire verse], "Let there be light, and there was light." God said, in fact: "Let the light of the human soul and human life come into being as an integral part of the Infinite Light of God." But the soul could not bear the blinding brilliance of the Divine Light. That's why God continued by saying, "*vayehi or*," meaning: Let the Infinite Light be hemmed in through *tzimtzum*, stricture, so that the world could come into being [and the act of restraining the Light is the "painful" element indicated by *vayehi*].

This thought is expressed in the verse, "For He spoke and it came to be [*vayehi*], He commanded and it stood firm" (*Tehillim* 33:9). In other words: By saying "*vayehi*" God restrained the Infinite Light, so that the world should be able to endure and stand firm.

Sefer Baal Shem Tov, Bereishis 23, 25

Thought and Speech

[Note: The *Sefiros* of *Chochmah* and *Binah* are known also as *Abba* and *Imma*. All human thought originates there.]

The thinking process unfolds along the lines of the ten *Sefiros*. Your ideas are conceived in *Abba* and *Imma* [i.e., *Chochmah* and *Binah*]. Therefore, the spark of an original Torah insight is called *Abba* and *Imma*. Your initial thought then expands in your mind and soars in all directions in an untamed flow of consciousness, in line with the *Sefirah* of *Chesed*. But now you need the power of the *Sefirah* of *Gevurah* to restrain and inhibit your free-flowing thoughts so that you can organize them, put them into words, and explain them to others. This gives you the serenity of *Tiferes*.

At this point you need faith [and the inner conviction to convey your thoughts]. Faith is symbolized by the *Sefiros* of *Netzach* and *Hod*, the "two thighs of truth" [the pillars that support the body]. The gratification you get from innovating your own Torah thoughts is akin to the *Sefirah Yesod*, which is symbolic of the male organ. Finally, you articulate your novel idea through speech, which conforms to *Malchus*, the *Sefirah* of the mouth, the organ of speech. [*Malchus*, the tenth and last *Sefirah*, receives but does not give. It epitomizes the mouth that receives food, the woman who receives the seed, and the oral Torah that is transmitted by word of mouth.]

Sefer Baal Shem Tov, Bereishis 64

Teshuvah, the Holy Spark Inherent in Sin

Kayin said, "My sin is too great to be forgiven."
(Bereishis 4:13)

[Note: As a result of Adam's transgression, the *Sefiros* were unable to hold the radiant Infinite Light flowing through them. In a cosmic catastrophe the vessels shattered (*sheviras hakeilim*), spilling sparks of holiness (*nitzotzos hakedushah*) all over the world. These holy sparks became trapped in shells (*klippos*) of impurity.]

It is a known fact that encased in all that exists there are sparks of holiness. In fact, there is nothing that is without a spark of holiness — even trees and rocks. And all your actions — even sinful ones — contain sparks of holiness. Now you will ask: What sparks of holiness can there be in a transgression? The answer is: The holy spark contained in sin is *teshuvah*. For when a person does *teshuvah* [his sin is forgiven, and] the holy sparks that were trapped in his sinful deed are freed and lifted all the way to the higher world. That is indicated in the passage, "God forgives sin [*nosei avon*]" (*Shemos* 34:7), which literally means, "God lifts up sin." And when Kayin said, "My sin is too great to be forgiven [*minneso*]," he meant, "My sin is too great to be lifted to the higher world."

Sefer Baal Shem Tov, Bereishis 167

The Beauty of Potifar's Wife

> One day, [Yosef] came to the house to do his work.
> (*Bereishis* 39:11)

[Note: Kabbalah teaches that Yaakov is the embodiment of *Tiferes*, which is a synthesis of the two opposite *Sefiros* of *Chesed* and *Gevurah*. Yaakov thus represents the spiritual beauty that is inherent in harmony, reconciliation, and unity.]

[The Gemara (*Sotah* 36b) relates that when Potifar's wife tried to seduce Yosef, at the critical moment,] Yosef saw his father's image, and as a result, his passion left him.

Let's explain. The Midrash (*Tanchuma, Vayeishev* 5) says that Potifar's wife did her utmost to entice Yosef. She adorned herself and changed into different alluring dresses three times a day. Seeing the physical beauty of Potifar's wife, Yosef realized that her beauty was a reflection of the spiritual beauty of *Tiferes*, the hallmark of his father Yaakov. This awareness immediately cooled his ardor, causing him "to run away and flee outside" (*Bereishis* 39:12). He ran away from the physical *Tiferes* of this woman, and rushed outside to the higher spiritual *Tiferes*, epitomized by his father Yaakov.

Sefer Baal Shem Tov, Vayeishev 6

Stepping into the Mud

> With this shall Aharon come into the Sanctuary [to perform the Yom Kippur service].
> (*Vayikra* 16:3)

The purpose of man in this world is to lift up those that are on lower level.

But in order to lift a person to a higher level, you have to lower yourself to that person's level. Your true essence is to be found in your inner worth. But in order to lift up a plain, unlearned person, you have to shed your superior inner worth and lower yourself to his frivolous level. As the Gemara (*Yerushalmi, Taanis* 2:7) says: "The prophet Shmuel put on ordinary, everyday clothes and said, 'We have sinned' [including himself with the plain people]. If you want to save someone who is drowning in a sea of mud, you have to get dirty yourself to pull him out.

Sefer Baal Shem Tov, Acharei Mos 2

Divine Justice

These are the ordinances that you shall place before them.

(*Shemos 21:1*)

Commenting on this verse, the *Zohar* says: "This [chapter contains] the mystery of reincarnation." This is puzzling, since the chapter deals mostly with monetary disputes and civil laws.

The explanation is this: Say a person files suit against his neighbor in the firm belief that he is right and will win the case. Yet, on the basis of Torah law, the judge rules against him. If that happens, the losing party should not protest, because the laws of the Torah are just and fair. Then why did he lose the case? Surely the reason is that in a previous incarnation he owed this person money, and now he is made to pay him in order to acquit himself. The fellow who won in this trial and was awarded the money will have to answer for that in his next incarnation.

The *Zohar* means to say: "These are the ordinances" concerning financial disputes which sometimes seem to be decided unfairly. Therein lies the mystery of reincarnation. For God, the Creator of all souls, knows what happened in previous incarnations between quarreling parties. He sets things right with kindness, compassion, and true justice, so that each person receives what is rightfully his.

Sefer Baal Shem Tov, Mishpatim 1

Sparks of Holiness

[In Yaakov's dream of the ladder reaching to heaven, God told him,] "The ground upon which you are lying, to you will I give it and to your descendants."

(Bereishis 28:13)

The Gemara says: " 'The ground upon which you are lying, to you I will give I will give it and to your descendants' — This teaches us that the Holy One, blessed be He, rolled up all of Eretz Yisrael and put it under our father Yaakov [to indicate to him] that it would be very easily conquered by his descendants [as the four cubits of ground on which he was lying]" (*Chullin* 91b).

The reason God rolled up all of Eretz Yisrael and put it under Yaakov is so that he should not have to travel around to retrieve the fallen sparks. This way, he would find all the sparks in one place.

Let me explain: The Ari teaches that when Adam sinned the sparks of holy souls fell among the shells of evil, and thereby good and evil became intermingled. These sparks need to be separated by the people through Torah study and the performance of mitzvos. For this reason it was necessary for the Jews to be sent into *galus* among the seventy nations where the holy sparks fell, so that they could redeem those sparks. Egypt is the only country that has no sparks of holiness, because when the Jews left Egypt they redeemed all the sparks that were lodged there. That is why it says, "You shall not see [Egypt] ever again!" (*Shemos* 14:13), since in Egypt there are no sparks left to be freed.

Sefer Baal Shem Tov, Vayeitzei 8, 9

Two Types of People

[The Baal Shem Tov teaches:] There are two types of people. There is the out-and-out evildoer who knows that God exists, but he deliberately wants to rebel against Him. Then there is the person who is blinded by his *yetzer hara* (evil inclination). He thinks he is a perfect tzaddik and that people admire him for his righteousness. He may learn Torah all day and pray and mortify himself, but it's worthless. He does not have true closeness to God, and his faith is not perfect.

The difference between the two is this: The evildoer may recover from his spiritual malady some day when he is stirred to do *teshuvah* and wholeheartedly returns to God. For the other fellow there is no hope. His eyes are too tightly closed for him to recognize God's greatness. He sees himself as the perfect tzaddik, so why should he do *teshuvah*? That's why, when the *yetzer hara* wants to lure a person into sin, he makes him believe that he is really doing a mitzvah and his conduct is flawless, so that he will never do *teshuvah*.

Seder HaDoros HeChadash[1]

Ebb and Flow

[The Baal Shem Tov teaches:] Nonstop pleasure is boring; you don't enjoy it anymore. To avoid such monotony a person experiences alternately fervor and coolness in his service of God. That way he continues to find delight in it. Therein lies the mystery of the angels "that ran to and fro" (*Yechezkel* 1:14). Since the soul comes from a holy place in heaven, it fervently yearns to return to its holy source. In order to prevent the soul from flying off to heaven, it is kept busy with earthly things like eating, drinking, doing business, and the like.

Keser Shem Tov[2]

Pulling the Beard

[The Baal Shem Tov teaches:] When the baby grabs his father's beard the father is not annoyed. On the contrary, he is delighted. We are doing the

---

1 By Rabbi Mendel Bodek, Lemberg, 1865.
2 By Rabbi Aharon of Apta, Zolkava, 1794.

same thing. We are grabbing, as it were, God's thoughts and pulling them down into our physical world. We go so far as to ask Him to bestow His flow of abundance on us. We even have the audacity to beg Him to have mercy on us.

Keser Shem Tov

Traveling to Distant Places

[The Baal Shem Tov teaches:] People travel to distant places with the intention of doing business there and earning profits. God has something else in mind. He knows better. Sometimes a person is destined to eat a loaf of bread or have a drink of water in a given place, at a given time, in order to set right a failing in his soul. For that purpose he has to travel hundreds of miles. God decreed for him to gather up holy sparks that have fallen in that place [by the mitzvah of reciting a *berachah* over his food]. This is alluded to in the verse, "By God are a man's footsteps established, but he chooses his way" (*Tehillim* 37:23). The truth is that God causes a person to take a trip, but he harbors the illusion that "he chooses his way," that he goes there for his own reasons.

[Consider this: When the traveler says a *berachah* over a meal of bread and meat, he redeems not only the holy sparks that were trapped in the meat and the bread, he releases also the sparks in the grass that nourished the animal that provided the meat and the sparks in the grain from which the bread was made, as well as the sparks in the soil in which the grass and the grain grew.]

Or HaMe'ir[1]

---

[1] By Rabbi Reuven Margolis, Lemberg, 1926.

Chapter 42
RABBI DOV BER
(The Maggid of Mezritch)

born: Lukatch, Volhynia (now Ukraine), 1704
died: Hanipol (now Ukraine), 1772

Young Dov Ber, the future Maggid of Mezritch, was the son of a poor *melamed* (teacher of young boys). A brilliant student, he went to Lemberg to study in the yeshivah of Rabbi Yaakov Yehoshua, the celebrated author of *P'nei Yehoshua*. Dov Ber married young and earned a meager living as a teacher in a small village. There, in the stillness of the modest hamlet, he perfected his knowledge of Torah and began to explore the mysteries of Kabbalah.

A gifted orator and original thinker, he served a *maggid* (preacher) in Turshin, Koritz, and Dubno. Like most of the early masters of Chassidism, he was initially a fierce opponent of the fledgling movement. Once, when he was gravely ill, someone suggested that he visit the Baal Shem Tov, who was known to be a healer.

The encounter proved to be the turning point in Rabbi Dov Ber's life. "He taught me the language of the birds and the secrets of the sages and the mystical meanings of many things," Rabbi Dov Ber declared. He became the Baal Shem's ardent follower and the foremost emissary for Chassidism of his time.

After the Baal Shem's death, the mantle of leadership passed to the Maggid, who established Mezritch as the new center of Chassidus. Under his guidance the movement expanded rapidly, despite its numerous adversaries. His students fanned out over the entire region, tirelessly spreading the chassidic message of hope, consolation, and faith — and above all, joy in serving God and fulfilling the mitzvos.

Some of the most illustrious scholars and Kabbalists were among the Maggid's disciples: Rabbi Schmelke of Nikolsburg and his brother Rabbi Zisha, Rabbi Levi Yitzchak of Berditchev, Rabbi Nachum of Chernobyl, Rabbi Shneur Zalman of Liadi, Rabbi Elimelech of Lizhensk, and many others. The Maggid's son was the saintly Rabbi Avraham HaMalach (the Angel), who was born in 1740 and died at an early age in 1776.

The Maggid himself did not write any books. His teachings were recorded and published by his students, mainly by Rabbi Shlomo of Lutzk, under the titles *Maggid Devarav LeYaakov*,[1] *Or Torah*,[2] and *Or HaEmes*.[3]

The Maggid's greatness was that he nurtured the seed that was sown by the Baal Shem Tov and made it grow into a healthy young tree, a tree that continues to bear fruit to this day.

Selections from the Commentaries of Rabbi Dov Ber

Esav's Holy Sparks

[Note: One of the themes of the Maggid's teachings is that there is a divine manifestation in all human actions, even in evil ones.]

Yitzchak loved Esav, for he was a trapper with his mouth.
(Bereishis 25:28)

The Ari teaches (*Sefer HaLikutim, Toldos*) that [although Esav was evil]

---

1 Koretz, 1780.
2 Koretz, 1804.
3 Husiatyn, 1899.

he possessed many holy sparks. Thousands of years later, these holy sparks surfaced in the great teachers of the Talmud [who were descendants of converts, and who descended from Esav]: Rabbi Meir,[1] Rabbi Akiva,[2] Shemayah and Avtalyon,[3] and other converts.

This is what happened. Esav did not allow the holy sparks to enter his heart for fear that they might overwhelm him and cause him to become a decent person. Therefore, he kept his holy sparks locked up in his mouth, preventing them from moving into his inner recesses. That is the deeper meaning of the passage, "He was a trapper with his mouth." The sparks literally were trapped in his mouth, unable to enter into the depths of his heart. That is where Yitzchak made his mistake [of favoring Esav], because when speaking to his father, Esav's words had the ring of refinement of the holy sparks that were in his mouth. [Rashi on the above verse says that he ensnared his father by asking sanctimonious questions, such as, "Father, how do you tithe salt and straw?"]

About such people it says, "A deceitful person will not succeed with his catch" (*Mishlei* 12:27). Esav deceived his father by bottling up his holy sparks in his mouth, preventing them from reaching his inner core. But he did not succeed in completely subduing the sparks, because eventually they were freed and emerged as the great teachers of the Talmud.

Maggid Devarav LeYaakov 186

Hovering over Its Young

[Note: The following remarks deal with the profound Kabbalistic principle of *ratzo vashov*, "run and return" (the ebb and flow of the universe). This rule of fluctuation dominates man's existence and is evident in the pulse of the heartbeat and the rhythm of the breathing lungs. It comes to the fore in

---

1 He was a descendant of converts (*Gittin* 56a).
2 His father, Yosef, was a convert who descended from the general Sisera (*Sanhedrin* 96a).
3 Both Shemayah and Avtalyon were descendants of Sancheiriv (*Gittin* 75b).

man's desire to free himself from the bonds of physicality and unite with the Creator and the opposing urge to remain in this world and partake of life.]

He was like an eagle arousing its nest, hovering over its young, spreading its wings and taking them.
(Devarim 32:11)

The Sages comment on this passage: God fluttered over them, touching them, yet not touching them *(Yerushalmi, Chagigah* 2:1). God is Infinite, and no one can exist in His Infinite Light. That's why He hovers, fluttering lightly with rapid vibrations. When He touches no one can survive; that's why He instantly pulls back, as it says, "The *Chayos* [a group of angels] ran to and fro like the appearance of a flash" *(Yechezkel* 1:14).

Maggid Devarav LeYaakov 237

Why Did Moshe Strike the Rock?

[Note: When the children of Israel complained about lack of water in the wilderness, God told Moshe to raise his staff and speak to the rock, which would then spout water. Instead of speaking to the rock Moshe struck it, whereupon abundant water came forth *(Bemidbar* 20:1–12).]

The *Zohar* says: "If Moshe had not struck the rock but had spoken to it [as God commanded], the Jewish people would not have suffered forgetfulness" *(Tikkunim* 21, 44a). What does this mean?

All the divine miracles came about after Moshe announced them; no action on his part was needed. That's why God said to Moshe [at the parting of the Red Sea], "Raise your staff" *(Shemos* 14:16) [and don't do anything else], and by merely [symbolically] raising your staff the sea will split. The reason is that Moshe was on the spiritual level of *Chochmah*, and wisdom is conveyed through the spoken word. The people who wandered through the wilderness [and witnessed the revelation at Sinai] also were on the level of *Chochmah*. In fact, they are called *"dor dei'ah,"* the generation of wisdom, for they received the Torah, and the Torah was conveyed to them through the spoken word....

Forgetfulness is essentially a slide from the spiritual level of wisdom to the level of tangible reality. After the death of the *dor dei'ah* — the generation that witnessed the giving of the Torah — a new generation arose that was no longer on the level of wisdom. Moshe saw them as a generation of doers, men of action, since they were the people that were destined to conquer Eretz Yisrael by force of arms. [Wanting to speak their language of action,] Moshe struck the rock. But God told Moshe that [instead of stooping to their more physical level] he should speak to the rock and thereby lift the new generation to the spiritual level of their parents, the *dor dei'ah*, the generation of wisdom. Moshe should have shown them that water comes forth just by speaking to the rock. By striking the rock he caused forgetfulness, which is the fall from the level of speech and thought to the level of physical action.

Maggid Devarav LeYaakov 129

God's Unrestricted Light

For a sun and a shield is God the Lord....

(*Tehillim* 84:12)

The analogy [of God and the sun] is fitting because the sun is surrounded by an insulating cover [the atmosphere]. This protective shield is needed, since the world could not take the full-blown brightness and heat of the sun. But only in this world is the sun wrapped in a sheath. When a person has shed his mortal shell and is connected to the higher world, he sees that God Himself is like the sun, in that His Godliness is covered by a shield. This means that in this world God has restricted His Infinite Light in the process of *tzimtzum*, but in the higher world God's Infinite Light reigns without *tzimtzum*, with unrestricted brilliance. This will come true in the future, as it says, "The sun will no longer be for you the light of day.... God will be an eternal light for you, and your God will be your splendor" (*Yeshayah* 60:19).

Maggid Devarav LeYaakov 184

Part of the *Shechinah*

[Note: In Kabbalistic writings the *Sefirah* of *Malchus* is thought of as the *Shechinah*, a kind of female aspect of God. The deeds of the righteous bring about the unification of the Holy One, blessed be He, and the *Shechinah*.]

When you need to ask something of God, bear in mind that your soul is a tiny particle of the *Shechinah*, like a drop in the ocean. [Thus, when you have a need, the *Shechinah* feels the same need.] So make your request on behalf of the *Shechinah*, and pray that the *Shechinah*'s want should be fulfilled [then automatically you will be helped, too]. But you have to believe firmly that your prayer on behalf of the *Shechinah* will be fulfilled. And only if you really attach yourself to the *Shechinah* and feel as part of the *Shechinah* will your prayer be answered. Then the divine flow of goodness will descend on you.

Let me give you an example: When you are jubilant, you spontaneously clap your hands, because the joy you experience spreads to your limbs. It is the same when you are attached to the *Shechinah*. [Since you are a limb of the *Shechinah*,] the flow of divine benevolence is poured out to you.

The *Zohar* puts it this way: "Just as a silkworm uses its mouth to make silk thread, so do the Jews produce words with their mouths with which they clothe the *Shechinah*" (*Zohar, Vayishlach* 178a).

Maggid Devarav LeYaakov 66

Letters, Vowels, and Cantillation Signs

The Hebrew letters are sometimes compared to horses, and the vowel marks (*nekudos*) are the reins. The intellect plays the role of the cantillation marks (*trop*). It represents the horse's rider. This means that basically the Hebrew letters are a shapeless mass, a body without a soul. The vowels make it possible for the letters to be pronounced [thus the vowels are the soul of the letters]. The cantillation signs are the intellect. They give meaning to the sentences. [The cantillation signs function as the punctuation marks that organize the thought expressed in the sentence.]

Maggid Devarav LeYaakov 180

The Root of the Seventy Nations

> You might say to yourself, "These nations are more numerous than we are. How will we be able to drive them out?"
>
> *(Devarim 7:17)*

We know that everything in this world has a root in the higher world. The Sages put it this way: "Every single blade of grass has a guardian angel in heaven that taps it lightly and says, 'Start growing!' " (*Zohar, Terumah* 171b).

The original seventy descendants of Yaakov who came with him to Egypt (see *Shemos* 1:5) are the root of the entire Jewish people. These seventy descendants in turn are rooted in the Seven Shepherds [Avraham, Yitzchak, Yaakov, Yosef, Moshe, Aharon, and David]. Consequently, the entire Jewish people derive from the Seven Shepherds.

Now everything on the side of holiness has a counterpart in the realm of the unholy, as it says, "God has made the one as well as the other" (*Koheles* 7:14). And so, [as counterparts to the seventy original descendants of Yaakov,] there are the seventy nations [of the world] on the side of the unholy. [Parallel to the Seven Shepherds,] the seventy nations of the world are rooted in the seven nations that occupied Eretz Yisrael [the Chiti, Girgashi, Emori, Kanaani, Perizi, Chivi, and Yevusi]. For this reason God commanded the Israelites to subdue these seven nations and bring them under the dominion of *kedushah*, holiness, for they are the spiritual root of all nations.

Maggid Devarav LeYaakov 122

Man Is a Microcosm

Man is a small-scale universe. He contains in miniature everything that exists in the spiritual world. He has the power to think, and thinking is a metaphysical process. He has wisdom, intelligence, understanding, memory, forgetfulness, and imagination, each of which has a quality that is unlike the others. From this you can figure out that in the spiritual universe each of these abilities is a separate world, and each of these faculties in man has a root in the corresponding higher world.

Or HaEmes 74

Chapter 43
RABBI YAAKOV YOSEF OF POLNOYE
(Toldos Yaakov Yosef)

born: c. 1710
died: Polnoye, Belarus, 1784

Rabbi Yaakov Yosef, the primary disciple of the Baal Shem Tov and one of the earliest supporters of the Chassidic Movement, was a descendant of the Kabbalist Rabbi Shimshon of Ostropole and of Rabbi Yom Tov Lipman Heller, author of *Tosefos Yom Tov*, the famed commentary to the Mishnah. His unique approach to Chassidus combines his ancestors' fields of expertise, blending scholarship in both Kabbalah and halachah.

While still a young man, Rabbi Yaakov Yosef was appointed to the rabbinate of Sharogrod. At that time he strongly opposed the new movement. However, on one occasion he met the Baal Shem and was closeted with him for several hours. Their heart-to-heart talk turned him into an ardent admirer of the new movement. His congregants, who disapproved of his changed mindset, forced him to leave his post. He served as rabbi of Rashkov and of Nemirov and in 1770 became the rabbi of Polnoye. He was revered for his deep piety and dedication to Torah study.

Although Rabbi Yaakov Yosef was the Baal Shem's closest disciple, he was not chosen to succeed the master upon his death. Instead, the more dynamic Maggid of Mezritch was selected, since Rabbi Yaakov Yosef's introverted and scholarly nature made him unsuitable to be the leader of a popular movement. But he was not piqued at being passed over and became a faithful follower of the Maggid.

Rabbi Yaakov Yosef's work, *Toldos Yaakov Yosef*,[1] is a highly intellectual exposition of the Kabbalistic underpinnings of chassidic philosophy. It occupies a preeminent place in chassidic literature and can be found on the shelf of every chassidic *beis midrash*. It was the first book published by chassidim and was highly praised by the eminent Sefardic Kabbalist, Rabbi Chaim Yosef David Azulai (the Chida). Rabbi Yaakov Yosef weaves together Kabbalistic and philosophic concepts, combining them with halachic themes, organizing his material according to the weekly Torah portions. He also authored *Ben Poras Yosef*,[2] *Tzofnas Paane'ach*,[3] and *Kesones Passim*.[4] Chassidim refer to this giant of the spirit simply as "the Toldos." By studying and quoting his writings, they lovingly keep his memory alive.

Selections from the Writings of Rabbi Yaakov Yosef

Body and Soul

The human body is made up of 248 limbs and 365 blood vessels, into which God breathed a living soul comprising also 248 spiritual limbs and 365 spiritual blood vessels. The spiritual parts are clothed by the corresponding physical limbs of the body.

So you see, the human body is not the essence of man. It is only a garment for the spiritual limbs of the soul, which is the real person. The spiri-

---

1   Koretz, 1780.
2   Koretz, 1741.
3   Koretz, 1742.
4   Lemberg, 1866.

tual limbs fulfill their tasks by means of the physical limbs; the spiritual limbs receive their nourishment through man's observance of the Torah, which is made up of 613 mitzvos, consistent with the 613 parts of the body (248 limbs and 365 blood vessels). Each limb of the body is nurtured by the particular mitzvah that is related to that limb....

And if a person fails to do a certain mitzvah, the limb that is associated with that mitzvah is deprived of the spiritual nourishment emanating from God. Therefore, you should do your utmost to fulfill all 613 mitzvos.... When you do, you attract the abundance that flows through the spiritual channels. Your soul then becomes a vehicle for God's holiness.

Toldos Yaakov Yosef, Introduction

Why Did Avram Become Avraham?

[Note: The divine Name *Elokim* has the same numerical value as *hateva*, "nature," both adding up to 86. The divine four-letter Name represents the supernatural. Note also that the human body has 248 limbs.]

Your name shall no longer be called Avram, but your name shall be Avraham.

(Bereishis 17:5)

[At the time of Avraham's circumcision God changed his name from Avram to Avraham by inserting the letter *hei*, which has the numeric value of 5.]

The name *Avram* has the numeric value of 243, the name *Avraham* equals 248. The Sages comment: "At first God gave him mastery over 243 of his limbs, and in the end He made him ruler over all of his 248 limbs" (*Nedarim* 32b). [The five limbs that were placed under his control are: his two eyes, two ears, and the male organ.]

The underlying idea is that when he was Avram, he was subject to the laws of nature (*hateva*), which equals the Name *Elokim*. For by nature, man has control over 243 limbs. But when he underwent *bris milah*, he received the letter *hei* of the four-letter divine Name, which placed him above nature. Thereby he was given mastery over the five limbs that until then were not under his control.

Toldos Yaakov Yosef, Introduction

Matter and Form

Man is a composite of matter and form; the two are diametrically opposed to each other. Matter is tangible matter; form is intangible and abstract. The purpose of man's existence is to elevate the physical to the level of the spiritual, "matter" to the level of "form." Just as each individual was created for this purpose, so is the purpose of the Jewish people as a whole to elevate "matter" to the level of "form" – raising the physical to the level of the spiritual.

The "matter" of the Jewish people are the masses of ordinary Jews who are involved in the day-to-day struggle for their existence. The tzaddik, being immersed in Torah study and worship of God, is the "form" of the Jewish people. It is his task to lift the "matter," the community, to his level of "form," of closeness to God. The same holds true on a global scale. The seventy nations of the world – the matter – draw their spiritual sustenance from Israel – the form – as the branches of a tree draw their vitality from the roots. The Jewish people attract the abundance of divine blessing and are the channel that conveys this abundance to the nations of the world.

Toldos Yaakov Yosef, Introduction

Predestination versus Free Will

Many of the towering Jewish sages, such as the Rambam, the Alshich,[1] and the Baal Ha'Akeidah, have been baffled by a statement in the Gemara: "The length of your life, how many children you will have, and your liveli-

---

1   See ch. 28.

hood are not dependent on your merits but on *mazal*, the stars under which you are born" (*Moed Katan* 28a). The obvious implication is that our lives are predetermined by the heavenly constellations and the horoscope, a notion that is completely at odds with the basic principles of free determination and reward and punishment.

Rabbi Moshe Alshich reconciles the conflicting theses as follows: The Holy One, blessed be He, created everyone with his predestined task to repair the sins he committed in a previous incarnation. If, in a previous existence, he was driven to sin because of the temptaions of affluence and the comforts of life, then in his next incarnation he is doomed to live in poverty. Conversely, if in an earlier life he was an upright and virtuous man living in dire straits, unable to give charity to the poor, he will return under a lucky star as a wealthy and prosperous man. Thus, while it is true that everything depends on your *mazal*, your lucky star, in the final analysis your fate is determined by your deeds in a previous existence.

This also answers the question as to why bad things happen to good people, and why the wicked are prospering: The good man who is suffering is being punished for a transgression he committed in a previous life; the thriving wicked person is being rewarded for a good deed he performed in a previous incarnation.

Toldos Yaakov Yosef, Kedoshim

Going Down in Order to Rise

This world is likened to a ladder that reaches toward heaven. Some of God's angels — meaning human beings, who came into this world to fulfill God's will — are going up, while others are going down. Life has its ups and downs. No one remains forever at the same level, for nonstop pleasure is no pleasure [it becomes monotonous]. That is why you go down a step sometimes, so that when you come back up you experience greater joy.

This is the figurative meaning of the verse, "It is not good for man to be alone" (*Bereishis* 2:18). "Alone" means without the *yetzer hara*, the evil impulse. It is not good for a person to live without the *yetzer hara*, for then he would remain unchanged forever. "I will make a helpmate for him who opposes him" — by virtue of his evil impulse a person sometimes sinks to a lower level, only to rise again, which is the source of genuine pleasure.

Ben Poras Yosef, p. 31

The Brothers and Yosef — Matter and Form

[Note: Think of matter as a shapeless chunk of clay that can be molded into any form. When you sculpt the clay into the form of a bird, it is the form that gives individuality and character to the shapeless mass. You could say that "matter" is the body of the sculpture, while "form" is its soul. It is the same with any material object: the substance from which it is made is its "body," its form is its "soul."]

Just as there is matter and form in the physical world, so is there matter and form in the spiritual world.

"Matter" is the feminine aspect of the spiritual world; it is represented by the *Sefirah* of *Gevurah*. "Form" is the masculine aspect of the spiritual world; it is personified by the *Sefirah* of *Chesed*. These two opposites blend in the *Sefirah* of *Tiferes*. The two extremes [*Chesed* and *Gevurah*] are epitomized by Avraham and Yitzchak respectively. Yaakov, the *bechir ha'avos*, "preferred patriarch," exemplifies the *sefirah* of *Tiferes*.

The *Zohar* says that Yosef's brothers are derived from the feminine aspect *Gevurah*, while Yosef stems from the male aspect *Chesed*. Taking this one step further, the brothers exemplify matter, while Yosef stands for form. That's why the brothers hated Yosef, for their roots were in opposite worlds; what the one favored, the others despised. The conflict was resolved when Yosef, who symbolized form [soul], subdued the element of mattter [i.e., the brothers].... This came to a head when "Yehudah approached [Yosef to plead on behalf of Binyamin]" (*Bereishis*

44:18). At that moment form (i.e., the characteristic of Yosef) subdued matter (i.e., the characteristic of the brothers).

Toldos Yaakov Yosef, Vayeishev

Half and Half

[A follow-up to the previous commentary:] The Gemara says, "A person should always consider himself as though his mitzvos and transgressions are evenly balanced — half and half; so that if he fulfills one more mitzvah, he tips the scale to the side of merit for himself and the whole world. By the same token, if he commits one transgression, he tips the scale to the side of guilt for himself and the whole world" (*Kiddushin* 40b).

The underlying thought is that every person has two components: matter and form — body and soul. If he keeps his matter under control [suppressing his bodily instincts] and lets his form [his spiritual part] gain the upper hand, he causes the same things to happen in the higher worlds. As a result, the fate of the whole will be tipped to the side of merit and kindness.

Toldos Yaakov Yosef, Vayeishev

Gehinnom and Gan Eden

The Sages say that when Mashiach comes, Gehinnom will be abolished. Is it fair that all evildoers will be admitted to Gan Eden? The answer is: The worst Gehinnom for an evildoer is to be sent to Gan Eden, a place where there is no eating and drinking and worldly pleasure. In Gan Eden the tzaddikim are sitting, wearing crowns on their heads, learning Torah. And the wicked man has to listen to this day and night. Can there be a worse punishment!

Sifran Shel Tzaddikim,[1] quoting *Toldos Yaakov Yosef*

---

[1] By Elazar Dov, Warsaw, 1914.

Chapter 44

RABBI ELIMELECH OF LIZHENSK

(No'am Elimelech)

born: Lapacha, near Tiktin, Poland, 1717
died: Lizhensk, Poland,1786

Rabbi Elimelech's father, Eliezer Lipa, a prosperous landowner, was known as a pious and charitable man. Of his seven sons, two rose to great fame in the world of Chassidism: Rabbi Elimelech of Lizhensk and Rabbi Zisha of Hanipol. Early in life the two brothers immersed themselves in Torah study, both in its revealed and its mystic forms, particularly the Kabbalistic teachings of the Ari HaKadosh.

Putting the Ari's words into action, the brothers went into self-imposed exile, wandering incognito for three years from town to town, spreading Torah and inspiring people to mend their ways. They became attracted to the emerging movement of Chassidus, eventually becoming outstanding disciples of the Maggid of Mezritch.

After the death of the Maggid in 1772, Rabbi Elimelech was recognized as the uncrowned head of the Chassidic Movement for the next thirty years. He developed the idea of making the personality of the tzaddik the focal point of a chassid's existence, believing that the tzaddik has the mission "to give life to all the worlds" by virtue of his divine soul.

Rabbi Elimelech taught that in a mystical way the rebbe could bind himself to his chassidim and purify their souls. This concept forms the basis of many of the expositions in his book *No'am Elimelech*,[1] a commentary on the weekly Torah portions. One of the principal works on Chassidus, *No'am Elimelech* has been printed more than fifty times, most recently in 1993.

Rabbi Elimelech had three sons, each of whom served as rabbi. His only daughter, Mirush, was admired for her piety and her prodigious Torah scholarship. Her lectures on her father's teachings, peppered with anecdotes about his life, drew large and enthusiastic audiences.

The grave of Rabbi Elimelech is visited by thousands of chassidim who come to Lizhensk from all over the world on annual pilgrimages.

Selections from No'am Elimelech

The Purpose of Avodah

> Open for me the gates of righteousness, I want enter them and thank God. This is the gate of God; the righteous shall enter through it.
>
> (Tehillim 118:9)

The more ardently a tzaddik serves God, the more he realizes that he can never attain God-like perfection. For God is infinite; His goodness is endless. In fact, the realization that perfection is beyond man's reach is the aim of *avodah*, of serving God.

The above verse expresses this thought. The tzaddik says, "Open for me the gates of service to God, so that I can enter and thank my Creator." Noting how distant he still is from achieving his goal of nearness to God, he imagines that until now his entire *avodah* (service) was futile, and that

---

1   Lemberg, 1788.

all his fervent prayers, meditations, and good deeds amount to nothing. The answer he receives is, "This is the gate of God" — the awareness that you fall short in your service of God and that God-like perfection is unattainable by its very nature, in itself is the main purpose of *avodah*, of serving the Almighty. [The realization that you are inadequate is the "gate of God," and you are well-suited to enter it.]

No'am Elimelech, Likutei Shoshanah

When Mashiach Comes (An Allegory)

Kabbalah teaches that when Mashiach gathers in the Jews from all over, the tzaddikim will stay close to him all the time. [But not everyone is a tzaddik.] There are good people who lead decent lives and avoid transgressions, but who love to make money and accumulate wealth. Mashiach will lead these people to the ocean and show them the hidden treasures lying there. They load up on silver, gold, and precious jewels and bring home a vast hoard of wealth. When the time comes for Mashiach to ascend to Gan Eden, the tzaddikim, buoyed up by their saintly way of life, rise upward along with him. The people who garnered piles of gold and silver also want to fly to Gan Eden, but the weight of their material goods prevents their liftoff. The tzaddikim who are used to serving God all their lives are not burdened with heavy baggage. When Mashiach comes they soar upward effortlessly. [The moral of the story: The accumulation of wealth and material goods stands in the way of spiritual growth.]

No'am Elimelech, Kedoshim

The Source of Anti-Semitism

> [Note: In Kabbalistic literature the *Shechinah* (the feminine aspect of the Divine) is God's manifestation in the *Sefirah* of *Malchus* which is the material world. The *Shechinah* yearns to be unified with the Holy One, blessed be He. We bring about this unification through the performance of mitzvos. This is expressed in the prayer *Leshem Yichud*, "For the sake of the unification of

> the Holy One, blessed be He, and His *Shechinah*," which chassidim say before the performance of a mitzvah.]

Kabbalah teaches that nothing can exist unless it holds within it a tiny spark of holiness which keeps it alive. If not for the holy spark residing in it, nothing in the world could survive. Trapped inside the shells of impurity, the holy spark envies the tzaddikim. Similarly, the holy sparks that are imprisoned among the nations are jealous of the Jewish people. This envy is the source of anti-Semitism. It is our job to extricate these caged holy sparks from the shells of impurity. When that is accomplished, the evil nations, having lost their life-sustaining force, will wither, and the *Shechinah* will rise upward [to be unified with the Holy One, blessed be He].

At the present time, the *Shechinah* is in this bitter exile together with us, but It is looking forward to the time when all sparks of holiness are set free [by means of the mitzvos we perform]. When that happens, the ultimate Redemption will come to pass, and the Messianic Era is ushered in, speedily in our days.

No'am Elimelech, Yisro

The Two Impulses

> Two men fight and one hits the other with a stone or with his fist. If [the victim] does not die, but becomes bedridden and then gets up and can walk with his cane, the one who struck him shall be acquitted. Still, he must pay for the victim's loss of work and his cure.
> (*Shemos* 21:18-19)

This passage lends itself to a beautiful allegorical interpretation: God created man with a good and an evil impulse. Both are characterized as "man." The Gemara tells us that we must serve God with both our impulses,[1] which means that the evil impulse, too, must be placed in the service of God. This is the import of the present verse. "When two men fight" — when the good and the evil impulses are battling one another; "and one hits the other" — the good impulse subdues the evil impulse, placing it in the service of the Almighty, so that the person now serves God with both his impulses. And how can he do that? "With a stone," that is, the Torah; for through Torah study you weaken the grip of the evil impulse..."or with the fist" — by bolstering your good character traits you sap the strength of the evil impulse.

No'am Elimelech, Mishpatim

You Must Be Holy

>[Note: The *Sefiros* of *Chochmah* and *Binah* are also known as *Abba* and *Imma*.]

You must be holy, since I am God, your Lord, [and] I am holy. Every person must respect his mother and father....
(Vayikra 19:2)

The phrase "You must be holy" suggests that a person should sanctify himself, believing that God sustains the world by illuminating it with His Light by way of the ten *Sefiros*. The nations of the world do not believe in God or in the chain of the ten successive *Sefiros*. The unbelievers go so far as to say that the world had no beginning and that it existed eternally. That is why it says, "You must be holy, since I am God, your Lord" — I brought all the worlds into being by the power of My Name. "I am *your* God," but not the God of the nations, who do not believe this.

"You must be holy" — You, living in the material world, must resemble the holiness of the upper worlds. For everything in the lower world has a counterpart in the higher world. And the passage, "Every person must respect his father and his mother [in this world]," has a counterpart in the higher world. It parallels the *Sefiros* that are known as *Abba* [Father, i.e.,

---

1 *Devarim* 6:5 states, "Love God, your Lord, with all your heart." Scripture uses the word *levavecha*, spelled with a double *beis*, to signify "your heart." Our Sages derive from the uncommon use of the double *beis* that we must love God with both our impulses, the *yetzer tov* and the *yetzer hara*. By subduing the *yetzer hara* we can transform it into an instrument for the service of God.

Chochmah] and *Imma* [Mother, i.e., *Binah*].

No'am Elimelech, Kedoshim

Complete Unity

> [Note: The word *erev*, "evening," can be read as *areiv*, "pleasant, sweet." Note also that the "Breaking of the Vessels" refers to *sheviras hakeilim*, the catastrophe that occurred after Adam's transgression. (See ch. 3.)]

> It was evening and it was morning, one day.
> (Bereishis 1:5)

God willing, when Mashiach comes everything will be set right. Then there will be complete unity. Scripture hints at this when it says, "It was *erev* (evening)," implying: When Mashiach comes, the darkness of evening will turn to sweetness (*areiv*). For all Creation will be rectified, and absolute unity will prevail, just as it did before the Breaking of the Vessels. "It was morning, one day" – When Mashiach comes, all existence will be unified. The night will become day; there will be total, all-embracing unity.

No'am Elimelech, Bereishis

The Seven Lamps

> [Note: The Menorah in the Beis HaMikdash had seven branches, three branches on each side of the central shaft (see *Shemos* 25:32).]

> Speak to Aharon and say to him: "When you kindle the lamps, the seven lamps shall cast light toward the face of the Menorah."
> (Bemidbar 8:2)

The Sages expound the phrase, "the seven lamps shall cast light toward the face of the Menorah," to mean that the [three lamps on either side of the center lamp] should be inclined toward the center lamp. This being so, shouldn't it say: "The six lamps [the three on either side] shall cast light toward the face of the Menorah"?

A possible answer may be that the six lamps represent the six days of the week, while the middle lamp exemplifies Shabbos and the *Shechinah*. On a spiritual level the idea behind inclining the seven lamps toward the middle lamp is that we should direct our thoughts toward the *Shechinah*, not only on Shabbos, but also on the six weekdays [so that on Shabbos and all week long we strive to attain *kedushah* and closeness to God].

No'am Elimelech, Beha'aloscha

Connecting with *K'lal Yisrael*

For there is no man so wholly righteous on earth that he [always] does good and never sins.
(Koheles 7:20).

This passage says that there is no tzaddik on earth who never transgresses. This being so, how can you do a mitzvah with one of your limbs, when that limb is tainted by sin? The answer is that you can do a mitzvah by including yourself in the community of Israel. For the totality of Israel is righteous, whole, and flawless. As it says, "Your people are all righteous" (*Yeshayah* 60:21). For this reason, even though the individual Jew may sometimes sin, the community as a whole retains its holiness and is immune to Satan's denunciations. The Kabbalists describe *k'lal Yisrael* (the community of Israel) as *Adam Kadmon*, "the First Man," and Adam was created free of sin. So when you connect with the community of Israel you are linked to purity and holiness. All your limbs are holy, and you can do the mitzvos in the name of all Israel.

No'am Elimelech, Koheles

Chapter 45
RABBI BARUCH OF KOSSOV

born: 1725
died: 1782

Rabbi Baruch of Kossov, one of the founders of Chassidus, was a great Talmudic scholar, Kabbalist, and profound thinker, who delved into Kabbalistic writings from a young age. Very little is known about his forebears. For many years he officiated as *maggid* (preacher) in the town of Kossov, Galicia. A disciple of the Maggid of Mezritch and Rabbi Menachem Mendel of Vitebsk, he was a prolific writer and an inspiring speaker. In his books he often quotes the Baal Shem Tov, the Maggid of Mezritch, and Rabbi Menachem Mendel of Premishlan. The latter has this to say about Rabbi Baruch: "He has a pleasing way of presenting the wisdom of Kabbalah and the talent to explain [Kabbalistic] ideas with absolute clarity" (from his approbation to Rabbi Baruch's *Amud HaAvodah*).

Rabbi Baruch wrote *Yesod HaEmunah*, in which he comments on Rashi, the Prophets, and the Talmud, and *Amud HaAvodah*,[1] in which he discusses the basic principles of Kabbalah. In a lucid style he explains abstruse Kabbalistic concepts, adding helpful illustrations to make a point. He en-

---

1 Both books first published in Czernovitz, 1854. *Amud HaAvodah* was reprinted in Jerusalem in 1968.

courages every learned Jew to study Kabbalah, but advises that no one should embark on the study of the *Zohar* before mastering the works of Rabbi Yitzchak Luria and Rabbi Chaim Vital.[1]

Selections from Amud HaAvodah

Prenatal Knowledge

Before the soul enters the body, it is in a nonphysical state, an immaterial being like an angel. Since the soul is purely spiritual and not wrapped in a dense curtain of physicality, it clearly and distinctly perceives supernal concepts. That is what the Sages had in mind when they said that before coming into this world, "The soul looks and sees from one end of the world to the other. As soon as it enters the world, an angel comes, taps the baby lightly on its mouth, and makes it forget completely all the Torah it learned" (*Niddah* 30b). For now the soul is enclosed in the physical body which erases all its prenatal knowledge.

That is why it is so hard to acquire Torah knowledge, because you need to weaken your bodily desires before spirituality can enter. The basic rule is that intellect and bodily cravings do not go together. Actually, all the Torah you learn in this world is just a rehashing of the wisdom you acquired before your soul entered your body, which you then forgot.

But not all souls are alike. There are saintly souls that emanate from a holy root in heaven, and there are ordinary souls that are less holy. The higher the soul, the more lofty the thoughts it can grasp.... And so a wise man takes great delight in the things he learns, whereas a fool does not enjoy learning and has no desire to listen to wise teachings.

Amud HaAvodah 103b

---

[1] Introduction to *Amud HaAvodah*, p. 1.

Love Your Fellow as Yourself

> Love your fellow as yourself — I am God.
> *(Vayikra 19:18)*

Let me explain the reason for the mitzvah to love your neighbor. We know that every deed you do in this world gives rise to a similar deed above, for your soul is a part of God. So when your soul is stirred to loving your neighbor, the *Shechinah* — on a grand scale — is stirred to fervently loving the Jewish people. Thus the present passage implies: If you love your fellow, you awaken love of Israel in God.

Perhaps this explains why the root cause of the destruction of the Beis HaMikdash was *sinas chinam*, "baseless hatred." You may ask: Baseless hatred surely is not a cardinal sin like idol worship, immorality, and bloodshed. [Then why the horrific punishment of the *churban*?] When you love someone you minimize his wrongdoing. Conversely, when you hate someone, his slightest offense is blown completely out of proportion and treated as a capital crime. Similarly, when there is hate and anger among Jews down in this world, divine anger is aroused above [and baseless hatred weighs very heavily] because, as we have said: Every action in this world brings forth a similar action above.

Amud HaAvodah 136b

An Analogy of *Chesed* and *Gevurah*

Nature mirrors the *Sefiros* of the higher world. So by studying the laws of nature you can gain an insight into the essence of the *Sefiros*.

We know that the *Sefiros* of *Chesed* and *Gevurah* are extreme opposites. In Kabbalistic literature *Chesed* is symbolized by water, which by nature flows downward. *Gevurah*, the *Sefirah* of Strict Judgment, is exemplified by fire, which rises upward.

You have to realize that all sweet things in the world evolve from *Chesed*, and all sharp, harsh, and tangy things — like strong wine, whiskey, and vinegar — stem from *Gevurah*.

[An analogy will explain this.] When you want to produce very strong brandy you pour ten gallons of weak brandy into the still, and you heat the liquid. The rising vapor is cooled in the condenser and flows into the receiving vessel, where the original ten gallons of weak brandy are reduced to one gallon of strong brandy.

The opposite happens when you distill honey wine. You start with ten gallons of weak honey wine that is not very sweet. When you heat the liquid, the condensed vapor is collected as water in the receiving vessel, and you end up with nine gallons of water and one gallon of exquisitely sweet honey wine.

The difference is that in the case of the honey wine the sweet beverage remains in the still, and the distilled water is discarded. By contrast, in the case of the brandy, the worthless residue remains in the still, and the good part — the strong liquor — rises up as vapor and is then collected. The analogy is: The vapors of the sharp brandy that rise upward represent *Gevurah*, the *Sefirah* that ascends, whereas the sweet honey wine that remains down in the still represents *Chesed*, the *Sefirah* that flows downward....

To sum it up: *Gevurah* — fire, heat, fury — rises upward; *Chesed* — cooling water, serenity — descends downward.

Amud HaAvodah 137a

Two Kinds of Light

You have to understand that there are two kinds of light: There is the physical light you perceive with your eyes. This includes the light of the sun, the moon, and a flame. Then there is the light of the intellect. By this I mean the understanding you get through your intellect. You don't need your eyesight to perceive this light. In fact, your eyesight is of no use in the dark. But the light of the intellect operates even in the dark, for you can contemplate with your eyes closed. The light of the intellect, which is a spiritual light, is far more treasured than physical light, which requires eyesight to be observed. The truth is that the light of the intellect is real light, whereas physical "light" is only a figurative, metaphoric term.

Let me give you an example to help you understand what is meant by intellectual light. Say you ram a round pole through a wall of a house so that the ends of the pole stick out on either side of the wall. Then you attach a tight-fitting wheel to each end of the pole, [so that the pole becomes the axle connecting the two wheels]. When an intelligent person standing inside the house sees the wheel on the wall turning, he concludes that someone standing outside must be turning the wheel. Another person standing outside plainly sees someone moving the wheel. The fellow inside is absolutely sure that someone outside is moving the wheel; he is just as sure as the fellow outside who actually sees the wheel being turned. Both "see" the same thing; only the fellow outside sees the turning wheel with physical light, while the fellow inside perceives it with intellectual light.

When you understand a verse in the Torah or you grasp the meaning of a *Rashi* or a *Tosafos*, you "see the light." The "light" you see stems from the essential light which is the light of your soul, that is, your intellect. Although you cannot possibly comprehend the essence of your soul, you still can infer logically that your soul is indeed the light of your intellect.

Amud HaAvodah 62a

The Six Extremes and *Gevurah*

[Note: It should be remembered that *Keser, Chochmah, Binah* — the three "*Sefiros* of the head" — are completely beyond human comprehension. The six lower *Sefiros, Chesed, Gevurah, Tiferes, Netzach, Hod,* and *Yesod,* are known as a group in Kabbalistic literature as *Shesh HaKetzavos,* "the Six Extremes." They are set off against *Malchus,* the seventh of the lower *Sefiros.*]

The Six Extremes are also called "Six Weekdays," and *Malchus* is called

Shabbos. Alternately, the following symbols are applied to them:

The Six Extremes are heaven and *Malchus* is earth;

the Six Extremes are day and *Malchus* is night;

the Six Extremes are sun and *Malchus* is moon;

the Six Extremes are male and *Malchus* is female;

the Six Extremes are water and *Malchus* is sand;

the Six Extremes are vegetation and *Malchus* is minerals.

The Six Extremes and *Malchus* have opposite charasteristics:

the Six Extremes are active and *Malchus* is passive;

the Six Extremes give and *Malchus* receives;

the Six Extremes are in motion and *Malchus* is at rest.

Similarly, the 365 prohibitions emanate from the side of *Gevurah*. This is the left side [of the *Sefiros*], the passive, female side, the side that is associated with *yirah* (fear of God), which is linked to leisure and inactivity and to the 365 prohibitions. In contrast, the 248 positive mitzvos emanate from the side of *Chesed*, the right side [of the *Sefiros*], the side associated with the positive mitzvos – the mitzvos you should actively perform.

This tells you that all these descriptions flow from one central idea. This idea points to the truth of the Torah and to the wisdom of Kabbalah, which we received from the saintly sages of old. They possessed the spirit of prophecy and certainly did not dream up these things by themselves. "For the ways of God are straight; the righteous walk in them and sinners will stumble over them" (*Hoshea* 14:10).

Amud HaAvodah 123b–124a

The Concept of Time

There are a great many profound and elusive concepts that a person cannot understand as long as he is alive, as a body and a soul, because of the dense physicality of the body. But when the soul leaves the body and is free of physicality, it can fathom these subtle ideas. Essentially, that is the reward and the spiritual delight a person receives in the World to Come. For there is nothing like the joy of grasping a profound thought that you could not understand before. But while the soul was in the body it could not possibly understand these concepts, any more than a cow can understand how a watch works. While you can figure out how a timepiece works, and you may even be able to assemble a new watch, a cow could never do that. Therefore, you should believe that there are things that a human being cannot comprehend.

To give you an example of an incomprehensible idea: Before Creation, time did not exist, for time came into being as part of Creation. Before Creation, concepts like past, present, and future did not exist. You cannot speak of a point in time "before Creation" because terms like "before" and "after" are meaningless when the whole concept of time does not exist. And even though you imagine that before Creation time extended into eternity, this is only a figment of your imagination. You think time existed when, in reality, it did not.

It is difficult to understand how there could be a period before Creation without "before" and "after." That's why the Gemara says: "You should not seriously inquire into things that are above and underneath [the universe]; what happened before [Creation], and what will happen [after the world ceases to exist]" (*Chagigah* 11b).

The limitations of the human intellect become clear when you think of an animal's instincts. An animal has the sense to search for food and to avoid being beaten or burned by fire. Surely it thinks that there is no greater wisdom than that. But we know that this is not so; the animal's mistaken idea stems from its ignorance. By the same token, we have to believe that there are many profound ideas that we are incapable of understanding.

This idea is expressed in the verse, "We can learn from the beasts of the land and from the birds of the sky" (*Iyov* 35:11). In other words, from the beasts that foolishly think that they possess the pinnacle of wisdom you should learn not to think that you possess the ultimate wisdom. If you do harbor such thoughts, you are just as foolish as the beast.

Amud HaAvodah 81a

Chapter 46
RABBI SHNEUR ZALMAN OF LIADI
(Baal HaTanya)

born: Laznia, Belarus, 1745
died: Piena, near Kursk, 1813

Rabbi Shneur Zalman, a descendant of the Maharal of Prague, is one of the pillars of the Chassidic Movement. Even as a youngster he displayed signs of genius, and at fifteen years of age he was known as a Torah scholar of high caliber. Later he became a disciple of the Maggid of Mezritch, the most prominent of the Baal Shem Tov's disciples, who initiated him into the world of Chassidism and introduced him to the Kabbalistic writings of the Ari HaKadosh. For twelve years he studied under the Maggid, becoming a member of his inner circle and one of his favorite disciples.

After the Maggid's death, Rabbi Shneur Zalman became the leader of the chassidim in Lithuania, the region of the *misnagdim* (opponents of Chassidism). Undaunted by their strident antagonism, he succeeded in creating a far-flung network of chassidic centers. His attempts at creating a dialogue with his chief adversary, the Vilna Gaon, were unsuccessful. In the wake of false denunciations he was sent to prison in Petersburg but was released miraculously a short time later. The nineteenth of Kislev, the day of his deliverance, is still celebrated by Lubavitch chassidim as a "holiday of liberation."

After that, Rabbi Shneur Zalman moved to Liadi, where the movement grew by leaps and bounds. He is the originator of Chabad Chassidus, also know as the Lubavitch chassidic movement. *Chabad* is an acronym of the words *Chochmah, Binah,* and *Daas* (the names of the three upper *Sefiros*). Chabad ideology seeks to create a synthesis between Chassidism and Torah scholarship and to establish a fusion of the mystical and the revealed aspects of the Torah.

Rabbi Shneur Zalman formulates his thoughts in *Likutei Amarim*,[1] better known as the *Sefer HaTanya*, or simply "the *Tanya*," which is the book's opening word. He expounds on such profound Kabbalistic themes as the Oneness of God, *tzimtzum*, and the *Sefiros*. He examines the opposing facets of the divine soul (*nefesh elokis*) and the animal soul (*nefesh habehamis*) and deals with many other fundamental subjects. He also wrote *Likutei Torah*,[2] reflections on the weekly Torah portions and on *Shir HaShirim*. In the realm of halachah he wrote the *Shulchan Aruch HaRav*,[3] a comprehensive code of Jewish law. His writings form the cornerstone of Lubavitch Chassidus and greatly influenced the Torah world as a whole. His thoughts on the portions of the week are collected in *Torah Or*[4] as well as in *Likutei Torah*.

Selections from the Teachings of Rabbi Shneur Zalman

Like a Candle

The 613 commandments of the Torah together with the seven commandments of the Rabbis add up to 620, which is the numeric value of *Keser*

---

1 Slavita, 1796.
2 Zhitomir, 1848.
3 Sadilkov, 1826.
4 Kapust, 1837.

[*kaf* (20) + *tav* (400) + *reish* (200)]....

The 613 mitzvos derive from God's Wisdom. Through these commandments the [flame of the] *Shechinah* clings to the "wick." This means that the *Shechinah* hangs onto the life-giving soul, which is compared to a wick. [To illustrate:] In the case of a wax candle, the light shines by dint of the destruction of the burning wicks. The same way, the light of the *Shechinah* rests on the *nefesh elokis* (the divine aspect of the soul) as a result of the destruction of the *nefesh habehamis* (the animal aspect of the soul), which is transformed from the darkness of the *klippos* to the Divine Light.... That is the underlying thought of the verse, "God, your Lord, is like a consuming fire" (*Devarim* 4:24). [In other words, by curbing your physical impulse you come closer to God.]

Tanya, ch. 53

The War between the Souls

The animal soul is [manifest] in the heart, specifically, in the left ventricle that is filled with blood [which is pumped out to the tissues throughout the body]. It says, "For the blood is the *nefesh* [i.e., the animal soul]" (*Devarim* 12:23). Therefore, lust, arrogance, anger, and similar emotions originate in the heart. From the heart these emotions spread through the whole body, rising to the brain, where you think and meditate about them and are affected by them.

By contrast, the divine soul is lodged in the brain [i.e., the intellect] that is in the head. From there it extends to all the limbs and also to the heart, namely to the right ventricle, where there is no [oxygenated] blood[1] [and there are no sensual emotions], as it says, "The heart of the wise man is on his right" (*Koheles* 10:2). It is the source of a person's fervent love of God. This love, like burning coals, flares up in the heart of a thinking person when he reflects on God's unfathomable greatness. [In the divine soul the

---

1   Actually, there is blood in the right ventricle, but it is low in life-going oxygen and high in carbon dioxide.

mind controls the emotions of the heart. Conversely, in the animal soul, the emotions of the heart affect the mind.]

Think of it in terms of two kings waging war over a town. Each wants to capture and rule it. Well, it is the same with the two souls. Your divine soul and animal soul fight over your body and your limbs. The divine soul wants to pervade the entire body so that all limbs obey it, including the [sensuous] left chamber of the heart. The soul wants to change the body from loving the pleasures of the world to loving God. And so the Torah says, "Love God, your Lord with all your heart [*levavecha*]" (*Devarim* 6:5). [*Levavecha*, written with the letter *beis* twice, signifies that you should love God with both your good and your carnal impulses (*Berachos* 54a)].

Tanya, ch. 9

The Era of Mashiach

The era of Mashiach and the resurrection of the dead are the ultimate objective of the creation of this world. It was for this reason that the world was created to begin with.

At the time of Mashiach, the Infinite Light will be revealed in this physical world. At that time, the materialism of the world will have been cleansed, and the world will be ready to receive the Divine Light that will radiate for the Jewish people through the Torah. [How can the world receive the Divine Light if it shines only for the Jewish people?] It is the leftovers of this Light that will illuminate the [spiritual] darkness of the nations of the world. As it says, "Nations will walk by your light, and kings by the brilliance of your shine" (*Yeshayah* 60:3).

But the coming of Mashiach depends on our actions throughout the duration of the *galus*. For the reward of a mitzvah is another mitzvah (*Avos* 4:2). This means that when you do a mitzvah you draw down a flow of the Infinite Light from above. This [spiritual] Light is clothed in the physicality of this world, in something that was previously under the dominion of the *klippos*. [When you do a mitzvah you set free the spark of holiness that was imprisoned in the *klippos*. When all the sparks of holiness have been released, Mashiach will come.]

Tanya, ch. 37.

Leah and Rachel

> God saw that Leah was unloved, so He opened her womb; but Rachel remained barren.
>
> *(Bereishis 29:31)*

You cannot love something you cannot understand. You may even dislike it. For example: When you have solved an intricate problem, you feel a sense of joy and delight, but when you are stumped by an question that is beyond your grasp you feel low and depressed. That explains why Leah was unloved. For [in Kabbalistic thought] Leah represents inwardness, the mystical world, the realm that is beyond human understanding; [remember, Leah had "weak eyes" (*Bereishis* 29:17), symbolizing the unfathomable]. And that's why Yaakov did not love Leah [as much as Rachel]. Rachel, on the other hand, represents outwardness, the revealed, the tangible world.

Toras Chaim,[1] *Vayeitzei*

The *Shechinah* Is Suffering

There is a well-known statement in the *Zohar* that the "*Shechinah* is suffering in the exile." In a figurative sense, the *Shechinah*'s sickness is like a physical ailment. A person's health or illness depends on the flow of blood from the heart to all the limbs and organs and back again to the heart. When your circulation is normal, you are in perfect health. All your limbs and organs are connected to the heart and receive their vitality from the heart through the circulatory system. But if there is a blockage clogging the flow of blood, then the bond that ties the organs to the heart is

---

1 An anthology of Torah insights of *gedolim*.

broken, and the person becomes sick, God forbid.

The same way, all Jewish souls are regarded as limbs of the *Shechinah*, which is the "heart" [of the Jewish people], as it says, "I will dwell among them" (*Shemos* 25:8).... This teaches us that when all souls are joined together, they are attached to "the Lord who is One." As it says, "You are standing this day, *all of you*, before God, your Lord" (*Devarim* 29:9).

Now you will understand what our Sages say about the destruction of the second Beis HaMikdash, the ensuing *galus*, and the withdrawal of the *Shechinah* into exile. The Sages tell us (*Yoma* 9b) that these calamities happened because of the sin of baseless hatred and divisiveness [among the Jewish people. As a result, the connection with the *Shechinah* was severed]. And that is why the *Shechinah* is suffering in *galus*.

Iggeres HaKodesh,[1] *ch. 31*

Elevating Food and Drinks

The Gemara says that thinking about something does not take the place of actually verbalizing your thoughts (*Berachos* 20b). Therefore, you have not fulfilled the mitzvah [of reciting the Shema by merely reflecting on the words]. You have to utter [the words] with your lips. Now the Gemara says that moving your lips is considered as "action" (*Bava Metzia* 90b). Therefore, the more intensity you put into your speech, the more energy you invest into the words you say. That is the meaning of the verse, "All my bones declare..." (*Tehillim* 35:10).

We know that our animal soul derives its strength and vitality from the blood. And the blood is nourished by the food and drink you consume which have been converted into blood. [Kabbalah teaches that] all food and drink is in the clutches of the *klippos*. But when you move your lips in

---

1   A letter the Baal HaTanya sent to all of his followers upon his release from prison, now printed in the back of the *Tanya*.

prayer or Torah study [the energy you use is supplied by your blood]. Thereby you convert the food and drink you ingested from evil to good, and your soul is elevated.

Tanya, ch. 37

Tangible Mitzvos

When you perform a mitzvah you literally draw the Infinite Light into your soul.... That's why a mitzvah is compared to a lamp. When you light a lamp the entire house is lit up; so too, when you do a mitzvah you illuminate the higher worlds....

The drawing down of the Divine Light by doing a mitzvah can be compared to planting seeds. Most seeds cannot be eaten. They are impalatable, tasteless kernels. But when you plant the seed in the earth it sprouts and grows into an savory fruit, this despite the fact that the seed from which it came was inedible.... It is the same with the mitzvos [which are purely spiritual in nature]. They come down from above and are clothed in tangible matter [the tangible scrolls inside] the tefillin, which are made of parchment, and the tzitzis, which are made of wool.... And when a Jew puts on tefillin there is an aura of divine manifestation.

Torah Or, Shemos

Chapter 47

RABBI CHAIM TIRER OF CHERNOVITZ

(Be'er Mayim Chaim)

born: near Butchatch, Galicia (now Poland), c. 1760
died: Tzefas, 1816

In his early years Rabbi Chaim Tirer, better known as the "Be'er Mayim Chaim," was introduced to Chassidus by Rabbi Yechiel Michel of Zlotchov, the Zlotchover Maggid. Later he studied under Rabbi Shmelke of Nikolsburg and the Maggid of Mezritch, becoming one of the trailblazers of Chassidus, spreading its teachings throughout Moldavia (now Moldava).

An eminent Torah scholar and noted Kabbalist, he served as rabbi in the communities of Mohilev, Batishan, Kishinev, Chernovitz, and the surrounding region of Bukovina. He was greatly admired for the kindness and love with which he dedicated himself to winning alienated Jews back to Torah observance.

Late in life Rabbi Chaim moved to Tzefas, the city of Kabbalists, where many rebbes and chassidim had settled. So great was the esteem in which he was held that for many years after his departure the Jews of Chernovitz refused to choose a new rabbi.

His book *Be'er Mayim Chaim*,[1] a commentary on the Torah, is considered one of the preeminent works on chassidic thought. Many of his expositions are based on the Kabbalistic teachings of the Ari. He also wrote the famous *Siduro shel Shabbos*[2] and *Shaar HaTefillah*.[3] His books can be found in the libraries of virtually every chassidic *shtiebel*, and his words are a source of inspiration and enlightenment to every serious student of Chassidism and Kabbalah.

Selections from Be'er Mayim Chaim

Groups of Four

> In the beginning God created heaven and earth.
> (*Bereishis 1:1*)

All of God's creations can be classified into four categories: mineral, vegetable, animal, and man. The four groupings are made up of four basic elements: earth, air, fire, and water. The four elements, in turn, are rooted in the four letters of God's ineffable Name, and they constantly draw their life force from these four letters, as Rabbi Chaim Vital points out. And so we say every morning in our *shacharis* prayer, "In His goodness He renews daily, perpetually, the work of creation."

Man was given a soul that emanates from the highest heaven, so that a Jewish soul ranks even higher than the angels. The soul comprises the four worlds: They are [in order from the highest to the lowest]: Atzilus, Beri'ah, Yetzirah, and Asiyah. Analogous to the four worlds, the soul has four dimensions: *nefesh, ruach, neshamah, chayah.*

God created man's body from the earth, which comprises the four elements that are the components of all creation: earth, air, fire, and water.

---

1   Chernovitz, 1836.
2   Mohilev, 1813.
3   Sadilkov, 1825.

[To summarize: There is a remarkable correlation among five sets of "four" — 1) the four elements, 2) the four basic components, 3) the four letters of the Tetragrammaton, 4) the four dimensions of the soul, 5) the four worlds.]

Be'er Mayim Chayim, Bereishis, p. 10

The Breaking of the Vessels

[Note: In the lineup of the *Sefiros*, each *Sefirah* is directly above the next. The higher *Sefirah* conveys the Divine Light to the *Sefirah* below it, so that the higher *Sefirah* is the "giver" and the lower one, the "receiver."]

> The earth was without form and empty, and the Divine Presence hovered upon the surface of the deep.
>
> (Bereishis 1:2)

In the wake of the Breaking of the Vessels, the earth was empty and without form. The receiving *Sefiros* were unable to hold the Infinite Light that flowed into them from the giving *Sefiros*. So they shattered and fell down.... The Ari says that as a result of the Breaking of the Vessels, 288 sparks of holiness descended to earth, and it is the mission of the Jewish people to gradually bring these fallen sparks back to their heavenly source by the power of prayer and good deeds.

"The Divine Presence hovered [*merachefes*]" — The letters of the word *merachefes* — *mem, reish, ches, pei, tav* — can be rearranged to read: *reish, pei, ches, mem, tav*. The numeric value of *reish, pei, ches* is 288; *mem, tav* reads *meis*, meaning "dead." This suggests that the 288 fallen sparks of holiness were left for dead among the *klippos*. This verse tells the Jewish people to make a mighty effort to return these sparks to the Creator.

Be'er Mayim Chaim, Bereishis, p. 32

Raising the Sparks

God said, "Behold, I have given you every seed-bearing plant on

> the face of the earth.... It shall be yours for food."
>
> *(Bereishis 1:29)*

Embedded in every herb and fruit you eat there is a spark of holiness that gives life to that food. The main purpose of partaking of food is to release the holy spark that is lodged in the food and to raise it to its root in heaven above. When you do that the food is set right, and thereby the whole world is brought closer to the Holy One, blessed be He. A person who has the proper intent and restrains his physical cravings when eating is ideally suited to raise the captive sparks of holiness in the food. In fact, the food literally jumps at the opportunity to be consumed by such a person because he will elevate it to the highest heaven. A person like that does not have to make an effort to find the food he needs; "it shall be yours for food" — the food comes looking for him, to be rectified through him.

Be'er Mayim Chaim, Bereishis, p. 61

Noach's Ark

> [Note: The six lower *Sefiros* (*Chesed, Gevurah, Tiferes, Netzach, Hod, Yesod*) are often referred to as *Ze'ir Anpin*, "the Small Face." *Keser*, the highest *Sefirah*, is also called *Arich Anpin*; *Chochmah* is called *Abba* (Father), and *Binah* is called *Imma* (Mother).]

> Noach was six hundred years old when the flood was water upon the earth.
>
> *(Bereishis 7:6)*

Kabbalah teaches that Noach was destined to enter the Ark since the six days of Creation. This is because Noach represents the *Sefirah* of *Yesod*, which is the sixth *Sefirah* of *Ze'ir Anpin*. For that reason he had to be reborn in the womb of *Imma* [i.e., *Binah*], which is symbolized by the Ark.

When Noach was six hundred years old, he reached the level of *tzaddik yesod olam*, "a tzaddik who is the foundation of the world," and God chose him to repair the world. God arranged for the souls that were born in the evil generation of the flood and in previous evil generations [to perish in the flood] in order to purify them, as the Ari sets forth (*Likutei Torah, Noach*). Of course, God could have obliterated these souls in a firestorm or some other calamity. But since He wanted Noach to come into the Ark [the symbol of the womb of *Imma/Binah*], He brought the flood upon those souls and drowned them in water. Thereby God's plan came to fruition.

Thus, in a Kabbalistic sense, our verse is saying: When Noach reached the level of *tzaddik yesod olam* at six hundred years of age, he was ready to enter the Ark, which represents the Ark of the Covenant. That's why "the flood was water upon the earth." It was a flood of water and not a flood of fire, because Noach was destined to enter the Ark that was prepared for him since primordial times.

Be'er Mayim Chaim, Noach, p. 162

Like a Fishless Pond

When the Jews left Egypt, all the holy sparks of Egypt flocked to them and departed with them. This is borne out by the verse, "[The Israelites] emptied Egypt" (*Shemos* 12:36), which the Gemara expounds to mean: "They turned Egypt into a fishless pond" (*Berachos* 9b). Explains the Ari: "Because they took with them all the sparks of holiness." As a result, a vast spiritual gap arose between the Jews, who were blessed, and the Egyptians, who, bereft of every trace of spirituality, were cursed.

That is why "The Egyptians were urging the people to hurry and leave the country. 'We are all dead men!' they were saying" (*Shemos* 12:33). They were right, for in a sense they were dead, since they did not have a single spark of holiness which is called "life" left in them. They lived off the *klippos*, which are equated with death, as the Sages say: "The wicked in their lifetime are called dead" (*Berachos* 18b). That is why the Egyptians said: We can't put up with the Jews anymore. And for that reason "[the Jews] were driven out of Egypt" (*Shemos* 12:39).

But since God wanted the Egyptians to drown in the Red Sea, He planted the idea in their minds to pursue the Jews. They chased the Jews although they had banished them completely from their thoughts, for the cursed cannot attach themselves to the blessed.

Be'er Mayim Chaim, Lech lecha, p. 289

Why Were the Jews Enslaved in Egypt?

We know from the Kabbalistic teachings of the Ari why our forefathers had to go down to Egypt and were forced "to do harsh labor involving mortar and bricks" (*Shemos* 1:14). The Ari explains that when Adam transgressed he caused an intermingling of good and evil. As a result, all souls were blemished. The Gemara tells us that for 130 years [after his expulsion from Gan Eden] Adam did not live with his wife, [as it says, "Adam lived 130 years, and he had a son," proof that until that time he did not have marital relations] (*Eiruvin* 18b). The semen he spilled in vain during those 130 years gave rise to numerous souls that were captured in the shells of evil. By spilling his seed Adam violated God's will for the second time [the first time was when he ate the forbidden fruit]. The souls he begat had to be purified by being reincarnated in three generations where they received their punishment.

The three generations were: the generation of the flood, the generation of Enosh [the first generation to practice idolatry], and the generation of the dispersion [the generation that built the Tower of Bavel in order to war against God]. Then those souls were further cleansed by being reincarnated in the generation that went into exile in Egypt. There they were punished for the sins of the generations of the flood and the dispersion. The punishment for the sins of the generation that drowned in the flood was that "every boy that is born must be cast into the Nile [to be drowned]" (*Shemos* 1:22). The punishment for the sins of the generation of the dispersion [which built the Tower with "bricks and mortar" (*Bereishis* 11:3)] was that the Jews had to do hard labor involving mortar and bricks [end of the Ari's commentary].

[Says the Be'er Mayim Chaim:] So you see that the children of Israel were forced to endure the Egyptian bondage in order to be cleansed and purified [of the stain of Adam's transgression]. Then they were worthy to enter Eretz Yisrael. Because inheriting Eretz Yisrael is contingent on the correction of the stain of spilling semen in vain. For their souls were tainted by the evil sparks of Adam's wasted seminal emissions. Until that blemish was set right they were not fit to inherit the Land. Only after being washed and purified did they receive the legacy of Yaakov. And Yaakov was the *tikkun* of Adam.

Indeed Yaakov testified, "Reuven, you are my firstborn, my strength and my initial vigor" (*Bereishis* 49:3). And the Sages interpret this to mean that Yaakov never had a wasted emission, and that Reuven came from his first seminal ejaculation. Since Yaakov was the *tikkun* of Adam who abused the *bris* [the organ of circumcision], Yaakov had to mend Adam's sin by guarding his *bris*.

Be'er Mayim Chaim, Lech Lecha, p. 305

In My Flesh I See God

> This is My covenant which you shall keep.... You must circumcise every male.
>
> (*Bereishis* 17:10)

The *Zohar* connects this verse with the passage, "In my flesh I see God" (*Iyov* 19:26). The implication is that the *bris milah* is performed on the organ that is all flesh and does not contain any bone. [Thus the verse, "In my flesh I see God" suggests that the male organ which is all flesh manifests God.] How is this to be understood? The crown of the male organ resembles the letter *yud*, the first letter of God's ineffable Name. *Yud* is also the last letter of the divine Name *Shakai*; it is the seal that closes the Name and shuts out any impure influence. Indeed, *milah* is the barrier against the *yetzer hara*....

You should realize that the body is nothing but a garment for the soul.

When you buy a cloth garment the sleeves and the pants fit your body. Similarly, your body's 248 limbs and 365 sinews are garments that fit the corresponding limbs and veins of your soul. And we know that the soul is a portion of God. So you could say, "In my flesh I see God" [meaning: In the crown of the male organ which is shaped like a *yud*, I recognize the Name of God]. In light of that, it does not sound far-fetched to say that the sign of the *bris milah* symbolizes the *yud*, the seal of God's Name.

Be'er Mayim Chaim, Lech Lecha, p. 317

Chapter 48

RABBI NACHMAN OF BRESLOV

born: Mizhbozh, Podolia, Russia, 1772
died: Uman, Podolia, Russia, 1811

Rabbi Nachman was a grandson of Adel, the Baal Shem Tov's daughter, and a grandson of Rabbi Nachman of Horodenko, a disciple of the Baal Shem Tov. He occupies a singular place in the world of Chassidus as an innovator who roused his followers to heretofore unknown heights of *deveikus*, attachment to God, coupled with sublime joy. Even as a youngster he showed signs of greatness, studying the Talmud without letup.

After his marriage at thirteen years of age, Rabbi Nachman would often retreat into seclusion, seeking communion with God through fervent prayer, fasting, and studying Kabbalah, a practice he maintained throughout his life. He would wander off into fields and forests, contemplating the mysteries of God's creation. Divesting himself of the mundane, he would reach a state of high exaltation and experience the purest form of spiritual joy. After he settled in Medvidovka, his fame as a holy man spread rapidly, and a steady stream of chassidim converged on his modest dwelling to be inspired by his saintly way of life.

In 1798, Rabbi Nachman traveled to Eretz Yisrael, the land of his dreams. Word of his imminent arrival spread rapidly, and many admirers, among them the well-known local Kabbalists, flocked to join his circle of ardent followers. His brief stay ended when Napoleon invaded the country. Returning to Poland, he settled in Breslov in 1802, which became a principal center of Chassidism.

His rise to prominence and his controversial leaning toward asceticism coupled with exuberant ecstasy provoked a great deal of criticism on the part of rebbes like Rabbi Aryeh Leib, the "Shpola Zeide," who claimed that Rabbi Nachman's service lacked dignity. On the heels a bitter dispute and a calamitous fire that ravaged his home in 1810, Rabbi Nachman left Breslov and settled in nearby Uman. On Sukkos the following year he died of tuberculosis without appointing a successor, and no new rebbe was chosen.

Although the Breslover chassidim still have no living rebbe, their movement continues to flourish and is today operating yeshivos and other institutions in America, Israel, and many other countries. It continues to attract many new adherents. Every year thousands of chassidim travel to Uman to visit the tomb of Rabbi Nachman, who has remained their rebbe. Since they have no living rebbe, Breslov chassidim are often good-naturedly referred to as *"toite* (dead) chassidim." The burgeoning growth of Breslover Chassidus certainly belies this appellation.

Before his death, Rabbi Nachman instructed his followers to destroy all his writings, but in spite of this admonition fifty-two of his books were published by his closest disciple, Rabbi Nassan (Sternharz).[1] Among these is *Likutei Moharan*,[2] a collection of Rabbi Nachman's thoughts. In his Torah insights he strongly opposes philosophical speculation, warning against the study of works of Jewish philosophy such as the *Moreh Nevuchim* by the Rambam. The true answer to questions of faith, says Rabbi Nachman, can be found in the Kabbalistic writings of the *Zohar* and Rabbi Yitzchak Luria, and in the Baal Shem Tov's teachings. He counseled his followers to serve God with simple, naive, childlike faith.

---

1   1780–1845.
2   Ostroh, 1806.

Rabbi Nachman is known for the intricate tales he wove of princes and beggars, horsemen and rabbis. These parables are based on Kabbalistic themes and carry profound moral messages. They were compiled by Rabbi Nassan in *Sippurei Maasiyos*.[1] Breslov Chassidus attracts numerous *baalei teshuvah*, who are drawn by the warmth of its enthusiastic fervor.

Selections from the Teachings of Rabbi Nachman

Scholarly Disputes

In a sense, a Torah dispute is akin to the concept underlying the creation of the world. Since God is omnipresent, His Divine Light fills all of existence. Before creating the universe, it was necessary for God to provide the space in which the universe could be placed. He did this by withdrawing His Divine Light and retreating into Himself, as it were, making room for the cosmos — in a process known as *tzimtzum*. He then created the world by means of His Word, as it says, "By the word of God the heavens were made and by the breath of His mouth all their hosts" (*Tehillim* 33:7).

The principle of *tzimtzum*, of withdrawal and creation, is also the foundation of all rabbinical disputes. If all sages were in perfect agreement on every issue, the Divine Light of Torah would reign supreme, filling the space of the universe, leaving no room for the creation of the world. Torah scholars, through their talmudic disputes and by presenting divergent views, are withdrawing to their respective positions. Thereby they are making "space" for the world.

This corresponds with the *tzimtzum* of the Divine Light and the subsequent creation of the world by means of the Word. By studying this Word — the Torah — and discovering new insights, the scholars continuously create the world. With their debates and disagreements, they maintain and preserve the entire universe, as the *Zohar* puts it, "[God says], 'Just as I

---
[1] Ostroh, 1816.

made heaven and earth by means of My word, so are you creating the world by means of your words' " (Introduction to the *Zohar*, p. 5).

Likutei Moharan 64:4

Heart and Lung

The *Zohar* says: "If the lungs did not cool off the heart, the [burning love of the] heart would set the whole body on fire" (*Tikkunei Zohar* 13, 27b).

The lungs have the quality of Yaakov, whereas the heart is symbolic of Yosef. How so? We know that Yaakov stands for truth, as it says, "Grant truth to Yaakov" (*Michah* 7:20), and truth is the essence of the Torah, as it says, "The Torah of truth" (*Malachi* 2:3). The Torah is made up of five books, matching the five lobes of the lung. [This indicates that Yaakov exemplifies the cooling quality of the lungs.]

Yosef has the quality of the heart, and when the fire in the heart burns uncontrolled, it consumes the entire body. But the rhythmic breathing of the five lobes of the lungs cools and dissipates the fiery heat of the heart.

[Explanation: The heart and the lungs represent two profound concepts. The heart is the source of the overwhelming desire of the soul to be united with its root, the *Ein Sof*, the Infinite. If this desire remained unchecked, the soul would escape from the body to be united with God. The five lobes of the lungs, which symbolize the five books of the Torah, cool off the blazing ardor of the heart and prevent the soul from leaving the body. In other words, the rational teachings of the Torah keep the emotions from getting out of hand. You could say Yaakov which equals truth, Torah, which equals five lobes of the lungs that cool the burning ardor of Yosef, the heart.]

Likutei Moharan 92

The Six Hundred Thousand Souls

The sum total of all Jewish souls in this world is 600,000. Of course, there are more than 600,000 souls, but the additional souls are offshoots of the 600,000 primary souls.

When a child is born, a soul [that is part of the 600,000 primary souls] comes down to this world to be cloaked with that child's body. But there are illustrious tzaddikim who beget souls that come from a heavenly source that is higher than the pool of 600,000 primary souls. By rights, these souls should not be incarnated in this world. But when they do come down to this world, the person they are assigned to inhabit grows up to be an otherworldly person of extraordinary saintliness.

Likutei Moharan 119b

The Hard Work of the Wicked

There are bad people who work very hard all their lives to cut themselves loose from God and His Torah. Although they are thoroughly wicked, there is still a tiny speck of Jewish holiness left in them. This small particle confuses them and stirs in them thoughts of *teshuvah* and fear of the Final Judgment. It grates their conscience and does not let them enjoy their sinful acts and their forbidden lustful pleasures. So they go to great lengths to uproot completely their belief in God, straining with all their might to get to the point where there is not a chance for them to be drawn to the truth. But that takes a great deal of hard work over a period of many years, because the Jewish spark in them does not give them peace and constantly throws them off balance. Some of these people manage to reach their goal of complete denial of God, to the point that they no longer hear the inner voice of Truth. The moment they reach that stage, they die. Then they see the Truth.

Likutei Moharan 119b

Relief of Pain

In the final analysis, the ultimate purpose of Creation is to spread the knowledge of God's Oneness. As it says, "On that day God will be One, and

His Name will be One" (*Zecharyah* 14:9). What this means is that the day will come when people recognize that whatever happens is good. They will realize that all the pain and distress a person suffers, God forbid, is for his good, either to remind him to do *teshuvah* or to rub out his transgressions. God wants only the best. If a person focuses on the ultimate purpose of life, he does not feel any pain at all.

This will help you understand a mysterious psychological phenomenon. We see that when a person experiences excruciating pain, he squeezes his eyes tightly shut. Why? Let me explain. When you gaze at a distant object you scrunch up your eyes. The reason is that vision is a function of the brain: the eye sends an image to the brain, and the brain recognizes the image. When you peer at a distant object you squint in order to concentrate on the object and filter out extraneous images.

The same way, in the spiritual realm, when you focus on the ultimate purpose you have to press your eyes tightly shut. You may even have to press your fingers on your eyelids in order to banish all worldly thoughts. [That is why when we recite the first verse of the Shema we cover our eyes.] When you do that you perceive the Light of the ultimate purpose which is all good, and then your pain and misery disappear. When you close your eyes when you are in pain, you don't realize what you are doing and why you are doing it. You do it instinctively, without thinking. But your soul knows.

Likutei Moharan 80b

The Two Sides of Seventy

Every Jewish soul is an offspring of the seventy descendants of Yaakov who came with him to Egypt. The spiritual root of these seventy descendants rests in the seventy levels of [understanding of] the Torah.[1] But we know that everything in the realm of *kedushah* has a counterpart in the world of the unclean. As it says, "God made the one as well as the other"

---

1   *Teshuvos Radvaz*, end of responsum #643; *Zohar* 1:47b, 54a.

(*Koheles* 7:14). And so as a counterpart to the [holiness of the] seventy descendants of Yaakov there are the seventy languages of the seventy nations of the world.[1]

Each of the seventy languages has an unholy element which places it completely out of reach of the seventy levels of Torah learning. [That is why a translation of the Hebrew text of the Torah can never capture the essence of the Scriptures.] And when a Jewish soul lives in exile under the domination of the seventy nations, it cries bitterly, like a woman in labor who howls seventy shrieks.[2] Her seventy shrieks correspond to the seventy words in the psalm that begins with the words, "May God answer you on the day of distress" (*Tehillim* 20). Without these seventy screams she cannot give birth.

And so it is with a Jewish soul. Before the Torah is revealed to the soul, it is tested and cleansed by living in the environment of the seventy nations. There it gives out seventy screams, since revelation is akin to giving birth. Before the Torah is revealed to the soul, it is like an unborn fetus. You can compare it to a fruit inside its shell. When you want to eat the fruit you first have to break the shell. That's why before the Torah is revealed to the Jewish soul, it has to live in exile and break the un-Jewish habits and customs of its environment. Only then can it receive the revelation.

The common denominator of the negative qualities of the seventy nations is their lust and moral looseness. And therein lies the key to a complete *tikkun*. For once you break the desire for promiscuity, you can easily break all other lusts.... That's why before Moshe received the Torah, he had to withdraw from all worldly desires, as it says, "[God said to Moshe,] 'As for you, stand here with Me' " (*Devarim* 5:28).

Bilam is at the other end of the spectrum. He was as great a prophet as Moshe, as it says, "[Bilam] knows the Highest One's Will" (*Bemidbar*

---

[1] *Shabbos* 88b, *Megillah* 13b, *Sanhedrin* 17a, *Sotah* 32a, *Zohar* 3:20a.
[2] *Zohar, Pinchas* 249b.

24:16). But whereas Moshe reached the pinnacle of holiness, Bilam sank to the bottom of immorality and was lodged in the corruption of the *klippos*.

Notice how the letters of Bilam's name allude to his antagonism to the values of the Torah. [*Bilam* is spelled *beis, lamed, ayin, mem.*] *Beis* is the first letter of the Torah [which begins with the word ***b****ereishis*]; *lamed* is the last letter of the Torah [which ends with the word *Yisrae****l***]. *Ayin* [whose numerical value is 70] corresponds to the seventy levels of understanding the Torah, and *mem* [whose numerical value is 40] correlates with the forty days Moshe sojourned on Mount Sinai before receiving the Torah. [Thus the name *Bilam* implies that he completely negated the teachings of the Torah.] Indeed, he was at the lowest level of the *klippah* of immorality [he committed bestiality with his female donkey (*Sanhedrin* 105b)].

Before Yosef was worthy of the revelation of the Torah, he had to be able to resist the lure of the all-encompassing vice of promiscuity of the seventy nations. By overcoming the seduction [of Potifar's wife], he cracked the shell around the fruit and earned the fruit, which is the revelation of the Torah.

Likutei Moharan 50a

Moshe's *Niggun*

Every field of study in the world has its own *niggun* (song, tune), and every science draws strength from its *niggun*. And so it says, "Sing, O enlightened one!" (*Tehillim* 47:8). Yes, even atheism has a special heresy-*niggun* all its own. There is a Gemara that confirms this. The Gemara (*Chagigah* 15b) asks: "How did Acher[1] become an apostate?" The Gemara answers: "Because he never stopped humming Greek songs. They said about Acher that [before he became an apostate] when he used to get up to leave the

---

1   Elisha ben Avuyah, a great talmudic sage and the teacher of Rabbi Meir, renounced the Torah and became an apostate. After that the Gemara refers to him as Acher, "someone else" (*Chagigah* 15b).

beis midrash many heretical books fell from his lap."

It was the heretical tunes that enticed him to study heretical books. By the same token, every level of Torah wisdom has its own melody. The higher the level of understanding, the more elevated is its *niggun*. You reach higher and higher on the wings of the *niggun* until you get to the absolute summit, namely the world of Atzilus. The only thing higher than that is the Infinite Light, for the Infinite Light is the Holy One, blessed be He, Himself, and His wisdom is beyond human comprehension. Then there is only faith in God. Faith, too, has its own melody. You can tell that this is so, because even non-Jewish creeds have their own religious chants they sing in their houses of worship.... In time to come, "when all nations will proclaim God's Name and worship Him with a united resolve" (*Tzefanyah* 3:9), then the *niggun* of the highest *emunah* will be sung, the *niggun* of Moshe, and all the other songs will dissolve in this song.

Likutei Moharan 79a

Chapter 49
RABBI SHLOMO RABINOWITZ OF RADOMSK
(Tiferes Shlomo)

born: Wlosziva, Poland, 1795
died: Radomsk, Poland, 1866

Rabbi Shlomo, the son of Rabbi Dov Tzvi, the rabbi of Wlosziva, was a descendant of the great Kabbalist Rabbi Nassan Nata Shapira, author of *Megaleh Amukos*. He studied under Rabbi Moshe Aharon of Kutno and Rabbi Avraham Tzvi Hirsch of Pietrkov, author of *Bris Avraham*.[1] At a young age he memorized the monumental *Shenei Luchos HaBris* by Rabbi Yeshayah Horowitz. In 1834 he became rabbi of Radomsk, which developed into a major center of Chassidus under his dynamic leadership.

Rabbi Shlomo, renowned for his beautiful singing voice, was an eminent Kabbalist and a great Torah scholar, which is evident in the profound insights in his work *Tiferes Shlomo*,[2] a two-volume compilation of his commentaries on the Torah and the *yamim tovim*. He often finds amazing allusions in the numerical values and letter permutations of certain words in the text. Although he loved the simple people who sought his advice about their mun-

---

1 Duhrenfurth, 1819.
2 Warsaw, 1867.

dane problems, his heart was drawn to the scholarly chassidim who were able to follow his discourses on the complexities of halachic and Kabbalistic themes. He is fondly remembered for his soul-stirring *niggunim*, with which he roused his chassidim to intense fervor as he conducted the services on Shabbos and *yom tov*. His book *Tiferes Shlomo* gained widespread popularity and was reprinted numerous times.

Selections from Tiferes Shlomo

Body and Soul

> [Note: Kabbalah teaches that, as a result of Adam's transgression, the vessels that conveyed the Infinite Light down to this world were unable to hold its intense radiance (see ch. 3). They broke, scattering 288 sparks of holiness (*nitzotzos hakedushah*) throughout the world. It is our task in the world to raise the 288 sparks back to their heavenly source by performing the mitzvos.]

> In the beginning God created heaven and earth. The earth was without form and empty, with darkness on the face of the depth, but God's spirit hovered [*merachefes*] on the water's surface. God said, "There shall be light" and light came into existence.
> (Bereishis 1:1-2)

Metaphorically, "heaven and earth" refers to man who is made up of body and soul, symbolized by earth and heaven. Our verse is telling us that man can reach perfection and keep Creation intact by making his earthly part – his body – "without form and empty" – having total disregard of his physical desires, in a spirit of self-denial and self-sacrifice. As before Creation, when nothingness preceded existence, man should live in terms of "physical emptiness."

This idea comes to the fore in the passage, "The spirit of God hovered [*merachefes*, written *mem, reish, ches, pei, tav*]." The letters of *merachefes* can be rearranged to read *reish, pei, ches, mem, tav* [*reish* (200) + *pei* (80) +

ches (8) = 288; *mem, tav* spells *meis*, which means "death"]. This carries the message that by self-denial and by deadening unbridled physical desires [*meis*] we elevate the 288 [*reish, pei, ches*] sparks of holiness and free them from their earthly husks. Thereby we draw the Light from above down to earth, as it says, "and light came into existence."

Liberating the Holy Sparks

> [God said to Noach,] "Take with you all the food that will be eaten, and keep it in storage. It shall be food for you and for them."
>
> *(Bereishis 6:21)*

Kabbalah teaches that encased in the food you eat there are sparks of holiness. These sparks are eager to be released from their imprisonment. They are liberated when you recite a *berachah* over food and eat it to gain the strength to serve God. That's what the verse wants to say, "Take with you all the food that will be eaten" – in order to liberate the imprisoned sparks of holiness. "It shall be food for you and for them" – food for you and for the holy sparks – for they will be elevated to their heavenly source when you eat the food [in which they are confined].

The Souls of Converts

> Avram took his wife Sarai, his nephew Lot, and all their belongings, as well as the souls they had made in Charan.
>
> *(Bereishis 12:5)*

Rashi explains the phrase, "the souls they had made in Charan," as referring to "the people they had brought in under the wings of the *Shechinah*," meaning, the heathens they had converted to the belief in one God. The Kabbalist Rabbi Menachem Recanati says that when tzaddikim bring out novel Torah thoughts they create souls in the higher world. That's how Avraham and Sarah created the souls of the converts they brought under the wings of the *Shechinah*. And that is why the book that Avraham wrote is called *Sefer Yetzirah* (Book of Creation). [With the novel Torah insights he developed and recorded in *Sefer Yetzirah*, he created the souls of converts.]

God Is Unknowable

> [God said to Moshe,] "I will take away My hand, and you will see My back, but My face will not be seen."
>
> (*Shemos* 33:23)

"You will see My back, but My face will not be seen" — What is meant by God's *achor*, "back," and *panim*, "face"?

We must realize that these are anthropomorphisms, spiritual concepts clothed in human language. God is infinite, not bound by time or space. Man, being finite, strives throughout his life to come close to God, to reach ever higher levels of *kedushah*. Each higher level he attains is called *panim*, "face, forward motion." His previous level, the level he left behind on his spiritual ascent, is called *achor*, "back, that which is behind you." No matter how lofty may be the sphere you reach, there will always be a *panim*, an even higher plateau to which you can aspire. The ultimate *panim* can never be attained, for God is Infinite. Therefore, "My face will not be seen." Man does, however, achieve the *achor*, the "back," the lower stages he leaves behind on his never-ending climb to perfection. Hence, "You will see My back."

This concept is implied in the saying, "The end goal of all knowledge is to know that God is unknowable" (*Bechinas Olam*[1] 13:45).

The Proper Time to Sing

> [At the parting of the Red Sea,] one did not come near the other all night.
>
> (*Shemos* 14:20)

---

1 A classic work by Rabbi Yedayah Bedrushi, dealing with the bliss of the World to Come and the vanity of this world. (Mantua, 1478.)

The Gemara (*Megillah* 10b) says that the phrase "one did not come near the other" refers to the ministering angels. The ministering angels wanted to sing a hymn [when the Egyptians were drowning in the Red Sea]. However, the Holy One, blessed be He, exclaimed: "My handiwork is drowning in the sea, and you sing a hymn of praise! [This is not the time for singing praises.]"

[Why was this not the right time for the angels to sing?] The true *tikkun* will come to pass when all the gentiles will turn to God, and all evil will convert to good. As it says, "It will happen in the end of days...the Temple of God will be firmly established, and all the nations will stream to it" (*Yeshayah* 2:2). [Obviously, at the parting of the sea the final *tikkun* was not yet at hand.] That being so, the sparks of holiness that were released because of the death of the Egyptians did not herald the final redemption, since the time of the ultimate *tikkun* had not yet arrived. Therefore, it was not right for the angels to sing a song of praise.

That is why God said: My handiwork is drowning in the sea, and the *tikkun* has not yet materialized. So why are you singing a song of praise? But in time to come, when "I will change the nations [to speak] a pure language, so that they all will proclaim the Name of God, to worship Him with a united resolve" (*Tzefanyah* 3:9), it will be appropriate to "sing to God, everyone on earth" (*Tehillim* 95:1).

The *Shechinah* in Exile

> God drove them [the Jewish people] from their land with anger, rage, and great fury, and He exiled them to another land, where they remain even today.
>
> (*Devarim* 29:27)

[Note: The Gemara says: "Wherever the Jews are exiled, the *Shechinah* is with them" (*Megillah* 29a). We find an allusion to this in the verse, "I am with him in distress" (*Tehillim* 91:15).]

The *Zohar* explains the concept of the *Shechinah* going into exile to mean that there are times when the *Shechinah* descends to the lowest levels of this world in order to safeguard the Jewish people. The *Shechinah* protects the Jews like a mother taking care of her children. For the sake of Israel, the *Shechinah* stoops to the point of slipping into the mind of one of the government officials who are planning evil decrees against the Jewish people [and who then vetoes the harmful statute]. This thought is expressed in the verse, "High above all nations is God, above the heavens is His glory" (*Tehillim* 112:4). Yes, God is exalted above all nations, nevertheless, "He bends down low [to see] what is below in heaven and on earth." He mingles with the humans where "He raises the needy from the dust, from the trash heaps He lifts the destitute [of Israel], to seat them with nobles...." When that happens, "[The *Shechinah* will be] a glad mother. Halleluyah!" (*Tehillim* 113:6–9)....

The nations will not be able to carry out their nefarious designs against the Jews, because the *Shechinah* infiltrates itself among people [and assumes the identity of one of their ministers] to abort their evil plans.... Indeed, we are witnesses to the obvious kindnesses of God that enable us to keep the Torah with "gladness, with goodness of heart, with plenty of everything" (*Devarim* 28:47).

The Holy Soul of a Convert

> You know full well that we lived in Egypt, and that we also passed through [the territories] of the nations you encountered. You saw the putrid idols they have.... Today, there must not be among you any man, woman, family or tribe...who goes and worships the gods of those nations.
>
> (*Devarim* 29:15–17)

For a better understanding of this passage, let us look at a statement that occurs very often in the Gemara [for example, *Yevamos* 47a]: "A convert who converts...." This is redundant. If he is a convert already, why does he convert again?

You have to realize that converts (*geirim*) have holy souls that were reincarnated and came back to life. As it says, "You were *geirim* in the land of Egypt" (*Shemos* 22:20). This refers to holy souls of non-Jews that intermingled with the Jews. These souls roamed about, because they did not have the *tikkun* to enable them to go down to Egypt with the children of Israel. "They wandered from nation to nation, and from one kingdom to another people. [God] allowed no man to oppress them" (*Divrei HaYamim* I 16:20–21).

This explains our verse, "You know full well that we lived in Egypt, and that we also passed [through the territories] of the nations you encountered." [The verse addresses the converts, telling them:] Your souls passed through Egypt. That's why you need special protection, lest you backslide to your original status. For even if your attachment [to your former situation] is broken, there always remains a trace of it [and there is the concern that you may have a relapse]. For this reason converts need strong protection from God to help them make a complete break with the past. [Thus, "a convert who converts" means a holy soul of a non-Jew who was always was a convert in spirit, but now he makes his conversion a reality.]

Chapter 50
RABBI YITZCHAK EIZIK SAFRIN OF KOMARNO

born: Zydatchov, Slovakia, 1806
died: Komarno, Slovakia, 1873

Rabbi Yitzchak Eizik, the only son of Rabbi Yissachar Berish of Zydatchov, is known for his saintly way of life and his prodigious greatness in Talmud and Kabbalah. He testified that he studied the Ari's *Eitz Chaim* one hundred times. When his father did not have a son at forty years of age, he petitioned the illustrious chassidic rebbe the Chozeh of Lublin,[1] who told him, "I see that you will have a son whose soul will be immeasurably great, but when this son will be ten years old, you will leave this world." And so it was. That year, a son, Yitzchak Eizik, was born who was exceptionally brilliant and endowed with spiritual power, so much so that at three years of age he correctly predicted future events in his family and the world at large.

As the Chozeh had foretold, when Yitzchak Eizik reached the age of ten his father passed away, and he was brought up by his uncle, the Kabbalist Rabbi Tzvi Hirsch of Zydatchov. The young orphan found solace in the

---

1   Rabbi Yaakov Yitzchak Horowitz, the "Seer" of Lublin.

study of Torah and Kabbalah, delving into the *Zohar* and the books of the Ari. After his marriage at sixteen years of age, he lived in abject poverty, to the point that his wife did not have enough money to buy two candles for Shabbos. He settled in Komarno, closeted himself in a small room, and totally absorbed himself in his studies, sleeping only two hours each night, living on bread and water. In his prayers, which lasted three hours, he rose to the loftiest spiritual heights.

When his uncle Rabbi Tzvi Hirsch died, Rabbi Yitzchak Eizik returned to Zydatchov where he became *dayan*, and in 1831, he became rebbe in Komarno. He often had dreams in which his uncle appeared to him. In other dreams he conversed with various souls in the hereafter. The ascetic and saintly Rabbi Yitzchak Eizik attracted thousands of chassidim, and even many rebbes sought his blessings and advice. The great chassidic master Rabbi Aharon of Chernobyl called him "an unblemished mirror."

His works include *Peirush Mahari*,[1] a commentary on the Midrash; *Likutei Torah VeHaShas*;[2] and *Zohar Chai*,[3] a commentary on the *Zohar*. In *Megillas Sesarim*,[4] he describes his visions and dreams.

Selections from the Writings of Rabbi Yitzchak Eizik

His First Vision

It happened early in the winter of 1823, that I was sitting in my unheated room studying Gemara, *Zohar*, and the works of Rabbi Moshe Cordovero. I was very depressed, and my mind was filled with evil thoughts of abandoning Torah study, for I subsisted only on bread and water. It was very cold, and my Torah studies and prayers did not give me any solace. It was

---

1   Lemberg, 1874.
2   Published in five volumes, Lemberg, 1877–1889.
3   Lemberg, 1875.
4   Jerusalem, 1944.

a critical juncture in my life. The seductive voices of the *klippos* were worse than a thousand deaths. But I remained firm like a rock, and I resisted the temptations. Suddenly, while I was studying tractate *Yevamos*, a glorious light of the *Shechinah* filled the entire house. It was the first time I experienced a small particle of the Divine Light. I sensed an exceedingly blissful feeling. From that moment on I served my Creator with renewed vigor, free of the former enticements....

Introduction to Megillas Sesarim

A Dream

On Friday night, the twenty-fifth of Cheshvan, 1847, I saw in a dream my friend Rabbi Yehoshua of Brody. I could not remember whether he was alive or dead. I asked him, "Where do you come from?"

"From the higher world," he replied.

"Tell me, dear friend," I asked, "what do they think of me in the higher world?"

"Very good," he answered. "You are highly respected there."

I then told him about an argument I had had with my wife the week before, and as a result, for two days I did not see any heavenly light, any souls, and any of the angels that always accompany me. "Did this cause great harm to me above?" I asked him. He did not reply. I said, "I am only asking you this because I want to be close to the Holy One, blessed be He."

"Everything is all right," he replied, whereupon I woke up.

Megillas Sesarim

Letters

You should know that there are letters written on every part of the human body [and which can be seen and read by a Kabbalist]. These letters, which appear mainly on the forehead, reveal a person's character. But letters can be detected also in the eyes, on the hair of the head and the beard, and on the rest of the body. The color, size, bent, and slant of the letters tell a great deal about a person, and much can be learned from them....

On weekdays the letters reflect a person's base instincts that stem from "the other side," the side of the *klippos*. But on Friday afternoon, after a person has immersed in the *mikveh* in honor of Shabbos, the gleam of the letters comes from the "side of holiness"....

When one comes out of the *mikveh*, tiny, delicate figures of the holiness of Shabbos radiate from his nails. They stay there until the conclusion of Shabbos. After Havdalah has been recited, the letters again take on their weekday look. That's why we hold our fingers up to the flame of the Havdalah candle and gaze at the light that falls on our nails.

Zohar Chai, Yisro, p. 92-93

The Musician

One day a musician came to play for the Baal Shem Tov. Listening to the beautiful music, the Baal Shem Tov could discern the sins the musician had committed throughout his life, and the man admitted his shortcomings. But although the Baal Shem Tov had the power to perceive all of a person's failings from the day he was born, he did not treat anyone with disdain. He followed God's example, as it says, "He discerns deceitful people; He sees iniquity, though He seems not to notice" (*Iyov* 11:11). The Baal Shem Tov allowed the artist to continue playing for him and let the music enter his holy ears.

Megillas Sesarim

Second Marriages

Sometimes a man's perfect match is assigned to him when he is born, but when he sins his soul undergoes a change. As a result, he loses his intended and marries another. Sometimes a man is reincarnated because of his sins, but without his wife, since she did not sin. So he remains alone in the world. He has no fitting mate, and he never will find a fitting match unless he takes a wife whose deeds match his. Occasionally a man is reincarnated because of a sin he committed, but since he had done many good deeds he merits that his wife is reincarnated together with him. That is called *zivug sheini*, "a second match," because both were already together in this world once before.

Zohar Chai, Lech Lecha

The Merit of Women

It is obvious that a man who is not married is completely disconnected from the *Shechinah*. The *Shechinah* does not associate with a man who does not have a wife, for the *Shechinah* rests on a man mainly because of his wife.

In point of fact, a man is positioned between two wives: one that takes, and one that gives. One, his wife here on earth, receives from him; the other, namely the *Shechinah* [i.e., the female aspect of the divine], bestows blessings on him. He receives spiritual illumination and holiness because he has a wife.

A person who does not have a wife, for whatever reason, does not live with the truth. I noticed that my saintly teachers, the Chozeh of Lublin, Rabbi Naftali of Ropshitz, the Maggid of Koznitz, my uncle Rabbi Moshe, and many other tzaddikim, remarried [late in life] although their physical desire had waned completely, and they were unable to fulfill the holy mitzvah. They united with their spouses in spiritual intimacy and in whispered words of endearment.

Notzeir Chesed

Two Kinds of Tzaddikim

There are tzaddikim who are called "Shabbos." Like Shabbos, they are completely detached from worldly affairs. All their thoughts are focused on spiritual matters. They do not mingle with the people. In their otherworldliness they cannot endure this world. Yet because of their righteousness and piety they raise the entire world to a higher level of service to God.

Then there are tzaddikim who are like *yom tov*, and on *yom tov* you are allowed to prepare, cook, and bake the food for the festival. These tzaddikim are involved in the needs of the community. They interact with the people. They draw down from heaven compassion, favor, sustenance, help, and healing, and they guide the people on the right path.

Heichal HaBerachah, Bereishis

Chapter 51
RABBI TZADOK HAKOHEN OF LUBLIN

born: Kreisburg, Latvia, 1823
died: Lublin, Poland, 1900

Rabbi Tzadok HaKohen, affectionately called Reb Tzadok, or simply "the Kohen," was a highly creative and original thinker. He was the son of Rabbi Yaakov, the rabbi of Kreisburg, and his mother was a descendant of the Shelah. When he was six years old his father died, and he was raised by his uncle, Rabbi Yosef HaKohen Katz, author of *Kapos Zahav Shtayim*.[1] As a youngster he was known as an *illuy* (child prodigy) of phenomenal versatility.

A saintly man, Reb Tzadok often withdrew from society into reclusive isolation. His personal life was filled with tragedy. Married three times, he never had children and lived in abject poverty on the meager income of the small store where his wife sold used clothing. As his reputation as a saintly talmudic and halachic scholar grew, he was swamped with queries from far and wide, and his wise answers solved the most complex problems.

At twenty-four years of age, Reb Tzadok began to study Kabbalah and

---

1 Vilna and Horodno, 1836.

Chassidus and became a disciple of the Rebbe of Izbitza, Rabbi Mordechai Yosef Leiner, a great Kabbalist, author of *Mei HaShilo'ach*. When the Izbitza Rebbe died in 1854, Reb Tzadok became a chassid of Rabbi Yehudah Leib Eiger of Lublin. Upon the latter's death, Reb Tzadok reluctantly agreed to become the leader of Rabbi Yehudah Leib Eiger's chassidim. He inspired his followers with his innovative homilies and profound teachings and counseled the thousands who sought his sage advice on personal and monetary matters.

He was a prolific writer. Integrating the teachings of the Maharal, Rabbi Nachman of Breslov, and the early Kabbalists, Reb Tzadok created a system of thought that brought together their ideas in a unique worldview. Although his writing is interspersed with obscure Kabbalistic terms, his thoughts have a timeless quality that addresses many questions of our time. It is not surprising that Reb Tzadok's writings are studied widely both in chassidic and non-chassidic circles. Among his published works are *Pri Tzaddik*,[1] *Tzidkas HaTzaddik*,[2] *Doveir Tzedek*,[3] *Pokeid Akarim*,[4] *Sichas Malachei HaShares*,[5] and *Yisrael Kedoshim*.[6]

Selections from the Writings of Rabbi Tzadok HaKohen

Three Names

Every Jew has three names: The name he acquires through his own efforts, the name he receives from his father, and his third name is derived from the heavenly root [of his soul, for every Jew is a portion of God], as it says, "For God's portion is His people, Yaakov is the rope of His inheri-

---

1. Lublin, 1901.
2. Lublin, 1902.
3. Piotrokov, 1911.
4. Piotrokov, 1922.
5. Lublin, 1927.
6. Lublin, 1928.

tance" (*Devarim* 32:9). [The "rope" in this verse suggests] that every Jew is linked to God by an unbreakable bond, and every Jew is a part of God....

The counterparts of the three names [a person acquires] are the three mitzvos that set Israel apart from the gentile nations [namely, Torah study, *milah*, and Shabbos]. Historically, the gentile nations have always begrudged us these three mitzvos and issued decrees forbidding Jews to observe them. And so [the Greeks, Romans, and later tyrants] prohibited the study of the Torah, the performance of *milah*, and the observance of Shabbos. Torah study [which takes a great deal of toil] corresponds to the name a Jew acquires through his own effort. The gentile nations [are jealous of the Torah], so much so that they translated it into Greek, claiming that they are the real Israelites, although they have no kinship with the Torah at all.

The name a Jew receives from his father is the name he is given at his *bris milah*, because a father [or his agent, the *mohel*] performs the *milah*, and the infant, without his consent and knowledge, is brought into the holiness of Israel, the covenant of Avraham. On the other hand, gentiles are uncircumcised, and even if a gentile were to undergo circumcision [for medical reasons], it would not do him any good, for he does not attain any holiness through his circumcision. The holiness of *milah* is conferred only on the Jewish people [including, of course, converts].

The name a Jew gains because of the root of his soul is through the sanctity of Shabbos. This *kedushah* is the sanctity that God confers on a Jew every Shabbos when he receives a *neshamah yeseirah*, an additional soul. And when a Jew eats and drinks on Shabbos and sings praises to God, he experiences a higher level of *kedushah*.

For this reason the nations of the world are determined to eliminate these three signs of holiness of the Jewish people, God forbid.

Yisrael Kedoshim, p. 93

Cheshek, Burning Desire

The burning desire to strive, to achieve, and to improve is the trait by which man stands higher than the angels. [Angels are standing still; they cannot aspire to improve and reach higher levels.] Man's yearning is evident in the *yetzer hatov* and the *yetzer hara* (the good and evil impulses). The Sages said: "The greater the man, the stronger is his drive" (*Sukkah* 52a). A greater desire to do good is what makes one person superior to the next, and the greater a person's desire to do evil, the more perverted he is. For the *yetzer hatov* and the *yetzer hara* are each other's counterparts, one the opposite of the other, seated in the two chambers of the heart, the good on the right side, the evil on the left side.

The three patriarchs had a burning *cheshek* (desire); they did not rest until their *cheshek* was fulfilled. Avraham, who represents the attribute of love and who is the epitome of the *Sefirah* of *Chesed*, did not rest until he achieved the ultimate love of God. Yitzchak [who represents *Gevurah*] had a burning desire to be in awe of God and a consummate hatred of evil. Yaakov's passionate desire was a combination of Avraham's love and Yitzchak's hatred of evil. [Yaakov represents the *Sefirah* of *Tiferes*, which mediates between *Chesed* and *Gevurah*.] With single-minded *cheshek* you can achieve any goal, even an immoral one. Desire is rooted in the *Sefirah* of *Malchus*, the feminine *Sefirah* [the *Sefirah* that yearns to receive the Infinite Light from *Yesod*]....

Tzidkas HaTzaddik 248

Haman's Consuming Hatred

Haman rose to prominence because of his burning desire to destroy the Jewish people. But his hatred was valuable because it prompted the Jews to "fight fire with fire" and rise to the occasion with their own *cheshek*. Haman demonstrated his hatred by giving King Achashveirosh ten thousand talents of silver [to obtain permission to annihilate the Jews] (*Esther*

4:9). And the Jews showed their more fervent love of God by contributing their shekalim [before the fourteenth of Adar, the day Haman planned to destroy the Jews, thereby overturning Haman's murderous plan].

Tzidkas HaTzaddik 250

Demons and Evil Spirits

All existence is influenced by the actions of man. So you could say that man is the life force of all creatures in the world. Commenting on the verse, "God said, 'Man has now become like one of us' " (*Bereishis* 3:22), the Sages say: "Just as the Holy One, blessed be He, is the life force of all higher beings, so is man the life force of the lower creatures..." (*Rashi, Bereishis* 3:22).

Now by ejaculating his seed into the proper place man produces a human being like himself. And even if his wife does not conceive, it is a known fact that souls are born [from that seed]. These souls are the souls of converts, like the souls Avraham and Sarah created, as it says, "The souls they had made" (*Bereishis* 12:5).

But when seed is wasted through masturbation, then evil spirits, demons, and *liliyos* (the female demons of the night) are born. And just as the highest holy *Sefirah* is *Keser*, which is closest to God Himself, so is there a *Keser* of the *klippos*, which are the *yetzer hara* and include all angels of destruction and the Angel of Death, as it says, "God has made the one as well as the other" (*Koheles* 7:14). These negative forces are called "angel," meaning messenger, because God wants evil to exist [so that man has a free will and earns a reward for resisting and overcoming evil]. The incarnation of evil are the satanic spirits, demons, and *liliyos*, all of which are agents of the *Keser* of Uncleanness.

Sichas Sheidim 1[1]

---

[1] Printed in the collected *Sifrei Rabbi Tzadok HaKohen*.

Man and Monkey

It says, "God has made the one as well as the other" (*Koheles* 7:14) [which means that every holy thing has a parallel in the realm of uncleanness]. The counterpart of man in the realm of uncleanness is the monkey. It emanates from the *Keser* [the highest *Sefirah* of the *klippos*, which is the counterpart of the highest *Sefirah* on the side of *kedushah*]. Just as it was God's will that man be created in His image, so it was His will that a counterpart of man [on the side of uncleanness] come into being in this world in the form of a monkey. Of course, when it comes to intellect and spiritual powers, a monkey has nothing in common with man; it just wants to look like him. This is what the Sages had in mind when they said, "Adam compares to the *Shechinah*, as a monkey to a human being" (*Bava Basra* 58a; *Zohar* 2:148b).

Now you will understand why it says that the people who built the Tower of Bavel in order to make war against God were transformed into monkeys, evil spirits, demons, and *liliyos* (female demons of the night).

You should be aware that everything has two extremes and a center. In the realm of the *Sefiros* of holiness the two extremes are *Chesed* and *Gevurah*, and the midpoint is *Tiferes*. Opposite these three *Sefiros* of holiness, there are *Sefiros* of the realm of the *klippos*. The *Sefiros* of evil are the source of the three cardinal sins: immorality, bloodshed, and idolatry.

Idolatry is the midpoint. It is the *Tiferes* of the *klippos*, the imitation of the holy *Sefirah* of *Tiferes*, for idolatry means worshiping a pseudo-God, a bogus diety.

On the extreme right is immorality, which is rooted in lust and counterfeit love. Its seat is in the unholy *Sefirah* of *Chesed* of the *klippos*. It is the opposite of the holy *Sefirah* of *Chesed*. Note that the spirit of promiscuity is evident in the verse, "If a man takes his sister…it is a disgrace [*chesed*]" (*Vayikra* 20:17). [The word *chesed* has two meanings: "kindness" and "disgrace." In the holy *Sefiros*, *Chesed* represents the highest form of spiritual love. In the realm of the *klippos*, *chesed* stands for the most sordid depravity.]

The *Sefirah* of *Gevurah* of the realm of the *klippos* becomes manifest in bloodshed and the killing of innocent people.

Sichas Sheidim

Why Was Rachel Barren?

When Yosef was born, the *kedushah* of *Yesod* became a tangible reality in this world. But there were heavenly accusers that argued that the time was not yet ripe for this *kedushah* to come to life in an offspring of Yaakov. The accusers were overruled. Since Yaakov knew that his faith was absolutely perfect, [he was sure that Rachel's inability to conceive was not his fault]. He suspected that perhaps she was infertile because she was unworthy to give birth to such a holy soul. That's why when Yosef was born Rachel said, "God has gathered away my humiliation" (*Bereishis* 30:23), for now it became clear that she was indeed worthy.

Then why was she barren until the birth of Yosef? Before a lofty soul like Yosef's could come down to this world, there had to be a community of ten people that was totally committed to God because whenever ten people gather [to pray] the *Shechinah* is present. Since the *Shechinah* rested on the ten sons of Yaakov, they constituted the Community of Israel. [Therefore, Yosef could only come into the world after his ten brothers were born.] They received the Stream of Abundance from their father, Yaakov, whose image is engraved on God's Throne. The Stream of Abundance flows down to this world through the channel of *Yesod*, embodied by Yosef, the *tzaddik yesod olam*.[1] For the world endures only in the merit of a tzaddik who safeguards the *bris* [covenant].

Pokeid Akarim, p. 20

---

1 See ch. 2.

Life Force, Heart, and Mind

Man is driven by three forces: [the basic life force, the heart, and the mind]. The basic life force [which he has in common with animals] corresponds to Olam HaAsiyah, the World of Doing. It is our world where God's actions in nature [in history and in daily life] are plain to see.

The heart is hidden beneath the surface of the body. It corresponds to Olam HaYetzirah, the World of Formation, which is the latent form of potential matter. So too, the heart is the hidden force that drives the organs of the body.

Our mind creates original ideas that did not exist before. Although intangible, ideas abound in our intellect. In that respect they are analogous to Olam HaBeri'ah, the World of Creation, for creation means bringing into being, *yesh me'ayin*, something out of nothing.

Sichos Malachei HaShareis, p. 49

A Jew Never Loses Hope

A Jew never despairs. He knows that Hashem Yisbarach can help in any situation. After all, the entire existence of the Jewish people came about in the wake of a hopeless state of affairs. For "Avraham and Sarah were already old, well on in years.... Who would have even suggested to Avraham that Sarah would be nursing children!" (*Bereishis* 18:11, 21:7). [Yet, miraculously, Sarah gave birth to Yitzchak, and eventually the Jewish people came into being.] The essence of a Jew is never to lose heart, and to believe steadfastly that Hashem Yisbarach can help, no matter what.

Divrei Sofrim 16[1]

---

1 Printed in the collected *Sifrei Rabbi Tzadok HaKohen*.

Part VIII
KABBALISTS OF THE TWENTIETH CENTURY

תמונת הגאון האדיר המפורסם בספריו היקרים בנסתר ובנגלה ריש גלותא דבבל
כמוהר״ר יוסף חיים זצוק״ל
בכמוהר״ר אליהו בכמוהר״ר משה חיים זצוק״ל
נולד בבגדאד כ״ז אב התקצ״ד, ועלה בקדושה השמימה י״ג אלול תרס״ם זיע״א

Introduction

KABBALISTS OF THE TWENTIETH CENTURY

The twentieth century brought tremendous upheavals on the Jewish people. The horrors of the Holocaust are still fresh in our minds, its wounds still festering. At the same time, the remarkable revival of Torah in Eretz Yisrael, in America, and around the world fills our hearts with joy, hope, and gratitude to Hashem, who said, "I put to death and I bring life; I struck down and I will heal" (*Devarim* 32:39). Yes, Hashem restores and heals our people. A burgeoning movement of *baalei teshuvah* sprouted, a mighty legion of returnees to Torah observance marching to the clarion call of our *gedolim*. Along with this awakening there emerged a growing interest in Kabbalah and the promise of *deveikus*, closeness to God, it holds out. The prophecy of Amos is coming true before our very eyes: "Behold days are coming when I will send hunger into the land; not a hunger for bread nor a thirst for water; but to hear the words of God" (*Amos* 8:11).

In addition to the great chassidic masters, the twentieth century has enriched us with a number of unique and outstanding Kabbalists. One of these is Rabbi Yosef of Baghdad, better known by the name "Ben Ish Chai," which is the title of his work. This great Torah authority led the Jewish community of Baghdad for half a century and has gained the admiration of both the

Sefardi and Ashkenazi communities all over the world.

Another renowned Kabbalist of the recent past is Rabbi Yehudah Leib Ashlag, whose interpretive translation of the *Zohar* has made its cryptic Aramaic text accessible to a wide circle of serious students.

Many people in Eretz Yisrael fondly remember Rabbi Yisrael Abuchatzeirah, the beloved Baba Sali, the humble miracle worker of Netivot in the Negev. May his memory and the memory of all the great tzaddikim be a blessing.

Chapter 52

RABBI YOSEF CHAIM OF BAGHDAD

(Ben Ish Chai)

born: Baghdad, Iraq, 1834
died: Baghdad, Iraq, 1909

Rabbi Yosef Chaim, the Ben Ish Chai, was one of the most illustrious rabbinical personalities of Sefardic Jewry in the last century. In 1859 he succeeded his father, Rabbi Eliyahu, as rabbi of Baghdad, the capital of present-day Iraq. A saintly and pure man of extraordinary greatness in Talmud, halachah, and Kabbalah, he was consulted by all the leading rabbis of his time. He was also an accomplished orator who captivated his audiences with his spellbinding eloquence. Among Sefardic Jews there is a saying that the Ben Ish Chai was originally destined to be one of the *tannaim* (teachers of the Mishnah), but Heaven had compassion on us and sent him to our generation instead, to enlighten us with the brilliance of his Torah.

The Ben Ish Chai's mastery of the Talmud was matched by his vast Kabbalistic knowledge, and he became the foremost exponent of the writings of the Ari HaKadosh and Rabbi Chaim Vital. He received inquiries from many countries ranging from questions on practical halachah to requests for interpretations of disturbing dreams. He was a prolific writer, but most of his books have not appeared in print. His responsa have been published under the title *Teshuvos Torah Lishmah*.[1] His most popular work is *Ben Ish Chai*, homiletics with halachah and Kabbalah. A compendium of the Kabbalistic teachings of the Ben Ish Chai, entitled *Otzeros Chaim*, was published in Yerushalayim in 1990.

In 1909 he fell ill while on a journey to pray at the tomb of the prophet Yechezkel in the village of Kifi, south of Baghdad, and he died shortly thereafter. He was laid to rest in Baghdad, having served as its rabbi for half a century. His fame has spread far beyond the Sefardic world to embrace the entire spectrum of Torah-observant Jewry.

Selections from the Writings of the Ben Ish Chai

Elevation of the Soul on Shabbos

> [Note: The *Zohar* (2:94b) teaches that the soul has three levels: *nefesh*, the lower animalistic, life-sustaining soul with which one is born; *ruach*, the divine soul, corresponding to the angels; and *neshamah*, the soul rooted in the Divine Throne. As Shabbos enters one receives the *neshamah yeseirah*, the additional soul which enables him to appreciate and benefit from the enhanced holiness of Shabbos.]

It is required that you close your eyes when you greet the Shabbos Bride with the words, "Enter, O bride! Enter, O bride!" [the closing stanza of *Lechah Dodi*]. You should be mindful of this because there is a mystical reason for it. However, people who have to read the words from a siddur must keep their eyes open. Don't criticize them for it.

On the eve of Shabbos, you experience a threefold spiritual elevation: First, there is an elevation in your *nefesh*. This happens when you welcome Shabbos by saying, "Enter, O bride!" Second, there is an elevation in your *ruach*. This comes about when you hear the chazzan say, "*Barechu —*

---

1 Jerusalem, 1973.

Bless God, the blessed One," and you respond, "Blessed is God, the blessed One, for all eternity" at the beginning of *maariv*. Third, there is an elevation in your *neshamah*, when you recite the prayer, "*U'Feros Aleinu* — And Spread over Us the Shelter of Your Peace..."

These are the attributes of Shabbos eve. Rabbi Chaim Vital says that you should stand when you respond to "*Barechu*" and receive the elevation of your *ruach*. You should also stand when you recite "*U'Feros Aleinu*" and receive the elevation of the *neshamah* element of your soul.

Otzeros Chaim, p. 129

An Upsetting Dream

Question: A man had a dream in which he was reciting the *alef beis* several times in succession. Each time, he skipped some letters and was unable to complete the entire *alef beis* flawlessly even once. He woke up feeling very upset, since he does not know what the dream portends. Please give us the true interpretation of the dream.

The Ben Ish Chai answers: Our teacher the Ari HaKadosh, in his *Shaar Ruach HaKodesh*, which we have in manuscript, writes, "The twenty-two letters of the *alef beis* are linked to the one hundred *berachos* a Jew recites each day. If a person skips a given *berachah*, the letter that is linked to that *berachah* is missing. If he did say the *berachah* properly but did not concentrate on its meaning, then the letter that is linked to it is obscure and murky." Therefore, the interpretation of the dream is that he lacks one of the one hundred *berachos*. He is being guided from heaven to do his best to recite with concentration the full one hundred *berachos* each day. If he is careful to do that from now on, all will be well with him.

Teshuvas Torah Lishmah, 466

Chapter 53

RABBI SHEM KLINGBERG OF ZALOSHITZ

(The Zaloshitzer Rebbe)

born: Skolya, Poland, 1870
died: Plaszow concentration camp, 1943

The Zaloshitzer Rebbe, one of the greatest Kabbalists of the pre-Holocaust era, was a scion of the Zidichov-Komarna lineage and a descendant of the famous Tosafos Yom Tov, who traced his ancestry to Rashi and King David.

A man of self-effacing modesty, he shunned controversy and treated everyone with warmth and kindness. He gained a reputation, not only as a pious and learned man, but also for the wisdom with which he settled family disputes and patched things up between litigants.

An outstanding Kabbalist, he published a book written by the Ari entitled *Likutei HaShas* together with his brother, Rabbi Zeide Moshe Chaim.

After his father's death in 1918, Rabbi Shem became the Zaloshitzer Rebbe in Cracow, where he ignited the hearts of the chassidim with the holy fire that burned within him. This gentle soul was as refined and gracious as a man can be, a father to every individual who needed him.

After the German conquest of Poland in 1939, he went into hiding but was forced to move into the Cracow Ghetto, where he devoted himself to helping others. From the ghetto he was transferred to the dreadful concentration camp of Plaszow, and even in the shadow of death he continued to infuse the camp inmates with hope and faith. It was there that he was shot to death on 28 Nissan, 1943.

The many books written by the Zaloshitzer Rebbe were all destroyed by the Germans, except for a few scattered manuscripts that survived the Holocaust. His son, Rabbi Moshe Klingberg, collected these writings and published them under the title *Ohalei Shem*.[1] The insights, many of which are based on *gematria*,[2] reflect the Rebbe's brilliant mind and original thoughts. In addition to Torah thoughts, the book contains a rich selection of moving anecdotes about the life of the great tzaddik.

Selections from Ohalei Shem

Why Did Yaakov Cross His Hands?

> Yisrael reached out with his right hand and placed it on Efrayim's head [even though] he was the younger son. He placed his left hand on Menashe's head. He deliberately crossed his hands, even though Menashe was the firstborn.
>
> (Bereishis 48:14)

Why did Yaakov cross his hands? Why didn't he simply tell the boys to change places? The reason is this: The Gemara says that the diagonal of a square is one and a third times the sides of the square (*Sukkah* 8a). With that in mind, Yaakov crossed his hands diagonally, so that the blessing he was about to give be increased by one-third.

Ohalei Shem, p. 37

---

1 Jerusalem, 1961.
2 A system whereby letters are used as numerals.

Do Not Erect a Sacred Pillar

The Zaloshitzer Rebbe prayed and performed the mitzvos with enthusiasm, fervor, and youthful freshness. He was wont to quote the verse, "Do not erect a stone pillar, since this is something God, your Lord, hates" (*Devarim* 16:22).

"This means," he would say, "do not serve God routinely, from force of habit, and without originality and creativity. Prayer that is cold and impassive like a stone pillar is hated by God."

Ohalei Shem, p. 12

The Word *Emes*

The three letters of the word *emes* [*alef, mem, tav*] are the first [*alef*], the last [*tav*], and the middle letters [*mem*] of the *alef beis*. If you include in the *alef beis* the five final letters, *kaf, mem, nun, pei,* and *tzaddi,* you obtain a total of twenty-seven letters. The *mem* is the fourteenth of these letters, so that there are thirteen letters before the *mem* and thirteen letters after the *mem*.

The two groups of thirteen letters on either side of the *mem* add up to twenty-six, which is the numeric value of the divine Name [*yud* (10) + *hei* (5) + *vav* (6) + *hei* (5)].

But there is more. The shape of the letter *mem* itself is a composite of a *vav* and a *chaf*, which again add up to twenty-six [*vav* = 6, *chaf* = 20]. Thus, the letters of the *alef beis* represent God's Name encapsulated within God's Name.

Embedded in this amazing *gematria* is the idea that the essence of God is contained in the Torah, which is the embodiment of *emes*, truth.

Ohalei Shem, p. 62

The Eye and the Heart

In the entire *Tanach*, no part of the human body is described as "good."

The only exceptions are the eye and the heart, which merit the adjective of "good": "He who has a good eye is blessed" (*Mishlei* 22:9), and "He that is of a good heart has a feast without end" (ibid. 15:15).

Why are only the eye and the heart termed "good"? According to the Sages, "The eye and the heart are the two agents of sin: What the eye sees, the heart lusts" (*Rashi, Bemidbar* 15:39; *Bemidbar Rabbah* 10:2). The things you see arouse your desire. To curb the excessive appetites of the eye and the heart we were given the mitzvah of tefillin. We place the arm-tefillin on the left biceps, opposite the heart, and the head-tefillin opposite the space between the eyes. We thereby decrease the power of the eye and the heart, the two agents of sin, and transform them into agents of virtue.

Only the eye and the heart, having the potential of enticing a person to do evil, can be turned into a force for good. This thought is echoed in the verse, "Give your *heart* to me, my son; let your *eyes* watch my ways" (*Mishlei* 23:26).

In the same vein, we say in the *shacharis* prayer, "Enlighten our *eyes* in Your Torah and attach our *hearts* to Your commandments."

Ohalei Shem, p. 85

Why Zaloshitz?

Rabbi Shem's father, Rabbi Avraham Mordechai Klingberg, was a chassid of the Divrei Chaim,[1] who encouraged him to become a chassidic rebbe. Once, on his way from Sanz to his hometown Komarno, Rabbi Avraham Mordechai passed through Zaloshitz. The local chassidim and leaders of the community urged him to stay and establish a *beis midrash* in their town. Initially, Rabbi Avraham Mordechai declined, but just then a terrible accident happened. Two children were buried alive in a landslide at a local quarry. The distraught parents and the members of the community implored Rabbi Avraham Mordechai to pray for the safe recovery of the children.

---

1 Rabbi Chaim Halberstam of Sanz, 1793–1896.

"If God helps," said the Rebbe, "and answers my prayers so that the two children will be saved, I consider that a sign that I should stay in Zaloshitz."

God heard his plea. The children emerged unscathed, and Rabbi Avraham Mordechai stayed to become the Zaloshitzer Rebbe.

Ohalei Shem, p. 8

In the Plaszow Concentration Camp

In 1943, Rabbi Shem was transported to the infamous Plaszow concentration camp near Cracow. This death camp was under the command of Amon Goeth, a rabid Nazi who took pleasure riding through the camp on his white horse, killing Jews with his pistol at point-blank range.

Once on a Shabbos, as the Zaloshitzer Rebbe huddled in the barracks for *shalosh seudos*, the third meal, together with his chassidim, he spoke these unforgettable words: "David HaMelech says in *Tehillim*, 'Until I entered God's sanctuary will I understand their fate' (*Tehillim* 73:17). The meaning of this cryptic passage is that only when Mashiach will come will I understand the secret of the divine stewardship in the present era. Only then will I comprehend the mystery of the killings and the carnage."

More he did not say and refused to discuss the situation further. Careful not to question the divine decree, he accepted his fate with love. Even there, at the threshhold of death, he continued to minister to his flock, in the spirit of, "Though He slay me, I will trust Him" (*Iyov* 13:15). On Purim, he arranged for the reading of the megillah and distributed the traditional gifts to the poor, a crust of bread to one, a few grains of corn to another.

With the onset of Pesach, the situation was getting worse. Every day Jews were rounded up to be shipped to the gas chambers of Auschwitz. On the seder night, in the dark barracks, the Rebbe, surrounded by brokenhearted, despondent Jews, recited the Haggadah by heart. He nourished them with spiritual food, telling them that God's salvation comes in the blink of an eye, that they would yet hear the footsteps of the Redeemer. "Only now that I am surrounded by these vile creatures," the Rebbe continued, "do I begin to grasp the full meaning of the *berachah* in which I thank God every morning for not having made me a goy."

Ohalei Shem, p. 17

His Final Moments

On 28 Nissan, 1943, the Germans, in an effort to totally demoralize their Jewish prisoners, combed the barracks of Plaszow in search of ten prominent rabbis whom they were going to execute publicly. When the beloved Zaloshitzer Rebbe was led to the execution site, thousands of Jews, observant and nonobservant alike, broke into bitter tears, but the venerable Rebbe begged them to accept the divine decree with love and joy.

He was ordered to remove his clothes, but he requested to be allowed to keep his shirt and his *tallis katan*[1] while reciting *Vidui*, his confession before death. When his request was granted, he rose to the pinnacle of *kedushah*. Absorbed in lofty thoughts, his face radiated an otherworldly glow. For a brief moment he glanced with deep compassion at his Jewish brothers who were forced to witness the execution. Then he lifted his eyes upward, crying out with a voice that pierced the heavens, "Let me be an atonement for Israel!"

He recited *Vidui*, covered his face with his *tallis katan*, and cried, "*Shema Yisrael, Hashem Elokeinu, Hashem echad!*" His face shone with a wondrous brilliance. Then, with a quick burst of machine-gun fire the German murderers felled this giant of Torah and Chassidus.

Ohalei Shem, p. 18

---

1   Fringed garment worn under clothes, also known as "tzitzis."

A Prolific Author

Rabbi Shem of Zaloshitz, an eminent scholar of Talmud and Kabbalah, wrote a commentary on the *Zohar* entitled *Ohalei Shem*. His library contained eight hundred volumes on Kabbalah and Chassidus and fifteen hundred volumes of responsa and talmudic novellae, all inscribed with his marginal notes. He avidly studied the works of the Vilna Gaon and had committed many of them to memory. All of his writings, except for a few scattered comments, were destroyed by the Germans.

Ohalei Shem, p. 15

What Is a Chassid?

"What is a chassid?" a prominent rabbi once asked the Zaloshitzer Rebbe.

"Nothing, a nobody, a zero without a number in front of it," replied the Rebbe. What he meant to say was that a chassid is a person who thinks of himself as a mere nothing, a nonentity. [This is a perfect decription of the Zaloshitzer Rebbe, a man of extraordinary humility and great love for every Jew.]

Ohalei Shem, p. 11

Chapter 54
RABBI YEHUDAH LEIB ASHLAG

born: Warsaw, Poland, 1886
died: Yerushalayim, 1955

Rabbi Yehudah Leib Ashlag, the great contemporary Kabbalist, gained worldwide acclaim for his monumental work *HaSulam*, an interpretive Hebrew translation of the *Zohar* that makes its obscure Aramaic text accessible to students of this holy book.

Rabbi Yehudah Leib was a chassidic leader, but unlike most chassidic rebbes, he was not a descendant of a chassidic dynasty. Very little is known about his early years. By the time he was thirteen years old he had a thorough knowledge of the entire Talmud. He became a chassid of Rabbi Meir Shalom of Kalushin and often traveled to Belz to be in the presence of the Belzer Rebbe, Rabbi Yissachar Dov.

As a young man he served as rabbi of a Warsaw congregation. However, after making the decision to devote himself to the study of Kabbalah, he gave up his position, withdrew from worldly pursuits, and lived in abject poverty. He was so poor that his commentaries were written on scraps of paper.

A deep mystery surrounds the person who introduced Rabbi Yehudah Leib Ashlag to the teachings of Kabbalah. The only information we have is contained in a letter by Rabbi Ashlag where he writes, "On Friday, the twelfth of Marcheshvan, 1919, a certain person visited me.... I immediately sensed that he was a holy man. He promised to reveal to me the wisdom of Kabbalah in all its facets. I studied under him for about three months....

"As I became more proficient, my saintly master gradually withdrew, until at the end of three months he disappeared altogether. I went looking for him but could not find him. On the morning of the ninth of Nissan I found him, at which time he revealed to me a deep mystery, which made me ecstatic.... Since he appeared to be very faint I stayed with him and did not leave his house. The next day, the tenth of Nissan, 1919, my saintly master passed away. He was a prominent Warsaw businessman, admired for his integrity, but no one knew that he was a great Kabbalist. He made me promise not to reveal his identity to anyone."

In 1922, Rabbi Yehudah Leib settled in Yerushalayim. There he lived with his family in a small attic apartment on an narrow alley near the Western Wall and pursued his studies of Kabbalah in Yeshivah Chayei Olam. Before long, his extraordinary piety and extensive knowledge of *chochmas nistar* (mysticism) were recognized, and a group of young disciples eagerly listened to his profound Kabbalistic expositions on the *Zohar* and the teachings of the Ari, as set forth in *Etz Chaim*. But extreme poverty forced him to accept a rabbinic position in Givat Shaul, a new section at the outskirts of Yerushalayim, where he established a *beis midrash* and *kollel* named Ittur Rabbanim. His lectures on Kabbalah, given in a lucid and systematic format, drew large audiences of devoted followers.

In the final decade of his life, Rabbi Yehudah Leib lived in B'nei Brak and Tel Aviv. It was there that he completed his magnum opus *HaSulam* (The Ladder), a twenty-one-volume interpretive Hebrew translation of the *Zohar*,[1] with a comprehensive introduction, which provides the key to the *Zohar*'s Kabbalistic concepts. He explains the title *HaSulam* by saying: "A person might have an attic filled with precious jewels. All he needs is a ladder to gain access to these great treasures."

Rabbi Ashlag's work bears a glowing approbation from Rabbi Yosef

---

1   Jerusalem, 1955.

Chaim Sonnenfeld, Chief Rabbi of the Ashkenazi community of Yerushalayim, who describes him as "one of the outstanding scholars of Yerushalayim, who studies the Torah *lishmah*, for its own sake." Rabbi Avraham Mordechai Alter, the Gerrer Rebbe (known as the "Imrei Emes"), also praised the work. Another laudatory approbation is from Rabbi Chaim Shaul Dewick, head of the Kabbalist scholars in Yerushalayim.

On Yom Kippur 1955, Rabbi Yehudah Leib Ashlag passed away. He was survived by two sons – Rabbi Baruch Shalom, who died in 1983, and Rabbi Binyamin, who established a *kollel* in B'nei Brak, where he spreads the teachings of Kabbalah among chassidim and students of *chen*.

Selections from HaSulam

The Present-Day Flowering of Kabbalah

The *Zohar* assures us, "The time will come when the teachings of Kabbalah will be revealed to all, even to children. And when the knowledge of Kabbalah is made known, the Jewish people will live to see the ultimate Redemption" (*Zohar, Naso* 125b).

Indeed, we see today that slowly but surely the words of the *Zohar* and the mystical teachings of Kabbalah are becoming better known. [The wisdom of Kabbalah will continue to spread] until we will merit a complete revelation of this knowledge. Then we will be worthy of the *geulah sheleimah*, the final complete Redemption.

HaSulam, Sefer HaHakdamos, p. 32

Why Did God Create the World?

God created the world in order to delight His creatures so that they recognize His truth and His majesty. This surely does not apply to inanimate things like the earth, the sun, the moon, and the stars. Neither does it apply to plants or animals. Since they do not have the capacity to feel for others, even for members of their own species, how can you expect them to appreciate God's benevolence! Only man has an innate feeling of compassion for others, and only he can fathom God's kindness. By fulfilling the Torah and the mitzvos, man brings God's plan to fruition. So you see, the only reason God created the entire universe was in order to benefit man.

I know that this does not sit well with certain philosophers. They cannot accept the fact that an insignificant, puny creature like man should be the focal point of this glorious, exalted universe. These people think like a little worm that was born inside a radish. It sees the world as a very small, bitter, dark, and harsh place. But the moment the worm breaks through the skin of the radish and has its first glimpse of the outside world it says, "I thought that the whole world was the radish where I was born. But seeing this splendid, dazzling universe, I realize that I was wrong."

It is the same with the people who are entangled deep inside the shell of the base instincts with which they were born. They have not tried to take the special potion — Torah and mitzvos — that is designed to crack that shell and convert their love of self to a love of God. If they did, their eyes would open. They would see the wealth of knowledge that is there for them to enjoy, the higher wisdom that is so sweet that the soul craves it. They would heartily agree with the saying of the Sages: "What does a good guest say? He says, 'All the trouble my host took to prepare this meal he did only for my sake' " (*Berachos* 58a).

HaSulam, Introduction to the Zohar, par. 39–40

Givers and Receivers

God derives the greatest satisfaction when His creations recognize His benevolence, like a father who is thrilled when his son is grateful for the many gifts he receives from him. And so it says, " 'Truly, Efrayim is a dear son to Me, a delightful child. Whenever I speak of him, I remember him more and more. That is why My heart yearns for him. I will surely take pity on him,' declared God" (*Yirmiyah* 31:19). To achieve this exquisite delight it was worth it for God to create the entire universe.

During Creation God bestowed His exalted beneficence in four stages: first to inanimate things, then to plants, then to animals, and finally to man — each successive stage having an increasingly greater capacity for receiving God's gifts.

Now, if you are a "receiver," you must have had a need, and when you have a need, you move toward the object you want. Thus you could say that need involves motion. Since inanimate things, like rocks, do not need anything, they do not move, and so they do not receive anything.

Plants are "receivers" to a very small degree [and their needs are very limited]. Therefore, plants move only very slightly: they turn toward the sun, and they absorb food and water. That's why plants cannot be considered out-and-out "receivers."

Animals manifest a much stronger drive to receive than plants. They have clearly defined needs, and so they have the ability to move about freely. However, animals do not display concern for the welfare of other animals. They do not share in the joy or the suffering of other animals. So how can they appreciate God's kindness?

Man has the strongest desire to receive, and he is also the only creature that has compassion for his fellow. His powerful desire to receive stems from an equally strong feeling of need. If left unbridled, his desire to receive and his concomitant deep-seated needs prompt him to accumulate untold wealth and property, as it says, "He who has a hundred *maneh* wants two hundred" (*Koheles Rabbah* 1:34). But by learning Torah and doing mitzvos, man's desire to receive is transformed into a desire to give. The "receiver" becomes a "giver." By becoming a "giver," man emulates his Creator and deserves God's benevolence, which is the whole idea why God created the world in the first place.

HaSulam, Introduction to the Zohar, par. 33–38

Yosef's Appointment as Viceroy of Egypt

> Then Pharaoh said to Yosef, "...There can be no one so discerning and wise as you. You shall be in charge of my palace, and by your command [lit., "by your mouth"] shall all my people be sustained [*yishak*]...." And Pharaoh removed his ring from his hand and put it on Yosef's hand. He then had him dressed in garments of fine linen and placed a gold chain upon his neck....
> *(Bereishis 41:39-44)*

> [Note: The word *yishak* (be sustained) from the root *nashak* (to kiss) can be translated as "be kissed."]

When Yosef was appointed viceroy over Egypt, God rewarded him for his moral conduct. [This is evident in the present verse.] The phrase "By your command [lit., your mouth] the people shall be sustained [lit., be kissed]" alludes to the fact that Yosef did not sin by kissing Potifar's wife. The phrase, "[Pharaoh] put the ring on Yosef's hand" alludes to the fact that Yosef's hand did not touch her. The phrase, "He put a gold chain upon his neck" alludes to the fact that Yosef's neck did not turn to do a sinful act. The phrase, "He had him dressed in garments of fine linen" alludes to the fact that his body did not come close to her. The phrase where Pharaoh called Yosef "discerning and wise" alludes to the fact that he did not entertain the thought of committing a sin.... All the favors Yosef received he earned with his virtuous conduct.

HaSulam, Zohar, Mikeitz 64

The Good and the Evil Impulse

> He will charge His angels for you, to protect you in all your ways.
> *(Tehillim 91:11)*

The moment a child comes into the world, the *yetzer hara* (evil impulse) takes hold of him. It tempts him without letup, as it says, "Sin [i.e., the *yetzer hara*] is crouching at the door [of the womb, at birth]" (*Bereishis 4:7*).

David also characterized the *yetzer hara* as "sin." For he said, "My sin is before me always" (*Tehillim* 51:5), meaning, the *yetzer hara* is making me sin against God every day. The *yetzer hara* does not leave you from the moment you are born until the end of life.

The *yetzer hatov* (good impulse) enters a person on the day he is mature enough to try to cleanse himself [of transgression]. When is that? The day he is thirteen years old. Then both impulses join him, the *yetzer hatov* on his right, the *yetzer hara* on his left. They really are two angels that stay with him all his life. When you want to do good, the right side subdues the left, and the *yetzer hara* surrenders to you. Then both the *yetzer hatov* and the *yetzer hara* work together to protect you wherever you go. That is the meaning of the verse, "He will charge His angels for you, to protect you on all your ways." [Meaning: The energy of the carnal impulse should be channeled and put to use for noble purposes.]

HaSulam, Zohar, Vayishlach, 1–4

Discourse about the Rose

[Note: The divine Name *Elokim* signifies God's attribute of strict justice.]

Rabbi Chizkiyah declared: It says, "Like a rose among thorns, so is my darling among the maidens" (*Shir HaShirim* 2:2). He asks: What is meant by "rose"? He answers: The rose symbolizes the Jewish people [which stands for the *Sefirah* of *Malchus*]. There are roses and there are roses. Just as there are red and white roses that bloom among thorns, so does the Jewish people have elements of justice and compassion. Just as the rose has thirteen petals, so is the Jewish people surrounded by the thirteen divine attributes of compassion.[1] You can tell that this is so, because following the first mention of the divine Name "*Elokim*" in the Torah ["*Bereishis bara Elokim*"], there are thirteen words until "*Elokim*" occurs the second time.

HaSulam, Introduction to the Zohar

---

1 See *Shemos* 34:6.

Reborn Souls

The Holy One, blessed be He, plants trees in this world. If they thrive, fine. If they don't thrive, He pulls them out and replants them someplace else. He will do this over and over again. God does this for the good of the soul, to set the world right.

[Explains *HaSulam*:] If a person is not able to reach perfection the first time he lives, he comes back to life a second time. He may be reincarnated many times until he is perfect.

HaSulam, Zohar, Vayeishev 176

Yibum and Reincarnation

> [Note: If a childless man dies, his brother has the obligation to marry the widow. This is called *yibum* (levirate marriage). See *Devarim* 25:5-10.]

> Yehudah said to Onan, "Marry your brother's wife, and thus fulfill the duty of a brother-in-law to her. You will then raise children to keep your brother's name alive."
>
> (Bereishis 38:8)

Although all men must face death and death separates man's body from its heavenly root, nevertheless, the connection is not completely severed. Each person remains attached to his heavenly root through his children. A son is part of his father's body; he is a link in the unbroken chain of life that begins with Adam and extends until the revival of the dead. As long as a person has a son, the chain of life remains intact, and death does not cause a break with eternity. It is as though the person is still alive.

A person who died without leaving children needs a *tikkun* so that his death should not cause a break with his eternal root, because his chain of life has been interrupted. To repair the separation caused by the death of a childless person, a body has to be created to enclose the soul of the departed, so that he can reestablish his connection with the chain of life. And when that person is reincarnated like this, he is praised in the World to Come, for God favors such souls....

But it is even better if a person is not reincarnated because that shows that he is a tzaddik who does not need to be reborn. For a person who is reborn has to suffer in this world for the sins he committed in a previous existence, but a tzaddik has a fitting place prepared for him in the World to Come.

HaSulam, Zohar, Vayeishev 177

Celebrating the Publication of HaSulam

Rabbi Yosef Weinstock, a student of Rabbi Yehudah Leib Ashlag, relates that when the *Zohar* with the commentary *HaSulam* came off the press, Rabbi Yehudah Leib, overcome with emotion, was unable to utter a single word. On Lag BaOmer 1953, the *yartzeit* of Rabbi Shimon bar Yochai [the author of the *Zohar*], Rabbi Ashlag arranged a festive banquet in Meron,[1] to celebrate the publication of his work. At the *seudas mitzvah* he told his chassidim to sing a wordless *niggun* (melody). He explained, "Words fail me to offer thanks to God for allowing me to write a commentary to the *Zohar*. That's why I'm asking you to sing a *niggun* without words."

Marbitzei Torah MeOlam HaChassidus,[2] p. 222

---

1 The town in the northern Galilee where the tomb of Rabbi Shimon bar Yochai is located.
2 By Rabbi Aharon Sorasky, B'nei Brak, 1989.

Chapter 55

RABBI YISRAEL ABUCHATZEIRAH

(Baba Sali)

born: Tafillalt, Morocco, 1890
died: Netivot, Israel, 1984

Rabbi Yisrael Abuchatzeirah, affectionately known as "Baba Sali," was the son of Rabbi Massoud Abuchatzeirah and a scion of the saintly Kabbalist Rabbi Yaakov Abuchatzeirah, the spiritual leader of tens of thousands of devoted followers. Even as a young boy Yisrael displayed extraordinary enthusiasm for Torah study and self-improvement. As he grew up, people began to see him as a person whose prayers brought miraculous results. While he was still at home with his parents, the brokenhearted and poor came flocking to him for his *berachah*.

Before long, he gained fame among Moroccan Jews as a miracle worker and became known as Baba Sali, "the father who will pray for you." Upon his father's death, he was chosen to succeed him as *rosh yeshivah* of the Tafillalt yeshivah. As he was an eminent Torah scholar and blessed with an infallible memory, Baba Sali's lectures drew students from far and wide. But he did not allow his students to take notes of his lectures. He feared that his astute comments would become public knowledge and that this might cause him to become proud. Therefore, none of his novel thoughts on halachah and Kabbalah were published.

His fondest wish came true when he visited Eretz Yisrael in 1921. On his arrival in Yerushalayim, the young Baba Sali (only thirty years old at the time) was welcomed by the great rabbis and prominent Kabbalists of the city. The news of the grand reception spread rapidly, and shortly masses of people lined up to receive a *berachah* from the saintly young Kabbalist. He stayed in Eretz Yisrael for an entire year, but when his brother, Rabbi David, the leader of the Tafillalt community, was brutally murdered by an Arab, he returned to Morocco to take his brother's place.

In 1964, after most Moroccan Jews had moved to Eretz Yisrael, and most of Baba Sali's children had also settled there, he fulfilled his long-time dream of making his home in Eretz Yisrael. He took up residence in Netivot, a small settlement in the Negev, northwest of Be'er Sheva. It did not take long for his modest residence to become a spiritual center. When news spread that his prayers effected miraculous cures, his home was besieged with petitioners. Large crowds, including chassidic rebbes, *roshei yeshivah*, students, common folk, and even Arabs, came to pay their respects, to receive advice and blessings, and to be inspired by his words and his saintly way of life.

After a lifetime devoted to serving God and helping others, Baba Sali passed away on 4 Shevat, 1984. More than 100,000 mourners escorted Baba Sali, the miracle worker of our generation, on his final journey. The impressive white tomb in the fields of Netivot is a landmark visited by thousands each year.

Anecdotes about the Life of Baba Sali

Don't Take Down My Lectures

Baba Sali had an uncanny ability of reading people's minds and seeing hidden things. Once, after a lengthy and difficult Talmudic discourse, Baba

Sali exhorted his students not to put down his lecture in writing. However, one of the students, unable to resist the temptation, planned to transcribe the brilliant *shiur*. Before taking it down, he reviewed the subject matter with a friend to commit it to memory and to make sure he had not missed any points. He then sat down, ready to transcribe the lecture.

But no sooner did he take pen in hand than his mind went blank. He could not recall a single detail of the lengthy discourse. The material he knew by heart faultlessly a minute before was erased from his memory. Once more he ran through the *shiur* with his friend, but when he wanted to jot it down it was gone again.

When he entered the *beis midrash*, Baba Sali went over to him and said, "If you want to remember my *shiur*, don't try to put it down on paper. I promise you, the moment you begin to write, you'll forget everything."

Praying in the Shul of the Ari

During Baba Sali's year-long stay in Eretz Yisrael in 1921, his mystical powers became evident to the local population when he visited Tzefas, the city of the Kabbalists. While there, he had long talks with the local Kabbalists, particularly with the elder Kabbalist Rabbi Alfandri. When he wanted to pray in the shul of the Ari, he learned that this was out of the question. "The Ari's shul has been closed and sealed shut for many years," he was told, "because whoever entered the shul did not come out alive."

His attendant, Rabbi Moshe Shitreet, relates: "Baba Sali asked me to get the key to the Ari's shul from the caretaker. Meanwhile, he went to immerse in the Ari's *mikveh*. But no matter how much I pleaded with the caretaker, he refused to release the key. 'Too many people have died while praying in there,' he said adamantly. 'If I gave you the key, I would be guilty of taking the rabbi's life.'

"But after my persistent urging, he gave in. Before handing me the key, he tied a long string to it, so that he would be able to retrieve it. He was convinced that the rabbi would not come out alive, and he was not about to venture inside and fetch the key.

"Baba Sali told me to hold on to his coat, and we entered the shul together. After walking across the courtyard, we opened the door to the shul. Silently we stood there, overawed. It was late in the afternoon, almost dark, but when the Rabbi crossed the threshhold, suddenly, the shul's interior was bathed in bright light. The Rabbi opened the *aron hakodesh* (holy ark), took out a *sefer Torah* (Torah scroll), and, his face aglow, read from it for a few minutes. We then sat down on a bench, and the rabbi calmly said to me, 'You may let go of my coat already.'

"After davening *minchah*, we left the shul. As we came out, the caretaker came running toward the rabbi. Unable to utter a word, he embraced him and tearfully kissed him."

Rabbi Shitreet concluded, "Baba Sali's visit to the Ari's shul was the talk of town. Ever since that day, people are coming again to pray in the holy Ari's shul."[1]

Don't Worry about Your Livelihood

Back in Tafillalt, Morocco, Baba Sali's attendant was a man named Avraham. He relates: "When I attended the rabbi, I was unable to take care of my business. I was running a store, but since helping the rabbi took up most of my time, I did not earn any money. One day I entered the rabbi's study and asked permission to leave in order to take care of my business. Smiling warmly, Baba Sali replied, 'Don't worry about your business. If you stay in your store for just half an hour each day, I promise you that you will earn as much as you used to earn working a whole day.'

"And that's exactly what happened. I made the same amount in half an hour as I previously earned staying in the store for a whole day. How did it happen? I have no idea. But let me tell you, that wasn't the only amazing thing I witnessed in Baba Sali's house. I can't explain it...."

---

[1] On a recent visit to Eretz Yisrael, I, like thousands of others, visited the Ari's shul in Tzefat and immersed in the Ari's *mikveh*. It is an exhilarating experience.

Instant Recovery

Baba Sali was invited to all festive occasions in the surrounding communities. At these banquets he would speak about the importance of the mitzvah that was being celebrated, a wedding, an engagement, a bris, a bar mitzvah, or a *siyum* (celebration at the completion of the study of a Talmudic tractate).

Rabbi Michael Alasari relates an incident that happened at one such feast: Once when Baba Sali visited a nearby town the city administration prepared a meal in his honor. The whole town was invited. The prominent citizens were seated inside the City Hall building, while the ordinary people sat at tables in the yard. When Baba Sali entered the building and took his seat at the head table, pandemonium broke out, as the people outside began to push forward for a view of the beloved Baba Sali. In the ensuing turmoil, two men got into an argument which soon turned into a nasty fist fight.

Suddenly one of the brawlers fell to the ground, unconscious, a deep gash on his head where a blow had landed. People ran to call a doctor. The victim's face turned blue; he stopped breathing. It was obvious that he was in the throes of death. Quickly Baba Sali was alerted. The fellow who had knocked him unconscious fell to his knees, begging the rabbi to save the dying man. "Please pray for the man," he pleaded.

Baba Sali calmly stepped outside. With his cane he tapped the comatose man on the sole of his foot. "Get up, brother! On your feet, my friend!" he called out. Instantly the man opened his eyes and stood up straight....

The Tank Was Still Full

Rabbi Eliyahu Alfasi, the rabbi's attendant, told the following story:

"It happened one cold wintry day that the rabbi asked me to prepare for a trip to Yerushalayim. 'I'd like to go right away,' he said firmly. I quickly called a friend, asking him to drive the rabbi to Yerushalayim. A few minutes later the car drove up, and the rabbi and I were on our way.

"We had not yet left Netivot when the rabbi asked me to tell the driver that he insisted on paying the full fare a taxi cab would charge. The driver replied, 'I should be paying the rabbi for allowing me to serve him. Don't make me forfeit the mitzvah by paying for it.'

"On the return trip the rabbi said, 'If the driver doesn't want to accept money for taking me, he should at least let me pay for the gas.'

"I told this to the driver and asked him to figure out the cost of the gas for the round trip. The driver looked at the gauge. Bewildered, he cried out, 'Unbelievable! I'm telling you, the tank is still full! I drove all the way to Yerushalayim and back, and it looks like I haven't used a drop. I can't ask you to pay me for the gas.'

"A faint smile lit up the rabbi's face. 'Let me tell you a story,' he said. 'Once I had to go on a long trip. I asked a good friend to take me in his car. He presently showed up, but before setting out on our journey, he wanted to fill his tank. "How long will the gas in your tank last us?" I asked. "For about half an hour's drive, and our trip will take more than two hours," came the reply. "Don't worry about it," I countered. "Let's get going, and I guarantee you we won't get stuck. You'll have enough gas to take us there and back."

" 'And that's how it was,' Baba Sali concluded. 'We drove there and back, with gasoline to spare.' Absorbed in deep thought, the rabbi added, 'I'm sure it was a *berachah* from Hashem.' "

Her Eyesight Restored

For many years, an elderly lady served as housekeeper in the rabbi's home in Netivot. She had taken care of the household in Morocco and knew the rabbi's father and grandfather, the great Kabbalist, Rabbi Yaakov Abuchatzeirah. She used to say, "There's one thing I don't have to worry about: losing my eyesight. Once when I had trouble with my eyes Rabbi Yaakov Abuchatzeirah blessed me and promised me that as long as I live I would have good vision."

Then it happened. While working in Baba Sali's home one day, she suddenly became dizzy, her eyes dimmed, and she slipped and fell on the floor. When she got up, to her great consternation, her vision was blurred; she could barely see. Heartbroken, she asked for the rabbi's blessing to restore her eyesight so that she could continue serving the rabbi for many more years. Besides, she argued, since she had the *berachah* of the rabbi's grandfather that her eyes would never fail her, then how could this have happened to her? Baba Sali consoled her and blessed her. Then he recommended that before retiring she should do *netilas yadayim* (ritual washing of the hands) the way it is done in the morning when arising. Pacified, the woman went home. Early the next morning she was back at her job, her vision fully restored, as if nothing had happened.

The Arrack Continued to Flow

From time to time Baba Sali would make a celebration on a festive occasion or on the anniversary of the death of a Rebbe or of one of his ancestors. Everyone was invited, the rich and the poor, and many of the students of the nearby yeshivah Be'er Yaakov joined the party to be close to the saintly Baba Sali and receive his *berachah*. The tables were set with a profusion of delectable dishes, and when the Rabbi spoke an aura of *kedushah* and true joy filled the hearts of the guests.

A bottle of arrack brandy always stood by the rabbi's side, and after the speech he would fill the glasses and pass around the drinks to all the guests, giving them a heartfelt *berachah*. There might be a hundred or more guests, but each received his glass of arrack poured from the same bottle. Everyone knew of the miracle of the arrack. No matter how many glasses Baba Sali filled, the bottle always remained full.

[I personally know of two eminently reliable persons who witnessed this; one, a well-known psychiatrist and former student of Yeshivah Be'er Yaakov in Netivot.]

His Prayers Cured the Young Girl

A young girl from Teveriah was critically injured in a car accident. All attempts to help her regain consciousness failed. After three weeks of hoping and praying, the disheartened parents gave up hope of seeing their daughter emerge from the coma. As a last resort they went to Netivot, to ask for Baba Sali's *berachah* and intercession.

Moved by the parents' sorrowful plea, he asked them to stay in the house until after *minchah*, when he would pray for the child's recovery. Following *minchah*, the rabbi prepared a bottle of water and instructed the parents to dab the child's forehead and wash her hands with the water. Filled with hope, the parents rushed to the hospital to carry out Baba Sali's instructions, after which they returned home. Late that night, the telephone rang. Excited but perplexed, the doctor gave them the happy news that the child had regained consciousness and would make a complete recovery. He had just one request. Would they please go back to Netivot and bring back a whole case of this miraculous water? [The doctor did not realize that it was not the water that cured the child, but that it was God's answer to Baba Sali's fervent prayer.]

GLOSSARY

Adam HaRishon — Adam, the first man

Aggadah (pl. Aggados) — the nonlegal partions of the Talmud

Aharon — Aaron

alef beis — the Hebrew alphabet

amora — teacher from the Gemara

aravos — willow branches, one of the four species waved on Sukkos

aron — ark

Aron HaKodesh — Holy Ark

Ashkenaz — Germany

Ashkenazi — originating from Germany

Asiyah — the World of Action

Atzilus — the World of Emanation

aveirah — sin

Avigayil — Abigail

Avos — Chapters of the Fathers, a tractate of the Mishnah

Avraham Avinu — the patriarch Abraham

Avram — Abram (the patriarch Abraham's original name)

baal teshuvah (pl. baalei teshuvah) – returnee to Torah observance

beis din – rabbinical court

beis midrash – house of study

Bemidbar – the book of Numbers

berachah – blessing

Bereishis – Genesis

Beri'ah – the World of Creation

Bilam – Balaam

Binah – Understanding

Binyamin – Benjamin

bris – lit. covenant; celebration on the occasion of a circumcision

bris milah – circumcision

Chanah – Hannah

chassid – chassidic Rebbe's disciple

Chavah – Eve

Chavakuk – Habakkuk

chen – an abbreviation of *chochmas nistar* (mysticism)

Chesed – Kindness

cheshek – desire

Chevron – Hebron

Chochmah – Wisdom

chochmas nistar – lit. hidden knowledge; Jewish mysticism

Chol HaMoed – intermediate days of the festivals of Passover and Sukkos

Choreiv – Horeb

Chumash – the Five Books of the Torah, the Pentateuch

churban – the destruction of the Temple

dagesh – a dot put in a consonant in a Hebrew word

daven – to pray

David HaMelech – King David

dayan – judge

Devarim – Deuteronomy

deveikus – attachment to God

Din – justice

Divrei HaYamim – Chronicles

dor dei'ah – the "generation of wisdom" that received the Torah

Efrayim – Ephraim

Ein Sof – the Infinite

Eliyahu HaNavi – Elijah the Prophet

emes – truth

emunah – faith

Eretz Yisrael – the Land of Israel

Esav – Esau

esrog – citron, one of the four species waved on Sukkos

gadol (pl. *gedolim*) – towering Torah sage

galus – exile, diaspora

Gan Eden – Garden of Eden

gaon – genius

Gehinnom – Hell

geirus – conversion

Gemara – a commentary on the Mishnah comprising the second part of the Talmud

***ger* (pl. *gerim*)** – convert

ger tzedek – righteous convert

geulah sheleimah – the final complete redemption

Gevurah – strength

gilgul – transmigration of souls

hadassim – myrtle twigs, one of the four species waved on Sukkos

Haggadah – the story of the Exodus told on the night of Passover

halachah – Torah and rabbinic law

Hashem – God

Hashem Yisbarach – God, blessed be He

Havdalah – blessings said at the conclusion of Sabbath and festivals

Hevel – Abel

Hod – Splendor

imahos – matriarchs

Iyov – Job

Kabbalah – lit. "tradition"; Jewish mysticism

Kayin – Cain

kedushah – holiness, sanctity

Keser – Crown

kiddush haShem – sanctification of God's name; a martyr's death

klippos – shells, husks of impurity

***kohein* (pl. *kohanim*)** – priest

Koheles – Ecclesiastes

kollel – advanced study center solely for higher Torah learning

Kuzari – classic philosophical work

Lavan – Laban

lulav – palm frond, one of the four species waved on Sukkos

Maaseh Merkavah – the Work of the Divine Chariot, Ezekiel ch. 1

maggid – preacher

Malchus – Kingdom

Marranos – Spanish Jews who were forced to convert to Christianity but continued to practice Judaism secretly

Mashiach – Messiah

Megillas Esther – the book of Esther

Michah – Micah

Midrash – the homiletic teachings of the Sages

***midrash* (pl. *midrashim*)** – a homiletic teaching of the Sages

mikveh – ritual pool used for immersion

milah – circumcision

minchah – afternoon prayer

Mishlei – Proverbs

Mishnah – the collection of halachic teachings of Sages, comprising the first part of the Talmud

misnagdim — opponents of Chassidism

mizbei'ach — altar

Moshe — Moses

mussaf — additional prayer service recited on Sabbath and festivals

mussar — Torah ethics

Naval — Nabal

nefesh — sensual soul

neshamah — soul

neshamah yeseirah — additional, higher soul, given on the Sabbath

Netzach — Eternity

Nevuchadnetzar — Nebuchadnezzar

niggun — melody, song

Nissan — one of the Jewish lunar months

nitzotzos hakedushah — sparks of holiness

Noach — Noah

Or Ein Sof — the Divine Infinite Light

pachad — fear

Pesach — Passover

Purim — festival celebrating the rescue of the Jews of Persia, as recorded in the book of Esther

Reuven — Reuben

Rivkah — Rebekah

Rosh Chodesh — beginning of a new lunar month

rosh yeshivah (**pl.** *rashei yeshivah*) — head of a yeshivah

ruach — spirit, instinct of self-preservation

ruach hakodesh — divine inspiration

Rus — Ruth

seder — meal at the night of Passover, commemorating the Exodus

Sefardi — originating from Spain and the Middle East

Sefardic — see *Sefardi*

sefer Torah — Torah scroll

Sefirah (**pl.** *Sefiros*) — Divine "vessels" or "emanations"

seudas mitzvah — meal at a religious ceremony

Shabbos — Sabbath

shacharis — the morning prayer

shalom — peace

Shavuos — holiday celebrating the giving of the Torah

Shechinah — Divine Presence

Shema — the fundamental declaration that God is One

shemittah — the seventh year in a seven-year cycle, during which the Torah commands that the Land of Israel lie fallow

Shemoneh Esrei — the daily prayer that forms the core of the daily prayer services, also called the "*Amidah*"

Shemos — Exodus

Shevat — one of the Jewish lunar months

sheviras hakeilim — shattering of the vessels

Shir HaShirim — Song of Songs

Shmuel — Samuel

shul — synagogue

Shulchan — the table in the Sanctuary

siyum — celebration at the conclusion of a Talmudic tractate

sofer — scribe of holy books

Sukkos — the holiday of Tabernacles

talmid (pl. *talmidim*) — student

Talmud Yerushalmi — Jerusalem Talmud

Tanach — the Bible, comprising the Torah, Prophets, and Writings

tanna (pl. *tannaim*) — teacher from the Mishnah

Tehillim — Psalms

teshuvah — repentance

Teveriah — Tiberias

Tiferes — Beauty

tikkun — cosmic rectification

Tishah B'Av — fast day commemorating the destruction of the Temple

Torah lishmah — Torah for its own sake

tractate — book of the Talmud

tzaddik (pl. *tzaddikim*) — righteous man

Tzefanyah — the prophet Zephaniah

Tzefas — Safed

tzimtzum — God withdrawing to make "room" for the cosmos

Vayikra – Leviticus

Vidui – confession of sins

Yaakov – Jacob

yartzeit – anniversary of the day of death

Yechezkel – Ezekiel

Yehoshua – Joshua

Yehudah – Judah

Yerushalayim – Jerusalem

Yerushalmi – Jerusalem Talmud

Yeshayah – Isaiah

Yesod – Foundation

yetzer hatov – the good impulse

yetzer hara – the evil impulse

Yetzirah – the World of Formation

Yirmiyah – Jeremiah

Yishmael – Ishmael

Yisrael – Israel (another name for Jacob; also refers to the Jewish people)

Yitzchak – Isaac

yod'ei chein – Kabbalists

yom tov – festival

Yonah – Jonah

Yosef – Joseph

yovel – Jubilee year

Zecharyah – Zachariah

NAME INDEX

A

Abuchatzeirah, Rabbi Yisrael.
  See Baba Sali
Abulafia, Rabbi Avraham, 87-90, 91
Alkabetz, Rabbi Shlomo, 179, 181-183, 190
Alshich, Rabbi Moshe, 66, 162, 179, 184-189, 208, 219, 305-306
Ari HaKadosh (Rabbi Yitzchak Luria Ashkenazi)
  and other Kabbalists, 80, 90, 91, 112, 126, 155, 169, 182, 184, 192, 213, 219, 226, 248, 254, 284, 309, 317, 324, 332, 340, 355-356, 373, 376, 384, 394-395
  and Rabbi Chaim Vital, 208-212
  biography, 179, 198-199, 207, 209, 210
  quoted in other works, 222, 229, 230, 233, 291, 295, 333, 335, 335-336, 375
  references to his teachings, 4, 16, 40, 47, 133
  selections from Eitz Chaim, 199-207
Arizal. *See* Ari HaKadosh
Ashlag, Rabbi Yehudah Leib, 48, 372, 383-391

R. Avraham Abulafia.
  See Abulafia, Rabbi Avraham
R. Avraham Azulai.
  See Azulai, Rabbi Avraham
R. Avraham ben David of Posquieres.
  See Ravad III
R. Azriel of Gerona, 63, 73, 74-78, 79
Azulai, Rabbi Avraham, 179, 212, 213-217
Azulai, Rabbi Chaim Yosef David. *See* Chida

B

Baal HaTanya (Rabbi Shneur Zalman of Liadi), 9, 145, 284, 295, 324-330
Baal Shem Tov (Rabbi Yisrael ben Eliezer), 283-284, 285-293, 294-295, 302, 316, 324, 339-340, 358
Baba Sali (Rabbi Yisrael Abuchatzeirah), 372, 392-399
R. Bachya ben Asher. *See* Rabbeinu Bachya
R. Baruch of Kossov, 316-323
Be'er Mayim Chaim (Rabbi Chaim Tirer), 331-338
Ben Ish Chai (Rabbi Yosef Chaim of

Baghdad), 371, 373–375
ben Israel, Rabbi Menashe.
　See Nishmas Chaim

C
R. Chaim Berlin of Volozhin.
　See R. Chaim Volozhiner
R. Chaim ibn Attar. See Or HaChaim
R. Chaim Tirer. See Be'er Mayim Chaim
R. Chaim Vital. See Vital, Rabbi Chaim
R. Chaim Volozhiner, 3, 240, 264, 271–279
R. Chaim Yosef David Azulai. See Chida
Chida (Rabbi Chaim Yosef David Azulai), 128, 132, 179, 214, 226, 227–236, 303
Cordovero, Rabbi Moshe (Remak), 5, 31, 48, 50, 60, 154, 157, 179, 182, 190–197, 199, 208, 210, 214, 243, 356

D
de Leon, Rabbi Moshe, 48, 63, 99–101
Donnolo, Rabbi Shabsai, 21, 65–69
R. Dov Ber. See Maggid of Mezritch

E
Eibeschutz, Rabbi Yonasan, 66, 239, 248–253
R. Elazar Rokeach of Worms.
　See Rokeach, Rabbi Elazar
R. Elimelech of Lizhensk.
　See No'am Elimelech
R. Eliyahu of Vilna. See Vilna Gaon

G
Gaon of Vilna. See Vilna Gaon
Gikatilla, Rabbi Yosef, 63, 89, 91–98, 99, 114
Gra. See Vilna Gaon

I
ibn Attar, Rabbi Chaim.
　See Or HaChaim
ibn Gabbai, Rabbi Meir, 74, 85, 98, 112–118, 191

K
Klingberg, Rabbi Shem.
　See Zaloshitzer Rebbe

L
Luria, Rabbi Yitzchak.
　See Ari HaKadosh
Luzzatto, Rabbi Moshe Chaim.
　See Ramchal

M
Maggid of Mezritch (Rabbi Dov Ber), 284, 294–301, 303, 309, 316, 324, 331
Maharal of Prague (Rabbi Yehudah Loewe), 66, 125–126, 145–153, 284, 324, 362
Megaleh Amukos (Rabbi Nassan Nata Shapira), 169–176, 248, 348
R. Meir ibn Gabbai.
　See ibn Gabbai, Rabbi Meir
R. Menachem Azaryah of Fano.
　See Rama of Fano
R. Menashe ben Israel.
　See Nishmas Chaim
Molcho, Rabbi Shlomo, 64, 119–121, 123
R. Moshe Alshich.
　See Alshich, Rabbi Moshe
R. Moshe ben Nachman.
　See Ramban
R. Moshe Chaim Luzzatto. See Ramchal
R. Moshe de Leon.
　See de Leon, Rabbi Moshe

N

R. Nachman of Breslov, 284, 339–347, 362

R. Nassan Nata Shapira.
　See Megaleh Amukos

R. Nechunya ben HaKanah.
　See Sefer HaBahir

Nishmas Chaim (Rabbi Menashe ben Israel), 239, 241–247

No'am Elimelech (Rabbi Elimelech of Lizhensk), 284, 295, 309–315

O

Or HaChaim (Rabbi Chaim ibn Attar), 180, 218–224, 227

R

Rabbeinu Bachya (Rabbi Bachya ben Asher), 63, 66, 72, 102–109

Rabinowitz, Rabbi Shlomo.
　See Tiferes Shlomo

Rama of Fano (Rabbi Menachem Azaryah of Fano), 126, 154–160, 192

Ramban (Rabbi Moshe ben Nachman), 33, 63, 66, 74, 79–86, 99, 102, 110, 245

Ramchal (Rabbi Moshe Chaim Luzzatto), 47, 239, 254–261

Rashash (Rabbi Shalom Mizrachi Sharabi), 180, 225–226, 227, 236

Ravad III (Rabbi Avraham ben David of Posquieres), 33, 38, 63, 66, 70–71, 72, 194

Raziel HaMalach, 21, 23–30

Recanati, Rabbi Menachem, 72, 110–111, 350

Remak. See Cordovero, Rabbi Moshe

Rokeach, Rabbi Elazar, 88, 110, 125, 128, 141–144

S

Safrin, Rabbi Yitzchak Eizik, 355–360

Sefer HaBahir, 21, 40–46, 116–117

Sefer HaZohar. See Zohar

Sefer Yetzirah, 9, 21, 29, 31–39, 40, 66, 68, 71, 73, 75, 88, 103, 125, 128, 142, 191, 192, 263, 351

R. Shabsai Donnolo.
　See Donnolo, Rabbi Shabsai

R. Shabsai Sheftl Horowitz.
　See Shefa Tal

R. Shalom Mizrachi Sharabi.
　See Rashash

Sharabi, Rabbi Shalom Mizrachi.
　See Rashash

Shefa Tal (Rabbi Shabsai Sheftl Horowitz), 157–160

Shelah (Rabbi Yeshayah Horowitz), 126, 157, 161–168, 219, 348, 361

R. Shem Klingberg.
　See Zaloshitzer Rebbe

R. Shimon bar Yochai. See Zohar

R. Shlomo Alkabetz.
　See Alkabetz, Rabbi Shlomo

R. Shlomo Molcho.
　See Molcho, Rabbi Shlomo

R. Shlomo Rabinowitz of Radomsk.
　See Tiferes Shlomo

R. Shneur Zalman of Liadi.
　See Baal HaTanya

T

Tiferes Shlomo (Rabbi Shlomo HaKohen Rabinowitz of Radomsk), 348–354

Tirer, Rabbi Chaim.
　See Be'er Mayim Chaim

Toldos Yaakov Yosef (Rabbi Yaakov Yosef of Polnoye), 283, 286, 302–308

R. Tzadok HaKohen, 48, 284, 361–368

V

Vilna Gaon (Rabbi Eliyahu of Vilna), 33, 38, 41, 66, 240, 251, 262–270, 271–272, 324, 382

Vital, Rabbi Chaim, 4, 90, 179, 184, 190, 192, 199, 202, 203, 207, 208–212, 213, 222, 226, 317, 332, 373, 375

Y

R. Yaakov Yosef of Polnoye.
See Toldos Yaakov Yosef

R. Yehudah HeChassid, 110, 125, 127–140, 141

R. Yehudah Leib Ashlag.
See Ashlag, Rabbi Yehudah Leib

R. Yehudah Loeve.
See Maharal of Prague

R. Yeshayah Horowitz. See Shelah

R. Yisrael Abuchatzeirah. See Baba Sali

R. Yisrael ben Eliezer. See Baal Shem Tov

R. Yitzchak Eizik Safrin.
See Safrin, Rabbi Yitzchak Eizik

R. Yitzchak Sagi Nahor, 63, 71, 72–73, 74

R. Yonasan Eibeschutz.
See Eibeschutz, Rabbi Yonasan

R. Yosef Chaim of Baghdad.
See Ben Ish Chai

R. Yosef Gikatilla.
See Gikatilla, Rabbi Yosef

Z

Zaloshitzer Rebbe (Rabbi Shem Klingberg), 376–382

Zohar

and Kabbalists, 102, 154, 162, 179, 190–191, 199, 207, 210, 248, 263, 278, 284, 317, 340, 356, 372, 382, 383–384, 391

background on, 21–22, 47–48, 99–100

quoted in other works, 129, 196, 206, 216, 219, 220, 223, 246, 247, 273–274, 274, 290, 297, 299, 300, 307, 328, 337, 341–342, 342, 352, 385

references to its teachings, 13–14, 15, 60, 113, 133, 374

selections from, 48–60

OTHER BOOKS BY THE AUTHOR

The Great Torah Commentators (Jason Aronson, Inc., 1990)

Responsa Anthology (Jason Aronson, Inc., 1990)

Dare to Survive (CIS Publishers, 1991)

Hardship and Hope (CIS Publishers, 1991)

Pressburg under Siege (CIS Publishers, 1991)

The Great Chasidic Masters (Jason Aronson, Inc., 1992)

The Essence of the Holy Days (Jason Aronson, Inc., 1993)

Itzik, Be Strong (CIS Publishers, 1993)

Songs of Hope (CIS Publishers, 1993)

Contemporary Sages (Jason Aronson, Inc., 1994)

Counterfeit Lives (CIS Publishers, 1994)

In My Flesh I See God (Jason Aronson, Inc., 1995)

The Essential Maimonides (Jason Aronson, Inc., 1996)

TRANSLATIONS BY THE AUTHOR

Torah Treasures (CIS Publishers, 1989)

The View from Above (CIS Publishers, 1992)

Introduction to the Rambam's Commentary on the Mishnah (Yeshivah Beth Moshe, Scranton, PA, 1993)

Iggeres Teiman, Letter to Yemen by the Rambam (Yeshivah Beth Moshe, 1994)

Shemonah Perakim by the Rambam (Yeshivah Beth Moshe, 1994)

Rambam's *Moreh Nevuchim: Part I, Chapters 1–49* (Yeshivah Beth Moshe, 1995)

Reb Aharon (CIS Publishers, 1995)

Chovos HaLevavos, four volumes (Yeshivah Beth Moshe, 1995–1998)

Reb Shlomo Zalman (CIS Publishers, 1996)

Ein Yaakov (Jason Aronson, Inc., 1999)

Ein Yaakov (CD-Rom, Davka, 1999)

Kuzari, two volumes (Yeshivah Beth Moshe, 2000)

Rambam's Mishneh Torah, Yad HaChazakah, to date four volumes (Yeshivah Beth Moshe, 2001–2002)

Ikvesa deMeshicha, The Era Preceding Mashiach by Rabbi Elchanan Wasserman (Yeshivah Gedolah of Los Angeles, 2002)